THOMAS JEFFERSON AND THE LAW

THE AUTHOR

EDWARD DUMBAULD, now United States judge for the Western District of Pennsylvania, was graduated from Princeton University and the Harvard Law School. He calls himself a lawyer by profession and a student of Jefferson by avocation. His interest in the former has led him to write such significant books as *The Declaration of Independence and What It Means Today, The Constitution of the United States,* and *The Bill of Rights and What It Means Today;* as a student of Jefferson he has written *Thomas Jefferson, American Tourist,* a work which is in its second printing. All of the above books were published by the University of Oklahoma Press.

THOMAS JEFFERSON by A. B. Doolittle.
    Here, more than in any other existing portrait, Jefferson resembles what a lawyer is commonly supposed to look like.
    Courtesy Thomas Jefferson Memorial Foundation.

Thomas Jefferson and the Law

By
Edward Dumbauld

UNIVERSITY OF OKLAHOMA PRESS
NORMAN

BY EDWARD DUMBAULD

Interim Measures of Protection in International Controversies (The Hague, 1932)
Thomas Jefferson, American Tourist (Norman, 1946; New edition, Norman, 1976)
The Declaration of Independence and What It Means Today (Norman, 1950; New
edition, Norman, 1968)
The Political Writings of Thomas Jefferson (New York, 1955)
The Bill of Rights and What It Means Today (Norman, 1957)
The Constitution of the United States (Norman, 1964)
Sayings of Jesus (Scottdale, 1967)
The Life and Legal Writings of Hugo Grotius (Norman, 1969)
Thomas Jefferson and the Law (Norman, 1978)

Library of Congress Cataloging in Publication Data

Dumbauld, Edward, 1905–
    Thomas Jefferson and the law.

    Bibliography: p.
    1. Jefferson, Thomas, Pres. U.S., 1743–1826—Law
practice. 2. Lawyers—Virginia—Biography. I. Title.
KF363.J4D8 1978   340'.092'4   78–5742
ISBN 0-8061-1441-X

To Lyman H. Butterfield
and to the memory of
Luther P. and Katharine Eisenhart

Preface

Being a lawyer by profession and a student of Jefferson by avocation, it was perhaps inevitable that I should write this book. But it was Lyman Butterfield, genial editor of Jefferson and Adams Papers, who actually suggested that I do it. As Justice Holmes might put it, he was the agency by which the inevitable comes to pass. He was a neighbor of Dean Luther P. Eisenhart and his wife Katharine at Princeton. When I called on them soon after publication of my book *Thomas Jefferson, American Tourist*, Mrs. Eisenhart brought us together. His friendship and encouragement and helpful insights have been warmly treasured during the years that have elapsed since then.

Diverted by professional responsibilities as well as other tasks of scholarly research which sprang up along the way, I have been long delayed in bringing this volume to fruition. But the bicentennial of the Declaration of Independence seemed an appropriate occasion for the completion of this tribute on behalf of the legal profession to one of its illustrious sons. It seemed prudent also to conclude the work *"donec virenti canities abest morosa."*

Through the good offices of Dean Eisenhart, I received from the Penrose Fund of the American Philosophical Society (an institution very dear to Jefferson) a grant for obtaining reproductions of manuscript materials. With gratitude I acknowledge this aid, as well as the courtesies and facilities extended by many individuals and institutions.

Foremost of course, in addition to Lyman Butterfield, I must name Julian Boyd, Dumas Malone, Merrill Peterson, and James A. Bear, Jr. Joseph H. Smith and Irwin S. Rhodes furnished helpful items. Dean Bernard Wolfman of the University of Pennsylvania Law School graciously provided a copy of the important letter on the study of law from Jefferson to John Minor; and Nelson B. Jones, clerk of the United States District Court for the Eastern District of Louisiana, made available court papers relating to litigation about the batture at New Orleans from which Edward Livingston had been unceremoniously evicted by the United States marshal at Jefferson's direction in 1808.

Libraries where I have enjoyed many happy and industrious hours include those of Princeton University, the University of Virginia, and the Harvard Law School, the Department of Justice Library and the Library of Congress in Washington, the Huntington Library in San Marino, the Massachusetts Historical Society in Boston, the Library Company of Philadelphia, the New York Public Library, and the British Museum.

May the third century of American independence bring to the hearts of every citizen a grateful remembrance of the labors of Thomas Jefferson, and rekindle in our lives the zeal which he exemplified to cherish law as an indispensable instrumentality in the perennial quest of all mankind for liberty and justice.

Edward Dumbauld

Uniontown, Pennsylvania

Contents

Illustrations

Introduction

That Thomas Jefferson was a lawyer by profession is often overlooked. The glamor of his political career and his prodigious versatility in many fields of intellectual endeavor overshadow his achievements in the prosaic realm of law.

Yet there is scarcely a branch of the profession in which he did not have some experience. After completing his academic studies at William and Mary,[1] he studied law for several years[2] under the preceptorship of the learned George Wythe, and came to the Virginia bar in 1767. For eight years he was active in private practice.[3] His business was extensive[4] and varied,[5] his clientele included leading citizens of the area,[6] and his earnings were lucrative as measured by the standards of the time.[7] His comments on "lawcraft"[8] show a perceptive practical judgment.[9]

Although not gifted with a voice suited to eminence as an orator,[10] Jefferson was an impressive speaker in the courtroom. Edmund Randolph, a well-qualified witness, reports hearing two "signal arguments" made by Jefferson in the General Court: "Without being an overwhelming orator, he was an impressive speaker, who fixed the attention. On two signal arguments before the general court in which Mr. Henry and himself were coadjutors, each characterized himself. Mr. Jefferson drew copiously from the depths of the law, Mr. Henry from the recesses of the human heart."[11] James Madison, an equally well-qualified authority, declared: "The Law itself he studied to the bottom, and in its greatest breadth, of which proofs were given at the Bar which he attended for a number of years, and occasionally throughout his career."[12] Aaron Burr, during his trial for treason at Richmond before Chief Justice John Marshall, had occasion to say: "Our president is a lawyer, and a great one too." Marshall himself, when reflecting upon a question which arose in the course of his law practice, doubted the correctness of his own view because of the contrary opinion of some of the "ablest men and soundest lawyers," including Jefferson among these.[13]

In the light of this testimony one may dismiss without hesitation the superficial observations of those who say "he was no lawyer."[14]

In addition to his private practice, Jefferson served with distinction as a lawmaker. He participated in the legislative process at all levels: as a member of the Virginia legislature,[15] of the Continental Congress, and as a draftsman of international treaties.[16]

An outstanding achievement of his career as a legislator was his program of law reform embodied in the revisal of Virginia's laws. He wished to bring the legal system of the commonwealth into conformity with republican principles and to eliminate those features which were the vestiges of English monarchical and ecclesiastical institutions. He believed that "our whole code must be renewed, adapted to our republican form of government, and, now that we had no negatives of Councils, Governors & Kings to restrain us from doing right, that it should be corrected, in all it's parts, with a single eye to reason, & the good of those for whose government it was framed."[17]

Jefferson's part of the work covered the common law and English statutes down to the establishment of the Virginia legislature in the fourth year of the reign of James I, thus including the law of descents and the criminal law.[18] The revisers embodied their work in a report containing 126 bills, which was printed in 1784.[19] From time to time, through the efforts of James Madison, some of these bills were enacted, notably the world-famous act for religious freedom, which became law in 1786, and the bill for abolishing primogeniture.[20] As Madison reported, "we went on slowly but successfully, till we arrived at the bill concerning crimes and punishments."[21] Jefferson's bill for proportioning crimes and punishments was one of his prized productions, based upon thorough study of the criminal law and inspired by the humanitarian philosophy of Beccaria.[22] It was too far in advance of public opinion for acceptance by the Virginia legislature and was lost by one vote.[23]

Some of Jefferson's legislative reforms were enacted during his own service in the House of Delegates. His bill abolishing entails passed promptly.[24] In Jefferson's view four of his proposed measures (abolition of primogeniture and of entail, freedom of religion, and diffusion of knowledge) would form "a system by which every fibre would be eradicated of antient or future aristocracy; and a foundation laid for a government truly republican."[25]

Judicial office was never held by Jefferson (except that he was named on March 5, 1777, as a justice of the peace for Albemarle County).[26] Edmund Pendleton wanted Jefferson to be a judge.[27] Nor did Jefferson ever serve as prosecuting attorney, although he displayed all the animus of a zealous prosecutor when giving instructions to George Hay, the United States attorney who was conducting Burr's trial for treason at Richmond in 1807.[28] Likewise, in drawing up the charges against the British government in the Declaration of Independence, he succeeded, contrary to Edmund Burke's dictum, in indicting a nation.[29]

It would not be farfetched to describe Jefferson as a law teacher. While governor of Virginia he reorganized the curriculum at William and Mary, establishing the first law professorship in America.[30] The chair was entrusted to Jefferson's old law preceptor, George Wythe, who served until 1800, and taught many distinguished pupils.

Jefferson advised many law students regarding their work, and drew up courses of professional reading for them to pursue.[31] He made his library available to them,[32] and counseled them. After his retirement from public office he wrote to a Virginia judge: "I still lend my counsel and books to such young students as will fix themselves in the neighborhood. Coke's institutes and reports are their first, and Blackstone their last book, after an intermediate course of two or three years."[33] Describing his life at Monticello to a European friend, he said: "A part of my occupation, and by no means the least pleasing, is the direction of the studies of such young men as ask it. They place themselves in the neighboring village, and have the use of my library and counsel, and make a part of my society. In advising the course of their reading, I endeavor to keep their attention fixed on the main objects of all science, the freedom and happiness of man. So that coming to bear a share in the councils and government of their country, they will keep ever in view the sole objects of all legitimate government."[34]

His concern for the University of Virginia led him to participate actively in the recruitment of the professor of law[35] and in the choice of textbooks[36] for that institution.

Jefferson's methods of legal education may be regarded as quite modern and effective. He favored the case method and moot courts.[37] "In reading the Reporters, enter in a Common-place book every case of value, condensed into the narrowest compass possible which will admit of presenting distinctly the principles of the case. This operation is doubly useful, inasmuch as it obliges the student to seek out the pith of the case, and habituates him to a condensation of thought, and to an acquisition of the most valuable of all talents, that of never using two words where one will do. It fixes the case too more indelibly in the mind."[38]

It is noteworthy also that the published books of which Jefferson was author were all, in whole or part, political or legal treatises.[39] His posthumously printed *Reports of Cases Determined in the General Court of Virginia. From 1730, to 1740; and from 1768, to 1772*[40] entitles Jefferson to be numbered among the estimable tribe of law reporters. As a collector of books (including law books) and public records,[41] he is also justly esteemed as a librarian and archivist.[42]

Notwithstanding these connections with practically every phase of the legal profession, Jefferson's time and talents were diverted into other channels when he became active in public life. Abroad as a diplomat, in the capital as secretary of state, vice-president, and president, there was no opportunity to keep abreast of legal developments, and his professional acumen became rusty.

Repeatedly he informed correspondents that so many years had elapsed since he had relinquished the practice of law that he was not qualified to advise them in their problems or answer their legal questions.[43] To one lady he explained that 52 years had passed since he had withdrawn from practice, and that "in the sale of his library to Congress he parted with every law book he owned, insomuch that he is obliged to apply to other counsel in all his own legal affairs."[44] Not only was that true,[45] but he also referred legal business to other lawyers, including Alexander Hamilton[46] and Aaron Burr.[47]

As he advanced in years, not only did Jefferson's unfamiliarity with current legal developments increase, but the incessant drudgery of answering letters exhausted his strength[48] and patience. Besides applications for public employment, he received requests for his opinions on scientific inventions[49] and literary works,[50] as well as for legal advice. He bewailed the voluminous torrent of communications "often from persons whose names I have never before heard" who "oppress me with their concerns, their pursuits, their projects, inventions and speculations, political, moral, religious, mechanical, historical &c., &c., &c."[51]

"I no longer meddle with questions of law," he replied, a decade before his death, when asked to give an opinion regarding interpretation of a treaty.[52] "I am now too old to read books solidly, unless they promise present amusement or future benefit. To me books of law offer neither."[53] In place of the doubts and conflicts of legal argumentation, he sought solace in the certainties of mathematics, which had ever been his favorite study, and in "the delights of classical reading."[54]

Yet the aging patriot with unabated fervor continued to cherish America's legal and political institutions as the supreme safeguard of the safety and happiness of the people.

In honor of the celebration at Washington of the fiftieth anniversary of the Declaration of Independence, its author (unable by reason of age and infirmity to be present) sent forth from his Virginia mountainside these ringing final words: "May it be to the world, what I believe it will be, (to some parts sooner, to others later, but finally to all,) the signal . . . to assume the blessings and security of self-government. . . . All eyes are opened, or opening, to the rights of man. The general spread of the light of science has already laid open to every view the palpable truth, that the mass of mankind has not been born with saddles on their backs, nor a favored few booted and spurred, ready to ride them legitimately, by the grace of God. These are grounds of hope for others. For ourselves, let the annual return of this day forever refresh our recollection of these rights, and an undiminished devotion to them."[55] Of the teachings proclaimed at Philadelphia in 1776 he spoke with earnest reverence in words which have not lost their timeliness: "I pray God that these principles may be eternal."[56]

THOMAS JEFFERSON AND THE LAW

I
A Methodical
Distribution of Hours

Before Thomas Jefferson began the practice of law, he had received an extensive classical and legal education. In view of his lifelong advocacy of "diffusion of knowledge" among all the people,[1] it seems fitting and appropriate that the earliest surviving letter from Jefferson's voluminous correspondence is one relating to his own schooling. Writing at the age of seventeen to one of his guardians, he discusses the desirability of pursuing his studies at William and Mary College: "I was at Colo. Peter Randolph's about a Fortnight ago, and my Schooling falling into Discourse he said he thought it would be to my Advantage to go to the College, and was desirous I should go, as indeed I am myself for several Reasons. In the first place, as long as I stay at the Mountain, the Loss of one-fourth of my Time is inevitable, by Company's coming here and detaining me from School. And likewise my Absence will in a great Measure, put a Stop to so much Company, and by that Means lessen the Expences of the Estate in House-Keeping. And on the other Hand by going to the College, I shall get a more universal Acquaintance; which may hereafter be serviceable to me; and I suppose I can pursue my Studies in the Greek and Latin as well there as here, and likewise learn something of the Mathematics. I shall be glad of your opinion."[2]

Regarding his study of the classics he said: "I think myself more indebted to my father for this than for all the other luxuries his cares and affections have placed within my reach; and more now than when younger, and more susceptible of delights from other sources."[3]

Jefferson's first formal instruction began when at the age of five he was placed in the English school at Tuckahoe, where his family had resided since he was two years old. At the age of nine, upon the return of the family to Shadwell, he was taught Latin, Greek, and French by a Scottish clergyman, the Reverend William Douglas. When Jefferson was fourteen, his father, Peter Jefferson, died, and the young pupil lived for two years in the home of the Reverend James Maury about fourteen miles from Shadwell.[4] Jefferson regarded Maury as "a correct classical scholar."[5]

In the course of reviewing his own youthful experiences for the edification of a grandson who was away from home at school, Jefferson wrote: "When I recollect that at 14 years of age, the whole care and direction of myself was thrown on myself entirely without a relation or friend qualified to guide me, and recollect the various sorts of bad company with which I associated from time to time, I am astonished I did not turn off with some of them, & become as worthless to society as they were. I had the good fortune to become acquainted very early with some characters of very high standing, and to feel the incessant wish that I could ever become what they were. Under temptations and difficulties, I would ask myself what would Dr. Small, Mr. Wythe, Peyton Randolph do in this situation. . . . I was often thrown into the society of horse racers, card players, fox hunters, scientific & professional men, and of dignified men; and many a time have I asked myself, in the enthusiastic moment of the death of a fox, the victory of a favorite horse, the issue of a question eloquently argued at the bar, or in the great council of the nation, well, which of these kinds of reputation should I prefer? That of a horse jockey? a fox hunter? an orator? or the honest advocate of my country's rights?"[6]

The prudent young scholar did carry out his plan of pursuing his studies at William and Mary College. From March 25, 1760, to April 25, 1762, he was enrolled in that institution and lived at Williamsburg, presumably in what is now called the Wren Building.[7] As a law student and public official, he continued to make his home in Williamsburg until 1780, when during his governorship Richmond became the capital of the Old Dominion.[8]

Of his college years Jefferson declared long afterward: "It was my great good fortune, and what probably fixed the destinies of my life that Dr. Wm. Small of Scotland was then professor of Mathematics, a man profound in most of the useful branches of science, with a happy talent of communication correct and gentlemanly manners, & an enlarged & liberal mind. He, most happily for me, became soon attached to me & made me his daily companion when not engaged in the school; and from his conversation I got my first views of the expansion of science & of the system of things in which we are placed. Fortunately the Philosophical chair became vacant soon after my arrival at college, and he was appointed to fill it per interim: and he was the first who ever gave in that college regular lectures in Ethics, Rhetoric & Belles lettres. He returned to Europe in 1762, having previously filled up the measure of his goodness to me, by procuring for me, from his most intimate friend G. Wythe, a reception as a student of law, under his direction, and introduced me to the acquaintance and familiar table of Governor Fauquier, the ablest man who had ever filled that office. With him, and at his table, Dr. Small & Mr. Wythe, his amici omnium horarum, & myself, formed a partie quarree, & to the habitual conversations on these occasions I owed much instruction. Mr. Wythe continued to be my faithful and beloved Mentor in youth, and my most affectionate friend through life. In 1767, he led me into the practice of the law at the bar of the General court, at which I continued until the revolution shut up the courts of justice."[9]

Classical and mathematical studies were regarded by Jefferson not only as indispensable to a law student from a utilitarian standpoint, but also as a source of intellectual pleasure. At the beginning of a plan of study prepared for a young friend he declared: "Before you enter on the study of the law a sufficient groundwork must be laid. For this purpose an acquaintance with the Latin and French languages is absolutely necessary. . . . Mathematics and Natural philosophy are so useful in the most familiar occurrences of life, and are so peculiarly engaging & delightful as would induce every person to wish an acquaintance with them. Besides this, the faculties of the mind, like the members of the body, are strengthened & improved by exercise. Mathematical reasonings & deductions are therefore a fine preparation for investigating the abstruse speculations of the law."[10]

Small's instruction in mathematics made a profound impression on the mind of the future Virginia barrister.[11] Nearing the age of seventy, Jefferson avowed: "When I was young, mathematics was the passion of my life. The same passion has returned upon me, but with unequal powers. Processes which I then read off with the facility of common discourse, now cost me labor, and time, and slow investigation."[12] But the effort was rewarding. "I have resumed that study with great avidity. It was ever my favorite one. We have no theories there, no uncertainties remain on the mind; all is demonstration and satisfaction."[13] Thus the aging statesman busied himself "to beguile the wearisomeness of declining life . . . by the delights of classical reading and of mathematical truths, and by the consolations of a sound philosophy, equally indifferent to hope and fear."[14]

The plan of law study recommended by Jefferson was presumably based on his own experience under the tutelage of George Wythe. It embraced not only strictly legal topics, but such "kindred sciences as will contribute to eminence" at the bar. These included "Physics, Ethics, Religion, Natural law, Belles lettres, Criticism, Rhetoric and Oratory." In this connection Jefferson noted that "carrying on several studies at a time is attended with advantage. Variety relieves the mind, as well as the eye, palled with too long attention to a single object." He also emphasized that "a great inequality is observable in the vigor of the mind at different periods of the day." Advantage should be taken of this fact "in marshalling the business of the day."[15]

Accordingly, the working hours of the day from early morning to bedtime were divided into five periods, each of which was to be devoted to a different type of subject matter. Until eight o'clock in the morning, the student was advised to give his attention to physical sciences, ethics, religion, and natural

GEORGE WYTHE by John Trumbull (detail from his familiar Declaration of Independence). Wythe was Jefferson's preceptor, associate, and adversary in the practice of law.

Copyright Yale University Art Gallery.

law. "From VIII. to XII. read Law," the outline directs. Then from twelve to one, "read Politics." In the afternoon, "read History." Finally, from dark to bedtime was the season for belles lettres, criticism, rhetoric, and oratory. Under each heading the books to be used were listed.[16]

The essence of law study for Jefferson was literally "reading law," an operation which the student must perform for himself, and which he can perform in any appropriate environment.[17] The professor or preceptor had but a small part to play in a student's progress toward mastery of his profession. "I always was of opinion that the placing a youth to study with an attorney was rather a prejudice than a help. We are all too apt by shifting on them our business, to incroach on that time which should be devoted to their studies. The only help a youth wants is to be directed what books to read and in what order to read them."[18]

However, when he reorganized the curriculum at William and Mary in 1779 while he was governor of Virginia, Jefferson established the first law professorship in America. The chair was entrusted to his old law preceptor, George Wythe, who served until 1800 and taught many distinguished pupils.[19] In 1788 Jefferson recommended sending to Williamsburg a young man destined for the law, pointing out that "the pride of the Institution is Mr. Wythe. . . . He is one of the greatest men of the age. . . . He gives lectures regularly, holds moot courts and parliaments wherein he presides and the young men debate regularly in law, and legislation, learn the rules of parliamentary proceeding, and acquire the habit of public speaking."[20]

The importance to a lawyer of "acquiring the art of writing and speaking correctly" was stressed by Jefferson. After analyzing the orations of Demosthenes, Cicero, and examples of English eloquence, the student was exhorted to prepare "orations on feigned cases," and urged to "suit your arguments to the audience before which it is supposed to be delivered." In this aspect of his training the student requires the participation of his fellows and of experienced counselors, and cannot rely upon his own reading in solitude. "If you have any person in your neighborhood engaged in the same study, take each of you different sides of the same cause and prepare pleadings according to the custom of the bar, where the pl[aintiff] opens, the def[endant] answers and the pl[aintiff] replies. It would farther be of great service to pronounce your orations (having only before you only short notes to assist the memory) in the presence of some person who may be considered as your judge."[21]

The general course of legal reading to be pursued during the hours from eight o'clock in the morning until noon was thus described by Jefferson: "Ld. Coke has given us the first view of the whole body of law worthy now of being studied: for so much of the admirable work of Bracton is now obsolete that the student should turn to it occasionally only, when tracing the history of particular portions of the law. Coke's Institutes are a perfect Digest of the law as it stood in his day. After this, new laws were added by the legislature, and new developments of the old laws by the Judges, until they had become so voluminous as to require a new Digest. This was ably executed by Matthew Bacon, altho' unfortunately under an alphabetical, instead of analytical arrangement of matter. The same process of new laws and new decisions on the old laws going on, called at length for the same operation again, and produced the inimitable Commentaries of Blackstone.

"In the department of the Chancery, a similar progress has taken place. Ld. Kaims has given us the first digest of the principles of that branch of our jurisprudence, more valuable for the arrangement of matter, than for it's exact conformity with the English decisions. The Reporters from the early times of that branch to that of the same Matthew Bacon are well digested, but alphabetically also in the Abridgment of the Cases in Equity, the 2d. volume of which is said to have been done by him. This was followed by a number of able reporters, of which Fonblanque has given us a summary digest."[22]

Jefferson's method of analyzing cases has a familiar ring to present-day law students. "In reading the Reporters, enter in a Common-place book every case of value, condensed into the narrowest compass possible which will admit of presenting distinctly the principles of the case. This operation is doubly useful, inasmuch as it obliges the student to seek out the pith of the case, and habituates him to a condensation of thought, and to an acquisition of the most valuable of all talents, that of never using two words where one will do. It fixes the case too more indelibly in the mind."[23]

The material dealing with the common law which Jefferson enumerated included:

Coke's institutes.
Select cases from the subsequent reporters to the time of Matthew Bacon.
Bacon's abridgment.
Select cases from the subsequent reporters to the present day.
Select tracts on Law, among which those of Baron Gilbert are all of the first merit.
The Virginia laws. Reports on them.[24]

On the subject of equity he specified:

Ld. Kaim's Principles of Equity. 3d edition.
Select cases from the Chancery reporters to the time of Matthew Bacon.
The Abridgment of Cases in Equity.
Select cases from the subsequent reporters to the present day.
Fonblanque's Treatise of Equity.[25]

In conclusion he named "Blackstone's Commentaries (Tucker's edition) as the last perfect Digest of both branches of law."[26]

The praise thus accorded to Blackstone contrasts with the unfavorable comments on the celebrated English institutional writer which Jefferson expressed subsequently.[27] In a letter written less than six months before his death, regarding the choice of a law professor for the newly founded University of Virginia, Jefferson exhorted Madison: "In the selection of our Law Professor, we must be rigorously attentive to his political principles. You will recollect that before the revolution, Coke Littleton was the universal elementary book of law students, and a sounder whig never wrote, nor of profounder learning in the orthodox doctrines of the British constitution, or in what were called English liberties. You remember also that our lawyers were then all whigs. But when his black-letter text, and uncouth but cunning learning got out of fashion, and the honied Mansfieldism[28] of Blackstone became the student's hornbook, from that moment, that profession (the nursery of our Congress) began to slide into toryism, and nearly all the young brood of lawyers now are of that hue. They suppose themselves, indeed, to be whigs, because they know no longer what whigism or republicanism means. It is in our seminary that that vestal flame is to be kept alive; it is thence it is to spread anew over our own and the sister States."[29]

Besides the political unacceptability of Blackstone's doctrines,[30] Jefferson believed that excessive dependence upon the *Commentaries* as the staple of legal education resulted in superficiality. "A student finds there a smattering of everything, and his indolence easily persuades him that if he understands that book, he is master of the whole body of the law. The distinction between these, and those who have drawn their store from the deep and rich mines of Coke and Littleton, seems well understood even by the unlettered common people, who apply the appellation of Blackstone lawyers to these ephemeral insects of the law."[31] He deprecated the prevalent view "that Blackstone is to us what the Alcoran is to the Mahometans, that everything which is necessary is in him, and what is not in him is not necessary. I still lend my counsel and books to such young students as will fix themselves in the neighborhood. Coke's institutes and reports are their first, and Blackstone their last book, after an intermediate course of two or three years. It is nothing more than an elegant digest of what they will then have acquired from the real fountains of the law."[32]

Perhaps Jefferson regarded the new matter appended to Blackstone's text by the Virginia editor as an adequate antidote to the English author's Tory sentiments.[33] In many respects the principles expounded by Tucker were congenial to Jefferson.[34] The Sage of Monticello would have agreed enthusiastically that "liberty and science are inseparable companions."[35] Likewise Jeffersonian is the assertion that "in a government founded on the basis of equal liberty among all its citizens, to be ignorant of the law and the constitution, is to be ignorant of the rights of the citizen." So too, knowledge of law is important for those who are to take part in the administration of government: "For what can be more absurd than that a person wholly ignorant of the constitution should presume to make laws pursuant thereto?"[36] Tucker's views on expatriation,[37] inheritance,[38] education,[39] the gradual abolition of slavery,[40] on freedom of speech and religion,[41] and on the nonexistence of federal common law[42] were characteristically Jeffersonian. Tucker disagreed with Jefferson's opinion[43] that the Virginia constitution of 1776 was an ordinary legislative enactment, not a fundamental law, emanating from the plenary power of the people and unalterable by the ordinary legislature.[44]

In addition to its doctrinal acceptability, Tucker's work was useful to a Virginia law student because of its convenient presentation of rare and inaccessible statutory materials,[45] as well as its analysis of the modes of practice in the various judicial tribunals functioning in Virginia.

Jefferson himself as a law student was not exposed to contamination by Blackstonian teachings, for the celebrated *Commentaries* were not completed until two years after Jefferson had been admitted to practice.[46] Nor was Tucker's edition available until Jefferson had served two years as president of the United States. The first American edition of Blackstone was published in Philadelphia by Robert Bell in 1771–72.[47] Perhaps more than a thousand copies had been imported from England before that. In 1775 Edmund Burke's well-known speech in Parliament on conciliation with America called attention to the popularity of Blackstone among the colonists.

That Jefferson carefully studied Blackstone is shown by his numerous annotations in his set of the 1770 edition now in the Library of Congress. Indeed, it may be from Blackstone's comment that Jefferson became aware of Coke's error in stating that homicide by accident *(per infortunium)* or in self-defense *(se defendendo)* was punishable by death as murder before the enactment of chapter 26 of the Statute of Marlebridge in 1267. As Jefferson noted in his copy of Coke's *Second Institute*, Hale, Hawkins, Foster, and Blackstone were "all of contrary opinion."[48] These authorities pointed out that the term *"murdrum"* in the statute referred to a secret killing where the slayer could not be found. In such a case, in order to protect the Norman conquerors against violence from the populace, the township or "hundred" where the death occurred was liable to an amercement of fifty-six marks unless (in a procedure known as "presentment of Englishry") it could be proved that the person killed was an Englishman and not a Norman. The intent of the statute of Marlebridge was to eliminate such liability in cases of killing by accident or in self-defense.

Blackstone's *Commentaries* is a work characterized by orderly and systematic sequence of presentation, as well as by the beguiling elegance of its literary style. It was rightly said of Blackstone by his severest critic, Jeremy Bentham, that "he it is . . . who first . . . taught Jurisprudence to speak the language of the Scholar and the Gentleman."[49] The pattern of treatment is based upon that of Justinian's *Institutes*.[50] The first of Blackstone's four books deals with the law of persons (including in addition to disabilities of infants, idiots, married women, and the like, the constitutional distinctions between the legal position of the crown and commoners); the second with the law of things, encompassing the complexities of property law; the third with the law of actions, explaining the intricacies of judicial procedure to remedy private wrongs; and the fourth with the law of crimes, or offenses against public order. Acknowledged as a legal classic, the *Commentaries* were nevertheless savagely attacked, especially by Jeremy Bentham and his followers, because of the complacent conservatism and "Blackstonian optimism" with which the author viewed British institutions as approaching perfection. This aspect of Blackstone's outlook would also tend to antagonize a leader of the American revolutionary movement such as Jefferson.

Coke's *Institutes*, on the other hand, are marked by a crabbed style and lack of coherence. Items of curious erudition are dumped in a confused mass before the reader, like the miscellaneous contents of a peddler's bag piled undiscriminatingly in front of a potential purchaser. Law students both before and after Jefferson's time have complained of the frustrations endured in attempting to master the learning embodied in Coke's pages.[51]

Of Coke's *Institutes* Jefferson wrote that "although the work loses much of its value by its chaotic form, it may still be considered as the fundamental code of the English law." Coke's uncouth style was also discouraging to learners. In his own student days Jefferson had exclaimed,"I do wish the Devil had old Cooke, for I am sure I never was so tired of an old dull scoundrel in my life." He was therefore very enthusiastic about the publication of Thomas's edition of Coke's first *Institute*, rearranging the material in accordance with Blackstone's systematic sequence, but "not omitting a sentence of Lord Coke's text, nor inserting one not his. . . . It can now be no longer doubted that this is the very best elementary work for a beginner in the study of the law."[52]

Coke's first *Institute* is more commonly known as Coke on Littleton. It consists of a commentary by Coke upon Thomas Littleton's *Tenures*, a treatise dealing with the English land law.[53] It was the only part of the *Institutes* published during Coke's lifetime, and was more comprehensive and elaborate than the others.[54] "It is a legal encyclopedia arranged on no plan, except that suggested by the words and sentences of Littleton."[55] Littleton's book, in Coke's judgment, was "a work of absolute perfection in its kind, and as free from error as any book that I have known to be written of any human learning."[56]

Coke's second *Institute* is a commentary on Magna Carta and other important statutes of the realm.[57] What is written here had significant consequences for the development of constitutional law, both in England and America.[58]

The third *Institute* contains an account of the criminal law.[59] Coke's long service as prosecutor and judge enabled him to furnish much information based upon his own practical experience.

The fourth *Institute* describes the courts which existed in England.[60] In addition to the familiar royal courts,[61] which effectively centralized the administration of justice,[62] numerous local and specialized tribunals, which were or soon became obsolete or dormant, are painstakingly described. Some scholars believe that the law which the colonists brought to America was significantly influenced by the local law developed in some of these lesser-known courts,[63] as distinguished from the nationally applicable common law (common to the whole kingdom) which was formulated by the king's courts.

One special tribunal colorfully described by Coke is the Court of the Lord High Steward of England, where peers are tried for treason. After an indictment has been returned, the king by commission under the great seal appoints a peer lord high steward *hac vice*, who summons twelve or more peers and fixes the date for convening. "At the day, the steward with six serjeants at armes before him takes his place under a cloth of estate, and then the clerk of the crown delivereth unto him his commission, who re-delivereth the same unto him. And the clerk of the crown causeth a serjeant at armes to make three oyes, and commandment given in the name of the lord high steward of England to keep silence: and then is the commission read. And then the usher delivereth to the steward a white rod, who re-delivereth the same to him againe, who holdeth it before the steward." Then the indictment is delivered into court, the prisoner brought in, the peers summoned answer to their names and take their places. "And when they be all in their places, and the prisoner at the bar, the high Steward declares to the prisoner the cause of their assembly, and perswades him to answer without feare, that he shall be heard with patience and that justice shall be done."

After reading of the indictment and arraignment, the lord high steward charges the peers "to try the prisoner indifferently [impartially] according to their evidence." Then the king's counsel presents evidence, the prisoner is heard, and the peers reach their verdict in the absence of the prisoner. He must be present if they wish to consult the judges in attendance or the steward. Like jurors, the peers must remain together until they arrive at a verdict. When the prisoner is brought in, the lord high steward acquaints him with the verdict, gives judgment accordingly, and commands execution to be done according to the judgment. If the king's pardon relieves the defendant of all the incidents of the judgment except beheading, this must be done under the great seal. When all is completed, "then is an oyes made for the dissolving of the commission; and then is the white rod, which hath been borne and holden before the Steward, by him taken in both his hands, and broken over his head." The record of the arraignment, trial, and judgment is delivered to the Court of King's Bench, there to be kept and enrolled.[64]

In addition to his *Institutes*, Lord Coke's *Reports* constituted a basic feature of Jefferson's program of law study.[65]

The availability of reported judicial decisions is an indispensable condition for the successful operation of the Anglo-American legal system. A distinctive feature of that system is the extent to which it relies primarily upon judge-made rules rather than upon legislative enactments or statutory codifications as a means of developing legal principles.[66] Under the doctrine of *stare decisis*[67] the courts diligently endeavor to decide questions confronting them in conformity with prior judicial decisions. Adequate written reports of such precedents are necessary if the system is to function effectively. Without such records of past determinations the courts would have to depend on what has been called "memory jurisprudence" based on oral tradition and personal recollections.[68]

At first the oral rulings made in English courts were recorded privately by bystanders and circulated in manuscript form. Later, in the fifteenth and sixteenth centuries, they were printed, and were called "Year Books" because the cases collected were grouped by regnal years.[69]

In the sixteenth century there was a transition from the anonymous Year Books to published reports written by, or ascribed to, named reporters, most of whom were eminent judges or lawyers.[70]

"The year 1600 is significant because in that year Sir Edward Coke brought forth the first of the eleven volumes of reports that he was to publish in his lifetime,"[71] the last in 1615. A second edition appeared before Coke's death on September 3, 1634. Parts twelve and thirteen were published posthumously, in 1656 and 1659 respectively, after most of Coke's papers (seized by the Crown as seditious while he lay on his deathbed) had been returned to his heir in 1641. Coke's acknowledged preeminence as an erudite expounder of the law and doughty champion of constitutional rights is such that when a lawyer cites simply "the Reports" (or, more briefly, "Rep."), the reference is to Coke's reports. When any other reports are cited, the name of the reporter, or of the jurisdiction referred to, must be given.

Coke's reports are distinctive not only because of their universal acceptance as authoritative, but also for the same thoroughness and learning which characterizes his *Institutes*. Moreover the prefaces to each volume of the *Reports* contain comments which add a quaint and almost romantic charm to the intricate legalism of the topics treated. In the preface to his first *Institute* Coke points out that "in the eleven Books of our *Reports* we have related the Opinions and Judgments of others; but herein we have set down our own."

In Jefferson's time, digests and abridgments not only served their present-day function as a guide or index to reported decisions, but often were the only repository in which such decisions were available to practitioners. The underlying law reports themselves were often not on hand in the relatively meager law libraries of the era.[72] In any event, Jefferson emphasized the importance of obtaining a knowledge of the state of the law at four important stages of its development by using Bracton, Coke, Matthew Bacon, and Blackstone, even at the expense of neglecting the reports intervening between those writers.[73]

Bacon's *New Abridgement,* recommended by Jefferson, first began to appear in 1736.[74] It was a favorite among American lawyers.[75] "As a text-book for students, it has long maintained an unrivalled reputation," Justice Story declared.[76] It consists of an alphabetical series of brief treatises on various topics of the law, generally illustrated by adjudications. These dissertations were largely taken from manuscripts of Sir Geoffrey Gilbert (1674–1726), Lord Chief Baron of the Exchequer. Although Bacon appropriated Gilbert's work without acknowledgment and made no effort to revise it or correct errors,[77] Bacon's *New Abridgement* was the first since Statham's which was not based on prior abridgments.[78]

The abridgment by Nicholas Statham (d. 1472), baron of the exchequer, was the earliest of such compilations. It was probably printed in 1490. Subsequently, Sir Anthony Fitzherbert (1470–1538), later a common pleas judge, published his *La Graunde Abridgement* in 1516. It was a digest of the Year Books, alphabetically arranged. After its fifth edition it was superseded by the work of Sir Robert Brooke (d. 1558), Speaker of the House of Commons and chief justice of the Court of Common Pleas, published in 1573/74. A supplement to Brooke was published by William Hughes in 1660–63, the first abridgment in English. Then in 1668, with a preface in English by Sir Matthew Hale (1609–76), chief justice of the Court of the King's Bench, was published (again in law French) the notable abridgment (which had been completed before 1640) by Sir Henry Rolle (1589?–1656), chief justice of the King's

Bench. Other works preceding Bacon's were those of William Sheppard in 1675; Knightley D'Anvers (1705–1737, never completed, containing a translation of Rolle with additional material); John Lilly in 1719; and William Nelson in 1725–26. After Bacon, Charles Viner (1678–1756) published at his own expense (1742–45) his *General Abridgment of Law and Equity*. Intending to supplement D'Anvers and Nelson, he started with the title "Factor." Later deciding to complete the work, he reverted to the beginning of the alphabet in the eleventh of his twenty-three volumes. From his profits he established the first chair of law at Oxford, of which Blackstone was the first incumbent.[79]

Rolle's abridgment, according to Chief Justice Matthew Hale's preface, was itself a sort of amplified commonplace book. Hale "commended the making and using of a commonplace book as the best expedient that I know for the orderly and profitable study of the law."[80] It was customary for law students in the seventeenth century to procure a blank folio volume in which appropriate headings were inserted to indicate the titles under which the matter was to be distributed. Abstracts of the cases read by the student were then placed under the appropriate rubric.[81] When Jefferson kept a commonplace book to serve as a repository of his reflections on the study of law, he did not use a huge folio volume with preordained headings, but simply recorded his material in consecutively numbered items on quarto sheets of paper which were subsequently bound.[82] Two such volumes have been preserved.[83] Because of the nature of their contents[84] one is commonly called his Legal Commonplace Book[85] and the other his Equity Commonplace Book.[86]

In Jefferson's Legal Commonplace Book an appearance of alphabetical arrangement is produced by the fact that Salkeld's reports,[87] which together with Lord Raymond's reports[88] form the most substantial portion of the early pages of his compilation,[89] are themselves arranged under alphabetical headings.[90] Modern scholars confirm the value and reliability of Salkeld's[91] and Lord Raymond's reports. Although some of the material in Lord Raymond's reports was not from the author's own notes but was furnished by others, the volumes are considered as providing the best account available of the decisions of Chief Justice Holt.[92]

The authorities recommended by Jefferson[93] in the field of equity, and digested in his Equity Commonplace Book, are likewise regarded as excellent. Henry Home, Lord Kames[94] (which Jefferson always spelled Kaims), was a Scottish judge whose writings on legal and philosophical[95] subjects considerably influenced Jefferson. Extensive extracts from his *Principles of Equity*[96] were included in Jefferson's Equity Commonplace Book. Modern scholarship has confirmed Jefferson's attribution to Matthew Bacon of *A General Abridg-*

ment of Cases in Equity.[97] William Peere Williams (1664–1736), whose *Reports of Cases argued and determined in the High Court of Chancery*[98] were used by Jefferson in both his Commonplace Books,[99] has been described as "the first full and clear reporter of Chancery cases."[100]

Likewise Fonblanque's revision of Henry Ballow's *A Treatise of Equity*[101] has enjoyed long-lived renown. Ballow's book was the "earliest systematic work upon modern equity," which was then in a transitional stage between the uncertainty of reliance upon the ethical promptings of the chancellor's conscience (as capricious a standard as the length of the chancellor's foot, according to Selden's witty observation) and the regularity of a settled body of doctrine.[102] A significant second period of this stage of development was about to begin under Lord Hardwicke.[103]

Ballow, a man of literary attainments, acquainted with Dr. Samuel Johnson and the poet Akenside,[104] set forth in skeletal form a systematized treatment of the subject, without citing any authorities.[105] Fonblanque not only added references, but supplied lengthy commentary dealing with developments between 1737 and 1793.[106] "Up to the publication of Joseph Story's books on equity, Fonblanque's *Equity* was for one hundred years the best elementary book on equity in use in America. 'It finally expired under the weight of its own notes.' "[107]

The other sources drawn upon by Jefferson in his Equity Commonplace Book were likewise standard authorities available to equity practitioners of the era.[108] Of Lord Kames, the *Abridgment of Cases in Equity*, and the reports of Salkeld and Peere Williams, we have already spoken.[109] The two posthumous volumes of William Vernon[110] (1654–1721), "an eminent practitioner in the court of Chancery," were published by William Peere Williams and William Melmoth in 1726–28 under the direction of the court after litigation among his survivors. They cover the period 1681–1720. A more satisfactory edition by Raithly appeared in 1806–1807.[111]

There were only two sets of chancery reports published before 1700.[112] Both were used by Jefferson.[113] He also noted cases from Richard Freeman's *Reports of Cases in Law and Equity: from 1670 to 1706*, published in 1742;[114] from *Precedents in Chancery*,[115] published in 1733;[116] and from the first volume (published in 1765)[117] of *Reports of Cases argued and determined in the High Court of Chancery, in the time of Lord Chancellor Hardwicke*[118] by John Tracy Atkyns of Lincoln's Inn, an English judge who died in 1773.[119] As the final item of his Equity Commonplace Book, Jefferson inserted a comment on statutory construction:

Acts of parl. are made with such gravity, wisdom & universal consent of all the realm, & for advantage of the public wealth; that they are not from the general & ambiguous words of a subsequent act to be abrogated. 11. Co. 63. Fortesc. c. 18. c. 40, L. parl. 65. Every proviso in an act is not a determination what the law was before; for they are often added for the satisfaction of them that are ignorant of the law. 1 Siderf. 155. Lex parl. 65.[120]

In Jefferson's Commonplace Books he recorded the results of his study of law reports and other authorities, as well as occasional reflections of his own on the topics covered.[121] To analyze these volumes in further detail would be unprofitable, since for the most part they are simply abstracts of the cases contained in law reports utilized by Jefferson in the course of his studies. As the original reports themselves are available to readers, anyone could make an abstract of them himself, in all probability just as satisfactory a compilation as the one Jefferson prepared. Jefferson's own comments, however, often illuminate distinctive aspects of his thinking, and enable us to understand better his attitude toward the law.

Perhaps the most characteristic example of Jefferson's own research and rumination as recorded in his Commonplace Books is his "disquisition" attacking the generally held view that Christianity was part of the English common law.[122] This was a favorite theme, to which he often recurred.[123] He included it with his collection of court decisions, which was posthumously published in 1829. His arguments on this subject will be treated in a subsequent chapter dealing with Jefferson's *Reports of Cases Determined in the General Court of Virginia.*[124]

II
Writings
Other Than Official

Other excellent illustrations of Jefferson's own reflections on legal topics are to be found in the books which he published during his lifetime. In a sense, all of these volumes, in whole or in part, may be regarded as legal treatises.

The earliest work of Jefferson's to be given to the press was *A Summary View of the Rights of British America,* printed at Williamsburg by Clementina Rind in 1774.[1] It is a forceful exposition of constitutional law and was undoubtedly the source of ideas later elaborated by Jefferson when drafting the Declaration of Independence.[2] According to Jefferson, "The *Summary View* was not written for publication. It was a draught I had prepared for a petition to the king, which I meant to propose in my place as a member of the convention of 1774. Being stopped on the road by sickness, I sent it on to the Speaker[3] who laid it on the table for the perusal of the members." It was read generally by the members, approved by many, and thought too bold for the state of affairs at the time, "but was printed by subscription of the members, with a short preface written by one of them."[4] Authorship of this stirring tract enhanced Jefferson's reputation and doubtless contributed to his selection as draftsman of the Declaration of Independence.[5]

The first proposition enunciated in the *Summary View* has a familiar Jeffersonian ring. It asserts the natural right of expatriation,[6] the establishment of government in America by consent of the inhabitants,[7] their voluntary adoption of a system of law to which they were accustomed,[8] and their union with other parts of the expanded empire through their submission to a common king.[9]

Jefferson forthrightly declared in the *Summary View:* "Our ancestors, before their emigration to America, were the free inhabitants of the British dominions in Europe and possessed a right which nature has given to all men, of departing from the country in which chance, not choice, has placed them, of going in quest of new habitations, and of there establishing new societies, under such laws and regulations as to them shall seem most likely to promote the public happiness. . . . America was conquered, and her settlements made, and firmly established, at the expence of individuals, and not of the British public. Their own blood was spilt in acquiring lands for their settlement, their own fortunes expended in making that settlement effectual;

for themselves they fought, for themselves they conquered, and for them-selves alone they have right to hold."[10] After settlements had been effected in the wilds of America, "the emigrants thought proper to adopt that system of laws under which they had hitherto lived in the mother country, and to continue their union with her by submitting themselves to the same common sovereign, who was thereby made the central link connecting the several parts of the empire thus newly multiplied."[11]

The natural right of a "free trade with all parts of the world" was next asserted, and the acts of Parliament detrimental to American trade were catalogued and condemned. "The true ground on which we declare these acts void is, that the British parliament has no right to exercise authority over us."[12] On behalf of the inhabitants of British America a "solemn and determined protest" was directed against these "acts of power, assumed by a body of men, foreign to our constitutions, and unacknowledged by our laws."[13]

Charges against the king as wielder of the executive power were then mar-shaled. While the royal veto had become dormant in Great Britain, it should be used, according to Jefferson, "to prevent the passage of laws by any one legislature of the empire which might bear injuriously on the rights and in-terests of another," that is to say, against acts of Parliament injurious to America.[14] At the same time the king was castigated for the "wanton exercise of this power which we have seen his majesty practise on the laws of the American legislatures. For the most trifling reasons, and sometimes for no conceivable reason at all, his majesty has rejected laws of the most salutary tendency."[15] In the Declaration of Independence the cognate charge against the king was that "he has refused his Assent to Laws, the most wholesome and necessary for the public good."[16] The Declaration also echoed the com-plaint in the *Summary View* concerning the practice of suspending the laws enacted in America until royal assent thereto had been obtained, and of utterly neglecting to attend to them when so suspended.[17] Likewise both the Declaration and the *Summary View* censure the king's refusal to permit the creation of new counties or other municipalities unless they "relinquish the Right of Representation in the Legislature, a Right inestimable to them, and formidable to Tyrants only."[18] Dissolution of the legislative body and refusal to summon another was also an abuse denounced in both documents.[19]

Jefferson next embarked, in his *Summary View,* upon a discussion of feudal and allodial land tenure.[20] He took the view that William the Conqueror introduced feudal tenure in England based upon the proposition that all land was ultimately "holden of the king." In Anglo-Saxon times landowners had enjoyed allodial tenure, that is to say, absolute ownership. However, Jefferson emphasized, "America was not conquered by William the Norman, nor its lands surrendered to him, or any of his successors. Possessions there are undoubedly of the allodial nature. Our ancestors, however, who migrated hither, were laborers, not lawyers. The fictitious principle that all lands belong originally to the king, they were early persuaded to believe real; and accordingly took grants of their own lands from the crown." This did little harm, however, until the terms of obtaining a grant were made more onerous to the purchaser "by which means the acquisition of lands being rendered difficult, the population of our country is likely to be checked."[21]

Another abuse strongly resented by Americans was the presence of English troops without the consent of the local legislature. If the king possessed "such a right as this, it might swallow up all our other rights whenever he should think proper."[22] It was a fundamental principle of English liberty, recognized in the English Bill of Rights, that a standing army could not be kept up in time of peace without the consent of Parliament, and the Declaration of Independence stressed this grievance.[23]

Compounding this evil, the king had violated the principle of supremacy of the civil over the military power.[24] "To render these proceedings still more criminal against our laws, instead of subjecting the military to the civil power, his majesty has expressly made the civil subordinate to the military. But can his majesty thus put down all law under his feet? Can he erect a power superior to that which erected himself?"[25]

This eloquent inquiry is reminiscent of Bracton's familiar pronouncement that the king ought not be under any man, but under God and the law, since it is the law that makes him king.[26]

The concluding paragraph of the *Summary View* cogently recapitulates "our grievances which we have thus laid before your majesty with that freedom of language and sentiment which becomes a free people claiming their rights, as derived from the laws of nature, and not as the gift of their chief magistrate: let those flatter who fear, it is not an American art. . . . [We] know, and will therefore say, that kings are the servants, not the proprietors of the people. . . . The whole art of government consists in the art of being honest. . . . [Let it not] be proposed that our properties within our own territories shall be taxed or regulated by any power on earth but our own. The God who gave us life gave us liberty at the same time; the hand of force may destroy, but cannot disjoin them."[27]

Jefferson's second, and best-known, book was his *Notes on the State of Virginia.* This was a compilation prepared in response to a questionnaire from a French diplomat, François de Barbé-Marbois, who was seeking to gather for his government information about the various American states. The twenty-two queries propounded by the Frenchman,[28] as revised by Jefferson and rearranged into twenty-three queries, furnished the topics treated in the book.[29] Geographical, scientific, economic, and historical materials preponderate; but for the lawyer query XIII, regarding the Virginia constitution of 1776, and query XIV, containing a succinct account of the state of Virginia law, form the most important parts of the work.

The *Notes* were begun in 1781 at Poplar Forest, Jefferson's rustic retreat near Lynchburg, where he was confined by injuries received in falling from a horse.[30] They were forwarded to Marbois in December of that year after additional data had been gathered at Monticello and at Richmond.[31] Jefferson continued to revise the *Notes,* and they soon trebled in bulk.[32] Finding that it would be too expensive to print them in Philadelphia while he was on his way to France on a diplomatic mission,[33] he later had an edition of two hundred copies privately printed in Paris in 1785 by Philippe-Denis Pierres,[34] who had probably been recommended by Benjamin Franklin.[35] Jefferson considered "the original edition printed at Paris" as "the only one almost perfectly correct."[36]

One of the presentation copies of the book, upon the recipient's death, fell into the hands of Barrois, a Paris publisher, who planned to bring out "a surreptitious translation," which Jefferson found "abominable." To forestall this piratical venture, the Abbé Morellet, a prominent man of letters, offered to translate the work himself, submitting his version for correction by the author. Jefferson had no alternative except to acquiesce in Morellet's "friendly proposition."[37] But he was not satisfied with the rearrangements made by the translator.[38] Publication of the unsatisfactory French edition,[39] which appeared some time in 1787,[40] made it desirable and almost inevitable that the *Notes* be "offered to the public in their original form and language."

Jefferson had feared to take this step because he thought that the vigorous strictures on slavery and on the Virginia constitution, which had been set forth in the *Notes,* might elicit an adverse reaction in his native state.[41] Upon learning from Madison and other friends that dissemination of his views would not be harmful[42] and that an accurate version in English would be desirable because of the likelihood of mistranslations based upon the French text,[43] Jefferson resolved to permit the London publisher John Stockdale to issue, in 1787,[44] the first trade edition of the book in its original language.[45]

The publisher was strictly admonished to print the *Notes* "precisely as they are, without additions, alterations, preface, or any thing else but what is there."[46]

Subsequent editions were reprints of Stockdale's, with the addition, after 1800, of an appendix published in that year[47] containing data in support of Jefferson's version of the circumstances under which the family of Logan, an Indian chief, had been murdered.[48] The edition published at Richmond in

1853 incorporated corrections marked by Jefferson in his own annotated copy of the London edition of 1787.[49] The latest edition is that of William Peden in 1954.[50]

Query XIII relates to "the constitution of the state, and its several charters."[51] After an account of these charters, beginning with that to Sir Walter Raleigh in 1584,[52] Jefferson, "having never seen [them] in print," sets forth in full the articles of March 12, 1651, whereby the Virginians accepted the authority of the English commonwealth government under Cromwell.[53] It was expressly stipulated that this submission be "acknowledged a voluntary act not forced nor constrained by a conquest upon the countrey, and that they shall have & enjoy such freedomes and priviledges as belong to the free borne people of England."[54]

In Jefferson's words, "The colony supposed that, by this solemn convention, entered into with arms in their hands, they had secured the antient limits of their country, its free trade, its exemption from taxation but by their own assembly, and exclusion of military force from among them."[55] Repeated violations of this convention and other injuries (particularly under George III) evinced "a fixed design of considering our rights natural, conventional and chartered as mere nullities."[56] A list of abuses reminiscent of the *Summary View* is then reviewed. "No alternative was presented but resistance, or unconditional submission. Between these could be no hesitation. [The colonies] closed in the appeal to arms. They declared themselves independant States. They confederated together into one great republic; thus securing to every state the benefit of an union of their whole force. In each state separately a new form of government was established. Of ours particularly, the following are the outlines."[57]

After a brief description of the Virginia government,[58] Jefferson proceeds to an extensive enumeration of its defects:[59] (1) less than half of those who support the state by paying taxes and serving as soldiers are granted the right to vote;[60] (2) representation is unequal, the tidewater area controlling practically a majority in both houses of the legislature;[61] (3) the Senate and House of Delegates are too homogeneous;[62] (4) legislative, executive, and judicial powers are all possessed indiscriminately by the legislature, and "concentrating these in the same hands is precisely the definition of despotic government";[63] (5) "the ordinary legislature may alter the constitution itself";[64] (6) the legislature determines the quorum required to legislate,[65] "and if they may fix it at one number, they may at another, till it loses its fundamental character of being a representative body,"[66] so that thereby the form of government might be imperceptibly changed into an oligarchy, or even a monarchy[67] or dictatorship.[68]

The last two topics (regarding the power of the legislature to alter the constitution or the conditions governing the exercise of authority to legislate) are of the utmost importance. In these passages Jefferson voices the basic principles underlying his views of American constitutional law.[69]

Jefferson here made clear his belief that a constitution is an embodiment of fundamental law. Since it delineates the powers of the ordinary legislature and prescribes the procedure by which legally binding rules may be created, it must be superior to, and not susceptible of being altered or affected by, ordinary legislation. Hence a true constitution, that is to say, a fundamental or basic law binding upon the ordinary organs of government and unchangeable by them, must be established by authority of the people itself. To this end the people must act through special agents appointed for that particular purpose, as in a constitutional convention.[70]

Jefferson cited instances where the Virginia legislature had exercised executive and judicial powers, thereby repealing *pro hac vice* the provision of the 1776 constitution establishing the doctrine of separation of powers. This proved that "the ordinance called the Constitution" was subject to legislative modification, and hence "that the state of Virginia has no fixed Constitution at all."[71]

An essential feature of "a real constitution,"[72] in his mind, was that it "bind up the several branches of government by certain laws, which when they transgress their acts shall become nullities,"[73] and that it should proclaim and "declare those fundamentals to which all our laws present and future shall be subordinate."[74] It was also needful that the constitution "be rendered permanent by a power superior to that of the ordinary legislature."[75] Where such a "real constitution" was in force, Jefferson declared, "the judges would consider any law as void, which was contrary to the constitution."[76]

The Virginia Convention of 1776, in Jefferson's opinion, had not been entrusted by the people with such basic power or designated as a constitution-forming body. Its function was to exercise the ordinary powers of government after the collapse of British royal authority, and to organize Virginia's opposition to British arms.[77] Historically, Jefferson was correct.[78] Legally, he was also on firm ground when he defined the nature and function of a constitution, and its supremacy over ordinary legislation.[79] But as a matter of actual practice, long-continued popular acquiescence (an omnific force in a government based upon the philosophy which ascribes binding force to the consent of the governed) had established the validity of the constitution of 1776 as a fundamental law of the sort to which Jefferson proclaimed allegiance.[80] Likewise the Virginia courts accepted the instrument emanating from the convention of 1776 as a true constitution.[81]

Jefferson's response to the argument that "the people have acquiesced and this has given it [the ordinance entitled a constitution] an authority superior to the laws" was to inquire: "Should a prudent acquiescence, at a critical time, be construed into a confirmation of every illegal thing done during that period? . . . On every unauthoritative exercise of power by the legislature must the people rise in rebellion, or their silence be construed into a surrender of that power to them?"[82]

He scorned the similar contention "that if the convention had meant that this instrument should be alterable, as their other ordinances were, they would have called it an ordinance: but they have called it a *constitution,* which ex vi termini means 'an act above the power of the ordinary legislature.'"[83] He inquired: "But of what consequence is their meaning, where their power is denied? If they meant to do more than they had power to do, did this give them power? It is not the name, but the authority, which renders an act obligatory. . . . To get rid of the magic supposed to be in the word *constitution,* let us translate it into its definition as given by those who think it above the power of the law; and let us suppose the convention instead of saying 'We, the ordinary legislature, establish a *constitution,'* had said, 'We, the ordinary legislature, establish an act *above the power of the ordinary legislature.'* Does not this expose the absurdity of the attempt?"[84]

Throughout his lifetime Jefferson continued to urge that a constitutional convention be called, to place Virginia's fundamental law upon a sound basis, as well as to liberalize suffrage and effectuate other reforms. In the summer of 1783, when it was expected that the Virginia legislature would call a convention for the establishment of a new constitution, he prepared a draft, intending to have it "proposed in such Convention, had it taken place."[85] But no convention was called. Jefferson in Paris had his draft constitution printed as a sixteen page supplement to his *Notes on Virginia.*[86] This plan was proposed "with a view to correct the faults of the existing Constitution, as well as to obtain the authentic sanction of the people."[87] In 1794 he again attempted to encourage calling a convention. But there was to be no new constitution for Virginia until 1830, four years after his death.[88]

In response to query XIV Jefferson gave an account of Virginia's court system and a description of the laws. The county court, composed of four or more justices of the peace, exercised civil jurisdiction in all matters not pertaining to the admiralty.[89] An appeal could be taken to a superior court in matters involving ten pounds sterling or concerning the title to lands or their boundaries.[90] In criminal cases the county court could itself try offenses less than felony,[91] and in offenses amounting to felony could bind the defendant over for the grand jury in the General Court. By vote of 13 or more of the 24 grand jurors, a defendant was held for trial in the general court "by a jury of 12 men of the county where the offence was committed, and by their verdict, which must be unanimous, he is acquitted or condemned without appeal. If the criminal be a slave the trial by the county court is final.[92] In every case however, except that of high treason, there resides in the governor a power of pardon. In high treason, the pardon can only flow from the general assembly."[93] In later years Jefferson criticized the county courts as a self-perpetuating oligarchy. It was largely the opposition of the justices of the peace that frustrated his efforts to reform the Virginia constitution of 1776.[94]

Of the three superior courts, the jurisdiction of the admiralty court was exclusively original. The General Court and the chancery court received appeals from the county courts, and also exercised "original jurisdiction where the subject of controversy is of the value of ten pounds sterling or where it concerns the title or bounds of land."[95] Final determination of appeals in civil cases from the three superior courts was entrusted to one supreme court, called the court of appeals, composed of the judges of the three superior courts.[96]

Controversies between foreigners of a nation in alliance with the United States were referred to the consul of that nation, unless the parties chose to submit to the local courts. If only one party was foreign, he was entitled to decision by a superior court. In cases of life and death, the foreigner was entitled to trial by a jury of "one half foreigners, the other natives."[97]

Settlement of public accounts was entrusted to a board of three auditors, appointed by the General Assembly, subject to review by a superior court.[98]

In his description of the laws, Jefferson restates the contentions set forth in his *Summary View* regarding the adoption of the English common law in America.[99] "The laws of England seem to have been adopted by consent of the settlers, which might easily enough be done whilst they were few and living all together. Of such adoption however we have no other proof than their practice till the year 1661, when they were expressly adopted by an act of assembly[100] except so far as 'a difference of condition' rendered them inapplicable. Under this adoption, the rule, in our courts of judicature, was that the common law of England, and the general statutes previous to the 4th of James, were in force here; but that no subsequent statutes were, *unless we were named in them,* said the judges and other partisans of the crown, but *named or not named,* said those who reflected freely. . . . To those which were established here, by the adoption of the legislature, have been since added a number of acts of assembly passed during the monarchy, and ordinances of convention and acts of assembly enacted since the establishment of the republic."[101]

Jefferson then enumerates a number of provisions which differed from English law. Bankrupt debtors were released from confinement upon surrendering their assets, but later-acquired property remained subject to past debts.[102] Describing the poor laws, Jefferson praises the system of placing persons unable to labor in the houses of good farmers, and furnishing those able to support themselves in part but not entirely "supplementory aids . . . which enable them to live comfortably in their own houses or in the houses of their friends."[103] He exclaims, "I never yet saw a native American begging in the streets or highways."[104]

Marriages might be solemnized by any religious society of Christians;[105] conveyances of land had to be registered in the county court, or the General Court, or they were void as to creditors and subsequent purchasers;[106] slaves "pass by descent and dower as lands do" and "were entailable during the monarchy: but, by an act of the first republican assembly, all donees in tail, present and future, were vested with the absolute dominion of the entailed subject";[107] protested bills of exchange carried 10 per cent interest, but in other cases 5 per cent simple interest was the maximum;[108] gaming debts were void.[109]

Jefferson then describes legislation for the encouragement of industry and improvement of agriculture, the inspection of tobacco, flour, beef, pork, tar, pitch, and turpentine, the extirpation of noxious animals, and protection of public health.[110]

The mode of acquiring lands is then reviewed. Originally grants were made upon petition to the General Assembly. Later a procedure was established requiring location and survey by a public officer, followed by a grant from the governor, and the grantee was obliged to improve the lands in a certain manner within a given time.[111] Where irregularities existed, grants could be set aside by *scire facias* or by bill in chancery.[112] There was little change in the procedure following the establishment of republican government. "An individual, wishing to appropriate to himself lands still unappropriated by any other, pays to the public treasurer a sum of money proportioned to the quantity he wants. He carries the treasurer's receipt to the auditors of public accounts, who thereupon debit the treasurer with the sum, and order the register of the land-office to give the party a warrant for his land. With this warrant from the register, he goes to the surveyor of the county where the land lies on which he has cast his eye. The Surveyor lays it off for him, gives him its exact description, in the form of a certificate, which certificate he returns to the land-office, where a grant is made out, and is signed by the governor. This vests in him a perfect dominion in his lands, transmissible to whom he pleases by deed or will, or by descent to his heirs if he die intestate."[113]

In his account of the method of obtaining land grants, Jefferson did not mention caveats, although use of that procedure was the predominant feature of his law practice.[114] If the petitioner for a grant does not comply with legal requirements, "any other person may enter a *caveat* in the land office against issuing a grant, expressing therein for what cause the grant should not issue: or if any person obtains a survey of lands to which another hath by law a better right, the latter may in like manner enter a *caveat,* to prevent the former obtaining a grant till the title can be determined."[115] Upon the filing of a caveat a summons was issued to the petitioner to appear at the next General Court for determination of the issue. The procedure resembled one of the same name in the English church courts to prevent installation of a clerk or probate of a will.[116]

Jefferson concludes his description of the laws by giving an account of the revisal,[117] a comprehensive program of law reform in which he was a chief actor. It was an attempt to eradicate features of Virginia's ancient legal system which were deemed to be "inconsistent with republicanism."[118] Discussion of the revisal will be postponed to a later chapter dealing with that important topic.[119] For the present, it will suffice to state that of the committee of five chosen by the legislature to perform this work, Jefferson was the most zealous and diligent. On June 18, 1779, after he had become governor, he laid before the House of Delegates the report of the committee, comprising 126 bills.[120] On June 1, 1784, the House of Delegates, for the information of the public, ordered 500 copies of the proposed legislation to be printed. It would not be farfetched to consider this *Report of the Committee of Revisors Appointed by the General Assembly of Virginia In MDCCLXXVI*[121] as being substantially a work of Jefferson's authorship, and to regard it as a monument of legal research and draftsmanship comparable in scholarship to his two earlier productions, the *Summary View* and *Notes on Virginia.*[122]

Besides his skill in draftsmanship, Jefferson had other qualities which contributed to his success as a member of legislative bodies. John Adams wrote: "Mr. Jefferson came into Congress in June, 1775, and brought with him a reputation for literature, science, and a happy talent of composition. Writings of his were handed about, remarkable for the peculiar felicity of expression. Though a silent member in Congress, he was so prompt, frank, explicit, and decisive upon committees and in conversation, not even Samuel Adams was more so, that he soon seized upon my heart."[123]

It was Jefferson's policy "that in measures brought forward by myself, I took the laboring oar, as was incumbent on me; but that in general I was willing to listen. If every sound argument or objection was used by some one or other of the numerous debaters, it was enough: if not, I thought it sufficient to suggest the omission, without going into a repetition of what had already been said by others. . . . If the present Congress errs in too much talking, how can it be otherwise in a body to which the people send 150. lawyers, whose trade it is to question everything, yield nothing, & talk by the hour? That 150. lawyers should do business together ought not to be expected."[124]

Jefferson's service in the Virginia House of Burgesses, under the royal government, began in 1769 and continued until that body ceased to function. He attended the second Virginia convention at Richmond in 1775,[125] where he was elected as a Virginia delegate to the Continental Congress.[126] The preceding year he had set out for the first Virginia convention at Williamsburg, but on account of illness was unable to attend.[127] After adoption of the Declaration of Independence on July 4, 1776, he left Congress and returned to Virginia in the autumn, in order to pursue as a member of the House of Delegates his program of law reform. Important legislation with which he was concerned dealt with entails, relief for religious dissenters, the establishment of courts of justice, and creation of a committee to revise the laws. Jefferson remained in the legislature until his election as governor on June 1, 1779.[128] He held that office until June 12, 1781. After the death of his wife in 1782, he returned to public life, taking his seat as a member of Congress on November 4, 1783, at Princeton, New Jersey.[129] On July 5, 1784, he sailed for France on a diplomatic mission. Returning in 1789, he served as secretary of state in the administration of George Washington until December 31, 1793. After another interval of private life at Monticello, he was sworn in as vice-president of the United States on March 4, 1797. He was inaugurated as the nation's third president on March 4, 1801.

It was in order to facilitate his task as presiding officer of the Senate during his term as vice-president that Jefferson prepared his next published book, *A Manual of Parliamentary Practice, for the Use of the Senate of the United States.*[130] Of the little volume he said "it was a mere compilation, into which nothing entered of my own but the arrangement, and a few observations necessary to explain that and some of the cases."[131]

In gathering material for his manual Jefferson called upon the experience of his long-time mentors George Wythe and Edmund Pendleton as well as upon his own research and recollection of the usages of legislative assemblies of which he had been a member.[132]

His basic source was a "Parliamentary Pocket-Book," now in the Massachusetts Historical Society, containing 145 numbered items, together with "Rules for conducting the business in the Senate of the United States" in 28 articles.[133] He informed Wythe: "I had, at an early period of life, read a good deal on the subject, & commonplaced what I read. This commonplace has been my pillow, but there are many questions of practice on which that is silent. Some of them are so minute indeed & belong so much to every day's practice that they have never been thought worthy of being written down."[134]

EDMUND PENDLETON by Thomas Sully.
    A wily, polished lawyer and politician, Pendleton constantly bested Wythe in their rivalry at the Virginia bar.
    Courtesy Virginia Historical Society.

On these points he sought the views of Wythe and Pendleton, writing his questions on paper with a wide margin, upon which they could answer yes or no. For the sake of his reputation he desired to state the customary practice correctly.[135] His mentors obligingly answered at length, but professing little confidence in the correctness of their opinions. Pendleton replied: "I am not only rusty in Parliamentary Rules, but never read much on the subject; my small stock of knowledge in that way I caught from Mr. Robinson & Gnl. Randolph, or was the result of my own reflexions dictated by the principle of having every question so put as to be well understood, & free as might be from embarrassment, or complexity. My mite however is freely cast into the Treasury, and I wish it was of more value." Wythe likewise concluded: "My language is didactic. Yet I am confident of nothing that I have written."[136]

Jefferson's working draft for the manual is in the Huntington Library.[137] There is a small notebook bearing the title "Rules of practice in the Senate of the U.S.," with 149 numbered items of data. There is also a list of 54 headings, all of which (except number 54) appear in the published work, which is divided into 53 topics. The items are allocated to the appropriate headings, and new matter is added. A new title was inscribed, "A manual of the Rules of proceeding in the Senate of the U S," and two new headings were inserted.[138]

In the published text, after the introductory heading on the importance of rules,[139] there follow a number of topics relating to the organization of the legislative body,[140] and then a lengthy list of rubrics relating to the various procedural steps to be pursued in enacting a bill into law.[141] Next are treated reconsideration, relations with the other house, and various formalities.[142] In conclusion the subjects of treaties and impeachment are dealt with.[143]

In a preface Jefferson refers to the extensive discretion conferred upon the presiding officer by the Constitution of the United States and the rules of the Senate, and the consequent necessity of his recurring "to some known system of rules, that he may neither leave himself free to indulge caprice or passion, nor open to the imputation of them." For this purpose the practice of the English Parliament, the prototype of American legislative bodies, is best known and most generally accepted. Moreover its rules are "wisely constructed" for governing the debates of a deliberative body "and obtaining its true sense." Accordingly, "I have here endeavored to collect and digest so much of these [precepts of the Constitution, regulations of the Senate, and rules of Parliament] as is called for in ordinary practice, collating the Parliamentary with the Senatorial rules, both where they agree and where they vary. I have done this, as well to have them at hand for my own government, as to deposit with the Senate the standard by which I am willing to judge and be judged."[144]

In the first section of the *Manual,* on the importance of rules, Jefferson emphasizes that "the only weapons by which the minority can defend themselves" against abuse of power by the majority "are the forms and rules of proceeding which have been adopted as they were found necessary from time to time, and are become the law of the house." He stresses that it is much more important "that there should be a rule to go by, than what that rule is."[145]

The vital role of parliamentary law as an aspect of constitutional law did not escape Jefferson's notice. The procedures observed by legislative bodies constitute a significant portion of the fundamental constitutional rules which prescribe how law shall validly come into being. "To suppose this branch of law, not existing in our code, would shake the foundation of our whole legal system; since every proposition which has been passed or rejected since the first establishment of a legislature in this country, has been determined to be law, or not law, by the forms of Parliamentary proceeding."[146]

The rules of parliamentary law, like other aspects of English law, became part of the law of the land in America because they were adopted by the settlers as their birthright. This was expounded by Jefferson on behalf of the Virginia House of Delegates in the course of a dispute with the Senate regarding the prerogatives of the House with respect to money bills. He declared that "the law and customs of their parliament, which include the usage as to 'money bills' are a part of the law of their land; our ancestors adopted their system of law in the general, making from time to time such alterations as local diversities required; but that part of their law which relates to the matter now in question was never altered by our legislature, in any period of its history; but on the contrary, the two Houses of Assembly, both under our regal and republican governments, have ever done business on the constant admission that the law of parliament was their law."[147]

Another subject of general interest discussed in the *Manual* is the topic of treaties.[148] Jefferson states emphatically that "Treaties are legislative acts. A treaty is a law of the land. It differs from other laws only as it must have the consent of a foreign nation, being but a contract with respect to that nation."[149] Hence only an act of legislation can declare a treaty infringed and rescinded.[150]

The scope of the treaty power, says Jefferson, is undefined and controversial; and so has it remained until today. The criteria enumerated by Jefferson for determining the propriety of dealing with a particular subject by treaty are substantially such as would command general acceptance at the present time: "1. . . . [I]t must concern the foreign nation, party to the contract. 2. [It must fall within] those objects which are usually regulated by treaty, and cannot be otherwise regulated. 3. [The Constitution] must have meant to except out of these the rights reserved to the States; for surely the President

31

and Senate cannot do by treaty what the whole government is interdicted from doing in any way."[151]

A fourth criterion discussed in the *Manual* would exclude from regulation by treaty "those subjects of legislation in which [the Constitution] gave a participation to the House of Representatives. This . . . exception is denied by some, on the ground that it would leave very little matter for the treaty power to work on. The less the better, say others."[152] Jefferson seems dubious regarding the validity of this fourth criterion, and history has vindicated his skepticism.[153]

Curiously enough, in 1785 under the Articles of Confederation Jefferson advocated entering into treaties in order to enable Congress to exercise powers over commerce which it did not possess in the absence of treaty.[154] Writing from Paris to James Monroe, he explained how concluding treaties would expand national control of commerce:

Congress, by the Confederation have no original and inherent power over the commerce of the states. But by the 9th. article they are authorized to enter into treaties of commerce. The moment those treaties are concluded the jurisdiction of Congress over the commerce of the states springs into existence, and that of the particular states is superseded so far as the articles of the treaty may have taken up the subject. There are two restrictions only on the exercise of the power of treaty by Congress, 1st. that they shall not by such treaty restrain the legislatures of the states from imposing such duties on foreigners as their own people are subject to. 2dly. nor from prohibiting the exportation or importation of any particular species of goods. Leaving these two points free, Congress may by treaty establish any system of commerce they please. But, as I before observed, it is by treaty only they can do it. Though they may exercise their other powers by resolution or ordinance, those over commerce can only be exercised by forming a treaty, and this probably by an accidental wording of our Confederation. If therefore it is better for the states that Congress should regulate their commerce, it is proper that they should form treaties with all nations with whom we may possibly treat. You see that my primary object in the formation of treaties is to take the commerce of the states out of the hands of the states, and to place it under the superintendence of Congress, so far as the imperfect provisions of our constitution will admit, and until the states shall by new compact make them more perfect. I would say then to every nation on earth, *by treaty,* your people shall trade freely with us, & ours with you, paying no more than the most favoured nation, in order to put an end to the right of individual states acting by fits and starts to interrupt our commerce or to embroil us with any nation.[155]

Another proposal by Jefferson, designed to prevent state legislation in violation of treaties, may have contributed to establishment of the doctrine of judicial review by the Supreme Court.

In the Constitutional Convention a proposal was made, which Madison strongly supported, to give the federal government a veto power over all state legislation.[156] It was thought that such power was necessary to effectuate the enforcement of treaties with foreign nations. But when this plan for a federal negative on state legislation "in all cases whatsoever" was communicated by Madison to Jefferson in Paris,[157] the latter replied, in an important letter, that the proposal was too broad and sweeping. It was defective in an essential feature, "that the hole & the patch should be commensurate."[158]

Instead of an all-embracing veto power permitting the federal government to veto state legislation on any subject, regardless of whether it was necessary or not in order to ensure compliance with treaties entered into by authority of the United States, Jefferson urged adoption of a provision extending the federal judicial power to cases where a treaty or federal law was controlling. This would be "as effectual a remedy & exactly commensurate with the defect."[159] There would then be a judicial question for decision by the courts whenever any conflict between a state law and a treaty was raised. This method of enforcement of treaty obligations, rather than the federal veto power favored by Madison, was eventually incorporated in the Constitution.[160]

Jefferson's suggestion may have been based on resolutions of the Continental Congress adopted in response to reports from John Adams, the American envoy in London, that Great Britain's refusal to return military posts along the Canadian frontier, as required by the treaty of peace of September 3, 1783, was based upon alleged violations by several states of provisions in that treaty intended to facilitate collection of debts in America by English creditors. Congress called upon the states to repeal, by description rather than by enumeration, any and all state laws which conflicted with treaties in force.[161] It was pointed out that "by repealing in general terms all Acts and clauses repugnant to the treaty, the business will be turned over to its proper Department, viz, the Judicial, and the Courts of Law will find no difficulty in deciding whether any particular Act or clause is or is not contrary to the treaty."[162]

When duty called Jefferson from the pleasures of Paris to the more onerous post of secretary of state, he himself prepared an able and thorough reply to British charges of treaty violation.[163] Other examples of his powers of legal argumentation on international subjects may be seen in his discussion of American navigation rights on the Mississippi,[164] and of the question whether treaties with France survived the abolition of the monarchy in that nation.[165] In the latter document he cited, in parallel columns, the views of recognized authorities on international law (Grotius, Pufendorf, Wolff, and Vattel).[166]

Jefferson's principal contributions to international law dealt with the rights and duties of neutral nations during war between other states.[167] This problem, serious as it was in Washington's time, became more acute during Jefferson's presidency. It was then that he embarked upon the ill-fated embargo laws,[168] as an experiment in "peaceable coercion."[169] Jefferson's attitude toward international affairs was dominated by a high-minded policy of enlightened self-interest. He recognized "but one system of ethics [and one code of morality] for men and for nations."[170]

Impeachment, the final topic treated in the *Manual,*[171] is another subject of greater interest to the general public than the formalities of the legislative process which fill most of the book's pages.[172]

After a review of the constitutional provisions relating to impeachment,[173] Jefferson outlines the English practice.[174] Points discussed include jurisdiction; accusation; process; articles; appearance; answer; replication, rejoinder, and the like; witnesses; jury;[175] presence of commons;[176] judgment; and continuance.[177]

In capital cases, the judgment must be strictly in accordance with law. The Lords "can neither omit any part of the legal judgment, nor add to it. Their sentences must be *secundum, non ultra legem.* "[178]

Continuing, Jefferson says: "This trial, though it varies in external ceremony, yet differs not in essentials from criminal prosecutions before inferior courts. The same rules of evidence, the same legal notions of crimes and punishments prevail. For impeachments are not framed to alter the law, but to carry it into more effectual execution against too powerful delinquents.[179] The judgment therefore is to be such as is warranted by legal principles or precedents."[180]

This passage should not be interpreted as supporting the contention advanced in 1974 by counsel for President Richard M. Nixon that an offense is not impeachable under the Constitution of the United States unless it is also a crime punishable under the ordinary criminal law. Although this position is often taken by defendants in impeachment proceedings, the consensus of legal scholars is that it is unsound.[181] It is contradicted by the teachings of both English[182] and American[183] history, as well as by the very language of the Constitution itself.[184]

The better view would include among impeachable offenses any grave and serious breach of public trust, disregard of duty, or usurpation or abuse of official power.[185] The purpose of impeachment is not so much to punish the offender as to protect the public from harm.[186] In England impeachment, like attainder, was a method of removing from office a person whose continuance therein was detrimental to the public interest.[187]

The passage in Jefferson's *Manual* (discussing only capital cases) seems to indicate that where an impeachment involves a charge of treason (in other words is based on a charge which *does* constitute a punishable offense under the criminal laws) the definition of the crime, the rules of evidence, and the penalty are the same as if the case were pending in a criminal court.[188]

At one period Jefferson considered impeachment as "the most formidable weapon for the purposes of a dominant faction that ever was contrived. . . . I know of no solid purposes of punishment which the courts of law are not equal to, and history shows, that in England, impeachment has been an engine more of passion than justice."[189] However, after the acquittal in 1805 of Justice Samuel Chase (whose impeachment Jefferson had instigated)[190] he regarded impeachment as an ineffectual "scarecrow" or "farce."[191]

III

The Plastic Nature
of Law

More than a decade after publication of his *Manual,* Jefferson sent to the printer in 1812 the last book written by him and published during his lifetime. This was *The Proceedings of the Government of the United States, in Maintaining the Public Right to the Beach of the Missisipi, Adjacent to New-Orleans, against the Intrusion of Edward Livingston.*[1] Of this volume the author confessed, "It is merely a law argument, and a very dry one."[2] Jefferson was then in retirement at Monticello but had become embroiled in a lawsuit brought against him in a Virginia federal court by Edward Livingston. In this proceeding the plaintiff claimed damages of $100,000 because of Jefferson's official action while president in authorizing the use of force to eject Livingston from the *batture* or beach at New Orleans. The book contains a detailed discussion of the facts and legal questions involved in the litigation.

Edward Livingston was born in 1764 of a prominent New York family. (His brother, Robert R. Livingston, administered the oath of office to George Washington in 1789 and was one of the envoys to France negotiating the Louisiana Purchase during Jefferson's first term as president.) Edward Livingston, who was likewise minister to France from 1833 to 1835, died in 1836. After serving three terms in Congress, he became mayor of New York City in 1801 and at the same time was appointed United States attorney by Jefferson. In that capacity he incurred liability to the government by reason of a $44,000 shortage in the accounts of a subordinate. Acknowledging his responsibility, he resigned both offices in 1803 and sought to improve his fortunes by land speculation in New Orleans, where he arrived on February 7, 1804. He represented Louisiana in Congress from 1823 to 1829 and then in the Senate from 1829 to 1831, when he became secretary of state in the cabinet of President Jackson. He held that office until his appointment to serve in France. A man of enormous ability, he drafted a code of criminal law in 1824 at the request of the Louisiana legislature. This was a notable piece of work which won the approbation of the English law reformer Jeremy Bentham and also of Jefferson, although it never was enacted into law either in Louisiana or in any other jurisdiction.[3]

Livingston's suit against Jefferson was dismissed in 1811 on a procedural technicality (becoming the leading American case for the proposition that actions for trespass to real estate are not "transitory" but must be brought in the jurisdiction where the land is situated and nowhere else).[4] Hence the former president, in justification of his official conduct, wished to convince the public that his position with regard to the merits of the controversy was well founded. So he decided to make available to a wider circle of readers the memorandum which he had originally prepared for use by his counsel.[5]

Before discussing Jefferson's analysis of the case, it will be helpful to outline the history of the dispute. Not only Jefferson's activities as an author, but also his behavior as a litigant, will thus be portrayed.

The basic question at issue was whether, under applicable law, new land (alluvion) formed by the action of the Mississippi River, in depositing soil along its bank during seasonal yearly inundations over a long period of time, belonged to the owner of the adjacent riparian land (title to which Livingston had acquired) or to the public (more specifically to the French king, to whose title the United States was successor in interest by virtue of the Louisiana Purchase).[6] Another controverted point was whether, even if the United States government had a valid claim to the alluvial land, Congress had authorized the president to remove intruding occupants. At Jefferson's direction the United States marshal had evicted Livingston's workmen from the batture as summarily and unceremoniously as General Douglas MacArthur, upon orders from President Herbert Hoover, expelled unemployed veterans from government-owned property at Washington in 1932.[7]

On May 16, 1810, suit was instituted against Jefferson on behalf of Livingston by John Wickham, a prominent Richmond attorney. Wickham anticipated at once that the action would be dismissed upon the grounds later elaborated in the court's opinion of December 5, 1811. He advised his client that if the time had not been so short he would have desired "a further communication with You before ordering the writ, as it is contrary to my usual practice to bring a suit in opposition to my own Judgment, & notwithstanding my respect for the opinions You mention, my present Impressions are unfavorable to your right of recovery, not upon the merits, but the Ground of Jurisdiction."[8]

The former president promptly engaged William Wirt and George Hay to defend him.[9] Later, with Wirt's approval, Littleton Waller Tazewell was added as a defense attorney.[10] Hay was the son-in-law of James Monroe (later to be Madison's successor as president). Wirt later served with distinction as attorney general of the United States from 1817 to 1828; and besides his professional attainments exhibited his literary talent by publishing *Letters of the British Spy* in 1803 and a biography of Patrick Henry in 1817. Tazewell, later a governor of Virginia, had as a boy lived in the house of George Wythe and studied Greek and Latin under him.

LITTLETON WALLER TAZEWELL by Charles Balthazar Julien Févret de St. Mémin.

As a youth Tazewell lived in George Wythe's house and was tutored by him in Greek.

Courtesy National Portrait Gallery, Smithsonian Institution.

Wickham had been one of Aaron Burr's counsel at his trial for treason at Richmond, over which Chief Justice John Marshall had presided.[11] Wirt and Hay acted as counsel for the prosecution in that case, while Tazewell was a member of the grand jury which had indicted Burr.[12] During the course of the proceedings against Burr, Marshall directed to President Jefferson a subpoena *duces tecum* calling for production of documents desired by Burr.[13] Jefferson refused to comply, but arranged for Hay to make available "anything proper for communication, & pertinent to any point" in Burr's defense. "Reserving the necessary right of the President of the U S to decide, independently of all other authority, what papers coming to him as President, the public interests permit to be communicated, & to whom, I assure you of

38

my readiness under that restriction, voluntarily to furnish on all occasions whatever the purposes of justice may require."[14]

He also offered consent to take in Washington his deposition or that of department heads. "As to our personal attendance at Richmond, I am persuaded the Court is sensible, that paramount duties to the nation at large control the obligation of compliance with their summons in this case. . . . To comply with such calls would leave the nation without an executive branch, whose agency, nevertheless, is understood to be so constantly necessary, that it is the sole branch which the constitution requires to be always in function."

With respect to papers, Jefferson observed that "there is certainly a public & a private side to our offices. To the former belong grants of land, patents for inventions, certain commissions, proclamations, & other papers patent in their nature. To the other belong mere executive proceedings. All nations have found it necessary, that for advantageous conduct of their affairs, some of these proceedings, at least, should remain known to their executive functionary only. He, of course, from the nature of the case, must be the sole judge of which of them the public interests will permit publication."[15]

After reading Marshall's opinion,[16] Jefferson responded with what Beveridge rightly calls "an answer of great ability, in which Jefferson the lawyer shines brilliantly forth."[17] The president wrote: "I did not see till last night the opinion of the Judge on the *subpoena duces tecum* against the President. Considering the question there as *coram non judice,* I did not read his argument with much attention. Yet I saw readily enough, that, as is usual where an opinion is to be supported, right or wrong, he dwells much on smaller objections, and passes over those which are solid. Laying down the position generally, that all persons owe obedience to subpoenas, he admits no exception unless it can be produced in his law books. But if the Constitution enjoins on a particular officer to be always engaged in a particular set of duties imposed on him, does not this supersede the general law, subjecting him to minor duties inconsistent with these? The Constitution enjoins his constant agency in the concerns of 6. millions of people. Is the law paramount to this, which calls on him on behalf of a single one? Let us apply the Judge's own doctrine to the case of himself & his brethren. The sheriff of Henrico summons him from the bench, to quell a riot somewhere in his county. The federal judge is, by the general law, a part of the *posse* of the State sheriff. Would the Judge abandon major duties to perform lesser ones? Again; the court of Orleans or Maine commands, by subpoenas, the attendance of all the judges of the Supreme Court. Would they abandon their posts as judges, and the interests of millions committed to them, to serve the purposes of a single individual?"

Jefferson emphasizes that "the leading principle of our Constitution is the independence of the Legislature, executive and judiciary of each other, and none are more jealous of this than the judiciary. But would the executive be independent of the judiciary, if he were subject to the *commands* of the latter, & to imprisonment for disobedience; if the several courts could bandy him from pillar to post, keep him constantly trudging from north to south & east to west, and withdraw him entirely from his constitutional duties?"[18]

Jefferson also resented, as a personal slur, Marshall's comment that *"'it is apparent* that the President's duties as chief magistrate do not demand his whole time, & are not unremitting.' If he alludes to our annual retirement from the seat of government, during the sickly season, he should be told that such arrangements are made for carrying on the public business . . . that it goes on as unremittingly . . . as if we were at the seat of government. I pass more hours in public business at Monticello than I do here, every day; and it is much more laborious, because all must be done in writing."[19]

Moreover, the president regarded the subpoena issued on Burr's behalf as a judicial interference with the executive branch, similar to Marshall's earlier opinion in the case of *Marbury* v. *Madison.*[20] Marbury had been nominated as a justice of the peace in the District of Columbia by President Adams on March 2, 1801 (two days before Jefferson's inauguration) and was confirmed by the Senate. But the commission had not been delivered to him before the new administration took office. Jefferson forbade its delivery (although it might have been delivered if Chief Justice Marshall, who had continued to act as secretary of state at Jefferson's request during his first day as chief executive, had been more diligent). Subsequently Marbury sought mandamus in the Supreme Court to compel Madison, as secretary of state, to deliver the commission. In his celebrated opinion in this case, Marshall declared that Marbury was entitled to his commission, and that mandamus was the proper remedy to obtain it. But the Chief Justice then went on to hold that the Court had no jurisdiction to award that remedy, because the act of Congress conferring such power was unconstitutional. He thus avoided making an order which Madison would probably have ignored, but at the same time he preempted for the Supreme Court the power to hold acts of Congress void. Today the case is best known as a precedent establishing this power of judicial review. But to Jefferson and his contemporaries "the case represented the determination of Marshall and his Associates to interfere with the authority of the Executive, and it derived its chief importance then from that aspect." It was Marshall's elaborate dicta, not necessary for the decision of the case, but affording an opportunity for gratuitous castigation of the executive department, that aroused Jefferson's lifelong resentment.[21]

Bitter frustration was also Jefferson's lot when, notwithstanding all his efforts as a zealous prosecutor, Burr was acquitted. He viewed Marshall's

JOHN MARSHALL by William Hubard.
    The chief justice's judicial instincts overcame his political antagonism to Jefferson and he decided the case of *Livingston* v. *Jefferson* in favor of the ex-president.
    Courtesy National Portrait Gallery, Smithsonian Institution.

instrumentality in that outcome with equal displeasure. In his seventh annual message to Congress on October 27, 1807, he said: "I shall think it my duty to lay before you the proceedings and the evidence publicly exhibited on the arraignment of the principal offenders before the circuit court of Virginia. You will be enabled to judge whether the defect was in the testimony, in the law, or in the administration of the law; and wherever it shall be found, the Legislature alone can apply or originate the remedy."[22]

It is not surprising, therefore, that when Livingston's suit about the batture was instituted, Jefferson considered it extremely unfortunate that Marshall was the judge by whom his case would be tried.[23] The hostility of the judge was a significant factor in Jefferson's mind at all times when he reflected upon the strategy and tactics to be employed in his defense.

When on May 25, 1810, Hay advised, "My impression is, that an action will not lie here, for a trespass committed in N. Orleans,"[24] Jefferson was reluctant to rely upon any pleas the sufficiency of which would raise questions of law for determination by his enemy on the bench. "I hope our practice in this country relieves us from the special plea which Mr. Rodney speaks of: this would place everything under the grip of the judge, who in the cases of Marbury & of Burr has given us lessons of the plastic nature of law in his hands. To him nothing is to be ultimately submitted. The plea to the jurisdiction which had occurred to you, & is repeated by Rodney, I am too rusty in my law to decide on: but I know how the judge will decide it but that is not to prevent it's being used if proper."[25] On the same subject he told Rodney that "the feelings of the judge are too deeply engraven to let this obstacle stand in the way of getting at his victim. My only chance is an appeal."[26] Two days later he wrote to Gallatin: "What the issue of the case ought to be, no unbiased man can doubt. What it will be, no one can tell. The judge's inveteracy is profound, and his mind of that gloomy malignity which will never let him forego the opportunity of satiating it on a victim. His decisions, his instructions to a jury, his allowances and disallowances and garblings of evidence, must all be subjects of appeal. . . . And to whom is my appeal? From the judge in Burr's case to himself and his associate judges in the case of Marbury v. Madison. Not exactly, however. I observe old Cushing is dead. At length, then, we have a chance of getting a Republican majority in the Supreme judiciary. . . . The event is a fortunate one, and so timed as to be a Godsend to me."[27]

Another significant aspect of Jefferson's conduct of the litigation is his control of the issues to be raised in pleading his defense. Although he professed not to be adept in the realm of procedural skills and declared, "I leave this to you gentlemen of the law,"[28] he in fact gave clear directions to his counsel how the case was to be handled. "I never had any relish or respect for the art of pleading; and therefore am no judge of it," he wrote to Hay. Yet he went on to state that a plea "that the action was official & without malice, could suffice for myself; but I stand pledged to a certain degree to the territory of Orleans not to abandon their title, and I suppose that our right of using several pleas may be made to protect their interests as well as my own. All this I leave to you gentlemen to settle." His own judgment with respect to the pleas to be filed, he professed, "was not worth anything; because of all branches of the law, that of the niceties of pleading least attracted my respect or attention; and our judges of that day being plain country gentlemen, gave no encouragement to scruples of pleading. . . . I must beg leave to rest this entirely on the judgment of my counsel."[29]

Jefferson was aware that the question of title to the batture was not necessary to his own defense.[30] But he was always sensitive to the political repercussions of the litigation, not only upon his own reputation but also upon the interests of the inhabitants of New Orleans. Hence he regarded it as important that the right of the public to the land in dispute should be established.[31] Hay[32] and Tazewell[33] also encouraged trial of the merits, feeling that the defendant had a strong case.

Jefferson's insistence on defending the rights of the people of New Orleans to their accustomed use of the batture may be an instance of the intense interest which he evinced at all times in Louisiana, the navigation of the Mississippi, and the development of the West.[34] He informed Governor Claiborne that he had been strongly advised to rest on his special plea of justification and "not to meddle with the question of [the public] right. This is urged from a desire to have the question constitutionally settled, whether one branch of the government is amenable to another for its official acts. But I think the right of Orleans a clear one, and will not abandon it. It is impossible the decision should be against it, if the proper evidence is collected."[35] However, the burden of obtaining evidence in New Orleans would be extensive,[36] and "the expense of defending the right to the batture ought not to be left on me. My defence would not require a single witness"[37] but could be established by official documents.

Any expectations Jefferson had entertained that the federal government or that of the Territory of Orleans would relieve him of the expense of defending the case were disappointed.[38] Ultimately, Jefferson's counsel concluded that his "interests ought not to be put in hazard even, for the benefit of settling either abstract political questions, or of trying a right of property in others who seemed to take no interest in the controversy."[39] The plea that the court could not entertain an action arising out of a trespass to land situated outside the jurisdiction was filed and was sustained by the court.

Jefferson himself had directed the filing of this plea as well as pleading the "general issue" under which the question of title could be litigated,[40] together with the special plea of justification[41] by virtue of official action without malice and pursuant to an act of Congress.[42] "With respect to pleas, I think, if the government should take an interest in the case I should omit none which may defeat the action in any way. The plea to the jurisdiction therefore, if it can be maintained, should be put in, and especially as it is recommended by the Atty. Genl. . . . If the action should be got rid of in any of these ways, I should immediately lay the case before the public, either directly, or by addressing the justification to Congress."[43]

Jefferson was thus contemplating publication of his memoir on the batture even before that suggestion was made by Hay when he announced to his illustrious client that the court had dismissed the case against him for lack of jurisdiction. Hay wrote: "You will pardon me for suggesting to you, that as the suit has gone off on a collateral point, it would afford great satisfaction to the public to see that its fate would have been no better if it had been tried on the merits. This they will see if the defence which you entrusted to my hands shall be made known. You will be so good as to say what shall be done with it, and with the books and documents belonging to the Cause."[44]

In his first communication to counsel (indeed in the very letter engaging their services) Jefferson indicated his intention of drawing up his statement of the case: "I have no information of the ground of the action & can only conjecture that it must be some act of mine, as President, respecting the Batture of N. Orleans. As soon as it shall be explained to me I shall make out a statement of the case for your government in pleading." He also instructed his attorneys to require the strictest observance of procedural formalities on the part of the plaintiff, even to the extent of disregarding the usual professional courtesies accorded to dilatory brethren. "Livingston residing out of the state & being bankrupt, I must pray you to call for security for the costs in the first place; & also that on any delay or failure in pleading which may authorize a dismission of his action, it be dismissed. The nature of the suit, as well as my duty to the public, requires this of me; & altho' it may be contrary to the courtesy of the bar towards one another, yet you may stand justified to your brethren by the positive instructions recieved. It will be important that I recieve a copy of his declaration, & any other information as to the ground of his action as soon as possible."[45]

The policy of insisting upon punctilious conformity by plaintiff with all procedural requirements had the disadvantage of reciprocity: the defendant would be held to equally strict compliance. Hence Jefferson's lawyers repeatedly importuned him to furnish them with his statement of the case without delay. Hay requested him on May 25, 1810, to "indicate the several laws under which the act is to be justified and to furnish copies of the documents,

GEORGE HAY by Cephas Thompson (formerly attributed to Rembrandt Peale).
Hay was also prosecutor in the trial of Aaron Burr for treason.
Courtesy Margaret N. Robins and Frick Art Reference Library.

if there be any, which may throw light on this subject. In doing this no time should be lost: as the defendants counsel requiring the utmost exactness on the part of the plaintiff will probably be required to observe equal exactness themselves."[46]

Jefferson lost no time in requesting President Madison's permission for the appropriate government offices to furnish necessary papers, and in writing directly to the heads of the departments involved.[47] The War Department supplied one item;[48] the secretary of state forwarded a voluminous mass of material.[49] State and Treasury each produced a further packet of pertinent papers.[50] The mayor of New Orleans also transmitted documents,[51] as did Governor Claiborne.[52]

But the process of gathering documents was lengthy and laborious, even though all the departments of government extended full cooperation. Jefferson wrote to his counsel: "I am busily engaged in collecting materials from the offices, arranging, extracting &c so as to be able to put a very plain case in your hands. . . .[53] But it will take me long. Every paper . . . is to be written for to Washington; & to await leisure for research &c. Every facility however which their occupations permit is most kindly extended to me there, and I trust that in the fulness of time I shall send you the case in such order as to give the least trouble possible where matter & materials are so voluminous."[54]

Additional time in preparing the memoir was consumed because Jefferson considered that the action upon which the suit was based had been an administration policy agreed to by his cabinet at the time. Accordingly he wished his formulation of the grounds of defense of that action to represent the views and receive the approval of his colleagues: Madison (Jefferson's secretary of state, now president); Caesar A. Rodney (Jefferson's attorney general at the time, and continuing to hold that post under Madison); Albert Gallatin (Treasury); and Robert Smith (secretary of the navy under Jefferson and secretary of state under Madison).[55]

Pressed by counsel for his statement of the case, which they needed before preparing the pleas to be filed,[56] Jefferson first forwarded a rough draft on August 1, 1810: "It has been impossible for me sooner to finish copying the inclosed. New matter occured as I went along, and you will find some additions of importance. It was ready for the last post; but just as I was concluding it Govr Claiborne arrived and I put it into his hands for correction. He set some local facts to right, so that it stands now with his entire approbation."[57]

Meanwhile an important memorandum had been received from Gallatin.[58] When counsel returned the draft, Jefferson added suggestions made by Gallatin.[59] Another substantial revision was incorporated after Jefferson finally received from Rodney, early in October, a memoir by Moreau[60] which he had

ALBERT GALLATIN by Rembrandt Peale.
   Although not a lawyer, Gallatin was familiar with legislation relating to the public lands, and gave Jefferson useful advice in the batture controversy with Livingston.
   Courtesy Independence Hall National Park.

long been endeavoring to procure.[61] That writer, according to Jefferson, "has treated the branch of the subject depending on the French law of alluvions & the edict of Louis XIV with great learning & ability."[62]

The day after Jefferson forwarded the final version of his statement of the case to his counsel, he sent copies to a member of the Senate and of the House,[63] in pursuance of a plan to assure that no action would be taken in Congress which might have an injurious effect upon the opinion of a jury regarding the issues in dispute.[64]

Jefferson decided to publish his memoir in the same form in which it had been submitted to his counsel, without revising it in order to make it more readable or comprehensible to the general public. In reply to Hay's letter announcing the court victory and suggesting publication,[65] he exclaimed: "I have not the courage & really not the time, to reform the Commentaries on the case which I sent you, and to put them into a more popular dress. They were written for those to whom the matters they contain were familiar; to common readers they will appear unnecessarily erudite and pedantic. But I repeat that I am too tired of the subject to go over it again, so I think I must publish it as it is. . . . I must request you therefore to return me the defence I put into your hands as also all the documents & papers that I may return them to their proper deposits."[66] This was duly accomplished.[67]

It is interesting to note that during the pendency of the Livingston litigation, Jefferson, in addition to preparing his "Commentaries on the case," was engaged in another burdensome and time-consuming literary enterprise. This was the publication of an English translation of Destutt de Tracy's *A Commentary and Review of Montesquieu's Spirit of Laws,*[68] which Jefferson hailed as "the most valuable political work of the present age."[69]

On September 29, 1809, the manuscript was received by Jefferson. On August 12, 1810, he sent to the Philadelphia publisher William Duane a portion of the work (Book II) in a translation by Jefferson himself. On September 16, 1810, he forwarded the entire manuscript to Duane, who had agreed to publish it in an English version.[70]

Jefferson wrote the preface, in which the author pretends to be a naturalized immigrant to the United States. He also corrected the translation, prepared or revised by Duane. Batches of the corrected English version were sent back to Duane on October 25, 1810, November 13, 1810, and January 26, 1811. On July 5, 1811, Duane sent Jefferson a copy of the published book, which was at once forwarded to Lafayette for delivery to the author in France.[71]

It was for a time rumored that Jefferson was author of the book, and Pierre Samuel Dupont de Nemours undertook to translate it into French. Jefferson immediately discouraged this enterprise, of "retranslating into French a work the original of which is so correct in it's diction that not a word can be altered but for the worse: and from a translation, too where the author's meaning has sometimes been illy understood, sometimes mistaken, and often expressed in words not the best chosen."[72]

It will be noted that the second batch of corrected translation was sent to Duane just two days after Jefferson's memoir on the batture case was finally dispatched to his counsel.[73]

The court's decision on December 5, 1811, dismissing Livingston's suit on jurisdictional grounds, provided the impetus for publication of Jefferson's *Proceedings*. The purpose of publishing the book was well summarized in a letter to a Virginia congressman: "It will doubtless be satisfactory to our citizens at large to see that no wrong has been done to Livingston, that the grounds of his complaint has been merely my maintaining the national right to the beach of the Missisipi adjacent to N. Orleans, and keeping it from such intrusions as might restrain individuals from making lawful use of it and preserve the city & country from destruction: and that in doing this I only obeyed the prescriptions of the law both as to matter & manner."[74]

Doubtless Livingston's object in bringing suit was to obtain judicial confirmation of his title, rather than to obtain money damages from Jefferson personally.[75] Otherwise, it would seem that the theory of the case could readily have been modified, so that Livingston's claim would have rested on other circumstances than the trespass *quare clausum fregit* to Louisiana land. Rodney, for example, before seeing the plaintiff's declaration, surmised that his action must be for assault and battery, or false imprisonment, by the defendant's agents, pursuant to the defendant's orders.[76] This type of allegation would present a transitory, rather than local, cause of action, and could be brought in any jurisdiction where the defendant could be served with process.

A famous decision by Lord Mansfield had established this principle.[77] An English subject born in Minorca had been awarded a verdict of £3000 against the governor of that island for assault and false imprisonment. The plaintiff, Fabrigas, a gentleman farmer, had been arrested by soldiers, imprisoned under harsh conditions, and banished to Spain, by order of the governor. The plaintiff had sought permission to sell twelve casks of wine from his vineyard at a price somewhat lower than the established market price fixed by public authority, in accordance with a regulation established by an order in council of May 17, 1752. The magistrate (whom Fabrigas accused of being himself illegally engaged in selling wine) refused permission, on the ground that a later regulation required the producers to take turns in selling their wine, since there were no storage facilities, and when all the wine came on the market at once the surplus turned sour and was detrimental to the health of soldiers in the garrison. The magistrate contended that only 41 persons concerned in the wine trade supported Fabrigas, while 93 favored the regulation requiring rotation by lot. Fabrigas repeatedly petitioned the governor, and said he would return with 150 or 250 supporters. The governor considered this to mean that a mob or mutiny might occur, the native Minorcans being restive under English rule. Hence he imprisoned and banished Fabrigas. The jury found that Fabrigas was not guilty of arousing mutiny or sedition, and awarded damages to the plaintiff.

On appeal to the Court of King's Bench, the questions at issue were whether the action could be brought in England when the cause of action arose beyond the seas, in Minorca; whether plaintiff has capacity to bring such an action; and whether the defendant, as governor, is a proper object of it.

Lord Mansfield quickly disposed of the second question: "Has not a subject of the king, born at Minorca, as good a right to apply to the king's courts of justice, as a person born within the sound of Bow-bell, in Cheapside?" On the third question, he held that the governor should have specially pleaded and proved his justification: "In this case, if the justification had been proved, perhaps the Court would have been of opinion that it was a sufficient answer. ... But ... to lay down in an English court of justice such monstrous propositions as that a governor ... can do what he pleases ... is a doctrine not to be maintained."[78]

Dealing with the first question (the pertinent issue in Livingston's case against Jefferson) Lord Mansfield held that the action brought by Fabrigas was transitory, and could be brought in any county in England, though the matter arises beyond the seas. He cited two cases "before me, going rather further than these transitory actions; that is, going to cases which in England would be local actions." One was against a naval officer for pulling down the houses of some sutlers who supplied sailors with spirituous liquors in Nova Scotia; another was for destroying fishing huts on the Labrador coast. In these *nisi prius* cases Mansfield had held that the reason for the rule forbidding local actions did not apply in those cases, which involved damages rather than title.[79]

Marshall did not have the "hardihood," in Livingston's case, to disregard a "technical distinction" which the illustrious Mansfield had tried in vain to demolish. He declared:

If however, this technical distinction be firmly established, if all other judges respect it, I cannot venture to disregard it. ... [I]t would require a hardihood which I do not possess, to pass this limit. ... From the cases which support this distinction, no exception, I believe, is to be found among those that have been decided in court, on solemn argument. One of the greatest judges who ever sat on any bench . . . was so struck with the weakness of the distinction . . . that he attempted to abolish it. . . . But this opinion . . . may be termed an obiter dictum. . . . Other judges have felt the weight of this argument [the total failure of justice, should a trespasser be declared to be amenable only to the court of that district in which the land lies, and in which he will never be found], and have struggled ineffectually against the distinction, which produces the inconvenience of a clear right without a remedy. I must submit to it. The law upon the demurrer is in favor of the defendant.[80]

Judge Tyler reached the same conclusion, but without reluctance.

The chief justice's professional instincts as a lawyer thus prevailed over his political and personal feelings of hostility to Jefferson, contrary to the latter's expectations. Marshall did, however, just as in *Marbury* v. *Madison,* clearly intimate that a "total failure of justice" might result from Jefferson's conduct, but that the court was without power to afford a remedy.

Perhaps Livingston's counsel thought that they had succeeded in pleading a transitory action of trespass *de bonis asportatis* for injury to personal property when in their first count they alleged that the defendant had entered the land and broken, destroyed, and carried away spades, tools, planks, rails, nails, and 200,000 cartloads of earth.[81] In Hay's letter forwarding the declaration to Jefferson, he took the view that no articles of personal property such as planks, timbers, and the like were taken by the marshal when evicting Livingston's workmen, and that any loss sustained with respect thereto was due to plaintiff's own negligence. The asportation or removal of sand did occur, but it was done by the inhabitants of New Orleans in accordance with their long-standing custom, and was not done by the marshal or pursuant to orders of the defendant.[82] Jefferson confirmed this view. The articles described in the declaration were never touched by the marshal. "If they left their tools &c it was their folly. . . . The earth said to have been taken, was I suppose by the people in the usual way." In a postscript he added "since writing the above Govr. Claiborne informs me that Livingston's people left nothing on the beach, but carried away their tools with them."[83]

All the counts of the declaration emphasize entry on the land, and deprivation of plaintiff's enjoyment of the land in some respect. On the whole, the wrongful acts alleged describe a typical case of trespass upon land *(quare clausum fregit)* and the court properly treated the case as such. Accordingly the issue for determination was whether such an action could be regarded as transitory. The correct conclusion, in accordance with established precedents, was reached that such an action must be brought in the district where the land is situated. Livingston and his counsel, desiring to try the question of title to the batture, probably hoped that Marshall would follow Mansfield's innovative views and accept jurisdiction of the case.

The unsuccessful suit against Jefferson was not the only remedy invoked by Livingston. His Philadelphia lawyers had also advised that an action could be brought against the United States marshal and all who assisted him in evicting Livingston from the batture.[84] On July 4, 1810, suit was filed in the federal district court of Orleans Territory against the marshal, Francis Joseph LeBreton d'Orgenois.[85] The defendant's answer, filed on July 16, 1810, set up as justification the instructions from the president contained in a letter of November 30, 1807, from Secretary of State James Madison.

Upon learning early in October that Livingston's purpose was not to obtain damages but to regain possession of the batture, the defendant on October 15, 1810, consented to the filing of an amended petition by plaintiff, which contained no claim for damages.[86] On the same date defendant answered the amended petition, plaintiff demurred, and defendant joined in demurrer. On October 22, 1810, when the demurrer was set for argument, a motion was made by United States Attorney Tully Robinson, that the proceedings be stayed as collusive, since the defendant had no interest in the case. He argued that the sole purpose of the suit was to affect the interest of a third party and obtain possession from the United States.

In support of this motion the affidavit of James Mather, mayor of New Orleans, was offered to show the exercise of dominion over the batture by the government during a period of several years. Other evidence was received, including the defendant's testimony "that he has no interest whatever in the property of the batture, nor any possession therein, that he dispossessed the plaintiff from the property in question by the commands of the president of the United States, . . . that on Mr. Paillette informing him as his counsel in the cause that no damages would be claimed from him . . . he consented to the amendment of the plaintiff's petition and would not have consented otherwise, but he had no conversation whatever with the plaintiff himself upon the subject and that he was glad to get rid of the business." On October 24, 1810, the court delivered an opinion and judgment staying the proceedings.[87]

On review by the Supreme Court, it appeared that writ of error was not the appropriate remedy, but on March 16, 1813, a *mandamus nisi* in the nature of a *procedendo* was granted, directing Judge Hall to "proceed to a final judgment of the said cause."[88]

Accordingly, on August 3, 1813, Judge Dominick Augustin Hall entered judgment in favor of Livingston: "The Court having advised of the Judgment to be rendered in this case & considered the pleadings & the arguments of

Counsel thereon, It is now considered that the demurrer filed by the plaintiff be allowed that Judgment be entered for the plaintiff & that a writ issue ordering the Marshal of the District to put the plaintiff in the peaceable & quiet possession of the premises mentioned in his said petition: and it is further ordered that the question of damages be reserved for the further consideration of this Court."[89] No opinion by the court has been found, giving the reasons for its decision.[90]

Governor Claiborne and the city of New Orleans, though admittedly not parties to the case, on August 10, 1813, petitioned Judge Hall for a writ of error.[91] Apparently this irregular application produced no results. Claiborne promptly notified Jefferson: "The . . . Judge . . . has decided, the dispossessing of Mr. Livingston of the Batture, by order of the late President to be illegal, & he directs the Plaintiff to be reinstated in his possession."[92]

This decision had an interesting sequel. On October 26, 1816, Livingston (in spite of his covenant with D'Orgenois and his heirs not to seek money damages) obtained a writ of *scire facias* against the heirs of the deceased marshal, requiring them to show cause why damages should not be assessed. Two months later the court held that the action did not survive against the heirs. On December 30, 1816, a writ of error was issued, but it may not have been pursued, as no trace of further action has been found.

In the fall of 1810 Livingston ostentatiously resumed possession of the batture. He published a newspaper notice, in both French and English, declaring that "the illegal force which deprived me of the enjoyment of my property on the BATTURE of the Suburb St. Mary, having now ceased to operate— the late Marshal, the present Marshal and the Attorney of the United States, having all declared under oath, in open Court, that they had no instructions from the Government relative to the said property—the claims of the City having been decided on, and the Mayor having later declared on oath, that the Corporation were not in possession, and claimed no title thereto—I have peaceably, in the presence of several magistrates and other respectable witnesses, resumed the possession of my said property." He announced that he would permit boats to load and unload without charge for wharfage, but would sue "every person who from henceforward shall dig the earth or commit any other trespass thereon."[93]

This action evoked an outburst in the press, which induced the United States attorney to direct the new marshal to evict Livingston again. Jefferson was kept abreast of these developments.[94] Livingston filed suit against the marshal, [John] Michel Fortier, on November 21, 1810. Less cautious than Jefferson,[95] the marshal did plead that Livingston was a resident of Orleans territory, but an affidavit was produced from a New York attorney to show that Livingston was practicing law in that city. The jury on April 24, 1812, found for the plaintiff on the issue of residence.[96] Trial on the merits began on May 23, 1812, but for some reason was abandoned and resumed before a different jury on July 31, 1812. Livingston tried his own case, while Pierre Derbigny and John R. Grymes represented the defendant.[97] On the following day the testimony, arguments, and charge of the court were concluded. On August 3, 1812, the jury was unable to agree upon a verdict and was discharged.

The litigation then languished until January 28, 1823, when Livingston notified Fortier that he must close up his affairs regarding the batture, and bring the case to trial for disposition. Accordingly Fortier filed an answer on June 6, 1823, setting up four defenses: (1) Livingston had illegally, on his own authority, resumed possession of the premises and thereby disturbed the possession which Fortier had received from his predecessor on behalf of the United States; (2) that the freehold and dominion of the property was in the United States; (3) that the land is part of a navigable river and not susceptible of private ownership; (4) that every citizen has a right of fishing on the batture during flood season, and a right of way over it the rest of the year. Livingston demurred to the second and fourth pleas; and traversed the first and third pleas, thus presenting jury questions.

On the first issue of fact, Livingston could take advantage of Fortier's deposition of November 7, 1816, in the D'Orgenois case, in which he testified that he never received any transfer of possession of the batture property from his predecessor D'Orgenois. On the other jury question, Livingston's assertion that the premises in question were not part of the river seems to be nothing more than a restatement of the legal problem whether the width of the bed of the river is to be measured at low water or at flood state.[98] On June 11 and 12, 1823, the court heard argument on the demurrers. On June 13 the court sustained Livingston's demurrers, and a jury was sworn. It began its deliberations on June 18, 1823, after completion of the trial, but was discharged the same day "shortly after sunset" on account of inability to agree upon a verdict.[99]

After the foregoing account of the litigation which generated Jefferson's "Commentaries on the case," we turn to analysis of the book itself. The material is arranged in narrative form, developing the facts and legal propositions as they arise, rather than in the argumentative form of a lawyer's brief.[100]

As Attorney General Rodney remarked: "It is true, it does not possess the strict method required in a legal argument, but the full & satisfactory explanation which it contains of the whole transaction is peculiarly gratifying. It treats by regular steps all the occurrences in the order in which they took place, & happily combining law & argument with the facts in their natural

WILLIAM WIRT by Samuel L. Waldo.
  Wirt, together with George Hay and Littleton W. Tazewell, represented Jefferson in the case brought by Livingston.
  Courtesy National Portrait Gallery, Smithsonian Institution.

course, leads us in an easy & familiar manner to a correct result." And William Wirt, himself a critic endowed with literary gifts, wrote that "your exposition of The Batture question . . . is by far the best piece of grecian architecture that I have ever seen, either from ancient or modern times. I did not think it possible that such a subject could be so deeply and at the same time so airily treated—because I never before had seen such an union of lightness and solidity, of beauty and power, in any investigation."[101]

In substance Jefferson begins his argument by contending that Livingston did not have title to the batture: "The plaintiff having had no right, can have sustained no wrong."[102] Gallatin's memorandum sustains this point upon five grounds: (1) that by law the batture cannot be the private property of any individual (relying upon Derbigny's view that it belongs to the crown, and Thierry's that only dry ground can be appropriated by private proprietors); (2) that Bertrand Gravier never had any title to the batture, as there is no sufficient evidence to demonstrate that his property extended beyond the road to the river; (3) that if he had, he lost it by erecting a *faubourg* or suburb;[103] (4) that whatever rights Bertrand Gravier had still belonged to his heirs, and did not pass to John Gravier when he purchased Bertrand Gravier's property with benefit of inventory; (5) that the sale by Gravier to Peter de la Bigarre, from whom Livingston purchased, was fraudulent and conveyed no title. As we shall see, Jefferson developed all these points in his book.

Livingston's lack of title seems to be a perfectly legitimate ground of defense in an action against Jefferson personally, seeking damages. Livingston in his *Answer* argues that it was indulging in "smear" technique to discuss Livingston's title and any possible defects therein. He contends that Jefferson should have asked only, "Did the land belong to the United States? Had the government a right to seize it?"[104] That would have been true enough if the lawsuit were one between Livingston and the government. But when liability is asserted against a former officer individually, he certainly can be expected to resist paying a huge sum from his private fortune to a person without any right to receive it. The plaintiff's title is a proper issue in such a case.

Jefferson's narrative thus begins appropriately with history of the title to the land involved, commencing with a lost grant of April 11, 1726, from Louis XIV of France to the Jesuits. When this religious order was suppressed in 1763, their property on the Mississippi was confiscated and sold, part of it to one Pradel, whose widow conveyed it to one Renard, whose widow married Bertrand Gravier. Gravier laid off the tract into lots. In 1788 he established them as a *faubourg* or addition to the city of New Orleans.

For the right of alluvion to exist, where newly formed land deposited by the river becomes part of the riparian owner's property, it is of course necessary in the first place that the proprietor be a *riparian* owner: in other words that his tract of land be bounded by the river, rather than by specific metes and bounds, such as particular courses and distances measured by a surveyor and described in a deed.[105]

Jefferson noted that the same wording appeared in the deeds *to* and *from* Gravier. "Whatever extent then, towards the river, passed to the Jesuits by the term 'face au fleuve,' or from the king to the purchasers of the Jesuits' property, under whom B. Gravier claimed, the same extent was, by the same expression 'face au fleuve,' or 'frente al rio,' passed by Bertrand Gravier to the purchasers of the front lots. If the words . . . gave him . . . to the water edge, then he sold to the water edge also, and having parted with all his right as riparian possessor, could transmit none to those claiming under him by subsequent title, as the plaintiff does. . . . If these words make the road your boundary, you never had a right to the batture beyond it. If they extend to the river what was conveyed *to you,* they extend to the river also what was conveyed *from you.*"[106]

But even if Bertrand Gravier retained any right to the batture when he died intestate in 1797, Jefferson continued, it did not pass to his brother, John Gravier, from whom Livingston took title.

Other brothers and sisters of the deceased remained in France. Bertrand Gravier was thought to have been insolvent when he came to America; and John Gravier, therefore, chose to decline the inheritance as heir and to take the estate as a purchaser with benefit of inventory and appraisement. Under Louisiana law he would therefore not be liable for debts of the decedent beyond the amount of the inventory and appraisement. But by the same token he would not inherit any property of the decedent except what was included in the inventory and appraisement.[107]

Jefferson contended that the inventory, under the heading "the lands of this habitation" did not include the batture,[108] and hence that it did not pass to John Gravier. Accordingly, it never was acquired by Livingston.

Another reason why Livingston's title was defective, according to Jefferson, was the fact that it was champertously acquired, in a manner contravening public policy. On March 27, 1804, Gravier conveyed a two-thirds interest in the batture to Peter de la Bigarre, from whom Livingston bought; and again on December 14, 1806, conveyed the entire batture, in a second secret deed which made no mention of the first one, and which was conditional upon the success of a lawsuit which Gravier commenced in his own name on October 22, 1805, against the city of New Orleans.[109] Jefferson declared that the transaction was criminal and void.[110] When on May 23, 1807, the Superior Court of Orleans Territory "adjudged the property wholly to the very man, who, if he had ever had any right, had conveyed away two thirds of it, before he brought his action, and the whole while it was pending" the decision was viewed with alarm and consternation by the citizens of New Orleans.[111]

Livingston was one of four lawyers who appeared on behalf of Gravier in this litigation. Moreau, Gurley, and Derbigny represented the city.[112] Soon after the judgment, Livingston says, he acquired the batture from Gravier, Girod, and de la Bigarre's heirs.[113]

The case had been before the court three times. On December 18, 1805, Judge John B. Prevost recused himself, but granted an injunction, which on April 9, 1806, was extended to continue until final determination of the case.[114] On May 2, 1807, a full bench, composed of judges William Sprigg, George Mathews, Jr., and Joshua Lewis sat.[115] On May 23, 1807, the court's opinion was handed down.[116]

The court held (1) that the tract was bounded, not by the road, but by the river; (2) that according to the civil and Spanish law, alluvion is an incident of riparian ownership; (3) that Bernard Gravier would therefore have been entitled to the alluvion if he had remained owner of the whole tract, but he had sold lots. If there was no alluvial land formed at the time when he sold the property, the alluvion which came into existence later would not belong to him. But the court found that there was sufficient alluvion already formed, and of sufficient height, that it could be considered as annexed to his property before he sold the land next to the river. The court further held (4) that he did not divest himself of the alluvial deposit; in fact he sold part of the batture as such to one of the front proprietors. He had not lost his property by the operation of prescription. Finally, the court decided that it did not need to determine the nature of the title of John Gravier. Whether he took by purchase or as heir, his right is strong enough against the city; and he is entitled to "be quieted in the lawful enjoyment of the Batture . . . against the claims & pretentions of the Defendants and that the Injunction heretofore granted in this cause be made perpetual."[117]

The lawyers representing the city then advanced a proposition which became one of the principal features of Jefferson's reasoning in the *Proceedings:* that John Gravier (and his successor in interest, Livingston) had no title because the United States was the true owner of the batture. After a hearing, the court denied a new trial which had been sought by the city on the basis of this theory.[118]

Governor Claiborne as early as May 20, 1807, entertained the "impression that the United States are the legal claimants to it [the land made by the river, and over which the city has heretofore exercised a right of ownership]."[119] But the major support for this thesis was derived from a widely published opinion given by Derbigny on August 21, 1807.[120] According to Jefferson, this "first brought into view the right of the United States."[121]

When Livingston's workmen began digging a canal on the property on August 24, 1807, Governor Claiborne anticipated danger of great "tumult, and *perhaps much bloodshed."* He repeated emphatically, "My opinion is that the title is in the United States." He also feared that Livingston's works would be injurious to navigation and might damage the levees along the river in the vicinity of New Orleans.[122] On November 14, 1807, a grand jury made a presentment that the "operations of Edward Livingston are calculated to obstruct the free navigation of the river . . . and . . . that all such measures should be taken as are consistent with law to arrest these operations which are injurious . . . and . . . hazardous in the extreme."[123]

Heeding the continued clamor of Claiborne, Jefferson obtained an opinion from Attorney General Rodney on October 28, 1807, and called a cabinet meeting on November 27, 1807. Rodney reported that he had received a lengthy statement of facts from Secretary of State Madison, which "I must presume to be correct, as it has been officially furnished." He read the legal opinions of Derbigny, Lisley [Moreau], and Gurley, the attorney general of Orleans Territory. He concluded: "Upon reflection, I concur with them."[124]

With regard to the remedy, Rodney said: "Under the first section of the act of the 3d of March, A.D. 1807[125] I am of opinion that military force may be employed by the President to remove from these lands any person who may have taken possession of them since the passage of the law. This, I think, appears to have been the fact in the present case, from the letter of Mr. Van Pradellers, of the 11th ultimo, which I return to you. At first I entertained doubts on this point, but further inquiry removed them. These observations contain the requisite answers to the two questions proposed, viz: 1. Have not the United States a claim to these lands? 2. If they have may not military possession be taken?"[126]

Accordingly, on November 30, 1807, Secretary of State Madison wrote to Governor Claiborne, enclosing instructions to the marshal "to remove immediately, by the civil power, any persons from the batture Ste. Marie, who had taken possession since the 3d of March, and authorising the Governor, if necessary, to use military force."[127]

On the morning of January 25, 1808, D'Orgenois received his instructions and ordered off Livingston's laborers. Later they returned, and refused to leave unless compelled by adequate force. In the meantime Livingston procured an injunction from the Superior Court of Orleans Territory forbidding the marshal from disturbing Livingston's possession of the batture. D'Orgenois obeyed the executive commands rather than the court order, collected a posse and ordered off the laborers. They peaceably retired and no further attempts were afterwards made to recommence the work.[128]

Livingston, after his eviction, was indefatigable in seeking recognition of his title to the batture and restoration of possession thereof. His suits against D'Orgenois and Fortier have previously been discussed, as well as that against Jefferson in Virginia. Before these attempts to secure judicial relief, Livingston traveled to Washington and sought interviews with Jefferson and Attorney General Rodney. Jefferson took the position that the only duty of the executive branch was to maintain the government's possession of the premises, and that the ultimate disposition of the property was a matter for Congress. He had on March 7, 1808, in a message to Congress referred the matter for consideration.[129] But in spite of Livingston's exertions, Congress took no action, except to refer both Livingston's petition[130] and one from the inhabitants of the city of New Orleans[131] to Attorney General Rodney for his opinion. In Rodney's opinion of June 12, 1809, he adhered to his earlier opinion of October 24, 1807, and viewed the purpose of the present reference to him as an effort to furnish a mode of settling the controversy. One such possible method would be for Congress to authorize an appeal to the Supreme Court from the decision of the Superior Court of Orleans Territory.[132] He noted: "It appears that the facts from which alone the law can arise are much controverted. These must be correctly ascertained before a satisfactory opinion can be formed. . . . The law itself, which should furnish the rule of determination, was also a matter of controversy."[133]

In negotiating with Rodney, Peter Samuel Duponceau (a prominent Philadelphia lawyer of French origin who had espoused Livingston's cause) tried to persuade the attorney general to report favorably to Congress on Livingston's claim. Duponceau's strategy was to prevent the batture issue from becoming a partisan conflict, since the anti-Jeffersonians were in the minority. He hoped to arouse antagonism on the part of the administration against the corporation of the city of New Orleans, on the ground that it had duped the government into taking action of doubtful legality, upon grounds later abandoned by the city itself. "I think you should urge this point strongly to Mr. Madison & to every body, & you have enough to excite the resentment of all who have acted against you, against the Corporation who have made them such dupes. . . . This has been the main object of my *Review.*" An alternative suggestion was to "let a second Injunction issue from the Superior Court of Orleans" which the government would agree not to resist, on the pretence that the marshal had "exceeded his orders when he resisted the first injunction. . . . He was only to take possession of the Batture, but not to resist the Judiciary."[134]

In a vain effort to avert his eviction from the property by convincing the government that it had no title, Livingston had prepared his *Examination of the Title of the United States to the Land Called the Batture.*[135] After his eviction he submitted thirteen questions[136] to eminent Philadelphia lawyers.

On August 3, 1808, Jared Ingersoll and William Rawle gave an opinion favorable to Livingston,[137] as did Edward Tilghman and William Lewis on August 16, 1808.[138] The most elaborate exposition of the law favorable to Livingston was set forth in Peter S. Duponceau's opinion of July 26, 1808.[139] Derbigny published a pamphlet to refute this opinion.[140] Duponceau issued a reply, dated February 27, 1809.[141] Other defenders of the government's title included Thierry,[142] Moreau,[143] and Poydras.[144] Livingston issued a voluminous publication entitled *An Address to the People of the United States, on the Measures Pursued by the Executive with respect to the Batture at New Orleans,* dated October 21, 1808.[145] In addition to an account of his own activities, this included the territorial court's decision, Derbigny's opinion, Livingston's *Examination,* Duponceau's opinion, the case stated and the responses of Ingersoll and Rawle, as well as of Tilghman and Lewis. All of these sources (in addition to other documents which he procured) were utilized by Jefferson in connection with the discussion of French law contained in his *Proceedings.* Not to be outdone in the contest for public approbation, Livingston promptly replied to Jefferson's book by publishing a lengthy *Answer,* which was an eloquent and forceful polemic, replete with barbed shafts of wit and erudition.[146]

According to Jefferson's exposition, French private law remained in effect after Louisiana was secretly ceded by France to Spain in 1762.[147] Spain did not receive possession until August 17, 1769. The territory was retroceded to France by the treaty of St. Ildefonso, dated October 1, 1800.[148] By the Louisiana Purchase treaty of April 30, 1803, the United States acquired it from France.[149]

It was generally agreed that under Spanish law, as under Roman law,[150] alluvion belongs to the riparian owner.[151] Therefore, if the alluvion which constituted the batture was formed during the sovereignty of Spain, between 1769 and 1800, it would belong to whoever was the riparian owner at the time when Spanish law took effect. This would be true whether the owner at that date was a private proprietor or the crown.

Under the law in force during the French domination of Louisiana, from the charter granted by Louis XIV on September 14, 1712, down to the transfer to Spain in 1769, the royal edicts, ordinances, and customs, together with the customary law of Paris, furnished the applicable rules.[152] Under the pertinent French law, Jefferson declared, quoting Pothier, "alluvions formed on the border of navigable streams and rivers belong to the king."[153] If, therefore, the batture was formed in part before 1769 and became public property of the crown, accretions during Spanish rule would under Spanish law belong to the same owner,[154] and would in due time become property of the United States by virtue of the Louisiana Purchase.[155]

Jefferson also interpreted an edict of Louis XIV of December 15, 1693, as establishing "incontestably" that alluvions in all navigable rivers belong to the king.[156]

What the preamble to this edict described as being incontestably established as belonging to the king as a consequence of his property in all navigable rivers were *"attérissements"* and *"accroissements"*[157] formed by the rivers. The operative part of the edict decrees that all possessors of *"attérissements,"* *"accroissements,"* *"alluvions,"* and other rights on navigable rivers, who produce title or proof of possession enjoyed before April 1, 1566, shall be confirmed in their possession upon paying to the treasury one year's revenue (and those without such muniments, upon paying two years revenue).[158] Duponceau regarded the edict as merely a fiscal device to raise money,[159] an abuse of feudal prerogative, similar to the sharp practices of Charles I.[160] They were resisted by the riparian proprietors, and in a famous case involving the *Parlement* of Bordeaux the king was forced to desist from his pretensions.[161] In any event, lands in Louisiana were allodial, and no feudal prerogatives (such as the sovereign's right to alluvion in navigable rivers) existed there.[162]

This reference to feudalism launched Jefferson upon a far-ranging philosophical disquisition.[163] He declared that "it is putting the cart before the horse to say, that the authority of the nation flows from the Feudal system, instead of the Feudal system flowing from the authority of the nation."[164] He endeavored to show by historical and sociological evidence that among primitive peoples the sovereign is recognized as the sole proprietor of the soil. "That the lands within the limits assumed by a nation belong to the nation as a body, has probably been the law of every people on earth at some period of their history. A right of property in moveable things is admitted before the establishment of government. A separate property in lands not till after that establishment."[165]

Jefferson next argued that, even under Roman law, the conversion of Gravier's plantation into a *faubourg* or suburb when he laid out lots and sold them, made the batture public property.[166] This contention, which Jefferson took over from Thierry,[167] was based on the supposition that "the Roman law gave Alluvion only to the Rural proprietor of the bank; Urban possessions being considered as praedia limitata."[168] It depended upon a narrow interpretation of the word *ager* as meaning only "field." Livingston easily demolished this argument by demonstrating that the word was used in Roman law texts in the broader sense of "land." It occurred in passages relating to land located in cities.[169]

A stronger argument based upon Bertrand Gravier's laying out a *faubourg* and selling his lots fronting on the Mississippi was that he had relinquished or abandoned any rights to the batture by his conduct at that time. Riparian owners were obligated to maintain the road and levee along the shore fronting their property. But after Gravier sold his front lots, he ceased to do so, and Governor Carondelet agreed that Gravier should be relieved of that burden. Thereafter the road was kept up at the public charge, as was customary within the city limits. When Gravier's *faubourg* was formed, the lots were thereby incorporated as a part of the city of New Orleans; indeed, they became a part of its port. Hence they were thereafter subject to the municipal laws governing New Orleans, including the provisions with respect to public use of the port and beach.[170]

According to a nineteenth century Louisiana lawyer, the question of dedication to public use disposed of the controversy, whether Livingston or Jefferson were correct as to the original ownership of the batture property.[171] However, in a case involving a similar issue the Louisiana Supreme Court held in 1841 (over the dissent of the renowned Judge François Xavier Martin) that dedication to the public had not been sufficiently established. In commenting on the 1807 decision, Martin said that John Gravier had won his case because opposing counsel neglected to show dedication except by proof of oral conversations.[172]

Jefferson then denied that the batture presented any characteristics of alluvion at all. He asserted that the addition of soil to the batture "is by *deposition* of particles of earth on it's face, not by their apposition or adhesion to the bank. . . . The deposition of earth on the bottom of a river, can be no more said to be an apposition to it's sides, than the coating the floor of a room can be said to be plaistering it's walls." Accordingly, "the whole claim of the plaintiff falls to the ground: for he has not pretended that it could be his under any other title than that of Alluvion."[173]

This basis of denying plaintiff's title seems quite farfetched and untenable. A deposit which builds the bank up from the bottom would seem to be alluvion just as much as one that builds it out from the side.[174] Livingston rightly ridicules the former president's erudite word juggling.[175]

Jefferson then undertakes to show what the batture is "which will further demonstrate what it is not." It is, he declares, part of the beach, that is to say, that portion of the bed of the river which lies between the high- and low-water marks.[176] Unquestionably the bed of the river, up to high-water mark, belongs to the sovereign (that is, in the United States, to the nation).[177] Since it has been the practice for riparian grants along the Mississippi to extend to the edge of the river when its waters are at their greatest height, it is evident that "neither the grant to the Jesuits, nor to Bernard Gravier, could have included the beach or batture."[178]

An obvious objection to this analysis is that "establishing the commencement of the bank at the high water mark, leaves in fact no bank at all, as the

63

high water regularly overflows the natural bank, or brim of the channel."[179] Under these circumstances, Jefferson maintains, the "real banks of the river" are the artificial banks or levees.[180] The analogy between the Mississippi and the Nile is developed.[181] According to Roman law, the Nile does not change its banks when it overflows.[182]

There seems to be considerable ambiguity regarding the location of the high-water mark, which determines where the bed of the river ends and the bank begins. Is it to be measured by the farthest extent of the river's inundation at flood stage? Or by the high-water mark ordinarily reached by the river in its natural state?[183] But since the Mississippi regularly overflows during six months (February to July inclusive) every year,[184] is its condition during that season to be regarded as an aspect of its natural state?

According to Jefferson, apparently where adequate natural or artifical banks exist, they constitute the barrier confining the river and marking the extent of its bed. When such banks exist, they do not change if the river sporadically or accidentally overflows them. But where no such banks exist, the entire area covered by inundation is part of the bed of the river, and constitutes public property. But the government, in order to encourage construction of adequate artificial banks and levees, grants the land belonging to it as part of the bed of the river to private proprietors "as far as to the natural, or incipient bank."[185]

Having completed his exposition of the reasons why he considers Livingston's title to the batture insufficient, Jefferson then lays down the rule that even privately owned riparian land beyond the river bed is nevertheless subject to various provisions of law designed to protect navigation and to prevent damage to the public.[186] With the eloquence of exaggeration he concludes: "Indeed, without all this appeal to such learned authorities, does not common sense, the foundation of all authorities, of the laws themselves, and of their construction, declare it impossible that Mr. Livingston, a single individual, should have a lawful right to drown the city of New-Orleans, or to injure, or change, of his own authority, the course or current of a river which is to give outlet to the productions of two thirds of the whole area of the United States?"[187]

Jefferson also calls attention to the fact that soon after Livingston's eviction from the batture the territorial legislature on February 15, 1808, passed an act providing that no levee should be constructed or completed in front of those presently existing without the approval of a jury of twelve riparian proprietors. Had Livingston proceeded in pursuance of that law, he could after that date have continued his operations. "The suspension of his works, therefore, by the general government was only during these 21 days."[188]

This would be a helpful defense in the trespass action against Jefferson, by limiting the period during which any wrongful or tortious act by the defendant was operative to produce damage to plaintiff. The defendant's tort would not be the proximate cause of any subsequent damages, since a supervening independent cause was responsible for Livingston's inability to continue his project.[189]

Had Livingston obtained permission to resume his enterprise under the procedure established by the territorial act of February 15, 1808, Jefferson says, "certainly it would have been duly respected by the National executive."[190]

Livingston castigated that statement with skepticism and scorn. Would Jefferson have respected the permission of a dozen fellow intruders to sanction Livingston's "intrusion" upon government property? If so, the president would have deserved impeachment.[191]

Such being the facts and the state of the law, what remedy could Jefferson and his cabinet apply?

First, the obstruction of a navigable river was subject to abatement as a nuisance.[192] To this justification, Livingston replied that it was not in keeping with the dignified station of the president of the United States to act as local constable or scavenger for the city of New Orleans. That was the function of the local government.[193]

Moreover, the president had not actually abated the nuisance. The premises were left *in statu quo;* all that was done was to remove Livingston, the "intruder," from the premises, which remained in the same condition as before, until the ravages of the river destroyed the incompleted works.[194] The instructions from Madison to the marshal did not speak of abating any nuisance. This defense was simply an afterthought.[195]

The second remedy open to the chief executive of the nation was the natural-law right of self-help.[196] In the case of private citizens this right was restricted in England by statutes prohibiting forcible entry. "When this natural right was first restrained among the Romans, I am not versed enough in their laws to say. It was not by the laws of the XII tables, which continued long their only laws."[197]

But the government itself is untrammeled by such limitations. "I believe that no nation has ever yet restrained itself in the exercise of this natural right of reseising it's own possessions, or bound up it's own hands in the manacles and cavils of litigation. It takes possession of it's own at short hand, and gives to the private claimant a specified mode of preferring his claim. . . . Indeed if the nation were put to an action against every Squatter, for the recovery of their lands, we should only have lawsuits, not lands for sale. . . . The correct doctrine is that so long as the Nation holds lands in it's own possession, so long they are under the jurisdiction of no court, but by special provision. The United States cannot be sued. The nation, by it's immediate representatives, administers justice itself to all who have claims upon it's public property. . . . But when once they have granted the lands to individuals, then the jurisdiction of the courts over them commences."[198]

The third remedy, and the one actually pursued by the government, was removal of Livingston by the marshal under the act of March 3, 1807.[199]

With regard to this topic, Livingston argues: (1) that the act did not apply under the circumstances; (2) that the procedures prescribed in the act were not followed; and (3) that in any event the act was unconstitutional.[200]

The claim of unconstitutionality is somewhat fanciful. It is based on the theory that the executive branch was usurping judicial powers, since issues such as whether the land belonged to the United States, whether Livingston had taken possession of it, and at what time he had done so, were judicial questions.[201] The cabinet council of November 27, 1807,[202] is pictured by Livingston as an extraconstitutional judicial tribunal, akin to the abhorred Star Chamber.[203]

Whether the statute was applicable, and whether the government's action was in accordance with its terms, are questions calling for examination in considerable detail.

The pertinent provision of the statute reads:

> That if any person or persons shall, after the passing of this act, take possession of, or make a settlement on any lands ceded or secured to the United States, by any treaty made with a foreign nation, or by a cession from any state to the United States, which lands shall not have been previously sold, ceded, or leased by the United States, or the claim to which lands, by such person or persons, shall not have been previously recognized and confirmed by the United States . . . it shall . . . be lawful for the President of the United States, to direct the marshal, or officer acting as marshal, in the manner herein after directed, and also to take such other measures, and to employ such military force as he may judge necessary and proper, to remove from lands ceded, or secured to the United States, by treaty, or cession as aforesaid, any person or persons who shall hereafter take possession of the same, or make, or attempt to make a settlement thereon, until thereunto authorized by law.[204]

Scrutinizing these words carefully and literally, a strong argument can be made that the law is applicable to Livingston's situation. He took possession of the batture after March 3, 1807.[205] The land was part of the Louisiana Purchase, ceded to the United States by a treaty with France, a foreign nation. The land had not been previously[206] sold by the United States, nor had Livingston's claim to the land been previously "recognized and confirmed" by the United States.

Livingston might have contended that the decision of the Superior Court of Orleans Territory amounted to recognition by the United States, through the territorial rather than the general or federal government. To this contention Gallatin (in point II of his memorandum) furnished several answers: (1) the recognition and confirmation contemplated by the act undoubtedly was of a sort binding upon the United States, and evidencing that the government had abandoned its claim to the land in question; but the decree of the territorial court was *res inter alios acta* insofar as the United States was concerned, and not binding upon the national government;[207] (2) the president's removal power extended to any person taking possession after passage of the act until such possession was "authorized by law"; this meant authorization by act of Congress, "not by the judgment or decree of a Court";[208] (3) the decree of the territorial court was a usurpation, since that tribunal lacked chancery powers and could not issue an injunction. These points were all duly incorporated by Jefferson in his book.

The policy of the law was to guard any land ceded by the treaty against the effect of fraudulent grants and to leave complete freedom of disposition in the hands of Congress.[209] Congress directed that persons claiming lands by virtue of "any legal French or Spanish grant made and completed" before October 1, 1800, and "during the time the government which made such grant had the actual possession" of the territory, *"may,"* and those claiming by virtue of any subsequent grant or incomplete title *"shall,"* file before March 1, 1806, a written notice "stating the nature and extent of their claims," together with supporting evidence.[210] A commission was created "for the purpose of ascertaining . . . the rights of persons claiming under any French or Spanish grant." The commissioner's report was to be transmitted to Congress for final action.[211] If the theory of French jurists who regarded the alluvion as property of the king is accepted (as Attorney General Rodney accepted it), and the monarch treated as the original owner of the batture, then it is difficult to find sufficient proof of any recognition, confirmation, or grant by the United States, after the transfer to it of Louisiana, of any private claim to ownership of the batture.[212]

Jefferson therefore had a prima facie case authorizing the removal of Livingston.[213] Were his instructions to the marshal transmitted "in the manner herein after directed," as required by section 1 of the act of March 3, 1807?[214]

The quoted phrase in section 1 doubtless refers to section 4 of the act, ordaining:

That it shall be lawful after the first day of January next,[215] for the . . . marshal, acting under such instructions as may for that purpose be given by the President of the United States, to remove from the lands aforesaid, any and every person or persons, who shall be found on the same, and who shall not have obtained permission to remain thereon as aforesaid.[216]

Livingston was obviously "found" on the land. It is equally obvious that he had not "obtained permission to remain thereon."[217]

A rather circuitous argument, of some possible merit, may be constructed to the effect that Livingston's removal was irregular under the combined effect of sections 1 and 4 of the act, because it was effected by the marshal, and no military force was used.[218] The requirement that removal by the marshal must take place "in the manner herein after directed" by section 4, does not apply to removal by military force.[219]

But with respect to the marshal it can be contended that, if he may act only in the manner directed in section 4, he has no authority whatever to act under circumstances where section 4 has been rendered totally inoperative by its second proviso.[220]

Assuming that the time limit of January 1, 1808, was correspondingly extended when the time for filing claims with the commission was extended until July 1, 1808,[221] it might be argued (as Livingston does)[222] that until July 1, 1808, it cannot be known whether he will or will not file a claim. Hence, he contends, it would be premature for the marshal to remove him before that date, because the purpose of the second proviso was to make section 4 (and the marshal's removal power derived therefrom) totally inapplicable to persons whose claims were filed on time with the commissioners. This reasoning is unsound, however, because section 4 of the later 1807 act expressly specified its own time limit (January 1, 1808) rather than adopting the date fixed by the earlier act.[223] Livingston's third point with respect to the act of 1807 therefore is likewise untenable.[224]

After his discussion of the available remedies and the action taken by the cabinet, Jefferson reviews the ground already covered in his memoir. Then he enters upon a discussion of the validity of the injunction of the territorial court, ordering the marshal not to obey his instructions to remove Livingston from the batture.[225] This line of argument had been suggested by Gallatin.[226]

Jefferson's contention is that the territorial court could not issue a valid injunction, because the act of Congress establishing the court had created it as a court of common law without chancery powers.[227]

He points out that the government of Orleans Territory was modeled upon that of Mississippi Territory, which incorporates provisions of the Northwest Ordinance of 1787 granting only a common law jurisdiction.[228] In the latter territory, when lack of chancery powers was felt to be inconvenient, they were supplied by legislation, rather than by usurpation on the part of the territorial courts.

But, as Livingston replies, the peculiar local law of Orleans Territory, based on Roman law, was continued in force by Congress. Indeed, Jefferson himself concedes that the term "common law" when applied to this territory does not mean the common law of England, but "the common law of that land, or the law of the land." When so understood, as meaning the system of law prevailing in that territory, does it not incorporate the Roman law equivalents of equity jurisdiction, including injunctive remedies?[229]

To this argument Gallatin suggests an answer. Under his explanation, while the Roman law provides the rule of decision for questions of substantive law, the procedural law available for the enforcement of substantive rights is limited to such remedies as can be furnished by a court having only common law jurisdiction. The nature and extent of the judicial power is a matter of public law, and must be consonant with the genius of the American government and its fundamental constitutional principles. In this area, therefore, the form of government established by the United States supersedes the judicial machinery that existed under French or Spanish rule.[230]

In conclusion, Jefferson warmly defends the rule of official immunity and his own good faith in the action taken with respect to Livingston. "Were the judge who, deluded by sophistry, takes the life of an innocent man, to repay it with his own; were he to replace, with his own fortune, that which his judgment has taken from another, under the beguilement of false deductions; were the Executive, in the vast mass of concerns of first magnitude, which he must direct, to place his whole fortune on the hazard of every opinion; were the members of the legislature to make good from their private sub-, stance every law productive of public or private injury; in short were every man engaged in rendering service to the public, bound in his body and goods to indemnification for all his errors, we must commit our public affairs to the paupers of the nation, to the sweepings of hospitals and poorhouses, who having nothing to lose, would have nothing to risk."[231]

In a lengthy peroration he expresses his confidence that even Livingston does not believe that there was corruption or malice involved in Jefferson's action. "What? was it my malice or corruption which prompted the Governors and Cabildoes to keep these grounds clear of intrusion? Did my malice and corruption excite the people to rise, and stay the parricide hand uplifted to destroy their city, or the grand jury to present this violation of their laws? Was it my malice and corruption which penned the opinion of the Attorney General, . . . and dictated the unanimous advice of the heads of departments, when officially called on for consultation and advice? . . . But I do say, that if human reason is not mere illusion, and law a labyrinth without a clue, no error has been committed; and, recurring to the tenor of a long life of public service, against the charges of malice and corruption I stand conscious and erect."[232]

The batture litigation and the publications which it engendered (including Jefferson's *Proceedings*) aroused extensive public interest. The other lawsuits in which Jefferson took part as a litigant were purely private in nature. Usually they involved boundary disputes with neighboring landowners,[233] or debts owed to British merchants by his father-in-law's estate,[234] or problems arising in connection with other estates where Jefferson had served as executor.[235]

In the letter in which he transmitted to William Wirt a fee of $100 for services in Livingston's lawsuit, he engaged Wirt and Hay to handle another case: "A love of peace and tranquility, strengthened by age and a lassitude of business, renders it extremely disquieting to me to be harrassed by vexatious lawsuits by persons who have no earthly claim on me, in cases where I have merely been acting for others. In Nov. last I was served with a subpoena in chancery at the suit of the executors of Mrs. Randolph (mother to Mr. E[dmund]. R[andolph].) in which Mr. Norborne Nicholas, & perhaps a dozen others, are also named defendants. . . . I never had any matter of business with Mrs. Randolph, nor saw a farthing of hers."[236] During the batture litigation Gallatin voiced indignation at the burdens thrust upon Jefferson: "Of the final result, as it relates to yourself there can be no doubt; but it is truly vexatious that your peace should be disturbed and your attention diverted from favorite pursuits by an unprincipled and delinquent speculator; and very unjust to compel you to incur the trouble of collecting . . . evidence."[237]

But the Sage of Monticello learned in the school of experience the bitter truth that, just as taxation is one of the inescapable incidents of life in a civilized society,[238] so is the necessity of defending unmeritorious litigation. No effective method has yet been devised for escaping this inexorable burden.[239]

For Livingston also the burden of litigation remained heavy. Entanglement in controversy about the batture did not end when his suit against Jefferson was dismissed, his possession of the premises restored, and his *Answer* to Jefferson's *Proceedings* published.[240] For more than a quarter of a century legal battles involving the batture continued. In many of these Livingston was concerned either as a party or as counsel.[241]

He first lost part of his batture holdings when in 1819 the French heirs of Bertrand Gravier were successful in a lawsuit to recover their share of the property which John Gravier (Livingston's vendor) had claimed *in toto* through purchase with benefit of inventory and appraisement.[242] The court

EDWARD LIVINGSTON by John Trumbull.

    Livingston had been evicted, while Jefferson was president, from land claimed by the government on the beach or batture of the Mississippi River at New Orleans, and later sued Jefferson in Virginia. Marshall sat on the court. This portrait hangs in the Governor's Room in the New York City Hall.

    Courtesy Art Commission of the City of New York.

thus upheld the contention which Jefferson and Gallatin had maintained, that Bertrand Gravier's title to the batture was vested in his heirs as co-owners, and did not pass to John Gravier with the inventoried property at the sale to him.[243]

In the same year Livingston lost a case in which he was both a defendant and counsel.[244] The plaintiff's title was derived from one Poeyfarré, to whom Bertrand Gravier had sold a piece of land "frente al rio" ("fronting on the river") in 1789.[245] The issues were similar to those in the case which John Gravier had won against the city of New Orleans, but Livingston's adversaries offered more convincing evidence than the city had done and emerged victorious.[246] It will be remembered that in the *Gravier* case the court held that if there was no alluvial land formed at the time when Gravier sold the property, the alluvion which came into existence later would not belong to him, but to his vendee, who would then be the owner of the riparian estate to which the increment accrued. But the court found in the *Gravier* case that there was sufficient alluvion already formed, and of sufficient height, that it could be considered as annexed to his land before he sold the tract next to the river.[247] The subsequently formed alluvial deposit therefore became his property.

But in the case of the sale to Poeyfarré in 1789, it was proved by the testimony of witnesses that at the time of the sale there was no alluvial deposit extending above the surface of the water.[248] The *Gravier* decision was between different parties, and in any event did not hold that *at the time of the sale to Poeyfarré* there was a deposit high enough above water to be susceptible of private ownership as Gravier's property.[249] Furthermore, it dealt with a different geographical area: the *Gravier* case involved the upper, rather than the lower, part of the *faubourg,* and the height of the alluvial deposit may well have been quite different.[250]

Another setback depriving Livingston of a substantial portion of his profits from land speculation occurred when the demands and needs of the inhabitants of New Orleans to dig and take earth from the batture, as they had done in times past, proved irresistible. The interests of the people of the city, which Jefferson had tried to protect, received definitive recognition.

On September 20, 1820, before Hugues Lavergne, a notary public, a compromise agreement was entered into between Jean Gravier and all other possessors of batture lands, on the one hand, and the corporation of the city of New Orleans, on the other. The front proprietors gave up in favor of the city, for public use, the levee and a portion of the batture. A line was drawn parallel to the levee, and alluvion between that line and the river was given to the city.[251] Among the public uses specifically secured in the compromise agreement was the right of all the inhabitants of the city to take earth from the part of the batture belonging to the city.[252]

Then in 1821 Livingston won a case involving the very tract of land from which he had been dispossessed by the marshal.[253] Unlike the deed to Poey-farré in the case previously discussed,[254] the grant from Gravier involved in this case extended only to the levee, not to the river.[255] Moreover it was established as a fact that at the time of the sale by Gravier there was a parcel of land, including augmentation by alluvion, situated between the levee and the river; and that this parcel was reclaimable and susceptible of private ownership.[256] Hence the defendant, not being a riparian owner at all, had no claim to alluvion.[257]

By 1823, according to Livingston's latest biographer, his title to the batture lots was clear enough to permit his selling part of the property.[258] Proceeds from the sale of such lots were used to pay off Livingston's indebtedness to the government when a settlement was arrived at on February 27, 1830.[259] The batture property also provided a competence for Livingston's widow after his death in 1836.[260]

As counsel for the city of New Orleans Livingston argued an important case[261] before the Supreme Court of the United States a few months before his death. Attorney General Benjamin F. Butler represented the United States.

The government brought suit to prevent the city from selling a vacant tract of land.[262] The site had formerly served as a quay for the loading and un-loading of vessels. It was no longer needed for such purposes, because the course of the river had shifted, and the addition of alluvial land had neces-sitated relocation of the levee. The United States claimed ownership of the area, contending that it had been part of the public domain belonging to the French and Spanish sovereigns, to which the United States had become suc-cessor in interest through the Louisiana Purchase treaty.[263]

In this litigation the claims of the federal government were being asserted in opposition to the interests of New Orleans rather than for the benefit of the people of the city, as had been the case in Jefferson's administration. But the city prevailed in the Supreme Court when its cause was supported by the combined talents of Livingston and Daniel Webster.[264] The court recognized (as Livingston had argued)[265] that if the extension of the quay by alluvion did not belong to the public by virtue of riparian ownership, "by the continual deposits of the Mississippi, the city of New Orleans would, in the course of a few years, be cut off from the river, and its prosperity impaired."[266]

The issue before the Supreme Court was not a contest between private landowners and the claims of the public (as it had been when Livingston and Jefferson had clashed). The question was whether the quays had been dedicated to public use for the benefit of all the inhabitants of the city (like streets and highways) or simply belonged to the crown as proprietor of the public domain (possessing the same rights of exclusive ownership of the soil as any property owner enjoys). If there had been no dedication to public use, the crown's proprietorship would have passed to the United States as successor in interest under the Louisiana Purchase treaty.[267]

The Supreme Court held that the early maps procured by Moreau[268] proved that early in the eighteenth century a chartered company owning Louisiana with power to grant land in allodial tenure had dedicated the space between the first row of buildings and the water's edge in New Orleans to public use as a quay for the benefit of the city's commerce and navigation.[269] The rights thus vested in the inhabitants were not destroyed by the retrocession of Louisiana by the company to the French crown, nor by the subsequent cessions of the territory by France to Spain, by Spain to France, and by France to the United States.[270] Under both French[271] and Spanish law,[272] this property was regarded as "land [which], having been dedicated to public use, was withdrawn from commerce" [res extra commercium],[273] and was not "considered as a part of the public domain or crown lands, which the king could sell and convey."[274] Thus victory came to New Orleans.

Responding to the attorney general's reference to Livingston's Answer, the adversary who had written a book[275] observed: "The pamphlet was written under circumstances, in which the author thought, and still thinks, he had suffered grievous wrongs; wrongs which he thought, and still thinks, justified the warmth of language in which some part of his arguments are couched: but which, his respect for the public and private character of his opponent, always obliged him to regret, that he had been forced to use. He is happy, however, to say, that at a subsequent period, the friendly intercourse, with which, prior to that breach, he had been honored, was renewed; that the offended party forgot the injury and that the other performed the more difficult task (if the maxim of a celebrated French author is true), of forgiving the man upon whom he had inflicted it. The court, I hope, will excuse this personal digression; but I could not avoid using this occasion of making known, that I have been spared the lasting regret of reflecting, that Jefferson had descended to the grave, with a feeling of ill-will towards me."[276]

Soon afterwards the time would come to say of both illustrious adversaries: "They . . . rest from their labours; and their works do follow them."[277] Just as the nation had profited from the earlier contest between Jefferson and Hamilton, receiving the benefits of each antagonist's contribution to the struggle, so did the people of New Orleans, standing at the gateway to a vast "empire for liberty,"[278] derive advantage from the vigorous controversy between Jefferson and Livingston.

IV

Some Leading Cases
of the Day

Besides English reports, digests, and treatises, Jefferson included "Virginia laws" and "Reports on them" in his list of materials to be mastered by law students.[1] The difficulty of access to Virginia legislative enactments has already been mentioned.[2] Virginia judicial decisions existed only in manuscript[3] and were infrequently available. Jefferson collected these whenever an opportunity occurred, and in 1768 himself "began to commit to writing some leading cases of the day." He "continued to do so until the year 1772, when the Revolution dissolved our courts of justice, and called those attached to them to find other occupations."

When Jefferson was at the bar of the General Court "there were in the possession of John Randolph, Attorney General, three volumes of MS. Reports of cases determined in that court; the one taken by his father, Sir John Randolph, a second by Mr. [Edward] Barradall, and a third by [William] Hopkins." From these materials, covering the years 1730–40, Jefferson extracted every case on topics distinctively pertaining to Virginia law. In that field the judgments of the General Court "whether formed on correct principles of law or not, were of conclusive authority." They established the rules "under which our property has been ever since transmitted, and is regulated and held to this day." But on general questions of English common law he considered the opinions of the Virginia court (a group of prominent country gentlemen chosen as privy councilors "without any regard for legal knowledge") to be "of little value."[4]

To four cases from Randolph, twenty-six from Barradall, and one from Hopkins, Jefferson added eleven of his own. The collection thus prepared by Jefferson was not published, however, until 1829, three years after his death. It formed a single volume, entitled *Reports of Cases Determined in the General Court of Virginia,*[5] covering the years 1730–40 and 1768–72. These are the earliest cases reported in any Virginia law reports,[6] but the volume itself is not the earliest volume of reports to be published. That distinction belongs to George Wythe's chancery decisions which appeared in 1795.[7]

Apparently no reports have been preserved of Virginia cases for the period 1740–68, and 1772–89. Cases in the General Court from 1789 to 1826 were reported in volumes edited by two judges of that court, William Brockenbrough and Hugh Holmes. Originally the General Court, composed of the governor and council, had been known as the quarter court, because it met quarterly; but in the revisal of the laws printed in 1662[8] it was ordained that the "Quarter-Courts . . . be henceforth called General-Courts; a name more suitable to the nature of them, as being places where all persons and causes have generally audience, and receive determination."[9] After the royal instructions of 1679 to the governor, there was no appeal from the General Court except to the King in Council in England (which required an amount in controversy of three hundred pounds sterling.)[10] In 1779 the General Court[11] continued to exist alongside the Court of Chancery[12] and the Court of Admiralty.[13] The judges of those three courts, sitting together at stated sessions, were constituted a Supreme Court of Appeals.[14] In 1788 it was reorganized as a tribunal of five judges chosen to sit on that court alone.[15] In course of time the Supreme Court of Appeals became the final authority in civil matters, while the General Court had the last word in criminal cases. The General Court was finally abolished in 1851.[16]

In 1820 an official reporter for the court of appeals was authorized by the legislature when the judges complained that private reporters were far in arrears. But this reporter's duties were confined to that court, and as a result there were no reports for the General Court after 1826. In 1828 an act was passed directing the reporter to include General Court cases as an appendix to each volume of the Supreme Court reports. This was done from 1828 to 1852.[17]

The first unofficial court of appeals report (and the second published Virginia law report, coming three years after Wythe's chancery *Decisions*)[18] appeared in 1798. This was Bushrod Washington's *Reports of Cases argued and determined in the Court of Appeals of Virginia.*[19] His reports cover decisions between 1790 and 1796. Daniel Call, William Waller Hening and William Munford are the other reporters prior to 1820.[20] Beginning in 1880, the official reports are cited by volume number.[21]

Examination of the cases in Jefferson's *Reports* indicates that more than half of them deal with some aspect of slavery.[22] This is not surprising, since that "peculiar institution" played a prominent role in Virginia's plantation economy, and Jefferson confined his selection of cases to those which illustrated points of law peculiar to Virginia, omitting those which involved only English law.[23]

Appended to his reported cases, Jefferson added "a Disquisition of my own" on "Whether Christianity is a part of the Common Law."[24] This dealt with what Jefferson called "the most remarkable instance of Judicial legislation, that has ever occurred in English jurisprudence, or perhaps in any other. It is that of the adoption in mass of the whole code of another nation, and its incorporation into the legitimate system, by usurpation of the Judges alone, without a particle of legislative will having ever been called on, or exercised towards its introduction or confirmation."[25] He excoriated the alliance between church and state in England which made the judges accomplices in the frauds of the clergy. "And thus they incorporated into the English code, laws made for the Jews alone, and the precepts of the gospel, intended by their benevolent author as obligatory only *in foro conscientiae*; and they arm the whole with the coercions of Municipal law."[26] In effect, Jefferson attacked a series of judicial decisions which, by holding that Christianity was a part of the law, brought into existence an establishment of religion by law, and thereby denied religious freedom to all dissenters from the Anglican church.[27]

The proposition that Christianity is part of the common law has been proclaimed by numerous authorities,[28] including Sir Matthew Hale[29] and Lord Mansfield.[30] But Jefferson traces these all back to a statement by Chief Justice Prisot[31] in a Year Book case of 1458.[32]

Besides Hale and Mansfield, Jefferson might have cited his favorite authority, Lord Coke, for the proposition that "the common law was grounded on the law of God."[33] Moreover, the Year Book case discussed by Jefferson was cited by Coke in support of a decision that a church court might deprive a clergyman of his office for preaching against the Book of Common Prayer, upon his first offense, although the statute prescribed the penalty of deprivation (together with one year's imprisonment) only for the second offense, the first being punishable by forfeiture of his living for one year and imprisonment for six months.

As reported by Coke, the king's court held "that the sentence given by the Bishop with the consent of his colleagues, was such as the Judges of the common law ought to allow to be given according to the ecclesiastical laws: for seeing their authority is to proceed and give sentence in ecclesiastical causes, according to the ecclesiastical law, and they have given a sentence in a cause ecclesiastical upon their proceedings, by force of that law; the Judges of the common law ought to give faith and credit to their sentence, and to allow it to be done according to the ecclesiastical law; for cuilibet in sua arte perito est credendum. And this is the common received opinion of all our books, as appeareth 11 H. 7.9.34 H. 6.14, &c."[34]

American cases likewise assert the proposition, controverted by Jefferson, that Christianity is part of the common law.[35] In a leading case from Delaware (in which Jefferson's discussion of the subject was commented on by the court) it is interesting to note how far the court goes toward asserting that the criminality of offenses against religion is a consequence of their tendency to subvert the foundation of civil society and disturb the public peace. The common law "took cognizance of offences against God only, when by their inevitable effects, they became offences against man and his temporal security." The state thus "avenged the wrong done to civil society alone."[36] This is reminiscent of the reasoning by which the present Supreme Court justifies Sunday observance laws on secular grounds.[37]

Likewise in 1802 when Connecticut Baptists protested against laws taxing all citizens "to support Presbyterian ministers and build Presbyterian churches," former Chief Justice Ellsworth, as chairman of a committee of the General Assembly, reported "that the primary objects of government are the peace, order, and prosperity of society. . . . To the promotion of these objects, particularly in a republican government, good morals are essential. Institutions for the promotion of good morals [including religious institutions] are therefore objects of legislative provision and support." Just as every citizen may be taxed for "the support of schools for the instruction of children, or of courts of justice for the protection of rights" even though he have no children of his own to be educated or no lawsuits to be adjudicated, so "on the same principle of general utility" his money may be used to support a church or religion from which he personally dissents and derives no direct benefit, but which the legislature regards as having a "benign influence on morals."[38] However, as Sir Frederick Pollock has made plain, it is doubtful whether morality really requires to be undergirded by religious orthodoxy. "Divers . . . persons holding opinions contrary to the official ones on divers matters of faith and speculation have, in sundry times and countries, perversely and obstinately continued to be good men, good companions, and good citizens. . . . The truth is that civilized morality . . . has been professed by . . . men holding the most widely discordant speculative opinions."[39]

The Year Book case referred to by Jefferson was an action of *quare impedit* against the Bishop of Lincoln. This type of proceeding (as Blackstone explains) was brought, by a patron having the proprietary right (*jus patronatus*, advowson) to name a clergyman to a benefice, against the bishop for failing to install the patron's candidate to fill the vacant church. If two persons claiming the right of patronage present different clerks to fill the vacancy, the church is said to be "litigious," and "if nothing further be done, the bishop may suspend the admission of either, and suffer a lapse to occur." In that case, the bishop himself may fill the vacancy. But if either contender requests him (within six months after the vacancy occurs) to determine who is the rightful patron he must award a commission *de jure patronatus* to summon six clergy and six laymen to determine that issue.[40]

Accordingly, in response to Bohun's claim, the Bishop of Lincoln pleaded that after a vacancy the plaintiff and another claimant had each presented a clerk, the church being thereby rendered litigious, so that "he was not obliged by the Ecclesiastical law to admit either, until an inquisition *de jure patronatus* in the Ecclesiastical court," but that neither party had demanded such an inquisition, and that six months had passed, whereupon he had filled the vacancy "as on a lapse" as he had a right to do. The plaintiff demurred. The question arose whether "the Ecclesiastical law was to be respected in this matter by the Common law court." Chief Justice Prisot, in the course of his discussion, said: "*a tiels leis que ils de seint eglise ont en ancien scripture, covient a nous a donner credence; car ceo Common ley sur quel touts manners leis sont fondes et auxy Sir, nous sumus obliges de conustre lour ley de saint eglise: et semblablement ils sont obliges de conustre nostre ley.*"[41]

To decide whether the Bishop's action was rightful, Jefferson points out, the judges "would have to turn to the ancient writings and records of the canon law, in which they would find evidence of the laws of advowsons, *quare impedit*, the duties of bishops and ordinaries, for which terms Prisot could never have meant to refer them to the Old or New Testament, *les saincts scriptures*, where surely they would not be found."[42]

But Sir Henry Finch, in his discourse on *Law*, published in 1613,[43] egregiously misinterpreted Prisot's language, according to Jefferson. He rendered *ancient writings* as *holy scripture* (that is, the Bible). Citing the Year Book case, he said: "to such laws of the church as have warrant in *holy scripture,* our law giveth credence."[44] Jefferson's comment is: "Here we find 'ancien scripture' converted into 'holy scripture' whereas it can only mean the antient written laws of the church."

Justice Story strongly disagreed with Jefferson's contention.[45] John Quincy Adams likewise rejected it. After recording Story's "severe remarks" on Jefferson's statement in his letter to Cartwright,[46] Adams remarked:

My own opinion has been, ever since I first read the letter, that it was Mr. Jefferson himself, and not the succession of English lawyers for three hundred years, who had mistaken the meaning of the dictum of Prisot. Judge Story said that he had looked into the case in the year-book, and found the exposition of it by Mr. Jefferson so manifestly erroneous that he cannot even consider it an involuntary mistake.[47]

Yet the distinction upon which Jefferson was insisting between ecclesiastical law and common law, the distinction between church government and civil government, is very clear and important. Its neglect leads only to confusion of thought.

Of equal importance is the distinction between church law and religious doctrine. Both may be professedly based upon Old and New Testament teachings. In the Presbyterian Church, for example, the Confession of Faith is separate from the Form of Government and the Book of Discipline. While the Confession is peppered with footnotes containing "proof texts" from the

Scriptures, such references are fewer (or absent) in the other two documents. Even though church officers believe "the Scriptures of the Old and New Testament to be the Word of God, the only infallible rule of faith and practice" and also accept "the Confession of Faith of this Church, as containing the system of doctrine taught in the holy Scriptures," there are many rules explicitly derived from deliverances of General Assemblies, or other sources. What scriptural authority can be relied upon, for example, to establish the rule that "a particular church shall not sell or mortgage its property in any amount without written permission of the presbytery"? Jefferson is surely right in saying that many matters of that kind (such as advowsons and *quare impedit*) are derived from other sources than the Bible.[48]

Some lack of clarity is apt to arise from the fact that in the middle ages, church and state were thought of as being simply different aspects of a single society.[49] After they became distinct entities, their relationship was the subject of controversy. The Hildebrandine view[50] ascribed supremacy to the church; the Erastian to the state;[51] and the Jeffersonian or American system erected a "wall of separation," excluding government from any intrusion into the realm of religion, and vice versa.[52] In Europe, even after the Reformation (as in the Netherlands in the time of Grotius) regulation of matters pertaining to religion was still regarded as a state function of the utmost importance.[53]

Notwithstanding the distinctions between church and state and between ecclesiastical polity and faith, which are clearly perceptible today[54] (largely as a result of Jefferson's own efforts), it is of course possible at a given time and place for the civil government to incorporate into its legal system both the organizational structure and the confessional doctrine of a particular church (in other words to set up an established church).

Thus in Puritan New England, there was a definite displacement of the English common law[55] in favor of local legislation supplemented by Biblical teachings.[56] Jefferson quipped that the New England law was composed of the law of God except where there were local statutes to the contrary.[57]

Jefferson's witticism was not without foundation. There was a Massachusetts enactment of 1636 directing the magistrates to "hear and determine all causes according to the laws now established, and where there is no law, then as near the law of God as they can."[58] At the same time John Cotton, a clergyman designated by the General Court as a member of a commission "to make a draught of laws agreeable to the word of God, which may be the fundamentals of this Commonwealth," prepared a code of laws called "Moses, his Judicials." The theory was that part of the law of Moses was ceremonial in character and was binding only upon Jews. Other precepts were considered as judicial, as being based upon the law of nature and hence binding upon all mankind.

Apparently Cotton's code was never actually in force as law in Massachusetts, but a later code, prepared by another clergyman, Nathaniel Ward, was accepted in 1641. It was known as the Body of Liberties. In Ward's code as in Cotton's, it was the word of God, not the English common law, that was prescribed as the rule by which the people were to walk.[59] In 1648 a comprehensive code was adopted, which was "no mere collection of English laws and customs, but was a fresh and considered effort to order men's lives and conduct in accordance with the religious and political ideas of Puritanism."[60]

So too in England the system of separate ecclesiastical courts, applying a separate system of law, long survived the secularization of the Church of England by Henry VIII.[61] Conflicts between the church courts and the common law courts had been a familiar feature in English jurisprudence and politics. Occasionally these controversies erupted into long-remembered incidents such as the death of Thomas à Becket in 1170 after his quarrel with Henry II and that of Thomas More in 1535 after his quarrel with Henry VIII. Another memorable instance was the removal of Lord Coke from the bench by James I in 1616 after acrimonious disputes over the practice whereby the common law courts directed writs of prohibition against the church courts, forbidding the latter from exercising jurisdiction in matters which the common law courts regarded as beyond the province of the church courts.[62]

The claims of the church courts are well summarized by Holdsworth:

> In the twelfth century the ecclesiastical courts claimed to exercise a wide jurisdiction. (1) They claimed criminal jurisdiction in all cases in which a clerk was accused, a jurisdiction over offences against religion, and a wide corrective jurisdiction over clergy and laity alike "pro salute animae." A branch of the latter jurisdiction was the claim to enforce all promises made with oath or pledge of faith. (2) They claimed a jurisdiction over matrimonial and testamentary causes. Under the former head came all questions of marriage, divorce, and legitimacy; under the latter came grants of probate and administration, and the supervision of the executor and administrator. (3) They claimed exclusive cognizance of all matters which were in their nature ecclesiastical, such as ordination, consecration, celebration of service, the status of ecclesiastical persons, ecclesiastical property such as advowsons, land held in frankalmoin, and spiritual dues.
>
> These claims were at no time admitted by the state in their entirety; and in course of time most of these branches of jurisdiction have been appropriated by the state.[63]

As early as 1166 under Henry II the Constitutions of Clarendon were enacted to settle (largely in favor of the king) controverted aspects of the relations

81

between church and state. Of uncertain date, but perhaps established by the Constitutions of Clarendon, was the assize utrum, a species of inquest by jury which contributed to the control of the king's courts over the land law.[64] "The Assize Utrum was introduced originally to determine the question whether land was held in frankalmoin, *i. e.* by a spiritual tenure, or by some lay tenure. This was an important question in the twelfth century because upon it depended whether the spiritual or lay court had jurisdiction."[65]

The Constitutions of Clarendon[66] contained a provision forbidding appeals to Rome from English courts without the king's permission. As early as 1354 criminal statutes of praemunire were enacted to prevent such appeals.[67] These statutes evinced a trend in national policy, which was intensified after Henry VIII declared himself head of the English church.[68] By that time "the position of the ecclesiastical courts had been fundamentally altered. The church had been brought within the state; and subjected to the power of the crown."[69] Yet the church courts remained in existence as a completely separate system, but one whose authority within their proper sphere the common law courts were bound to recognize, just as in Prisot's time.[70]

In America, however, where no resident English bishop had been established,[71] the functions of English ecclesiastical courts were performed by the ordinary courts of justice. The separate church courts were doubtless regarded as an aspect of English law which, by reason of local conditions, was inapplicable in the colonies;[72] and in any event, after the Revolution, would have been deemed one of the vestiges of monarchy which Jefferson's program of law reform was designed to obliterate.[73]

Having concluded our comments on the disquisition appended to his *Reports*, we shall now consider the cases reported in which Jefferson himself took part as counsel. One of these[74] involved recondite points of church law similar to those treated in his argument whether Christianity was part of the common law.

Wythe and Jefferson appeared for the libellants (plaintiffs), who were vestrymen and churchwardens in Nansemond County and sought the removal of a curate "of evil fame and profligate manners." He also, it was alleged, neglected his parochial duties and avowed his disbelief in the religion of Christ. He cared not of what religion he was so he got the tobacco which constituted his remuneration, "nor what became of the flock so that he could get the fleece." They prayed "that the said Patrick Lunan might be corrected, punished and deprived, or otherwise, that right and justice might be administered." The defendant pleaded to the jurisdiction of the court. The court held that it possessed ecclesiastical jurisdiction in general and might proceed to censure or deprive the defendant, if there should be just cause.[75]

Noting that he was of counsel in the case, Jefferson observed, "This circumstance is the apology for the little justice done to the arguments of the other counsel in this case; being prevented taking them minutely by the necessity of considering in the instant, how they might be answered."[76]

While Jefferson "thought the ecclesiastical jurisdiction of the court established beyond a doubt, yet I conceived it did not follow thence that they might deprive the defendant of his parish, because visitation and deprivation are no parts of the office of an ecclesiastical judge."[77]

He therefore entered upon an extensive inquiry into the rights of advowson held by patrons of churches. He agreed with Blackstone[78] in classifying churches into three groups: donative, presentative, and collative. Donatives are churches where the patron (either the crown or a subject) who endowed the church has the complete right by his deed of donation to invest the clerk, without presentation to the bishop or any other ceremony. Presentatives are those where by custom the candidate must be presented to the bishop for examination and admission or rejection. If the bishop refuses to admit the clerk presented, the patron may bring an action of *quare impedit* in the temporal court (as has been seen).[79] Collatives are churches where the bishop himself is patron. Incident to patronage is the right of visitation, which includes deprivation, censure, and other forms of punishment. Where the crown is patron of a donative church, the king may entrust visitation to commissioners, but if none are appointed the chancellor visits *ex officio*. It is punishable by *praemunire*[80] for an ecclesiastical court to undertake visitation of a donative church, where the patron alone has the right to visit.

Virginia churches, Jefferson argues, are donative. Legislation has given vestries the right to nominate within a year after a vacancy, but the crown retains the right of investiture (which puts the clerk into possession of the church and entitles him to his temporal emoluments).

Thus Jefferson concludes, by this roundabout route, that the General Court does have the right of visitation on behalf of the king as patron by virtue of their having the powers of a chancellor, since the king has never appointed commissioners to exercise his right of visitation.[81]

Colonel Richard Bland came to the bar as *amicus curiae*, admitting that the court had ecclesiastical jurisdiction, but claimed for the vestries the right of visitation. Attorney General John Randolph confined himself to answering Mr. Wythe, but contended further that the court had no general ecclesiastical jurisdiction. The court ruled, as has been seen,[82] against the defendant; but on the importunity of the attorney general a rehearing was granted.[83]

In the other case argued by Jefferson,[84] his eloquent and ingenious appeal to the law of nature, under which all men are born free,[85] on behalf of a mulatto seeking release from servitude, fell on deaf ears.[86] The court did not wish to hear from opposing counsel. "Wythe, for the defendant, was about to answer, but the court interrupted him and gave judgment in favor of his client."[87] Fortunately, Jefferson's passion for liberty was not quenched by this humiliating defeat at the hands of his former preceptor.

The court's conclusion seems to be clearly correct. The case turned upon the application of statutory provisions. Jefferson's interpretation is plausible, but not persuasive.

The Act of 1705 provided that "if any woman servant shall have a bastard child by a negro or mulatto, or if a free Christian white woman shall have such bastard child by a negro or mulatto; in both the said cases the church-wardens shall bind the said child to be a servant until it shall be of thirty one years of age."[88] Pursuant to this statute, plaintiff's grandmother, "begotten of a white woman by a negro man, after the year 1705," was bound to service until the age of thirty-one.

After 1723, but during her servitude, she bore plaintiff's mother. In 1723 a statute had been enacted providing that "where any female mulatto or Indian, by law obliged to serve till the age of thirty or thirty one years shall, during the time of her servitude, have any child born of her body, every such child shall serve the master or mistress of such mulatto or Indian, until it shall attain the same age, the mother of such child was obliged, by law, to serve unto."[89] By virtue of this provision plaintiff's mother was bound to servitude until she attained thirty-one years of age. During her servitude, in 1742, plaintiff was born. He was sold to defendant by the person to whom plaintiff's grandmother was bound. Defendant claimed a right to the service of plaintiff until plaintiff became thirty-one years of age.

Jefferson contended that the Act of 1723 operated to impose servitude upon plaintiff's mother, but not upon plaintiff, since the statute says that the "child" (not grandchild or more remote issue) of a female mulatto subject to servitude shall be subjected to similar servitude.

This is true, but Jefferson adroitly ignores the fact that the statute operates with equal effect upon plaintiff's mother in the same manner as it did upon his grandmother. The mother was also a "female mulatto"; she too was "by law obliged to serve" till the age of thirty-one; she too, "during the time of her servitude," had a "child born of her body" [to wit, the plaintiff]. Therefore, by virtue of the Act of 1723, "such *child*"[90] [the plaintiff] must serve his mother's master or mistress until he attains the same age [thirty-one] to which "the mother of such child" [that is, plaintiff's mother] "was obliged, by law, to serve unto."

So Jefferson's poetic peroration misses the point when he claims to have proved "that the act of 1705, makes servants of the first mulatto, that of 1723, extends it to her children, but that it remains for some future legislature, if any shall be found wicked enough, to extend it to the grandchildren and other issue more remote, to the '*nati natorum et qui nascentur ab illis*'."[91]

Jefferson may have had in mind some of his youthful forensic frays when he observed to Madison that "Men come into business at first with visionary principles. It is practice alone which can correct and conform them to the actual current of affairs. In the meantime, those to whom their errors were first applied, have been their victims."[92]

Wythe was less successful in his courtroom contests with Edmund Pendleton. Jefferson's *Reports* substantiate the generally accepted view that the shrewd and polished Pendleton had the better of the gentle and scholarly Wythe in their rivalry for leadership of the bar at the General Court.[93] There is no case reported by Jefferson in which the decision was in favor of Wythe and against Pendleton.[94]

Pendleton defeated Thomson Mason in an interesting case[95] involving questions of servitude similar to those dealt with by Jefferson in his contest with Wythe. Betty Bugg, daughter of a white Christian woman and a black father, was born between 1723 and 1768, and was bound to service until she attained the age of thirty-one. During her servitude she was delivered of the defendant Bugg, who was sold by his master to the plaintiff. At the age of twenty-six, having cause of complaint for lack of proper clothing and diet, he sought his freedom. Three points were made on his behalf: (1) He had never been bound out by the churchwardens, so the master of his mother had no right to his service. (2) The master had forfeited whatever rights he had by transferring Bugg to the plaintiff. (3) The master had forfeited whatever rights he had by failing to provide necessaries for Bugg's maintenance. Mason, for the defendant, relied principally on the second point.[96]

Pendleton argued that emancipation was not the proper remedy for ill-treatment. The court decided in his favor. Jefferson noted a query whether "the great clearness of the first and third points, which alone were assigned in the record as the grounds of the judgment, might not prevent the court from attending minutely to the second, which seems to be in favor of the pauper."[97]

Mason defeated Bland in another case involving slavery.[98] Mason represented plaintiffs in an action of trespass for assault and battery against persons holding them as slaves. This was an action to try their title to freedom.[99] They were descendants of an Indian woman brought into Virginia between 1682 and 1748. The question was whether an act of 1682,[100] on which defendant relied, permitting such persons to be sold as slaves had or had not been repealed.

Mason, as befitted a kinsman of the author of the Virginia Bill of Rights, and undeterred by Jefferson's defeat two years earlier, again invoked the law of nature. In terms reminiscent of the denunciation of writs of assistance by James Otis in 1761,[101] he declared that the Act of 1682 enslaving Indians was contrary to natural right and justice; hence it was void *ab initio*. He reminded the judges that "Indians of every denomination were free, and independent of us; they were not subject to our empire; not represented in our legislature; they derived no protection from our laws, nor could be subjected to their bonds. . . . Now all acts of legislature apparently contrary to natural right and justice, are, in our laws, and must be in the nature of things, considered as void. The laws of nature are the laws of God; whose authority can be superseded by no power on earth. A legislature must not obstruct our obedience to him from whose punishments they can not protect us. All human constitutions which contradict his laws, we are in conscience bound to disobey. Such have been the adjudications of our courts of justice.[102] . . . And so he concluded the act [of 1682] is originally void, because contrary to natural right and justice."[103]

Mason also argued[104] that the Act of 1682 was virtually repealed by an act of 1684[105] and one of 1691[106] and was actually repealed by the Revisal of 1705.[107]

Jefferson felt that "these arguments are so contradictory that I can hardly suppose the plaintiff's counsel so used them; yet do my notes, taken while he was speaking, confirm them in so many places, that I can as little suppose the error in myself."[108]

Mason expounded the legislation of 1705 as specifying who shall thereafter be slaves; the description includes two characteristics not possessed by Indians: they must be *servants* and they must be *shipped* into Virginia. All other acts relating to slaves and servants are repealed; hence the Act of 1682 was repealed, if it was then still in force.[109]

Colonel Bland, for the defendant, denied that the Act of 1682 was void. He cited Pufendorf to show the legitimacy of slavery.[110] To enslave Indians was not as unjust as to enslave blacks, for the former by warlike incursions destroyed inhabitants and property. Even if the act were contrary to natural justice, it could not be disregarded by a court of law.[111]

"Mason, in reply denied that Puffendorf [*sic*] justified slavery on the principles of natural law. That on the contrary[112] . . . he proves it to have no foundation in nature, but to be derived from contract alone."[113]

The court held that neither the Act of 1684 nor that of 1691 had repealed the Act of 1682, but that the Act of 1705 had done so.[114] Mason's clients were thus entitled to their freedom, since their ancestor had arrived in Virginia after 1705.[115] Later, as will be seen,[116] the court of appeals by use of a manuscript from Monticello established the existence of an act of 1691[117] which was the means of assuring freedom to Indians arriving in Virginia between 1691 and 1705.

V

Subtle Reasonings
of the Law

In addition to the description in Jefferson's *Reports* of cases in which he participated as counsel, various other available sources of information shed light on his professional labors during the period when he was actively engaged in private practice as a lawyer.

First of all must be mentioned his account books. He conscientiously recorded his expenditures and other memoranda in notebooks (for some of the earlier years, in the blank pages of almanacs); and these methodically kept volumes make it possible "to follow Jefferson's movements almost, if not quite, day by day."[1] They begin in 1767, the year he became a lawyer, and continue until his death in 1826.[2] Many entries relate to legal business, interspersed among expenditures for clothing, horses, books, and visits to the "play house," as well as at taverns and ferries along the way.[3]

Besides the notes on legal matters found in the account books, a number of similar memoranda have been preserved separately among Jefferson's papers. These are of a rather fragmentary nature and of no particular value as illustrative examples of his legal skill.[4] Many papers relating to his law practice (as well as all his law books except one, which was lent out at the time) were destroyed by the fire at Shadwell, his boyhood home, on February 1, 1770. He was obliged to seek continuance for the cases which should have been heard at the April session of the General Court.[5] Several specimens of Jefferson's opinions advising clients about their affairs have been preserved.[6] Occasional references to law business occur in his voluminous correspondence.[7]

A more systematic survey of Jefferson's law practice is obtainable from his Case Book.[8] This handsomely written volume, now in the Huntington Library, lists in numbered sequence 939 cases,[9] over a period of time from February 12, 1767, to November 9, 1774. On the margin of left-hand pages appears the number of the case with the names of the parties. To the right of the neatly ruled margin Jefferson entered a brief description of the case, beginning with the date, followed by the full names and county of residence of the parties. Then the nature of the case and the action to be taken is recorded, as well as any fee received, or sometimes the amount to be charged. The items vary in length but usually do not exceed four lines, and there is room for eight or more cases to a page. A neatly ruled line extends from the marginal ruling across both the left- and right-hand pages.[10] The space on the right-hand page is ordinarily used to show later developments or disposition of the case. It is often blank; and in many instances merely states "———— 1774. Aug. 11. E. R. to finish," indicating that the case is one turned over to Edmund Randolph (later governor of Virginia[11] and attorney general of the United States under George Washington) when Jefferson withdrew from practice of the law in 1774. Sometimes the entry is "E. R. to finish & receive fee," indicating the amount (usually £2 10s. or £5).

Jefferson's first case should be set forth in full. In the ruled-off box on the left-hand page he wrote: "1767. Feb. 12. Gabriel Jones (Augusta) v. Andrew Lewis (Augusta) enter caveat for 100 acres of land near Warm spring Augusta. see state of case. ———— Mar. 20. recd. of Jones £3. ———— Apr. 13. pd L. Savage for tax and Sum. 8/3 ———— 1768. June 18. took out N.S. pd Walthoe 5/9." On the right-hand page the entries continue: "———— July 6. inclosed Sum. to mr Jones. ———— 1769. Mar. 21. the identity of the lands in Jones's and Lewis's entries is proved by Lewis's letter which I have. ———— 1770. June 13. obtd. ord. conc. ———— July 12. wrote to pl. ———— July 14. inclosd him copy ord. conc. ———— Aug. 22. recd. 29/6."[12]

The final entry in the book (Case 939) reads: "1774. Nov. 9. Charles Smith (Orange) I am to give him opn on John Jones's will. recd 14/9. ———— 20. comm[itte]d opn to writing."[13]

Caveats (to prevent the grant of land to another claimant) and petitions (to procure a grant to the applicant himself) constituted the predominant feature of Jefferson's law practice.[14] Less than a year and a half after he came to the bar, a volume of such business was turned over to him by George Wythe.[15] Presumably Wythe had already collected a fee,[16] so Jefferson in those cases received only such compensation as the clients voluntarily offered.[17]

A sampling of other items from the Case Book will illustrate the variety of his practice. He represented plaintiffs and defendants with approximately equal frequency.

In one case "to recover a number of slaves" Jefferson wrote to his client,[18] the plaintiff, on March 23, 1769, "advising him to drop this and the suit No. 182. on cond[ition] Daniel [the defendant] would pay costs." The companion case[19] was an action of slander for these words: "If the s[ai]d Betty [the wife plaintiff] has a child it positively is not the child of James Devire but is a bastard; and tho' it is hard to say so of my child, I really think it so." Both cases languished and were turned over to Randolph to finish.

On June 9, 1767, Jefferson wrote: "Gordon (a seafaring man) v. George Wythe (my friend) defend him totis viribus. take no fee."[20] Friendship was probably also the reason for charging no fee to Francis Willis, Jr.,[21] and

Francis Eppes.[22] Jefferson on his own account brought a friendly caveat against Thomas Mann Randolph for four hundred acres on Southwest Mountain, near Edgehill;[23] and defended Randolph against another claimant for the same land.[24]

Jefferson also declined fees in actions to establish the liberty of persons claimed as slaves. One such case was *Howell* v. *Netherland*, which he included in his *Reports*.[25] In the Case Book a briefer account is given: "Samuel Howell, a pauper v. Wade Netherland (Cumbd.) the pl's great-grandmother was a white woman and had a daur. by a negro man, whose grandson the pl. is; and sues for freedom. charge no fee."[26] In another such case Jefferson won a verdict and judgment for £50 and costs.[27]

Indigent parties also received the benefit of his professional services without charge. In a caveat proceeding he "undertook before Gov. & council to appear gratis for def. who was too poor to employ counsel."[28] In a replevin[29] proceeding he noted: "The pl. being poor charge no fee."[30]

The most frequent occasion for remitting a fee was where for some reason the work for which the fee was to be charged was not performed. Abatement of the proceeding by reason of the death of a party[31] would be a frequent example of this situation, or the decision of a litigant not to pursue his claim.[32] Sometimes the failure to prosecute a case may have been due to lack of diligence on the part of counsel rather than to change of heart on the part of the client. In one instance where Jefferson was to "bring writ of AB. by journey's accounts for the battery formerly sued for" the notation on the right-hand page of the book tersely states: "not done. so make no charge."[33] Under the same policy of *quantum meruit*, no additional fee would be charged by Jefferson in a matter relating to the same land as was involved in a proceeding already pending.[34] Likewise, where a caveat was filed but dismissed as inappropriate because the land was already patented, Jefferson concluded it was proper to make no charge. In June of 1774 such a case was "Dismd with costs because the caveat was unnecessary, the Council declaring they could not meddle with patd. lands."[35]

The fee was also remitted in cases where Jefferson refused to represent the client.[36] Thus when Isaac Bates, an overseer for John Cannon, a plantation owner in Buckingham County, sued for his share of the crop, Jefferson notified the sheriff of that county "that I decline appearing for pl. and remit fee."[37] Perhaps Jefferson had already gotten wind of the overseer's unsavory reputation. Less than two years later Jefferson sued Bates on behalf of his brother Randolph:[38] "the def. was overseer for my bro[the]r and by a cruel whipping killed a negro woman Hannah."[39]

Conflicts of interest account for another group of cases where Jefferson remitted fees which he was not in a position to earn. Thus in a caveat entered for Matthew Harrison against Alexander White, Jefferson had the summons issued,[40] and "inclosd [it] to pl. and declined prosecuting it, and informed White I should appear for him."[41]

In another caveat proceeding, by Joseph Pleasants against John Bibee, Jefferson wrote: "Bibee informs me this is the land I recovered for him in Biby v. Norvell. so decline appearing & refund £2–10."[42] However, in a "friendly petition" for four hundred acres in Albemarle County by Thomas Pleasants against Joseph Pleasants, Jefferson was "empl[oye]d. by T. Pleasants and also by Joseph Pleasants."[43]

On another occasion Jefferson had prepared a declaration (the original pleading or complaint setting forth the plaintiff's claim in the traditional legal language) in ejectment[44] for Thomas Lucas against Ambrose Rucker. But he found himself unable to go forward with the case, "having been formerly retained by Rucker in these cases (as he says) I retire from them and remit the balance due from Lucas, who is satisfied I should keep what I have for the trouble I have been at."[45]

Similarly, with regard to an action of slander by John Fitz-patrick against Thomas Turk (both residents of Augusta County), "pl. applied to me to bring it but declined, having been retained by Turk. informed Turk. rcd. of 25/."[46]

Sometimes Jefferson remitted fees simply for reasons of convenience rather than because of professional ethics. In a caveat case where he had received £2 3s. 6d. on June 15, 1769, he then on August 17, 1771, made an entry to "remit the balance of 9 d. to save trouble of repeating it yearly in list of balances."[47]

Procedural quirks could also prove costly to a neophyte practitioner. On one occasion Jefferson, representing defendants, received a note from the plaintiff agreeing to dismissal of the suit; whereupon he "imprudently de-liv[ere]d it and got the suit dism[isse]d before I ent[ere]d appearance so that my clients recover no costs. I think I ought not to charge them but get any fees of pl[aintiff]. as well as I can. he promises to pay."[48] Regarding an appeal where Wythe was cocounsel, he wrote: "charge no fee unless we prevail."[49] On another occasion he comments: "I promised to be patient for my fee."[50]

An unusual action of trespass was brought by Jefferson "for taking pl[ain-tiff]'s son and keeping him 2. or 3. days. also for entering his house and taking forcibly a bottle of whiskey and shirt."[51] The tenuous distinctions between trespass and trespass on the case under common law pleading[52] were sometimes troublesome to Jefferson. On one occasion after issuing a writ of trespass for assault and battery he became "apprehensive this suit is bro[ugh]t wrong iss[ue]d writ in Case."[53]

In another caveat proceeding he was "emploied by def. but with no other

91

WILLIAM BYRD III by an unknown artist (perhaps Cosmo Alexander).
Byrd was a prominent Virginian, and one of Jefferson's clients on retainer.
Courtesy Virginia State Library.

views than to keep it off as long as we can in hopes the pl. may run away."[54] Similarly in a chancery case he was employed by defendant "to delay as long as possible."[55]

Jefferson may have felt he was achieving recognition in the profession when on June 14, 1768, he noted that "the Honble Wm. Byrd (Charles city) retains me generally."[56] He received additional fees from Byrd for actual litigation.[57]

It was also a sign of his standing as a capable practitioner that when Robert Carter Nicholas retired from the bar in April, 1771, he "put his business into my hands to be finished." Finding himself, however, "under a necessity of declining it," Jefferson made no entries of cases except to note payments actually received in half a dozen matters.[58] Two years later he successfully obtained money judgments in a group of cases which he "took on mr Blair's leaving the business."[59]

Other aspects of Jefferson's practice deserve notice. Once he was employed in a chancery suit against George Washington and the Custis heirs "which has been pending these 30 years" (and which was still pending when Edmund Randolph took over Jefferson's practice).[60] By drawing a bill for an injunction on behalf of William Byrd against Edmund Pendleton and Peter Lyons, administrators of John Robinson (late Speaker of the House of Burgesses and treasurer of the Colony of Virginia),[61] Jefferson became involved peripherally in the notorious Robinson affair.[62] As a result of the treasurer's recirculating paper money which by law should have been retired and burned up, the Robinson estate owed the colony over £100,700, and doubtfully collectible debts of over £138,000 were owing to the estate. Byrd was the largest debtor, owing £14,921 to Robinson's administrators.[63]

Jefferson brought an action of assault and battery on behalf of another prominent Virginian, Carter Henry Harrison, against John Mayo, a county justice and the acting coroner of Cumberland County, "for committing the pl. while sheriff and confining him 48 hours."[64] Cases involving various public officials were not infrequent. On one occasion (perhaps a precursor of present-day civil rights complaints charging "police brutality") Jefferson brought an action of assault and battery "ag[ains]t def. a constable who struck the pl. tho' he surrend[ere]d. himself."[65] An action of trespass on the case was brought (on behalf of Thomas Turk)[66] "for malversation in office of surveior."[67] Action was taken against the sheriff of Culpepper County to compel him to pay over to the plaintiff money collected on an execution against a debtor.[68]

Jefferson appeared on behalf of the defendant when the sheriff of Bedford County was sued "on some pretend[e]d contract with pl. about farming the office."[69] Another case where Jefferson represented the defendant was in connection with an "Inform[atio]n of Gab[riel]. Jones et al. before the council

. . . to prevent his hav[in]g comm[issio]n of sheriff" for Augusta County.[70] On another occasion Jefferson represented the contestant, Zachariah Taliaferro, against Cornelius Thomas in "a dispute before the council for the Sheriff's place in Amherst County."[71] The same was true when he appeared, two weeks later, for John Coleman against John Jones in a "dispute before council for sheriff's place" in Brunswick County.[72] He advocated the case of the incumbent, John Bowyer, in a proceeding "before the council to remove him from his office of Justice of the peace" in Botetourt County.[73] He defended Luke Bowyer, of the same county, "for mal-practices as atty."[74]

Somewhat akin to disciplinary proceedings against attorneys as officers of the court, or to proceedings for removal of public officials, were the legal procedures available against beneficed clergymen in the colonial era before Jefferson had succeeded in disestablishing the state church.[75] In 1769 Jefferson was employed by the inhabitants of Fairfax parish in an ecclesiastical case against their rector.[76] The nature of the dispute is not stated. It may have been about tithes, like the famous "Parsons' Case" which added to the fame of Patrick Henry.[77] Or it may have been an attempt to remove the clergyman from office for unbecoming conduct.[78] In any event this controversy may have whetted Jefferson's interest in church law, and prepared him for participation (two years later) in the better-known case of *Goodwin* v. *Lunan*,[79] described in his *Reports*.[80]

Some idea of the range and scope of Jefferson's law practice will have been gained from the preceding review of illustrative examples drawn from the Case Book. But the meager data there recorded (only one to four lines to each item) afford no indication of the erudite learning and resourceful professional skills which Jefferson brought to bear upon the matters which he had occasion to handle.

Concerning the case of *Bolling* v. *Bolling*, for instance, all that the three lines devoted to that case disclose is the following succinct statement: "1770. Dec. 2. Archbd Bolling ( ) v. Robt. Bolling (Buckingham) case in canc. referrd to arbitration. desired by R. Bolling to state it with written arguments at length in writing. charge £5. ——— 1771. Sep. 13. recd. £9-17."[81]

Fortunately, however, in this case the skimpy information thus provided can be supplemented by the text of the written arguments themselves which are preserved in a volume in the Huntington Library.[82]

After a two-page statement of the facts of the case[83] George Wythe's opening argument for the plaintiff appears,[84] followed by Jefferson's argument for defendant.[85] Appended is a transcript of an English case relied on by both sides.[86] In Jefferson's argument he says, "This case is too long to be transcribed, but if there be any doubt on this question [that making a debtor of the testator his executor is an extinguishment of the debt] I beg it may be turned to and read, because I rely on it as decisive."[87] Next comes the second argument for plaintiff.[88] Then, again in Jefferson's hand, is his second argument for defendant. The concluding reply on behalf of the plaintiff[89] completes the arguments. Thus Jefferson wrote 110 pages, and opposing counsel 125, of the volume as it now stands.[90]

The controversy being argued related to the proper distribution of the estate of one Edward Bolling, and the interpretation of his last will and testament. The litigation involved a prominent Virginia family. The testator's father, John Bolling of Cobbs, was born January 20, 1700, and died September 5, 1757. John's second son (John) born June 24, 1737, married Jefferson's sister Martha. Both plaintiff and defendant were brothers of the testator (who was born September 9, 1746, and died August 18, 1770, unmarried). Jefferson's client, the defendant Robert Bolling of Chellowe, was born August 28, 1738, and died July 21, 1775, having been twice married and the father of six children. The plaintiff Archibald Bolling (the youngest son of John Bolling of Cobbs) was born March 20, 1750, and died July 11, 1827. He was married four times, and had four children.[91]

Edward Bolling made his will on July 13, 1769, and gave his Buffalo Lick plantation, along with certain slaves, to his brother Robert Bolling, the defendant. To his youngest brother, Archibald Bolling, the plaintiff, he devised other lands (including "my warehouse at a place called Pocahontas"). Archibald was also made residuary devisee and legatee[92] by a later provision in the will which gave to him "the rest of my estate, negroes, horses, clothes, and every other part of my estate not already given."

Between the two gifts to Archibald, the testator gave a slave to his sister Mary Bland; a legacy of £100 to his sister Sarah Tazewell; a slave to his sister Anne Bolling; a slave to his friend Richard Meade; and a slave to his cousin Bolling Eldridge.

Between the legacies to Meade and to Eldridge, the testator inserted the following language (which gave rise to one of the hotly contested issues in the case): "it is my will and desire that my Book be given up to my brother Robert and that he recieve all the debts due to me, and pay all that I owe."[93]

The testator died on August 18, 1770. Between the date of his will and of his death, he sold the Pocahontas warehouse to Neill Buchanan for £500. According to the defendant, the decedent in contemplation of the money due from the sale of the warehouse purchased other property in an even greater amount than £500, all of which purchases (except one of £20) passed to plaintiff as residuary legatee.

After testator's death, defendant Robert Bolling probated the will and undertook to act as executor. The propriety of his so doing was not contested by Archibald Bolling.[94]

The two principal questions in the case were: (1) whether the defendant Robert Bolling was entitled to the crops growing on the Buffalo Lick plantation at the time of the testator's death,[95] or whether as part of the decedent's personal estate they should pass to his residuary legatee, the plaintiff; and (2) whether the language about the testator's "Book" of accounts was a legacy to defendant Robert Bolling of the surplus of receivables collected over debts of the testator to be paid, or whether that surplus also was an otherwise undisposed of part of the decedent's personal property which should pass under the residuary clause of the will to plaintiff.

With great thoroughness, resourcefulness, and legal acumen counsel for plaintiff and defendant developed every possible argument to support the position of their respective clients with respect to these disputed points. They canvassed pertinent English decisions, evaluated the accuracy of the reporters, and debated the tenor of the *ratio decidendi* attributed to the judges deciding those cases. They minutely scrutinized every word of applicable Virginia statutes, and every word of the disputed passages in the testator's will, as well as every possible circumstance which might shed light on his intent when he wrote the words whose lack of clarity gave rise to the controversy. It was a notable performance, truly typical of the titans of the Virginia bar of that era.

Much erudition was displayed by both sides on the subject of "emblements," the term which designates a growing crop which the law, for the sake of encouraging agriculture, preserves to the sower even if the land on which it is planted passes to someone else before harvest time. As Blackstone explains, if a tenant having a life estate sows the lands and dies before harvest, his executors shall have the crop, not the remainderman who succeeds to the lands. The same rule applies to a tenant *pur autre vie*, holding during another person's life, when that person dies before harvest time. The same is also true of a tenant at will, whose interest is of uncertain duration and subject to termination at the landlord's pleasure. But a tenant for years, who knows with certainty when his term of occupancy will end, shall not have the emblements; for it was his own folly to sow what he knows he cannot reap. So too, in the case of any tenant whose term is ended by his own voluntary act.[96]

Wythe's opening argument was not particularly effective. Acting in accordance with Aaron Burr's maxim that law is whatever is boldly asserted and plausibly maintained,[97] he declared broadly that emblements were *mobilia*[98] or personal property in all respects, and therefore passed to the administrator or executor of the decedent and ultimately into the residue. They did not, he contended, pass to the devisee of land. He stressed the difficulty of segregating the crops that had been harvested on August 18, 1770, and those ripening later, especially since they had been intermingled in the same storage facilities. Hence "the distinction . . . between crops growing and crops gathered, is unsound and not warranted."[99]

Anticipating that defendant would cite certain cases, Wythe undertook to weaken their force by showing that they were not directly in point, or that the judges were not in accord as to their reasons, or that the reporters were inaccurate or not authoritative.[100]

Briefly referring to a Virginia statute,[101] Wythe interprets it as uniting the emblements with the use of the testator's slaves, and directing both the crop and the labor of the slaves to be treated as assets or personal estate (hence ultimately part of the legacy to Wythe's client as residuary legatee). He points out that "our lands being cultivated mostly if not altogether by slaves, if they should be removed immediately after the owner's death the crop on his ground must perish. To prevent this public as well as private loss, the act directs the crop . . . to be finished by the slaves, who should for that purpose be continued on the plant[atio]n till Christmas." Wythe asserts that "by this confusion of the emblements of the land with the profits of slaves the legislature has declared them to be homogeneous, and the former . . . must go as all other personal chattels go, without distinguishing such plants &c as are cut from what are standing."[102]

Turning to the clause in the will about the testator's "Book," Wythe contends that this language is nothing more than the appointment of defendant as executor. It is not a legacy of the surplus of the debts to Robert Bolling. That being so, the residuary bequest to Archibald Bolling prevents operation of the rule that an executor is entitled to the surplus in his hands by reason of the implied gift to him by virtue of his appointment as executor.[103] Wythe also argued that under the equitable maxim *qui sentit onus sentire debet et commodum*[104] it would not be fair for defendant to receive the surplus of receivables over debts of the testator when plaintiff would have had to bear the loss if the testator's debts had exceeded what was owing to him.[105]

Jefferson sets forth a clear and lawyerlike synopsis of the points defendant undertakes to establish:

I. Under the devise of the Buffalo lick plant[atio]n
    he claims
    1. the Emblements unsevered at the death of
        the test[ato]r.
    2. the Rents growing and not paiable till after
        his death.[106]
II. Under the bequest of the test[ato]r's Book he claims
    His test[ato]r's Credits burthened with
    his Debts. but

1. in the Credits he means to include
the £500 due from Buchanan. and
2. among the Debts charged on this fund he does not reckon
   (a) Edward Bolling's proportion
   of his father's debts. nor
   (b) the legacy of £100 to Sarah Tazewell.
   but if it should be thought the bequest of
   the book was merely fiduciary he then insists
III. That the debt of £235 due from him to the
test[ato]r is extinguished.[107]

Jefferson begins his discussion of the first point by laying a comprehensive philosophical foundation. "What first presents itself to us as a guide thro' this enquiry is the maxim 'quicquid plantatur solo, solo cedit,' a maxim derived from our earliest ideas of property."[108] In support of this proposition he cites Pufendorf and Justinian's *Institutes.*[109] In some instances, however, this basic principle must yield, on public policy grounds for the encouragement of agriculture, in favor of recognition of rights accorded to the sower of the crop, in accordance with a second maxim "he who sows shall reap."[110]

Jefferson then reviews the authorities[111] in order to demonstrate that a devise is simply one mode of transferring or conveying property; hence a devisee's rights are not identical with those of an heir to whom land descends by operation of law, but are like those of one to whom an estate in land is conveyed by deed.[112] Summing up, Jefferson found his conclusion identical with Wythe's (that emblements follow the person of the sower, if he have an interest in the land which is of uncertain duration, "unless his estate determine by his own act") "only the pl's counsel does not consider a conveiance by deed, or will, as a determination 'by the act of the party.' "[113]

One of Jefferson's tricks of advocacy[114] is displayed when he states: "Having now settled what I think the rule with respect to Emblements, I shall answer the objections made to my authorities, which I was unwilling to do as I cited them, lest it should interrupt the course of our ideas, and divert our attention from what was then to be proven."[115]

Wythe had objected to the authority of a case reported in Winch that "this is another unauthoritative publication, translated, as it is said, from a fair copy of Sr. Humphrey Winch's in French. But all the cases were not collected by him, for in one of them (pa. 125) there is an eulogy of himself upon occasion of his death."[116]

Jefferson effectively replies to this threefold criticism. As to lack of authority, he answers: "I have so few of the old reporters, in my posess[io]n, that I cannot fully state which have, or have not, the license of the judges. Noy has it not. T. Jones has it signed faintly by one judge only. Shower's parliamentary

98

SIR HUMPHREY WINCH by an unknown artist.

According to Dean Roscoe Pound of the Harvard Law School, x-ray examination reveals that this portrait of Sir Humphrey Winch (the authority of whose *Reports* was debated by Jefferson and Wythe) was painted over the portraits of two wives of King Henry VIII.

Courtesy of Harvard Law School.

cases, and I believe his reports[117] which are not in my possess[io]n, have it not. To my editions of Plowden and Coke, no license is prefixed; but they are English ed[itio]ns, the former a very late one, and perhaps it may be omitted, as the license has been lately thought of little consequence. Yet these books are cited universally, without objection for want of the license. These are the only Reporters, prior to Winch, of whom I can speak with certainty. Among the moderns, the license is utterly laid aside. Foster, Andrews, Burrow, Prec. in Chanc. Cases temp. Talbot, Barnardiston, Atkyns, prove this. The character of Sr. Humph. Winch however, as a judge, should seem to give as much authority to *his* book, as it would have given to that of *any other*, to have had an imprimatur prefixed, signed by him. And yet such signature would have made such book authoritative."[118]

Numerous instances are mentioned where Winch was cited (even in the presence of Lord Holt) without cavil. "I never before met with an objection to his authority. Indeed I have ever considered 'all Reporters to be authoritative, whether licensed or not, if they have been usually cited by, and before, the judges in Westminster hall, and were never, by them, denied.' "[119]

In reply to the objection that the book is a translation, Jefferson observes that "Coke's, Plowden's, Noy's Levintz's, Lutwyche's cases, were collected and published in French" and later translated. Yet "the English editions are held equally authoritative with the French, and are most sought after." With regard to the eulogy, he retorted that "we might as well endeavor to destroy the authority of the Pentateuch, by observing, that all the chapters thereof were not written by Moses, because in one of them, Deut. XXXIV. 5–12 'is an eulogy on himself, on occasion of his death.' In both cases the passage, which could not be by the author himself, is easily and equally distinguishable."[120]

Rising to the defense of Godbolt,[121] Jefferson asserts: "That the cases in any reporter were all *taken* in court by the reporter himself, is I believe in no instance true."[122] In a mathematical mode of argument characteristic of Jefferson,[123] he tabulates the dates of cases in seven often cited reporters[124] and observes: "Now we know it impossible men should have lived at all, much less enjoyed that vigor of mind requisite for such works, thro' so long spaces of time. And tho' we know they could not have *taken* all the cases themselves, yet as they declare *they collected them*, we are satisfied with their judgment and fidelity" and admit their authority. Accordingly, all reporters named in the table "are acknoleged authorities."[125]

In response to the objection that Godbolt's cases were not published by himself but by William Hughes, Jefferson replies that the same is true of many other authoritative reporters (including Leonard, cited by Wythe, published "by the very same Wm. Hughes who published Godbolt"). According to

Jefferson, the two questions "which determine him authoritative or not, are these, Is he cited in Westminster hall? Ans. he is. . . . Was he ever *there* denied to be authority? ans. Never."[126]

Jefferson then devotes five pages to refuting six objections urged against a case[127] which was a strong authority in defendant's favor. It was supported by Lord Coke, "and his opinion, when clear, I consider as no mean authority." To the objection that this was an extrajudicial opinion, Jefferson replied: "If to an *adjudged* case it be essential that there be a *judgm[en]t entered of record*, this is not entitled to be so called. . . . It was a friendly reference to Sr. Edward Coke, who took the advice of the court, and the parties were ready to perform their dictum of what was the law. But I conceive the *opinion* of the judges is the essence of every authority; and if that opinion be given on a full state of the case, on mature deliberation and on the point, in support of which it is adduced; then their opinion so given must influence ours, i.e. it becomes as authority, whether, when they pronounced it, their clerk took a minute of it or not."

In response to Wythe's remark that the reporter, Sir George Croke, was then but 27 years of age, Jefferson spoke with deference to his mentor: "Far be it from me to detract from that superiority of wisdom to which years give title, because they bring it. The longer a man has lived, the more facts have come under his observation, and the more time he has had for reflection. But the understanding of Sr. Geo. Croke must have been of slow growth indeed if at the age of 27. he was yet unable to apprehend a case so simplified as this, when canvassed among the judges and counsel in court, and again explained to him in conversation with Coke: besides if this part of his book be not authority because of his youth, say whereabouts he begins to be old enough, that at that place we may draw a line in the book. Our law books do not inform us; they cite equally every part of his work." Jefferson then shows in confirmation of Croke's report of this case, that it was cited in a later case reported by Croke when he was 36 years of age.[128]

Of a passage in a textbook[129] Wythe had remarked that "Wentworth was a compiler only, and what he sais . . . since he quotes no authority is but his opinion, which was probably founded upon that leading case in Cro. El. 61."[130] Jefferson retorted: "What are the authorities produced in support of the pl's right? Swinburne a compiler; Blackstone a compiler; Broke [*sic*] a compiler; Perkins a compiler; and Viner a compiler. . . . Then, as to the merit of Wentworth's book, I shall only observe the credit given him by two of our best modern compilers. Blackstone quotes him in almost every page, while treating on Wentworth's subject; and Bacon has transcribed I believe every word in the book."[131]

After his review of the authorities, Jefferson concludes that Wythe is taking too much for granted when he asserts that emblements are to be treated in all respects as personal chattels. Coke and Blackstone are "properly cautious" in considering them as "subject to *many*, tho' *not to all* the incidents attending personal chattels." In some aspects they are not "meerly personal but savor of the realty."

Satisfied that the decided cases are in his favor, Jefferson bursts forth into an eloquent encomium in favor of *stare decisis*. "And here I cannot suppress the anxiety I ever feel when an attempt is made to unhinge those principles, on which alone we depend for security in all the property we hold, and to set us again adrift to search for new. And by the time these are found, they will again be sent off after the old. When rules of property have been settled, on their faith we buy things, and call them our own. They should therefore be sacred, and not wantonly set aside when ingenuity can persuade us to believe they are unfit, or inconsonant with other decisions. We should not, under a momentary impression, demolish what has been the growth of ages. This deference to adjudged cases is enjoined by our laws."[132]

Jefferson concluded therefore that the cases establish the rule that at common law " 'Emblem[en]ts go to the ex[ecuto]r of the sower if his estate was rightful, not joint, of incertain continuance, and determined by the act of god or of the law: but if it was wrongful, or joint, or of certain continuance, or determined by his own act, as by desertion, forfeiture, alienation without reserve &c. they go with the lands.' To apply it. E. Bolling's estate was indeed rightful, not joint, and of incertain continuance. But it was determined by his own act, i.e. by devise without reserving the emblem[en]ts when he had opportunity to reserve them if he had meant to do so. They therefore return to their natural channel and pass with the land to Robert Bolling."[133]

Jefferson's exhaustive analysis of the authorities regarding emblements at common law was successful to the extent that it persuaded opposing counsel to concede that at common law the crops not severed at the testator's death would pass with the land devised to defendant.[134]

It remained for Jefferson to consider what effect Virginia legislation had produced with respect to the common law rules. As Jefferson points out, the first statute dealing with this subject was enacted in 1711.[135] It was followed by additional acts of assembly in 1730[136] and 1748.[137] Because of the previously mentioned dependence of the Virginia agricultural economy upon slave labor,[138] the legislature enacted that, in the case of a person dying whilst his crop of Indian corn, wheat, or other grain, or tobacco is in the ground, all servants and slaves employed on the said crop at the time of his death shall continue on the plantation and work on said crop until December 25, and that then the said crop shall be deemed and taken to be assets in the hands of the executors or administrators, and the slaves shall then be delivered to the heir or legatees.[139]

Jefferson's interpretation of this act was that it annexed the benefit of the labor of the slaves to the emblements, but did not affect in any manner the ownership of the emblements. These would go to whoever was entitled to them at common law, but their value would have been preserved and enhanced by the labor of slaves belonging to other persons. "The legislature have not given the emblem[en]ts to the labor of the slaves, for then they would go to legatees, but the labor of the slave to the emblem[en]t." The emblements are the principal thing to which the labor of the slaves is made accessory.[140]

This statute applies, as Jefferson points out, only to crops *already in the ground* at the testator's death. "Under this act the owner of the emblem[en]ts could only finish what was actually in the ground; he could not put in a single new seed." To encourage efficient production the Act of 1730 authorized retention of the slaves for the purpose of "making" as well as "finishing" a crop, thus permitting additional planting. To prevent unduly long detention of the land, the application of the act was limited to persons dying between March 1 and December 25. Another amendment directed deduction of the expenses of the crop, whereas the old law had made the whole crop assets, without allowance for the necessary production costs.[141]

The common law as to who was entitled to emblements was unchanged by the Virginia legislation, according to Jefferson. The statutory provisions merely made the emblements more valuable, by annexing to them the right to plant additional crops and to use the labor of slaves not belonging to the owner of the emblements. "So that it appears from a view of these three acts that the act of 1711. meddled not with the right to the Emblem[en]ts, but annexed thereto the Labor of the slaves till Dec. 25 ———— that the act of 1730. made a new annexation of a right to sow or plant more emblem[en]ts, and the labor of the same slaves to finish them. ———— and the act of 1748. as to this matter made no alteration. The conclusion then is . . . 'that the labor of slaves is by the laws annexed to the Emblem[en]ts . . . and goes to him who can entitle himself to the emblem[en]ts.' That right then being determined, this follows of course."[142]

Jefferson then confronts the consequences of the statutory provision that the crop is to be deemed "assets" in the hands of the decedent's executor or administrator. Ordinarily this would mean that, subject to payment of debts and pecuniary legacies, they would become part of the residue (bequeathed to Archibald Bolling) and not go with the testator's lands to his heir or devisees.

Ingeniously arguing that the term "assets" is derived from the French word "*assez*" (meaning enough), Jefferson contends that there can be no authority produced "where this term is used to denote the *personal estate* in general, abstracted from the idea of paying debts and legacies, or in other words, it is never used to denote the *distributable or residuary surplus*. What I infer from all this is, that the word *assets* denotes that part of the personal estate which will actually be applied to the paiment of debts and legacies, and that as soon as these are paid there are no such things as *assets* in existence. So that where an act of assembly directs that any thing 'shall be *assets* in the hands of exrs and admrs' it means only that 'it shall be considered as a *chattel* for the purpose of paying *debts* and *legacies*, if there be a deficiency without it' but if not, it remains in the hands in which it would have remained had such act never been made. So that this is my position, a thing by being made *assets*, is only subjected to the paiment of *debts* and *legacies*: . . . but if not so applied, it remains as it would have done, had no act been made."[143]

Plausible support for this position is adduced by citing various types of property which have been made subject to payment of debts but without losing their original status if not needed for that purpose: slaves,[144] American lands,[145] trust estates,[146] estates *pur autre vie*.[147]

Jefferson then concludes his discussion of emblements with an appeal for adoption of a simple, uniform rule: "I think it is to be wished that now, when questions on this subject are first arising, an end should be put to them, by carrying the Labor of the slaves with the Emblem[en]ts, and subjecting them at once to the same rules. If that were done, we have a set of rules, already formed, which will apply to every case that can arise; and judges will determine, counsel advise, and even the people themselves proceed, at once with certainty and precision. But on the other hand, if a set of rules is to be now built up express for this particular property, I fear we shall find that (like the jumble of real and personal rules which our legislature made it necessary to compound when they altered the legal nature of the slaves themselves) it will introduce infinite contest, and time, and expence, before they can be framed consistent with themselves, and with the other parts of the law."[148]

Proceeding to the second point of his argument, Jefferson undertakes to establish that the testator's intention, when he wrote the clause about his "Book," was "to transfer to [defendant Robert Bolling] the right to his credits, paying thereout his debts."[149] Jefferson skillfully scrutinizes the testator's language[150] and circumstances and marshals every piece of evidence which leads to this conclusion. Just as in point I of the argument Jefferson displayed the extent of his profound erudition as a legal scholar, so in point II he displays the resourceful ingenuity of astute trial counsel in artfully arranging facts and emphasizing particular facets and aspects of them so as to derive from them the most favorable inferences of which they are susceptible.

The first argument advanced is that "a beneficial bequest" is evidenced by "the import or efficacy of the word 'give' " itself. "The word '*give*' imports a transfer of the *use*, as well as *legal property*, of the thing given. . . . The bequest of the book then by the word '*give*' carried both an use and property in the paper and leather of which it was made. But how idle and nugatory would the gift of the paper and leather be, if their appendages, the *Credits*, were not to follow them? No body can suppose the test[ato]r intended to give his brother merely a parcel of waste paper."[151]

With equal sprightliness Wythe in his reply retorted that Jefferson was attaching an extraordinary sense to the words "given up" when he interpreted them as importing a legacy to the recipient of the book. "To give up the ghost is to die, an apostate is said to give up his religion; a woman to give up her virtue, when she becomes a prostitute. To give up a friend is to betray him, to desert him, to have no further connection with him. . . . To give up an argument is no longer to continue the dispute; which was the meaning of the defendant's counsel when he said 'I might venture to give up the question.' "[152]

Jefferson's second argument is that the word "receive" is "sufficiently expressive of an intention . . . that he should have the property." Suppose someone else had been appointed executor in another clause of the will, the word "receive" in this clause would certainly "have transferred the right to these monies. This proves it proper and sufficient then to carry a legacy. Indeed no technical term, no precise form of words is requisite to dispose of property in a will. Any expressions, from which the intention of the test[ato]r can even be collected, shall be effective of that intention. . . . The benevolence of the test[ato]r . . . is supposed to actuate every movement of his mind" throughout every part of the will, and every gift is presumably for the use of the donee "till the contrary be proved."[153]

Here again Wythe replied pointedly: "Does barely desiring one to *receive* my money *ex vi termini*, authorise him to *spend* it? When my property is taken out of the hand of this man, and put into your hand, does it cease to be mine?"[154]

The third argument emphasizes the context in which the words are used. "Words of doubtful meaning may recieve illustration from others in their neighborhood." If there were doubt whether the direction to receive the debts were meant to be beneficial or fiduciary, it would be resolved in the former sense by its juxtaposition with the words constituting a gift of the book. This circumstance shows that a gift of the debts was also effected. The donative intent in the one instance carries over into the other. "The context, to wit, the '*gift* of the book' explains the doubt and proves a beneficial devise intended."[155]

The fourth argument is grounded upon "the manner in which the several parts of this sentence operate." If the testator had merely said, "I give to my

105

brother Rob. my Book, and will that he recieve my debts," Jefferson says, "I think his meaning could not have been doubted. The addition then 'that he pay all I owe' operated only by way of exception. It abridges the bequest pro tanto, but does not destroy it in the whole. It is as if he had said, 'I give him my outstanding debts, except so much as is requisite to pay what I owe.' "[156]

Jefferson's fifth argument derives donative intent "from the *location* or *situation* of this clause. . . .[157] Observe it comes in a little below the middle of the will. The testator was going on in a full career of donation. To one who attends to the usual operations of the human mind, it is inconcievable that he should all of a sudden fly off from a tract of thought in which he was proceeding, in the midst of his benevolences to erect a barren ex[ecuto]rship, and then again return to giving. Reason as well as constant practice has placed the appointment of an ex[ecuto]r after all those purposes are expressed which he is desired to execute. But here, while the test[ato]r is intently pursuing an uniform and connected train of purposes, a scrap of a sentence is laid hold of, withdrawn from it's context which might alone explain it, and by the subtle reasonings of the law, it is distorted into a circumlocutory form of appointing an ex[ecuto]r, tho capable of another, and a most obvious construction, which would preserve, instead of interrupting that uniform tendency of mind in the test[ato]r."[158]

The sixth and last argument urged by Jefferson in support of his construction of the clause is grounded upon "the most unusual and *circumlocutory* form of this appointment of an ex[ecuto]r, if considered merely as such." Even "the lowest and most illiterate of the people" are familiar with the term "executor" and would ordinarily use it rather than trying to catalogue that functionary's duties. "No man would chuse to build up an appointment by enumerating the several branches of his duty, as superintending the labor of his slaves, buying clothes and provisions for them, selling his crops or other estate, recieving, paying &c. when he could do the same thing more completely in three words."[159]

Jefferson goes on to point out that Edward Bolling was familiar with the term "executor" by reason of his dealing with the executors of his father's estate. "But I am persuaded that by the clause now in question he had not a thought of appointing an ex[ecuto]r, but totally forgot to do it: and that had he been asked, after writing his will, whom he had appointed ex[ecuto]r? his answer would have been 'I have forgotten to appoint one.' I do not mean by this that the clause now under consideration shall not have the effect of constituting Rob. Bolling his ex[ecuto]r. . . . But I contend that the test[ato]r had not then in contemplation the appointment of an ex[ecuto]r, and consequently that his purpose was something else, to wit, to give a legacy."[160]

As a final thrust, Jefferson points out that the residuary clause under which plaintiff claims,[161] when interpreted under the rule of *ejusdem generis*,[162] was probably not intended by the testator to include debts owing to him. Had he considered the money due to him (which was substantial in amount) as a part of his estate "not already given [to Robert Bolling by the clause about his "Book"], would he not have mentioned it in the residuary clause"? "We cannot believe that in enumerating the principal articles of the residuum he was giving he would mention such trifles as his horses and clothes, and omit the capital article of outstanding debts."[163]

This point was forcefully emphasized by a homespun analogy: "So a man who had just made the tour of America, would hardly say 'he had visited the towns of Contocook, Kenderhook, Concord, and all the other towns of America.' Boston, New York, Philadelphia, as being the great and principal objects, would first strike his mind in recollecting and enumerating the places he had visited, and would most certainly be mentioned."[164]

From all "these several circumstances" Jefferson concluded that the testator's intention was "that his brother Rob' should recieve these debts, in his private right, and that Arch' should not have them: and that this appears on the *Face of the Will.*"[165]

Having established that Robert Bolling received as a beneficial bequest "the Credits, paying the Debts," Jefferson proceeds to inquire, "1. What are the Credits, and 2. What the Debts, included in these general terms?"[166] Defendant claimed as one of the Credits, the £500 due from Buchanan for the warehouse at Pocahontas. The sale by the testator during his lifetime amounted to a revocation or ademption of the devise to plaintiff.[167] Moreover, it would not be just for plaintiff to receive the property purchased with the proceeds from the sale of the warehouse and also the proceeds themselves.[168]

Defendant also contended that his proportion (one fifth) of his father's debts was not properly chargeable on the legacy to him. Under the will of testator's father, John Bolling, his debts were charged against the undistributed corpus in the hands of his executors, who were to distribute to each son as he became of age his share of the estate, leaving any unpaid debts as a charge against the shares of the minor sons. When Archibald, the youngest son, came of age, it was discovered that there remained unpaid a large debt to a firm of English merchants.[169]

Jefferson contested the propriety of paying Robert Bolling's share of John Bolling's debt out of the money collected by defendant from testator's debtors listed in the "Book." Several reasons were urged in support of this position. First, the debt had not been incurred by the testator, nor was it chargeable on his estate at the time when the will was written. The debt was then chargeable against plaintiff's estate; hence it "does not come within the words of the will" ["pay all that I owe"]. The testator "had every imaginable reason to

107

believe it [his father's debt] was long ago paid, and that he should never be called on for a shilling of it. He could not therefore have it in contemplation when he directed that his brother Rob. should pay all that *he* owed."[170]

Secondly, "the words of the clause shew he only meant his own private debts," because the "Book" which he bequeathed to Robert Bolling contained none but his private accounts."[171] Hence the debts directed to be paid by defendant were "*debts ejusdum generis* with those in his book, i.e. his private debts."[172]

Thirdly, the testator "*knew not* of this debt, so had it not in view." Hence, "as *his words* do not include his father's debts, so neither did *his intention.*" This unexpected call from his father's executor "was not under his contemplation when he wrote the will"; and in interpreting wills "the object which the test[ato]r had in his view, is what we are to pursue."[173]

Fourthly, the testator's benevolent purpose would be defeated by including his father's debt as a deduction from the amount willed to Robert Bolling. "But what most of all evinces that he did not include *his father's*, within the idea of *his own debts*, is that by this bequest he meant to give his brother something." An additional disbursement of £550 instead of leaving Robert Bolling a surplus of about £200 would produce a deficit of £350.[174]

After a brief summary of point II, Jefferson proceeds to point III: Even if the clause about the "Book" amounted to nothing more than the appointment of Robert Bolling as executor, it operated as an *Extinguishment* of his debt of £235 to the testator. On this point he relied on an English case "as decisive."[175] He declared it to be settled law that making a debtor executor extinguishes the debt, provided (1) that there be no deficiency of other assets to pay the testator's debts; and (2) that no legacy is particularly charged on it.

Jefferson's argument, which has now been analyzed, covers practically all the points at issue in the case. The second argument for plaintiff, Jefferson's second argument for defendant, and Wythe's reply for plaintiff are largely repetitious; they develop and reinforce, elaborate and refine, emphasize and reiterate the respective positions already taken. Only the highlights of these debates, where particularly effective or new contentions are advanced, need be mentioned here.

The second argument for plaintiff begins with a philosophical explanation of the right of the sower to emblements as flowing from the fruits of his labor. Locke is not mentioned, but the labor theory of property is expounded.[176] But the exceptions to the rule favoring the sower are reviewed, and on the strength of a passage from Baron Gilbert the plaintiff concedes defendant's proposition that at common law the emblements would go to the devisee under the circumstances of the case at bar. Plaintiff strongly insists, however, that the Virginia legislation has changed this situation.[177] Plaintiff contends that the act of assembly *suspends* the devisee's right to the land until the crop is harvested; hence the emblements cannot go to the devisee as an incident of his right to the land, when even the land is not his to enjoy until after the crop has been severed from the soil: "How then can the crop, as emblements, belong to him, who has no right to take possession of the land till after the crop is finished, and actually severed?"[178]

Against Jefferson's definition of assets as what is actually used to pay debts, plaintiff objects that this is repugnant to the statute, which makes the crop assets not when it is paid out (which sometimes might never happen at all) but so soon as it is made and finished by the labor of the slaves. "If no part of the estate be assets but what will actually be applied in payment of debts and legacies; and if consequently, it is not assets before it be so applied; it seems there is no such thing as assets." For the moment it is paid away it is not the decedent's assets but the payee's property; and if it "be not assets *before* or *after* it be paid away it is not assets at all."[179]

With regard to the clause about the "Book" plaintiff makes the point that in that clause the "testator appointed his brother Robert not only his receiver, but his Bursar." The person executing these two offices undoubtedly acts in the same capacity in both: "He must either act for himself, or for the testator in both. If he received for himself, he must pay for himself, if he paid for the testator he must receive for the testator." Suppose the testator had died before selling the Pocahontas warehouse, and thus had owed more than was due him, would Robert Bolling have made good the deficiency out of his own, or out of the testator's assets? If out of the latter, "it will follow that he received the debts for, and as representative of, the testator, and consequently is accountable for them to the residuary legatee."[180]

On the issue of extinguishment of the executor's debt to the testator, plaintiff narrows the issue to the question whether the debt "is bequeathed to Archibald Bolling or not?"[181] Plaintiff contended that the debt was part of the decedent's estate, and passed under the residuary bequest of everything "not already given"; and that it is entirely immaterial "in what order the clauses were inserted."[182]

As to Robert Bolling's share of his father's debts, plaintiff urges that "a man may owe a debt which he did not contract."[183] Jefferson's argument that the testator meant to give something to Robert is applied by plaintiff as a reason "against expounding this clause as a legacy at all," if it be assumed that the testator "meant the same by it at the time he made his will, as when he died." Until the sale of the Pocahontas warehouse the testator's debts *did* exceed what was owing to him. Hence when the will was made, the clause could not have been beneficial to Robert Bolling. If the warehouse had not been sold, defendant would probably have argued that the clause merely appointed him as executor.[184]

In Jefferson's second argument, he emphasizes that there is no express language in the Virginia legislation which would deprive the devisee of emblements. He then inquires whether the addition of the labor of the slaves could have had that effect. In this connection he reviews the Roman law on "accession" (where the property of one person is mingled with that of another) and the doctrines of Bracton and Blackstone on the same topic. He finds the rule to be that the owner may reclaim his property unless its nature has been changed and it has become a new article: as grain made into bread, grapes into wine, olives into oil, or the like.[185] His contention is that since the legislature has not decided "to whom the plants thus improved [by the labor of the slaves] shall belong, then Justice and Analogy with the fabric of the law in similar cases carry it to the proprietor of the soil, and authorize my position that the labor of the slaves is annexed, or is an accession to the Emblements . . . and consequently is the property of him who can entitle himself to them: i.e. of the devisee of the lands in the present case."[186]

In reply to the argument that the act of assembly suspends the devisee's right of possession until the crop is harvested,[187] Jefferson maintains that "by suspending the right of the devisee to call for his emblements till it be seen whether they may not be wanting to pay debts, it cannot be supposed that his right to them is altogether taken away. Or in other words, the bare suspension of the use of a right is no extinguishment of it. If it is, then no distributee can recover his distributory part, because his use of it is suspended for a year by the statute of distributions that the adm[instrato]r may have time to see that there is enough besides to pay his test[ato]r's debts."[188]

He then grapples again with the difficulty presented by the statutory provision making the crop "assets." He reiterates his contention that "those things are assets . . . which are *liable* to the test[ato]r's debts. But when all the debts are paid, the emblem[en]ts of Rob. Boll[ing] are no longer *liable* to debts, because there are no debts for them to be *liable* to . . . and consequently are no longer *assets*, because they have lost that quality of *liableness* which is essential in the definition of assets."[189] He points out that no one ever supposed that specific legacies "because they are *assets* they are therefore taken from the specific, and given to the residuary legatee." And in law the gift of the land is a specific bequest of the emblements as perfectly as if it had been stated expressly in the will.[190]

Jefferson chides plaintiff's counsel for failing to answer defendant's argument based on the liability of slaves as assets for the payment of debts without losing their nature as real estate.[191] American lands, trust estates, and estates *pur autre vie* were similar examples of the same proposition. He again analyzed *Oldham* v. *Pickering* at length, setting forth the details of the case as contained in three different reports.[192]

In that case the owner of an estate for the life of another person (still living) died. The owner's next of kin sued his administrator in the ecclesiastical court to require inclusion of the estate *pur autre vie* in the inventory to be distributed (there being enough other assets to pay all the decedent's debts). The administrator sought a writ of prohibition to prevent the church court from meddling with the estate *pur autre vie*.[193] The Court of King's Bench upheld issuance of the writ, holding that although "an estate pur autre vie is made assets by the stat. 29. Car. 2. yet 'tis not distributable within the stat. 22. Car. 2. for distribution of intestates estates, because *distribution* is a quality not necessarily included in the notion of *assets* as paiment of *debts* is; now an estate pur autre vie is not properly goods or chattels, but remains a freehold tho' 'tis assets by the first statute." Notwithstanding the fact that it is made assets by that statute "it remains a freehold still: and the amendment of the law in this particular was only designed for the relief of Creditors."[194] From the report of the case by Holt, Jefferson quotes a passage that "such an estate still remains a freehold, the design of the stat. being only in respect to creditors; but in *all other respects the quality of the estate remains the same as it was before at Common law*: & the Spiritual court never had any jurisdiction in cases of *freehold*." From a third report he quotes: "Tho an estate pur autre vie is made *assets* by the stat. yet 'tis not *distributable*, because *distribution is a quality not necessarily included in the notion of assets, as paiment of debts is*."[195]

Jefferson thus developed a very solid argument in favor of his client by comparison of the status of emblements with that of an estate *pur autre vie* as expounded by the court in the case relied upon. He emphasized that it was not some magical quality in a freehold estate "which will exempt that from being made distributable by words which would at the same time make any other estate, not possessing that particular magic quality, liable to distribution," which was the ground of the court's decision, but that the issue as to the jurisdiction of the church court turned upon "that particular quality of the estate, which, if unaltered by the act, withdrew it from Ecclesiastical cognisance." Hence Jefferson regarded the case as establishing a rule "that an act introducing new alterations in the nature of any estate, shall not be intended to reverse the whole nature of that estate in every point, but only to alter those qualities particularly expressed to be altered."

Under this rule the Virginia legislation "by making emblements liable to *debts,* has not taken away their deviseable quality, nor yet given them a distributable one where they had it not before."[196] The statute of distributions applies only to chattels not disposed of by will, chattels as to which the decedent dies intestate. Hence "tho' these devised emblements are of a chattel nature & by the act are made assets in the hands of ex[ecuto]rs & adm[inistrato]rs, yet notwithstanding this alteration by the act they remain a *devised estate* and consequently are not within the stat[ute]. of distribution."[197]

The enactment of a later statute[198] making estates *pur autre vie* distributable Jefferson regards as "rather evidence that it was not so before" than that it weakened the holding in *Oldham* v. *Pickering*.[199] He comments interestingly on the skepticism with which the recitals in preambles to statutes are to be viewed: "Nothing is less to be depended on than the allegations in the preambles of modern statutes. The facts set forth in them, are most commonly mere creatures of the brain of the penman, & which never existed but in his brain. That this is true with respect to our own acts of ass[embly]. we all know too well to require instances of proof. That it is also true with respect to the English acts" he demonstrated by examples. "The truth is it was become necessary to supply a defect in the stat[ute]. of frauds, which had omitted to give a valuable part of a man's estate to his relations; and the drawer of the act which was intended to effect that alteration of the law recites currente calamo 'that doubts had arisen' which probably he well knew to have also subsided" [by reason of the decision in *Oldham* v. *Pickering* itself, which settled the law on the point].[200]

After replying tellingly to some other points advanced by plaintiff, and summarizing lucidly his own argument on the subject of emblements,[201] he recurs to the topic of the clause in the will about the testator's "Book."[202] Confident that his prior argument "does not appear to be shaken" by anything advanced by the other side, he confines himself to giving "short answers to some passages" in plaintiff's argument.[203]

Plaintiff had responded to Jefferson's case cited to show that the word "receive" imports a legacy by saying that this doctrine applies only to things in the testator's possession, and not to things in the possession of other parties.[204] To this interpretation Jefferson replied: "Now this is answering an authority not from any circumstance found or even hinted in the book, but from one picked up 'in the field of conjecture,' a liberty by the help of which . . . any authority whatever may be disarmed & even pointed in it's opposite direction. In the present instance the words of the authority are general, & there is nothing to establish the conjecture of the pl's counsel that they were not intended to be taken generally."[205]

Answering another point, Jefferson admits that defendant received the debts due the testator "as representative of the test[ato]r," but denies that this means that he is accountable for them to the residuary legatee. For in like manner defendant "as representative of the testator"[that is, as executor]

112

received the slaves bequeathed to various legatees; but that does not mean that he was accountable for them to Archibald Bolling, rather than to the persons to whom they were bequeathed.[206]

Passing to the third point in the case (whether the appointment of defendant as executor extinguished his debt to the testator) Jefferson reaffirms his reliance on *Wankford* v. *Wankford*.[207]

With nonchalant bravado Jefferson answers plaintiff's reference to a statement of Lord Hardwicke that a will is to be interpreted by looking at it as a whole, and that the order in which the various clauses stand is immaterial:[208] "This might be true in cases resembling the one then before the Chancellor. What that was I know not, as I do not possess the book. But this I may assert that Ld. Hardwicke would never say that where the relative terms 'before' & 'hereafter' are used descriptively, it is not material in what order clauses stand." He puts a hypothetical case: the owner of six slaves gives to S a life estate in "my slaves A. & B."; to T a life estate in "my slaves C. and D." Then the testator adds: "The remainder in the slaves *before* given I bequeath to X. I give to my friend Z. my slaves E. & F. for his life." Under the will as so written, the remainderman X receives a remainder in four slaves. If the bequest to X stood after the bequest to S, X would be entitled to a remainder "in but two. If it stood as the last clause in the will it would entitle him to a rem[ainde]r in six. And can any body suppose Ld. Hardwicke would say in this case that 'it is not material in what order the clauses stand'?"[209]

Twitting plaintiff's counsel for citing a case where Lord Talbot, after saying that in the case before him it is not necessary to determine whether a debt from an executor be assets to pay legacies in general, adds, "I am inclined to think it may,"[210] Jefferson gleefully reproaches his adversary: "All delicacy about authorities seems now to have subsided.[211] Here is the *inclination* of a Chancellor on a point which had not been argued, which was not in question, which could never come but incidentally before the court of which he was judge but belonged properly to the department of the Common law, and on which he does not pronounce even an obiter dictum, but expressly reserves his opinion till the case should happen; this I say is produced to contradict a judge within whose proper province the question lay, who declared it to be his opinion, not merely his inclination, who supported this opinion by authorities, & whose judgment in a question of Common law (tho' perhaps it might give way to that of a Holt, as would the opinion of any Judge who had lived since the days of Lord Coke, yet) surely is not to be controlled by that of a Ld Chancellor Talbot."[212]

Distinguishing another case cited by plaintiff,[213] Jefferson remarks of Lord Hardwicke (with respect to the controversial question whether legacies were to be paid before the lands of the heir are exonerated): "Considering this as a

113

'quaestio diu vexata' had he meant to decide upon it, he would certainly have paid to the understandings of mankind the compliment of a little reasoning. . . . He could not mean to give this as a judicial opinion on the question on mature deliberation; because there was no such question then before him."[214]

But even if a debt due from the executor could be used toward payment of legacies, only legatees bequeathed pecuniary legacies of a specific sum could benefit by that rule, not the legatee of the residue, which "is only a bequest of what remains when all other donations whether expressed in words or implied by law, are made good."[215] In any event, the executor's debt "would . . . only be subject to legacies as it is to debts, that is, *on a deficiency of other assets.*" In the case at bar Archibald Bolling could not receive anything from that source. In Edward Bolling's estate "there is enough to pay debts. enough to satisfy legacies specific and pecuniary, enough to comply with the operations of law, and then a good residuum for the pl[aintiff]."[216] Succinctly summarizing his discussion of point III, Jefferson concludes: "For all these reasons the debt of Rob. Boll. to E. B. is in the present case extinguished by the appointment of him ex[ecuto]r."[217]

The last word in the argument was Wythe's. His final reply on behalf of the plaintiff (occupying 62 pages of Anderson Bryant's "elegant hand writing") was likewise largely a repetition of previous points, punctuated with cunning jabs at any maladroit expressions which Jefferson had chanced to use in the course of his discussion of the case.[218]

Acquisition of property by "accession" or intermingling,[219] Wythe insists, occurs only when the intermingling is brought about wrongfully or tortiously. But the use of the decedent's slaves to complete the crop is done lawfully, by direction of the legislature.[220]

He reiterates that by the wording of the Virginia legislation the right of the persons to whom land or slaves are given by will to take possession of the property thus becoming theirs is suspended until after Christmas.[221] Wythe distinguishes the case of a crop under the statute from the case of a distributee (whose right is likewise suspended, as Jefferson had pointed out) by asserting that "here the crop is not due to the devisee of the land at all, unless he had a right to the possession of the land, whilst the crop was growing, or when it was severed; and he [the devisee, Robert Bolling] had not any such right, but it was in the executor or administrator" [who by chance was the same person].[222] In other words, Wythe contends, it is only "by his *right of possession* the original owner of a thing becomes intitled to it's accession." This proposition "defendant's counsel must admit, or reject the authority quoted by himself."[223]

Wythe ingeniously argues that the design of the legislature (for the encouragement of agricultural production) was "to put things in the state they would have been in if the testator or intestate had lived to reap the fruits of his industry; . . . [just as if he] had not died until the 25 Dec." [in which case, of course, the severed crop would admittedly constitute personal property].[224]

Discussing at length Jefferson's definition of "assets," Wythe goes on to observe that "lawyers and judges frequently speak of a sufficiency of assets, and a deficiency of assets; the defendant's counsel uses that language several times in the last page of his argument[225] of which this explanation makes as good english as a sufficiency of a sufficiency and a deficiency of a sufficiency, or enough of enough and not enough of enough. But enough of this logomachy; especially as the defendant's counsel emancipating the word we have so much reason to be tired with, objects not to the adoption of another, to wit, liableness, the effect of which shall be now considered."[226] Wythe's word play on "liableness" then continues. He undertakes to show, "1. what kind of estate the crop is; and 2. whose estate it is."[227] He concludes that it is personal estate, and is the personal estate of the testator; and hence is subject to debts, legacies, and distribution like all the testator's personal estate.[228]

Plaintiff's admission that at common law the devisee would have been entitled to the emblements as a specific legacy is paradoxically transformed into an argument that under the statute the devisee is not entitled to them: "For a specific legacy, altho' liable to debts, cannot be taken to satisfy pecuniary legacies, if there be a deficiency of assets: then the act of assembly having, by saying the crop shall be assets, made it liable to pecuniary legacies, the crop ceases to be a specific legacy and consequently is no legacy, but falls into, and makes part of the residuum, which in this case is bequeathed to Archibald."[229]

Wythe compares in parallel columns his and Jefferson's views regarding "assets."[230] He emphasizes that crops are basically chattels; and "that if it should be proved, that a thing which is a real estate, by being made assets is subject to payment of debts only, it would not concern the present question whether a crop, which is a *personal* estate, being declared assets, be subject to *debts only*." He thus distinguishes (but does discuss at length) the illustrations given by Jefferson, which he had been criticized for ignoring.[231]

After briefly summarizing his argument on emblements, Wythe proceeds to discuss point II (about the "Book").[232] He points out that the testator was familiar with the usual words "give and bequeath" when he meant to give a legacy, and in fact used them ten times in his will. Would he have used the unusual expression which he did, when speaking of his "Book," if he had intended that clause of the will to constitute a bequest to Robert Bolling?[233]

Regarding the unpaid debt of John Bolling, Wythe points to a conflict between the reasons given by the defendant and by his counsel, for excluding that debt. As to Jefferson's assertion that Robert Bolling did not know of the existence of this debt, Wythe exclaimed: "It cannot be pretended that he did not know himself to be liable to pay his proportion of his father's debts in general, because his estate is chargeable therewith by the same will as he derived his title to that estate by. So that if he knew of the one, he must know of the other too, and it cannot be now discovered, but by necromancers, that this debt alone had escaped his knowledge."[234]

Jefferson's other reasons for excluding the father's debts[235] were attacked as spurious derivatives from Jefferson's "paraphrase" of the actual words of the will. "If indeed the words of the paraphrase had been in the will instead of what it contains, it would have been inconsistent and absurd to say he should pay out of the debts more than they amounted to; but this is chargeable, not upon the will, but upon the mutilation and metamorphosis it suffers by such a paraphrase."[236] To rely upon "a paraphrase, as it is called, supposed to be more expressive of the testator's meaning than his own language" Wythe regards as "a dangerous kind of reasoning. Two or three paraphrases have been made of this clause, and then the author singling out one of them makes it his thesis for an argument, leaving the will [behind] as if we had nothing more to do with it."[237]

Concluding his discussion of point II, Wythe declares "that the foundations upon which Rob. Bolling claims the debts as bequeathed to him are not only 'shaken' but intirely demolished; it is . . . manifest that the words of the clause in question do not in themselves create a legacy; and that it was not the testator's intention they should; and that this clause is no more than an appointment of Rob. Bolling to be executor, which appointment he [the testator] might express in this manner, because he might suppose the executor would have little or nothing to do in that office besides receiving and paying debts."[238]

On point III, Wythe concedes that the executor's debt to the testator would have been extinguished if it had not been bequeathed to someone else. He contends that the residuary legacy to Archibald Bolling constitutes such a bequest.[239]

In the final seven pages of his argument Wythe pertinaciously repeats points he has continually dwelt upon, but develops them with powerful emphasis and effect. Adroitly he exploits to full advantage a concession earlier made by Jefferson. Wythe's final appeal thus closes on a note of strength, just as he finished point II by urging a strong point not previously mentioned during the debate (when he suggested a plausible reason why the testator used the unusual form of appointing an executor which is found in the clause about the "Book").[240]

It will be remembered that in his first argument Jefferson relied on *Wank-*

ford v. *Wankford* "as decisive" to prove that a debt to a testator is discharged by appointment of the debtor as executor; provided this asset is not needed to pay the testator's debts, and provided that it is not specifically bequeathed to another person.[241]

In that case the testator's son-in-law had been appointed his executor, and had undertaken to administer the affairs of the estate to some extent, but died before offering the will for probate. The precise question for determination seems to be whether his failure to probate the will prevented extinguishment of the debt.[242] The Court of King's Bench affirmed the judgment of the Court of Common Pleas in favor of the defendant (the son and heir of the debtor),[243] thus holding that the debt was extinguished. The justices were unanimous in this conclusion.

The reasons, however, set forth in their *seriatim* opinions, were somewhat divergent. In particular, Justice Powell said "that this extinguishment was not wrought by way of effectual release, because then the debt could not be assets; but by way of legacy or gift of the debt by the will; and where that debt, or any part of it, is expressly devised by the will to pay a legacy, it will be assets to pay such legacy, because the testator did not intend to extinguish the whole debt. . . . but where there is no such special devise, the debt shall be extinguished notwithstanding any other legacies."[244]

Chief Justice Holt, on the other hand, said that "by being made executor he is the person, that is intitled to receive the money due upon the bond before probate, and . . . he is also the person that is to pay it; and the same hand being to receive and pay, that amounts to an extinguishment." As another reason he asserted "That when the obligee makes the obligor his executor, tho' it is a discharge of the action, yet the debt is assets, and the making him executor does not amount to a legacy, but to payment and release. If H. be bound to I. S. in a bond of 100 £. and then I. S. makes H. his executor; H. has actually received so much money, and is answerable for it, and if he does not administer so much, it is a devastavit."[245]

Plaintiff's counsel vigorously attacked Powell's view,[246] which Jefferson had put forth in his first argument. Powell's opinion was subjected "minutely to be scrutinized and finally condemned as extrajudicial, unwarranted by his authorities, singular,[247] and absurd," as Jefferson observed in his second argument.[248]

Whereupon Jefferson made what was perhaps an unfortunate concession. He declared his willingness to rely upon Holt's analysis. He professed that he was "so well assured that it is immaterial whether this operation is by way of legacy, or of paiment & release, that without losing time in defending Powell's or examining Holt's hypothesis, he is willing to rest it on the latter. Let it

117

be then . . . that it is as if the debtor had made paiment to the debtee in his life and the debtee had given him a release. Now I cannot see what the pl[aintiff]. gains by this."[249]

To the question of plaintiff's counsel, "Do these words 'I constitute Robert Bolling my executor,' . . . mean the same thing as 'I give and bequeath to Robert Bolling the money he owes me' " Jefferson explicitly acknowledges, "Justice Powell sais Yes. Justice Holt, No. But both say it extinguishes the debt, and that is enough for Rob. Boll. who, if he is entitled to retain the money will not be very anxious whether it be by way of legacy, or of release."[250]

Pouncing upon Jefferson's concession, Wythe proceeds to turn it to his advantage. First he points out that Jefferson misapprehended the effect of Holt's view. It did not result therefrom that the situation was as if the debtor had made payment to the testator during the latter's lifetime and received a release from the testator. Since the appointment of the executor, like every other part of the testament, has "no operation whatever, until after the death of the testator, if it should amount to payment and release by him in his life of what the executor owed to him, it would not be less preposterous than that an effect should be prior to its cause, or that a thing should act before it exists." Furthermore, if released, the debt could not be assets, but concededly it does constitute assets for the payment of the testator's debts if needed for that purpose. Moreover, if the debt were specially bequeathed, its release would result in revocation or ademption of the legacy. Hence Jefferson's interpretation is saying "more than Holt said, or appears . . . to have intended."[251]

Wythe explains that the person to whom the payment is supposed to be made and by whom the release is given is not the testator, but his executor: it is the executor in whom the duty to receive and the duty to pay are united, and according to Holt "*he actually receives* and is afterwards *answerable* for the money." The debt disappeared "in the same manner as if any other debtor of the testator had made payment to the executor, after the death of the testator, and the executor had given him a release."[252]

Wythe then repeats his previous contention that a residuary bequest constitutes a sufficient bequest of the executor's debt to require him to account for it to Archibald Bolling.[253] As before, he relied on a case decided by Chancellor Talbot.[254] The case is interesting as a strict application of the rule excluding parol evidence. Talbot was convinced "privately" that the testator intended Selwin, the executor, to be forgiven his entire debt. The headstrong lawyer, one Viner, who wrote the will, disregarding instructions, refused to mention this debt in the document, being of opinion that the appointment as executor would effect the intention without the insertion of express language in the will.

118

The chancellor, however, felt obliged to follow the words of the will as written. "I privately think it was intended the £3000 should go to Mr. Selwin. Privately I think so. But I am not at liberty, by private opinion, to make a construction against the plain words of a will." Accordingly he concluded that Selwin must account for half of the debt to his coexecutor, the plaintiff. Both plaintiff and defendant had been given other legacies by the will. The residuary clause gave to them in addition all the testator's estate "which I have not herein and hereby . . . given." Talbot held "that this debt . . . falls within the description. The testator was entitled to this debt when he made his will and at the time of his death; he had not disposed of it, nor had he appointed Mr. Selwin executor."[255]

In his first argument, Jefferson had distinguished this case from the Bolling case by arguing that Edward Bolling had first appointed Robert Bolling his executor "which is a legacy of the debt" and then bequeathed to Archibald Bolling the residue composed of whatever was not "already given." But "the debt of R. B. was *already* given by having *already* appointed him ex[ecuto]r, and so this residuary clause *does not describe it* nor carry it to A. B." Jefferson argued that "the case of Brown v. Selwin is in our favor because it confines the residuary legatee to the articles described in the residuary clause, & our debt is not within that description."[256]

By abandoning the contention that the appointment was a legacy, under Justice Powell's view, Jefferson demolished the effectiveness of the distinction he had previously drawn. Whatever authority the case of *Brown* v. *Selwin* carried would now weigh in favor of Wythe's position. Inexorably and cogently Wythe demonstrated the consequences of Jefferson's concession: although Edward Bolling had made Robert Bolling executor, "such an appointment hath been proved, and is now admitted not to be a legacy, and so no gift or disposition." And Wythe's client was entitled to whatever was not "already given," if Talbot's ruling in *Brown* v. *Selwin* was applicable and authoritative.[257]

In conclusion Wythe re-emphasized that it is entirely immaterial in what order the clauses appointing the executor, and bequeathing the residue in this will, were inserted, "the former being neither a legacy, as is now admitted, nor a release by the testator, so that the debt remaining part of the testator's estate not already given was consequently given and bequeathed to Archi[bald] Bolling." The final paragraph of his argument claimed interest "upon whatever balance may be in Rob. Bolling's hands" with the expectation that this "will be thought a reasonable demand."[258]

The arguments of counsel in *Bolling* v. *Bolling* constitute a splendid specimen of the professional powers and proficiency of the Virginia bar in the years immediately preceding the American Revolution. Both Thomas Jefferson and his former preceptor George Wythe displayed enormous erudition and handled with skill and resourcefulness the pertinent legal materials relating to the novel, intricate, and difficult questions under consideration. Statutory provisions were scrutinized with thoroughness;[259] the language of judicial decisions and authoritative treatises was analyzed with acute perceptivity. Considerations of logic, history, and public policy were attentively weighed.[260] But likewise both adversaries exhibited astute alertness in the rough and tumble combat of forensic conflict, in quoting an opponent's own words against himself, in sprightly sallies of wit, in resort to *argumentum ad hominem* and *reductio ad absurdum*, in clearness and cogency of expression.[261] In every respect their performance was worthy of renown, and added lustre to the high esteem in which both men were held by fellow lawyers and their countrymen.

VI

Lubberly Volumes
of the Law

In addition to his *Reports* of early judicial decisions, Jefferson's services to Virginia jurisprudence included heroic exertions with a view to preservation and publication of early Virginia statutes. He carefully collected legislative acts sparing "neither time, trouble, nor expense." He preserved the decaying manuscripts "by wrapping & sewing them up in oiled cloth, so that neither air nor moisture can have access to them." However, he considered "a multiplication of printed copies" as the only effective way of preventing their loss, and urged "that there should be printed at public expense, an edition of all the laws ever passed by our legislatures which can now be found."[1]

Jefferson displayed similar interest in the publication of state papers and historical records. "At an early part of my life, from 1769. to 1775. I passed much time in going through the public records in Virginia, then in the Secretary's office, and especially those of a very early date of our settlement." He encouraged and assisted Ebenezer Hazard in publishing a collection of such documents: "Time & accident are committing daily havoc on the originals deposited in our public offices. The late war has done the work of centuries in this business. The lost cannot be recovered; but let us save what remains: not by vaults and locks which fence them from the public eye and use, in consigning them to the waste of time, but by such a multiplication of copies as shall place them beyond the reach of accident."[2]

Jefferson's proposal for a complete edition of all the laws was made in response to a request from George Wythe for use of Jefferson's materials in connection with the work of a committee appointed by the General Assembly in 1795 to collect the statutes relating to land law. The committee was composed of Wythe, John Marshall, and several others. Jefferson promptly sent Wythe "my whole & precious collection of the printed laws of Virginia," giving instructions that they be bound into seven volumes before Wythe used them.[3] A few days later Jefferson wrote to Wythe urging that the project be broadened so as to include publication of all the Virginia laws.[4]

Wythe's committee "declined proceeding in the business" relating to the land laws "in hope the general assembly may be persuaded, by the reasons which you suggested, to extend the work." Wythe obtained permission to print Jefferson's letter as a broadside and distributed a copy to every member

121

of the legislature.[5] However, nothing came of Wythe's effort to obtain favorable action by the General Assembly, or of a subsequent attempt by Governor James Monroe in 1800. Jefferson's hope of publishing the Virginia laws which he had diligently collected and preserved did not come to fruition until many years later, when (using materials furnished by Jefferson) William Waller Hening published his monumental collection of Virginia statutes.[6]

Meanwhile the Virginia courts relied upon Jefferson's collection of laws from time to time when pending litigation required reference to statutes otherwise unavailable. In particular, a bound volume belonging to him which contained the Virginia statutes from 1734 to 1772 was frequently resorted to in judicial proceedings in all parts of the state. Until after 1733 the acts passed at each session of the legislature were preserved only in handwritten copies read to the people at the beginning of every monthly court and filed in the clerk's office of each county court. Sometimes the new acts would be inserted as a manuscript continuation at the end of the copy of Purvis (or other printed volume of statutes) in the clerk's office. Even after it became the practice for these session laws to be printed regularly, no one but Jefferson seems to have taken the pains to assemble a consecutive series of them.[7]

The treasures assembled at Monticello were thus described in a letter to a historian desiring to consult them:

> I have a collection, nearly compleat, of the laws from 1624 to 1662 where Purvis's printed collection begins. But some of the volumes are in such a state of decay, that the leaf falls to pieces on being turned over. Consequently as they never can be examined but once I reserve that to the moment when the legislature shall decide to have an authentic copy taken. In the meantime I have sewed them up in oil cloth, and seared the joints to preserve them from the air.[8]

Enumerating the contents of his eight bound volumes of printed laws,[9] of which the fifth contained "Fugitive sheets published each session 1734–1772," Jefferson pointed out:

> The 5th volume is the only one of which there exists probably no other collection. This fact being generally known, the courts in the different parts of the state are in the practice of resorting to this volume for copies of particular acts called for in the cases before them. For this reason I have always refused to let it go from Monticello not only because it might be lost, but because while it was gone out in the service of one person, many might have occasion to recur to it.[10]

The courts treated Jefferson's library as being in substance a depository of public records and would accept a copy from Jefferson of any particular act of assembly involved in proceedings before them "instead of requiring the volume itself to be produced to them as evidence."[11]

This precious volume was entrusted in 1809 to William Waller Hening,[12] who had finally undertaken the task of publishing the laws of Virginia, an enterprise which Jefferson had long hoped to see accomplished and had sought to stimulate.[13] Hening's first volume appeared on October 21, 1809.[14] Succeeding volumes were issued in 1810, 1812, and 1814. Publication was resumed in 1819 (when volumes V and VI appeared), followed by volume VII in 1820, and volumes VIII and IX in 1821. Volume X came out in 1822; and the three final volumes in 1823.[15] In the same year a second edition of the first three volumes was published. Volume IV had been reissued in 1820, all the sheets except for 150 copies or so having been destroyed in a fire on July 16, 1815, at Petersburg, where they had been sent to be bound.[16]

It was largely due to Jefferson's impetus and assistance that Hening's publication of the Virginia statutes was made possible at all. In the preface to his first volume, Hening justly made the acknowledgment that "Thomas Jefferson, late President of the United States, has contributed more than any other individual to the preservation of our ancient laws. He very early employed himself in collecting them for the public use; and to his assistance the editor is chiefly indebted for the materials which compose the present work."[17]

When Jefferson looked for his bound volume of session laws from 1734 to 1772 in order to send it to Hening, he found that the book was missing from his library. "Having received often applications from courts & individuals for copies from that volume, I imagine it has been trusted to some one in the neighborhood to copy some act, & not returned. I shall immediately enquire for it & hold it at your service."[18]

Fortunately, he soon learned that it was in the hands of his kinsman George Jefferson, a Richmond merchant, "with an injunction not to let it out of his possession."[19] Thus Hening was able to procure the volume, which he retained, after the sale of Jefferson's library to Congress in 1814,[20] until completion of volume VIII of the *Statutes at Large.*[21]

Besides making use from time to time of Jefferson's unique volume of printed statutes, the Virginia courts on at least one important occasion consulted his collection of manuscript laws in order to ascertain whether or not a particular piece of legislation had in fact been enacted.

In a case before the Virginia Court of Appeals in 1808,[22] human liberty was at stake. The slender reed upon which it hung was a manuscript from Monticello.[23] The plaintiffs in that case, whom the defendants sought to hold as slaves, sued for their liberty.[24]

It was indisputable law that the Act of 1705[25] relating to trade with the

Indians had been construed by the Virginia courts as a complete bar to slavery insofar as American Indians were concerned.[26] But the proof in the case showed that Indian Bess, from whom plaintiffs were descended, had been brought to Virginia in 1703, two years too soon to receive the benefits of that statute.

However, Judge Tucker recollected having seen on the eastern shore a volume of laws which contained an Act of 1691, inserted in handwriting at the back of the book following the printed statutes. It was Judge Tucker's belief that it was this Act of 1691, not the Act of 1705, which first authorized free trade with the Indians and abolished Indian slavery.[27]

If Indian slavery was abolished by an Act of 1691, then the plaintiffs, descendants of Indian Bess who was brought to Virginia in 1703, were free. If no such act had become law, they would be slaves. Whether or not there existed an Act of 1691 was the question before the court.

When the case came up for argument, the court's reporter, William Waller Hening, produced a manuscript from Northumberland County which contained the Act of 1691.[28] After seeing this, Judge Roane proposed that application be made to Jefferson to see whether the Act of 1691 appeared in his collection of ancient Virginia laws.[29] As a large amount of property was involved, the court did not wish to decide the question upon the authority of a single manuscript, and postponed the case until the next term in order that inquiry might be made of Jefferson.[30]

On February 7, 1808, Hening wrote to Jefferson, who was then president of the United States, transmitting the request of the court.[31] Aware of Jefferson's solicitude for his fragile manuscripts,[32] Hening said: "I am not certain whether your MSS are in such a state of preservation as will admit of their being opened more than once. Should this be the case I could not expect to be furnished with the act even were you at Monticello. But if it can be obtained thro' the agency of any of your friends who may have access to your library, it will confer a singular favour on the judges, and will be aiding the cause of humanity."[33]

Jefferson replied on February 26, 1808, that he had written to his son-in-law Thomas Mann Randolph to procure a copy of the act.[34]

When the case was reached at the following term, Hening on March 15, 1808, produced a copy of the manuscript from Monticello containing the Act of 1691. He also had obtained a copy of the eastern shore manuscript which Judge Tucker had recalled seeing.

The court was convinced by the agreement of the three independent manuscripts that nothing but a miracle or the genuineness of the statute could have produced such uniformity among the three texts. Accordingly on March 22, 1808, the court of appeals rendered its decision, holding that the plaintiffs were not slaves.[35] The manuscript from Monticello thus tipped the scales in favor of freedom.

In the same letter in which he asked for a copy of the 1691 statute, Hening informed Jefferson that the General Assembly had authorized publication of the Virginia laws.[36] Jefferson's prompt response was encouraging: "You shall have the free use of my collection." He offered the suggestion that "the various readings of different MS.S. should be noted," and that octavo volumes would be preferable to unwieldy folios. Calling attention to the fact that the law books recently printed in Virginia "are really, from their paper & type, a scandal to our state," he urged that if the work could not be well done at Richmond, it would be advisable to have it done more cheaply at New York, Philadelphia, Baltimore, or Washington, where "as good printing is done as in Europe."[37]

Jefferson was not remiss in providing the promised aid. In addition to supplying Hening with his unique volume of printed session laws,[38] he furnished valuable manuscripts of the earlier Virginia statutes.[39] Eight such items[40] were specified in a list[41] of materials sent to Hening.[42] Two additional manuscripts[43] had been enumerated in the list of printed and unprinted laws in Jefferson's possession sent to George Wythe in 1796.[44]

One of the manuscripts furnished to Hening[45] had been found by Jefferson in a tavern, where it was being used for waste paper. The clerk of the court, who was the legal custodian of the paper thus rescued by Jefferson, "very readily" gave it to him for his collection at Monticello.[46]

Another manuscript belonging to Jefferson and used by Hening[47] experienced a strange fate before it finally found a safe haven in the Library of Congress.[48] Hening had obtained this manuscript from Edmund Randolph, the first attorney general of the United States, Jefferson's colleague in Washington's cabinet and successor as secretary of state.[49] In the *Statutes at Large* he referred to MS.D as "belonging to Edmund Randolph, Esq. which was once the property of his grandfather Sir John Randolph."[50] In the second edition he inserted a correction showing the provenance of this manuscript and its transmission through Jefferson.[51]

What had happened was that Edmund Randolph, planning to write a history of Virginia, had borrowed MS.D, along with other manuscripts, from Jefferson's library while the latter was abroad as minister to France. The attorney general had taken them to New York, but when he moved to Philadelphia at the time the nation's temporary capital was transferred to that city, the box containing them was lost. Some years later it was found in a warehouse, and the manuscripts were returned to Jefferson. However, the most valuable one (MS.D) was missing. With great joy Jefferson learned in 1815 that it was still in existence and had come into Hening's hands.[52]

Truly, Hening's *Statutes at Large* stand as an abiding monument of Jefferson's legal and historical scholarship, just as much as Jefferson's own revisal of the laws of Virginia[53] after the Revolution, in order to adapt them to republican principles of government "with a single eye to reason and the good of" the people[54] for whom they were framed.

Before the monumental work of Hening had been undertaken, a number of publications containing legislative enactments were available to Virginia lawyers.[55]

The earliest printed laws for Virginia antedated the establishment of representative government in the colony. The first settlers landed in 1607 and were governed by a council in accordance with the royal charter of April 10, 1606. Famine, disease, dissension, and Indian wars soon resulted in a new form of government under the auspices of a new charter of May 23, 1609. This instrument was drafted by Sir Edwin Sandys. It gave complete control to the Virginia Company in London, and (by delegation) to a governor general. In May, 1610, Lieutenant Governor Sir Thomas Gates arrived with the new charter, and a stern regime began. Gates had fought against the Spaniards in the Netherlands, and he promptly posted in the church at Jamestown a set of laws exceedingly severe in their terms. These were not enforced vigorously, however, until the arrival of Sir Thomas Dale, also a veteran of the Dutch wars, as deputy governor in 1611. Dale put the harsh code into execution, supplemented by rules derived from martial law as practiced by English forces in the Netherlands. This strict regime did enable the colony to survive, but was ill-suited to a population composed of free-born Englishmen. It was also in conflict with the charter. "The Colony . . . remained in great want and misery under most severe and Cruell lawes sent over in printe." Dale returned to England in 1616.

Meanwhile a third charter had been granted on March 12, 1611/12, pursuant to which the company in London authorized Governor George Yeardley to establish a representative assembly, the first in the New World, which met in Jamestown on August 9, 1619. Soon after Yeardley's arrival on April 29, 1619, he issued a proclamation "that those cruel laws by which we had so long been governed were now abrogated, and that now we were to be governed by those free laws which his Majesty's subjects live under in England."[56] Thus the first revision of Virginia laws may be deemed to have taken place when Dale's code[57] was superseded by the legislation of the 1619 Assembly.[58]

Dale's code, issued June 22, 1611, "enlarged" the laws first established by Gates on May 24, 1610, and confirmed by Sir Thomas West (Lord Delaware, governor and captain general) on June 12, 1610.[59] It begins with a series of strict provisions relating to religious observances and moral transgressions.[60] Other "Ciuill and Politique Lawes" relate to the economy of the settlement.[61] Some offenses are punishable both by the martial and civil power.[62] Other offenses are specifically military.[63] Strict sanitary regulations were prescribed,[64] and deceptive trade practices forbidden.[65] Penalties were severe: death, whipping, a bodkin thrust through the tongue, loss of ears, burning in the hand, head and heels fastened together, condemnation to the galleys.[66] Numerous offenses were punishable by death.[67]

Soldiers moreover faced peculiarly military penalties, such as "to passe the pikes" or to be "put to death with the Armes which he carrieth."[68] Officers, as well as men, were subject to stern discipline. "No officer shall strike any souldier, for any thing not concerning the order, and duty of service, and the publique worke of the Colony, and if any officer shall so doe, hee shall be punished as a private man in that case, and bee held vnworthy to command, so peruerting the power of his place and authority."[69]

It is not surprising that Virginians rejoiced when the harsh regime under Dale's code was replaced by a legislative assembly representing the people.

The first printed collection of Virginia laws, compiled after the establishment of representative government in the colony and after the restoration of King Charles II as sovereign, was published at London in 1662.[70] Its title page reads: "THE LAWES OF VIRGINIA Now in Force. Collected out of the *Assembly Records,* and Digested into one Volume. Revised and Confirmed by the *Grand Assembly* held at *James-City,* by Prorogation, the 23d of *March,* 1661. in the 13th. Year of the Reign of our Soveraign Lord King Charles the II. *LONDON:* Printed by E. Cotes, for A. Seile over against St. *Dunstans* Church in *Fleet-street.* M.DC.LXII."[71]

This book contains 138 acts in 80 pages. These constitute the revisal of March 23, 1661/2,[72] which Colonel Francis Morrison, deputy governor, and Henry Randolph, clerk of the assembly, had been directed to prepare. Only four years had elapsed since the previous revisal of 1657/58, but the restoration of the monarchy on May 29, 1660, signaled an important change of government, which necessitated corresponding changes in the laws.

In his "epistle dedicatory" to Sir William Berkeley, Francis "Moryson" reported that "the charge to peruse our Laws, and to reduce them into as good a Form, as our weak abilities could perform" might perhaps "have been better done, had not the Troubles of the Indians, and Quakers, and other emergent Occasions of the Publique, depriv'd me of much of that time I had devoted to that most serious Imployment." However, "as they are (since the Assembly hath approv'd them, and Ordered them to be put in Print) I thought it my duty to Dedicate them to your Patronage, who, of the most and best of them, was the only Author."

Continuing, he notes that "Little addition there is to what your self had done in the time of your Government, only what vitious Excrescencies had

127

grown in the body of them, by the corrupt humor of the times, we have thoroughly purg'd them of, that we might not any where leave unrazed the memory of our enforc'd Defection from his Sacred Majesty; for whom, your prudent care so long preserved the Countrey."

In the same adulatory vein, he concludes: "Sir, though the remoteness of this place, hath veild the glory of these, and other your Honourable Actions; yet I, and all that here with me were witnesses of them, must, and each will, acknowledg that to you, next to his Majesties goodness, we owe both the Laws we Govern by, and the Countrey it self now Govern'd by those Laws."

The preamble declared that "the late unhappy Distractions caused frequent Change in the Government of this Countrey, and those produced so many Alterations in the Laws, that the People knew not well what to obey, nor the Judges what to punish; by which means, Injustice was hardly to be avoided, and the just freedom of the people, by the uncertainty and licentiousness of the Laws, hardly to be preserved."[73] The acts passed were to be written in a book, signed by the deputy governor and speaker, and a copy sent to England for royal confirmation, with a ten-year exclusive license to print.[74] This volume is quite rare and it was apparently never seen by Jefferson or Hening.[75] This 1662 publication (not Purvis)[76] is meant when references are made in several early documents to the "printed laws."[77]

The most widely used collection of laws was that known as "Purvis" (which Jefferson continually spelled "Pervis"). The title page of this volume reads: "A Complete Collection OF ALL THE LAVVS OF VIRGINIA NOW IN FORCE. Carefully Copied from the ASSEMBLY RECORDS. To which is Annexed an ALPHABETICAL TABLE. *LONDON,* Printed by *T.J.* for *J.P.* and are to be sold by Tho. Mercer at the Sign of the *Half Moon* the Corner Shop of the *Royal-Exchange* in *Cornhil.*"[78]

It will be noted that no date of publication is given. It has been generally stated that the book was issued some time between 1684 and 1687.[79] However, a later writer thinks it probable that the book "was compiled and printed in London during 1683, or in the early part of 1684," or possibly even in 1682.[80] This view is supported by the fact that the General Assembly, on April 26, 1684, presented an address to Lord Howard humbly praying that the book be suppressed and that "Capt *John Puruis* Commander of . . . ye Shipp Duke of *Yorke,* who is Said to be ye publisher and Importer of diuers printed Copies of ye sd Booke, be Commanded forthwith to appeare before this Genll Assembly to Answer for his misdemeanor in presumeing to publish withoute Licence a booke of yt title & Contents, to ye Great Scandall & Contempte of ye Gour of this his Maties [Majesty's] dominion."[81] The Governor and Council concurred in this presentment, and made an order which "shall speedily Goe forth, into all Counties ord'ring signifying & declareing to every Respectiue Countie . . . not to Receiue admitt or allow in any Courte of Judicature the aforesaid Booke or any pte ther'in Contained to be the Lawes of this his Maties Colony & dominion of *Virga.*" He also declared that "Whereas you present Capt *John Puruis* as the author therof he shall receiue my reprehention for yt his presumption & forwardnesse."[82]

Although the resolution and address stated that the book was "found to be very false and imperfect,"[83] it seems clear that the chief offense was publication without licence. Perhaps the interests of competitors were being jeopardized.[84]

These proceedings against the presumptuous mariner are likewise the source of the generally held belief that *J. P.* means John Purvis. The writer who first drew public attention to the 1662 collection says: "Nor is it certainly known who John Purvis was. At the time of this publication, which was some time between 1684 and 1687, there was a merchant trader doing a large business with Virginia—a Captain John Purvis by name—commanding 'The Duke of York;' and on one occasion he acted as jailer for the colony, keeping imprisoned on his ship Major Robert Beverly, who had been the ringleader of the Plantcutting riots, in which, by destroying the tobacco crop that year, the colonists sought to increase its value—a misguided but Spartan method of bolstering up a currency which had been depreciated by overproduction.

"As no other Purvis is mentioned at that period, and as Captain John Purvis had great need to know the laws of Virginia, it is probable that he was the compiler of this much-used and more abused book."[85]

In the preface to Purvis the compiler emphasizes how impossible it is "for any number of Men to be at Peace or to flourish and prosper without good *Laws,* which are the firm Pillars of Government, and the strong Bonds of all Humane Society. One had as good live in a Desart amongst Savage Beasts, as among Men without *Law* to defend him; for *Laws* are the Hedges on either side the Road, which hinders from breaking into other Mens Propriety." He goes on to observe that laws are every man's "Civil Armour," and are useful "not only to be our Guide, but also our Shield."

In chronological order (though of much less practical value than Purvis) the next printed volume containing Virginia laws[86] was a mediocre compilation[87] commonly known as the "Plantation Laws."[88] It enjoys the temporal distinction of being the first printed digest of Virginia statutes.[89] However, had Phillip Ludwell's[90] 1694 abridgment[91] been published in due season it would have been entitled to make that claim to fame. But it did not appear in print until 1903. According to its own statement, "this Abridgment was made in Sepr [September] in 1694." It also points out: "Note all ye printed laws were made in ye year 1661 in ye 13th year of King Charles ye 2nd, Sr Wm. Berkley, Governor."[92]

In 1722 a better known and widely used medium of finding Virginia legislation was made available to the legal profession. This was William[93] Beverley's *Abridgement*.[94]

In the dedication to Lieutenant Governor Alexander Spotswood the author says:

> Having observed a great Desire in the People for some Years past, and their many Petitions to late Assemblies, to obtain the Printing of their Laws; and that those Desires were also countenanced by the last Assembly; but not hearing that the laws at Large are likely to receive that Benefit in any short time; I was willing to make an Offering to my Country of the following Abridgement, which I had made for my private Use and this may be an Ease and Satisfaction to many, 'till the larger Volume can be procured.[95]

The popularity of Beverley's volume is shown by Hening's statement that "Except Purvis, & Beverley's Abridgment, the laws of Virginia existed entirely in MS. till after the revisal of 1733."[96]

Five years after Beverley's *Abridgement* there was published in London "ACTS OF ASSEMBLY, PASSED in the Colony of *VIRGINIA,* From 1662, to 1715. VOLUME I. *LONDON,* Printed by *John Baskett,* Printer to the King's most Excellent Majesty, MDCCXXVII." A second edition, apparently differing from the first only in the title page, appeared in 1728.[97] "These are the most ignored of all the editions of the Codes and yet they are the only authentic printing of the laws after a lapse of sixty-five years.[98] They are believed to be an accurate and full compilation of all laws in force from 1662 to 1715 . . . Yet no mention is made of either of these editions in all the realm of Virginia Legal Literature until in 1898 Mr. Bryan brought them out of oblivion. No reference is made to them by contemporary writers or in contemporary documents. They were either ignored by Jefferson, Hening and Tucker or unknown to them."[99] Probably publication was stimulated by Governor Spotswood's complaint that "a perfect collection of those [laws] in force has never yet been attained to, and that the want thereof is no small inconvenience, both to ye Courts of Justice and to the people."[100]

A watershed in the publication of Virginia legislation was reached when in 1733 William Parks printed "A COLLECTION OF ALL THE ACTS OF ASSEMBLY, Now in Force, in the Colony of *VIRGINIA.* WITH THE TITLES of Such as are Expir'd, or Repeal'd. And NOTES in the Margin, shewing how, and at what Time, they were Repeal'd. Examin'd with the Records, by a COMMITTEE appointed for that Purpose. Who have added Many useful *Marginal Notes,* and *References.* And an exact TABLE. *Publish'd, pursuant to an Order of the* GENERAL ASSEMBLY, *held at* WIL-

LIAMSBURG, *in the Year* M,DCC,XXVII. *WILLIAMSBURG:* Printed by WILLIAM PARKS. M,DCC,XXXIII."[101]

The editor of this compilation[102] was George Webb,[103] and it was very useful to the profession. It was one of the earliest Virginia imprints, and the first law book printed in Virginia.[104] Parks inaugurated the practice of supplementing the collection by regularly printing the new laws subsequently enacted at each session of the General Assembly.[105] Jefferson preserved a complete set of such session laws, as we have seen, from which Hening printed the legislation from 1734 to 1772.[106] The acts of 1734 were often bound with copies of the 1733 compilation.[107]

Another useful work[108] soon followed, when Mercer's *Abridgment* was published by Parks in 1737.[109] Copies of the second edition of this book were supplied at public expense to every county court.[110] In Jefferson's copy of that edition he filled the interleaved blank pages with manuscript material, and also made marginal annotations.[111]

William Parks died in 1750, and, under an arrangement with his executors, William Hunter in 1752 printed the next important collection of Virginia laws.[112] This embodied the revisal of October 27, 1748.[113] It is said to be the only printed code (except the *Lawes* of 1662) ever issued by a committee directly authorized by the General Assembly to collect and publish "the whole body of the laws."[114] It was known in later years, after being reprinted as supplemented in 1769,[115] as "the old body of the laws."[116] When the 1748 revisal was sent to England, it was confirmed except for ten acts which were disallowed on October 1, 1751. This was not made known to the General Assembly until April 8, 1752, and the printing was too far advanced to omit the disallowed acts from the publication.[117] However, twenty old laws which had been repealed by the disallowed acts were revived by reason of the disallowance. These were printed by Hunter at the direction of the Speaker of the House of Burgesses.[118]

VII
Laws Friendly to Liberty

The next program of statutory revision in Virginia was one in which Jefferson himself took a leading part. After the Revolution, it seemed necessary and desirable, in his view, to bring the laws into conformity with republican principles of government, and to eliminate any remaining vestiges of monarchy.[1] Accordingly, within less than four months after the Declaration of Independence, the General Assembly adopted an act for the revision of the laws.[2] The terms of this enactment clearly show that what was intended was not a mere compilation of existing law. Substantial change was contemplated, corresponding to the new state of affairs created by separation from the royal government across the sea. The laws were henceforth to be in keeping with "the republican spirit," appropriately "adapted to our present circumstances of time and place," as well as "friendly to liberty and the rights of mankind." Accordingly, the committee of five persons to be appointed by joint ballot of both houses was given "full power and authority to revise, alter, amend, repeal, or introduce all or any of the said laws, to form the same into bills, and report them to . . . the General Assembly." Under these circumstances it was natural, by way of precaution, that a proviso was added to the act explicitly stating that such bills would have "no force or authority" until passed by both houses in the usual manner.

On November 5, 1776, when the balloting procedures were completed, the tellers reported that the committee would be composed of Thomas Jefferson, Edmund Pendleton, George Wythe, George Mason, and Thomas Ludwell Lee. "To be chosen, at the age of thirty-three, head of so important a committee and in competition with some of the finest legal minds in America, indicates" the impact upon Jefferson's colleagues of his professional prowess and unwearying dedication to the task of law reform.[3]

The committee met at Fredericksburg on January 13, 1777. A memorandum by George Mason describes the plan agreed upon for carrying out the work.[4]

The following general principles were adopted:

> The Common Law not to be med[d]led with, except where Alterations are necessary.

The Statutes to be revised and digested, alterations proper for us to be made; the Diction, where obsolete or redundant, to be reformed; but otherwise to undergo as few Changes as possible.

The Acts of the English Common-wealth to be examined.

The Statutes to be divided into Periods:[5] the Acts of Assembly, made on the same subject, to be incorporated into them.

The Laws of the other Colonies to be examined, and any good ones to be adopted.

Provisoes &c. which wou'd do only what the Law wou'd do without them, to be omitted.

Bills to be short; not to include Matters of different Natures; not to insert an unnecessary word, nor omit a useful one.

Laws to be made on the Spur of the present Occasion, and all innovating Laws, to be limited in their Duration.[6]

The memorandum then outlines the principal points to be observed in treating the criminal law, the law of intestate descent, and the land law. The punishment of death was to be abolished except for treason and murder; suicide was to be "considered as a Disease" rather than a crime;[7] whether pardons should be permitted was deferred for consideration at a later time.[8]

The English rule of primogeniture (inheritance by the eldest son alone) was abolished;[9] property was to pass to all children "Males and Females, in Equal Portions." New grants of land should not exceed 400 acres in any one county. Lands not improved were to lapse, with right of jury trial. "Lands to be recovered by one uniform rational Action."[10]

Further details of the discussion at Fredericksburg are given in Jefferson's Autobiography (written in 1821 at the age of 77). The revisers first considered whether "to abolish the whole existing system of laws, and prepare a new and complete Institute, or preserve the general system, and only modify it to the present state of things." Surprisingly, "Mr. Pendleton, contrary to his usual disposition in favor of antient things, was for the former proposition, in which he was joined by Mr. Lee." Wythe, Mason, and Jefferson took the opposite view: "that to abrogate our whole system would be a bold measure, and probably far beyond the views of the legislature" which probably intended that the revisers should follow the customary practice of "omitting the expired, the repealed and the obsolete [laws], amending only those retained" except that the process should in this case be applied to "the British statutes as well as our own." The objection was also made "that to compose a new Institute like those of Justinian and Bracton, or that of Blackstone, which was the model proposed by Mr. Pendleton, would be an arduous undertaking," requiring extensive research and deliberation. Moreover, when completed every word of the text agreed upon would become the subject of litigation "and render property uncertain until, like the statutes of old, every word had been tried, and settled by numerous decisions, and by new volumes of reports & commentaries." In addition, such a work "to be systematical, must be the work of one hand," and none of the revisers would probably be willing to undertake such a task.[11]

In an earlier account of the work of the committee, Jefferson commented that

the question was discussed whether we would attempt to reduce the whole body of law into a code, the text of which should become the law of the land? We decided against that, because every word and phrase in that text would become a new subject of criticism and litigation, until its sense should have been settled by numerous decisions, and that, in the meantime, the rights of property would be in the air. We concluded not to meddle with the common law, *i.e.,* the law preceding the existence of the statutes, further than to accommodate it to our new principles and circumstances; but to take up the whole body of statutes and Virginia laws, to leave out everything obsolete or improper, insert what was wanting, and reduce the whole within as moderate a compass as it would bear, and to the plain language of common sense, divested of the verbiage, the barbarous tautologies and redundancies which render the British statutes unintelligible.[12] From this, however, were excepted the ancient statutes, particularly those commented on by Lord Coke, the language of which is simple, and the meaning of every word so well settled by decisions, as to make it safest not to change words where the sense was to be retained.[13] After setting our plan, Colonel Mason declined undertaking the execution of any part of it, as not being sufficiently read in the law. Mr. Lee very soon afterwards died, and the work was distributed between Mr. Wythe, Mr. Pendleton and myself. To me was assigned the common law, (so far as we thought of altering it,) and the statutes down to the Reformation, or end of the reign of Elizabeth; to Mr. Wythe, the subsequent body of the statutes, and to Mr. Pendleton the Virginia laws. This distribution threw into my part the laws concerning crimes and punishments, the law of descents, and the laws concerning religion. After completing our work separately, we met, (Mr. W., Mr. P. and myself,) in Williamsburg, and held a long session, in which we went over the first and second parts in the order of time, weighing and correcting every word, and reducing them to the form in which they were afterwards reported. When we proceeded to the third part, we found that Mr. Pendleton had not exactly seized the intentions of the committee, which were to reform the language of the Virginia laws, and reduce the matter to a simple style and form. He had copied the acts *verbatim,* only omitting what was disapproved; and some family occurrence calling him indispensably home, he desired Mr. Wythe and myself to make it what we thought it ought to be, and authorized us to report him as concurring in the work. We accordingly divided the work, and re-executed it entirely, so as to assimilate its plan and execution to the other parts, as well as the shortness of the time would admit, and we brought the whole body of British statutes and laws of Virginia into 127 acts most of them short.[14]

The industrious scholarship and careful weighing of considerations of public policy which Jefferson devoted to the revision of Virginia's laws is perhaps comparable to the work of a reporter drafting a restatement of some branch of the law for the American Law Institute today. He did not shirk laborious toil. Concerning one notable bill which he prepared, that for proportioning crime and punishment, he remarked that formulation of that proposal "employed me longer than I believe all the rest of the work, for it rendered it necessary for me to go with great care over Bracton, Britton, the Saxon statutes, and the works of authority on criminal law; and it gave me great satisfaction to find that in general I had only to reduce the law to its ancient Saxon condition, stripping it of all the innovations and rigorisms of subsequent times, to make it what it should be."[15]

The philosophical reflections on penology of Montesquieu and Beccaria also influenced Jefferson's proposals concerning this topic.[16] As Dumas Malone says: "The bill he drew after all this labor is notable for its studied simplicity, and the draft he submitted in advance to George Wythe represents, probably, the highest point he had yet attained in craftsmanship. This is certainly true of its physical form, for it is an extraordinarily beautiful document. For the benefit of his own memory, he attached notes in Anglo-Saxon characters, in Latin, old French, and English, attesting the meticulous carefulness of his procedure. In printed versions these are naturally put at the bottom of the pages, but Jefferson himself placed them in columns, parallel with the text, after the manner of his old lawbook, *Coke upon Littleton;* and, as in the work of the old master, they frequently encroach upon the text. The penmanship is beautifully clear, and no other document that Jefferson ever drew better exhibits his artistry as a literary draftsman."[17]

But "he never regarded the bill on which he labored most as his greatest contribution to the Revisal. At last, he gave that honor to his bill for establishing religious freedom."[18] Ironically, no manuscripts in his own hand of his bills on religion and education are known to exist, while "the Bill for Proportioning Crimes and Punishments, which never was adopted and which in many respects was a harshly reactionary piece of legislation" is preserved "in two self-consciously precious and meticulously drafted manuscripts."[19]

In language, as well as appearance, the bill is characteristically Jeffersonian. The preamble has a sonorous rhythm (though not so noble as that of the bill for religious freedom): "Whereas it frequently happens that wicked and dissolute men, resigning themselves to the dominion of inordinate passions, com-

135

mit violations on the lives, liberties and property of others, and, the secure enjoyment of these having principally induced men to enter into society, government would be defective in it's principal purpose were it not to restrain such criminal acts, by inflicting due punishments on those who perpetrate them . . . it becomes a duty in the legislature to arrange in a proper scale the crimes which it may be necessary for them to repress, and to adjust thereto a corresponding gradation of punishments." He notes also that "capital punishments . . . exterminate instead of reforming, and should be the last melancholy resource against those whose existence is become inconsistent with the safety of their fellow citizens."[20] Likewise he comments that "the experience of all ages hath shewn that cruel and sanguinary laws defeat their own purposes" because "the benevolence of mankind" produces a reaction resulting in their nonenforcement.[21]

After two and a half years of work, the revisers submitted their report. On June 18, 1779, the speaker laid before the House of Delegates a letter from Jefferson (who had become governor of the commonwealth on the first day of that month) and George Wythe, reporting (with the approval of Pendleton) on behalf of the committee.[22] They had prepared 126 bills, the titles of which were set forth in a catalogue accompanying the letter.[23] "Some of these bills have been presented to the House of Delegates in the course of the present session," the revisers continued. Two or three were "delivered to members of that House at their request to be presented, the rest are in the two bundles which accompany this; these we take the liberty through you of presenting to the General Assembly." It was ordered "that the said letter with its enclosures do lie on the table."

It may have been Jefferson himself who selected the bills that were presented by members for enactment at the May, 1779, session. In any event, ten bills were promptly passed.[24] These dealt with matters relating to the organization and operation of the government. One declared "who shall be deemed citizens of this Commonwealth" and provided how they might exercise the "natural right" of expatriation.[25]

Except for such matters of immediate urgency, the proposals submitted by the revisers lay ignored for almost five years. Perhaps this was because of the pressure of wartime exigencies, or of uncertainty as to the outcome of the war.[26] On June 1, 1784, "for the purpose of affording to the citizens at large an opportunity of exam'ning and considering a work which proposes such various and material changes in our legal code," the House of Delegates ordered 500 copies of "a complete set of the bills contained in the said revisal" to be printed and distributed.[27] A rather "rare and inacessible" book[28] resulted, the *Report of the Committee of Revisors Appointed by the General Assembly of Virginia In MDCCLXXVI.*[29] Julian Boyd, in his excellent treatment of the revisal,[30] does not reprint the *Report of the Revisors* literally, but (in addition to editorial changes and corrections) supplements it by manuscript materials whenever such are available.[31] As he points out, even a full and correct reprint of the *Report* would not adequately portray the scope of the revision. To do that it would be necessary to ascertain: "(1) the law as it stood before the Committee of Revisors began work; (2) the alterations that the Committee proposed; and (3) the extent to which these alterations were adopted by the General Assembly." Boyd's analysis covers the second and third stages of this inquiry (and occasionally the first) by comparison of available texts.[32]

Meanwhile, perhaps because of need for clear understanding of the first point (the state of existing law), the General Assembly, almost a year before ordering the *Report of the Revisors* to be printed, directed that acts since the 1769 revisal, together with ordinances of Convention in force "be collected into one code, with a proper index, and marginal notes, to be revised and examined by any two judges of the High Court of Chancery."[33] The chancery judges were Edmund Pendleton, George Wythe, and John Blair. This compilation,[34] printed in 1785, was consequently often called the "Chancellors' Revisal."[35]

By virtue of Madison's strenuous efforts a substantial part of the neglected bills in the *Report of the Revisors* became law in 1785 and 1786.[36] On October 31, 1785, Madison presented from the committee for courts of justice, according to order, 117 of the bills contained in the *Report of the Revisors,* not yet enacted into law, and not of a temporary nature.[37] His exertions resulted in the adoption of 35 bills at this session.[38] These measures included the abolition of primogeniture[39] and the establishment of religious freedom.[40] At the next session in October, 1786, 23 more bills were enacted into law.[41]

Madison found sentiment in the legislature much more favorable to the revisal than he had anticipated.[42] He reported to Jefferson (who was then in Paris as minister to France) that "we went on slowly but successfully, till we arrived at the bill concerning crimes and punishments."[43] The combined effect of opposition and shortness of time necessitated postponement until the next session. "After the completion of the work at this Session was despaired of it was proposed and decided that a few of the bills following the bill concerning crimes and punishments should be taken up as of peculiar importance. The only one of these which was pursued into an Act is the Bill concerning Religious freedom."[44]

The same hindrances were encountered at the session of October, 1786. On November 1, 1786, "Mr. Innes reported, from the committee for Courts of Justice, that the committee had, according to order, examined the Journal of the last session, and found 61 of the printed bills contained in the Revised

Code of laws, which were committed to a committee of the whole House, were at the end of the session, depending and undetermined." The said bills were read twice and committed to a committee of the whole house, and a standing order made that on three days a week no other business be "considered after 12 o'clock of the day, other than the bills contained in the said Revised Code, or such other as respects the interest of the Commonwealth at large, or messages from the Executive or the Senate."[45]

The following month Madison informed Jefferson:

The consideration of the Revised Code has been resumed and prosecuted pretty far towards its conclusion. I find however that it will be impossible as well as unsafe to give an ultimate fiat to the System at this Session.[46] The expedient I have in view is to provide for a supplemental revision by a Committee who shall accomodate the bills skipped over, and the subsequent laws, to such part of the Code as has been adopted, suspending the operation of the latter for one year longer. Such a work is rendered indispensible by the al[te]rations made in some of the bills in their passage, by the change of circumstances which call for corresponding changes in sundry bills which have been laid by, and by the incoherence between the whole code and the laws in force of posterior date to the Code. This business has consumed a great deal of the time of two Sessions, and has given infinite trouble to some of us. We have never been without opponents who contest at least every innovation inch by inch. The bill proportioning crimes and punishments, on which we were wrecked last year, has after undergoing a number of alterations got thro' a Committee of the Whole; but it has not yet been reported to the House, where it will meet with the most vigorous attack. I think the chance is rather against its final passage in that branch of the Assembly, and if it should not miscarry there, it will have another guantlet to run through the Senate.[47]

Madison's forebodings were verified by "rejection of the Bill on crimes and punishments, which after being altered so as to remove most of the objections as was thought, was lost by a single vote. The rage against Horse stealers had a great influence on the fate of the Bill. Our old bloody code is by this event fully restored."[48]

The intensity of public revulsion against horse thieves was doubtless no surprise to Jefferson. The preceding year, in commenting on the draft of a French writer's article being prepared on the United States for the *Encyclopédie,* Jefferson had philosophized that: "in forming a scale of crimes and punishments, two considerations have principal weight. 1. The atrocity of the crime. 2. The peculiar circumstances of a country which furnish greater temptations to commit it, or greater facilities for escaping detection. The punishment must be heavier to counterbalance this. . . . For this reason the stealing of a horse in America is punished more severely than stealing the same value in any other form. . . . In some countries of Europe, stealing fruit from trees is punished capitally. The reason is that it being impossible to lock fruit trees up in coffers, as we do our money, it is impossible to oppose physical bars to this species of theft. Moral ones are therefore opposed by the laws. This to an unreflecting American appears the most enormous of all the abuses of power; he has been used to see fruits hanging in such quantities that if not taken by men they would rot."[49]

Finding it impossible, for a variety of reasons, to complete the enactment of the revisal at the 1786 session, Madison put into effect his plan to appoint a committee (composed of Pendleton, Wythe, and Blair) "to amend the unpassed bills and also to prepare a supplemental revision of the laws which have been passed since the original work was executed." However, it was deemed advisable not to suspend the portions of the revisal which had already been passed. By leaving them in effect they were put "out of the reach of a succeeding Assembly, which might possibly be unfriendly to the system altogether."[50] But this committee never acted. Nothing more was ever done with respect to the enactment into law of Jefferson's revisal.[51] The faithful and industrious Madison had left the legislative arena at Richmond to gain new laurels on the national scene as Father of the federal Constitution.[52] In a few years another committee for revision of the Virginia laws would be created.[53] Publication of that version was authorized in 1792,[54] and completed in 1794.[55] This was the last collection of Virginia statutes published before Hening's monumental enterprise began to bear fruit.[56] It was also the last folio edition of the laws.[57]

What, then, is to be said as to the abiding importance and value of Jefferson's revisal? His own earliest estimates make no grandiose claims. The account given in his *Notes on Virginia*[58] summarizes concisely what he considered to be notable features of the work:

> The plan of the revisal was this. The common law of England, by which is meant that part of the English law which was anterior to the date of the oldest statutes extant,[59] is made the basis of the work. It was thought dangerous to attempt to reduce it to a text: it was therefore left to be collected from the usual monuments of it. Necessary alterations in that, and so much of the old body of the British statutes, and acts of assembly, as were thought proper to be retained, were digested into 126 new acts, in which simplicity of stile was aimed at, as far as was safe. The following are the most remarkable alterations proposed:
>
> To change the rules of descent [so as to introduce equal partition].
> To make slaves . . . moveables.[60]

To have all public expences . . . supplied by assessments on the citizens, in proportion to their property.[61]

To hire undertakers [contractors] for keeping the public roads in repair,[62] and indemnify individuals through whose lands new roads shall be opened.[63]

To define with precision the rules whereby aliens should become citizens, and citizens make themselves aliens.[64]

To establish religious freedom on the broadest bottom.[65]

To emancipate all slaves born after passing the act. . . .[66]

The revised code further proposes to proportion crimes and punishments. . . .[67]

Another object of the revisal is, to diffuse knowledge more generally through the mass of the people. . . .[68]

Lastly, it is proposed, by a bill in this revisal, to begin a public library and gallery, by laying out a certain sum annually in books, paintings and statues.[69]

To a Dutch friend who had read the *Notes on Virginia* Jefferson wrote in 1785:

If you had formed any considerable expectations from our Revised code of laws you will be much disappointed. It contains not more than three or four laws which could strike the attention of a foreigner.[70]

Among these would surely have been numbered the laws changing the ancient rules of intestate succession,[71] as well as those concerning expatriation,[72] crime and punishment,[73] education,[74] and the establishment of religious freedom.[75]

In later years Jefferson singled out four of his proposals for reform, and considered them "as forming a system by which every fibre would be eradicated of antient or future aristocracy; and a foundation laid for a government truly republican."

These were the abolition of entail (which would prevent "the accumulation and perpetuation of wealth in select families"); the abolition of primogeniture ("substituting equal partition, the best of all Agrarian laws" in place of a vestige of feudalism "which made one member of every family rich and all the rest poor"); the establishment of religious freedom (which relieved the people from taxation for the support of a religion not their own); and the diffusion of knowledge by means of public education (which would enable the people "to understand their rights, to maintain them, and to exercise with intelligence their parts in self-government").[76]

As has been seen, three of these four significant measures were enacted into law as part of Jefferson's youthful labors for law reform.[77] The fourth (public education) was not to be achieved in its full extent until, as the crowning accomplishment of his old age, he was hailed as Father of the University

140

of Virginia[78] when that institution opened its doors at Charlottesville on March 7, 1825.[79] Truly had he spoken when he declared: "A system of general instruction which shall reach every description of our citizens from the richest to the poorest, as it was the earliest, so will it be the latest of all the public concerns in which I shall permit myself to take an interest."[80]

In the *Report of the Revisors* there were three bills dealing with education. Of these the most celebrated was *A Bill for the More General Diffusion of Knowledge*[81] whose stirring preamble echoed the sentiments expressed in the *Notes on Virginia.*[82] Jefferson goes on to declare that it is "expedient for promoting the public happiness that those persons, whom nature hath endowed with genius and virtue, should be rendered by liberal education worthy to receive, and able to guard the sacred deposit of the rights and liberties of their fellow citizens, and that they should be called to that charge without regard to wealth, birth or other accidental condition or circumstance." But since the indigence of many parents prevents them "from so educating, at their own expence, those of their children whom nature hath fitly formed and disposed to become useful instruments for the public, it is better that such should be sought for and educated at the common expence of all, than that the happiness of all should be confided to the weak or wicked."[83]

Accordingly, a system of ward or "hundred" schools was to be set up, from each of which a student would be chosen to attend the "grammer schools" to be established in twenty districts. Each of these schools, every other year, would send its best student to William and Mary, for three years of education at public expense.[84]

The second bill on education sought to reorganize William and Mary, so that it might serve more effectively as a state university at the topmost level of the Virginia educational system.[85] Besides modification in the governing body, revision of the curriculum was also prescribed. The third bill was one for "Establishing a Public Library."[86]

Jefferson's proposed reorganization of the governing body of William and Mary College resembled what was undertaken at Dartmouth College and Harvard College, and might have given rise to litigation similar to the Dartmouth College case.[87] Interestingly enough, it was John Marshall (author of the celebrated Dartmouth College case opinion) who as counsel for William and Mary College successfully defended the reorganization effected in 1779 during Jefferson's governorship. The litigation arose upon the initiative of a "grammer master and professor of humanity" who had been ousted from his post by reason of the discontinuance of the grammar school as a result of Jefferson's reforms.[88]

As time went on, Jefferson came to the conclusion that the state university should be a new institution, in a new locality. After his return from France

141

in 1789, he displayed no further interest in the reorganization of William and Mary. By 1800 he was contemplating a new university in "a healthier and more central" location.[89] In 1817 he drafted a bill for establishing a system of public education.[90] This proposal provided for primary schools, district colleges, and a university. In 1818, as an amendment to a bill providing for education of the children of the poor, the General Assembly made an appropriation of $15,000 from the literary fund for the support of a university.[91] The act called for appointment of commissioners from the twenty-four senatorial districts. They met at Rockfish Gap on August 1, 1818, to plan for the establishment of the newly authorized institution of higher education.

The most crucial matter for their determination was the site of the university. Several rival locations advanced their respective claims, but Jefferson adroitly managed to demonstrate by population statistics and a map that the most central and suitable site would be Charlottesville.[92] Central College had been established there in 1816,[93] as successor to Albemarle Academy, a school chartered in 1803 of which Jefferson had become a trustee in 1814.[94] It was his plan to make Central College the nucleus of the new university.[95] After a struggle in the legislature the decision of the commissioners was confirmed on January 25, 1819, and Central College became the University of Virginia.[96]

Jefferson superintended the designing and construction of buildings, as well as the recruiting of faculty, purchase of books and equipment, and establishment of the curriculum. These tasks filled his remaining years with anxiety and anticipation.

He was resolute in refusing to open the university before the buildings were completed, knowing that operating expenses would drain away available funds, "and nothing remain ever to finish the buildings." With equal determination he insisted that the institution must be a "real University" on a full scale "embracing the whole circle of sciences; and we consider a compleat, tho' later institution, as preferable to an earlier but defective one." He rejoiced to report that "our University is now so far advanced as to be worth seeing. It exhibits already the appearance of a beautiful Academical village, of the finest models of building and of classical architecture, in the United States. It begins to be much visited by strangers and admired by all, for the beauty, originality and convenience of its plan."[97] At last the joyful day came, on March 7, 1825, when the university commenced to function. The fourth important feature of the revisal had become a reality.

Jefferson never wavered in his belief in the importance of these achievements in the field of law reform. Shortly before his election as president, pondering "whether my country is the better for my having lived at all," he enumerates among his accomplishments "the demolition of the church establishment" by degrees, culminating in the act for religious freedom, which he "prepared in 1777, as part of the revisal."[98] Listing other important legislative acts, he mentions abolition of entails,[99] prohibiting importation of slaves, equal inheritance, and apportioning crimes and punishments.[100] And shortly before the end of his life, when reviewing his public services,[101] he specifies the same items, except that he adds "the establishment of our University."[102] These, in his judgment, were works worthy of acclaim.

VIII
Puritan Precedents
of that Day

Jefferson's proposals for law reform and those advanced in England by Puritans during the interregnum[1] exhibit significant similarities. It is highly probable that to some extent Jefferson patterned his plan to extirpate the vestiges of royal government in America upon the earlier efforts of Englishmen to abolish monarchy. In preparing a protest in 1774 against the Boston port bill he and some of his colleagues in the Virginia House of Burgessess used "Rushworth, whom we rummaged over for the revolutionary precedents & forms of the Puritans of that day."[2] Perhaps in other respects also the stream of Puritan principles[3] passed into his thinking through the influence of Rushworth and other "elementary books of public right."[4]

Many points of resemblance, however, are more likely to have originated independently as natural outgrowths of a shared philosophy of republicanism in general than to have been derived directly from specific English precedents. Jefferson could not possibly have been familiar with all the particular facets of Puritanism which modern scholars have brought to light.[5]

The term "Puritanism" originated as a description of the religious views of persons who did not believe that the Elizabethan established church had carried the Reformation far enough.[6] Later it was used generically to describe the political and social philosophies of various Protestant dissenters.[7] The basic feature of Puritanism was its ideal of a "holy community," set apart from the unregenerate secular world.[8]

Different factions of Puritans viewed in conflicting fashion the relationship between the church and secular society. The Presbyterians (influential in Parliament and the City of London) were less interested in liberty than in reform.[9] They believed that it was the duty of the civil magistrate to protect the true reformed religion; and that the holy elect should dominate and govern the secular world. They opposed toleration and favored adoption of Presbyterianism as an established national church. Indeed, in this endeavor they were successful for a brief interval. Parliament found it expedient to make concessions in order to obtain the help of the Scottish army in the struggle against the king. In substance Presbyterianism was accepted as the established religion when the Solemn League and Covenant was taken by the House of Commons on September 25, 1643.[10] On January 4, 1645, the Anglican Book

144

of Common Prayer was replaced by the Presbyterian Directory of Worship.[11] On August 16, 1645, an ordinance was adopted providing for the election of elders.[12] No elders were actually chosen, however, until the latter half of 1646, because of dissatisfaction on the part of the clergy, until a compromise was reached regarding the procedure for excluding scandalous or improper persons from the sacrament.[13] This was effected by an ordinance adopted on June 15, 1646.[14] "Thus the presbyterian form of church government became the national establishment . . . as far as an ordinance of parliament could make it."[15]

The Independents, numerous in Cromwell's army, formed a second faction of Puritans. Like the Presbyterians, they were strong supporters of public order and of the rights of private property.[16] But they became the party of toleration. They were descended from Congregationalists, who believed in the autonomy of the individual congregation rather than in a national church with a centralized organization having control over the local congregations. They conceived of the church as a body of believers voluntarily gathered together by covenant, rather than as a portion of the state's governmental apparatus. The original Separatists (who withdrew from the establishment) were often called "Brownists" by reason of being followers of Robert Browne, who in 1582 called for "Reformation without Tarrying for anie" official approbation.[17]

Likewise influential in the army were the Levellers, a third Puritan faction. They favored total separation of church and state, and demanded complete liberty of conscience.[18] They recognized that the spiritual virtues required of church members could not be expected among the populace at large. The concern of the holy community for its own religious affairs resulted in leaving the outside world to its own devices. The scriptural regime of grace was contrasted with the law of nature. The spiritualization of the church went hand in hand with the secularization of the state.[19] Levellers stressed the political liberty of individuals and the need for government by a democratically selected Parliament.[20] Though somewhat less devoted to protection of property rights than were the Presbyterians and Independents, they rejected any kinship with a more revolutionary group known as Diggers, who called themselves "true levellers" and who advocated abolition of private property in land.[21]

On the furthest fanatical fringe of Puritanism were the Fifth Monarchy men.[22] They believed that only the godly were fit to govern, and hence that the saints should rule over the entire social order.[23] "These enthusiasts called for nothing less than an entire abolition of the existing law, and a substitution for it of a simple code based on the law of Moses. . . . Office and authority were to be given to the Saints alone, and all institutions derived from William the Conqueror—the Little Horn concerning whom Daniel had prophesied—

were to be swept away without hesitation."[24] The Fifth Monarchy men were as revolutionary as the Diggers[25] but as Hildebrandine as the Presbyterians in their claim that the elect should dominate the civil government.[26]

In spite of the divergent tenets and idiosyncrasies of these sects, the desire for reform was a trait common to all varieties of Puritanism.[27] The resulting political activism was most marked, however, in the ferment produced by the Levellers. It was this sect which contributed most prominently to the movement for law reform[28] and constitutional development.[29]

The Puritan movement for law reform was widespread. Besides the propaganda of Levellers,[30] there was interest in government circles.[31] Cromwell himself endorsed the objective.[32] Painstaking work was performed by the committee created by the Rump Parliament under the chairmanship of Matthew Hale (who later became chief justice of the Court of King's Bench). Sixteen bills were prepared but none was enacted during the life of the Rump Parliament (which was dissolved in April, 1653).[33] When later in 1653 the Barebones Parliament met, it published the bills reported by the Hale Commission.[34] It set up a committee on law reform, abolished the Court of Chancery, and on August 19, 1653, passed a motion calling for "a new body of the law" which was to be "easy, plain and short" as well as consonant with "the word of God and right reason." In pursuance of this resolution a parliamentary committee was set up to draft a new code. "The committee began with the criminal law and the making of punishments more proportionate to offences." Other social reforms were contemplated.

On December 12, 1653, a maneuver by conservative members who met in advance of the usual time of assembly carried a motion for the dissolution of Parliament.[35] A few days later, on December 16, 1653, the Protectorate was established, under a written constitution, the Instrument of Government.[36] The Parliament of 1654 was conservative and short-lived; nothing came of Cromwell's intention, announced at the opening of Parliament, to reform the laws so as to make them short, plain, and less expensive.[37] The next Parliament, in 1656, displayed less interest in law reform than its predecessors during the commonwealth period.[38] But it was in October of that year that *Englands Balme* by William Sheppard was published. This book presented one of the most detailed and comprehensive programs for law reform formulated during the interregnum.[39]

Sheppard, best known as author of a much-used work on conveyancing,[40] outlined in *Englands Balme* the grievances felt by the people against the legal system, and then proceeded to propose remedies therefor. In many instances the remedy is left blank, as if the author had made a list of the grievances to be enumerated, but had been unable to devise an effective cure for a particular evil, or the deadline for publication had come too soon.[41] In other instances he offers only a less inarticulate uncertainty: "And as to these, it is offered to consideration what to do herein."[42] Sometimes the remedy is simply that existing laws be enforced,[43] or a pious admonition to the effect that "there ought to be a law" on the subject. Sometimes the author's proposal is merely to do what needs to be done, as the remedy for lack of a perfect translation of scripture is to prepare one,[44] and the remedy of a person aggrieved by destruction of his house in time of war is to pay him for his loss.[45]

Illustrative of Sheppard's treatment is his discussion of the prolixity of court proceedings:

> It is objected,
> That the long Arguments
> of the Lawyers and Judges, do much lengthen the Suits.
> It is offered to be considered,
> That they be taken
> away, or shortned; and
> that the Judges give their
> Judgment without solemne
> Argument, expressing briefly
> their reasons.[46]

Occasionally, the cure may be somewhat drastic or unworkable, or even worse than the disease, as when abolition of jury trial is proposed because jurors render erroneous verdicts;[47] or that offenders be punished without trial upon the oath of one witness and the certificate of a constable and parish minister;[48] and that for minor offenses such as swearing, drunkenness, whoring, vagrancy, roguery, and the like, any person whatever may on his own suspicion and without any other warrant bring the suspect before a justice of the peace to be examined as to the fact.[49] Of similar nature is Sheppard's exhortation that lawsuits without good cause be prevented, while meritorious litigation should be encouraged.[50]

Often Sheppard seems to rely upon a naive hope of transcending the weaknesses of human nature, as when he urges that officers be chosen from the most able men;[51] that good judges be provided in all courts, high and low;[52] that only the most honest and substantial persons be chosen as jurors;[53] and that sheriffs "be chosen out of the most Godly men in the County."[54]

Another proposal was that there be kept in every county a book in which the justices of the peace would list the names of "godly men" in two groups: one of persons fit to be grand jurors and constables, the other of persons fit to serve in other offices. Another list would contain the names of "all sober and civil men, not pretending more to religion than every man." A third list was to be kept of all godless and wicked men, or "dangerous in their Principles;

147

as Ranters, Quakers, and such like: Or any way notoriously wicked, or scandalous in their lives." These were to be incapable of holding any office.[55]

However, most of Sheppard's proposals for reform are practical and effective. Many have been adopted during the course of legal development, and some are still the topic of perennial discussion in our day.

With respect to the law in general the following prevalent objections were noted:

> 1. The length and tediousness of it,
> that it is so large and voluminous, that it
> can hardly be read in many years.
> 2. The obscurity of it, that it is not to
> be understood, when it is read.
> 3. The incertainty of it, that the Judges
> do not agree amongst themselves.[56]

To remedy these evils, the author proposed: "To make one plain, compleat, and Methodical Treatise or Abridgment of the whole Common and Statute Law, comprehending the Heads thereof, to which all cases may be referred: And therein, to make those things that are now obscure and incertain, cleer and certain. And to have all the Judges subscribe it for the setled Law, and to have it confirmed by the Parliament."[57]

Sheppard points out that some existing laws are repugnant to the laws of God, and evil in themselves. These include those regarding religious observances.[58] Other laws, he continues, are cruel and oppressive to the people, as where the law "doth impose anything it ought not impose, and wherein the people ought to be free," or punishes an action "which is no offence at all," or "where the punishment doth exceed the offence."[59] Examples of such are the manner of death for treason, of *peine forte et dure* for refusal to plead, the death penalty for trifling thefts. Unjustifiable discriminations exist "where one Man is punished lesse for a greater, and another more for a lesser offence: As, where one escapeth by [benefit of] Clergy for Man-slaughter, and another is hanged for stealing, because he cannot read."[60]

Furthermore, in spite of the fact "that the Laws are exceeding long and voluminous," they nevertheless are defective in many respects, often furnishing no remedy for the protection of rights, and in other cases no apt or complete remedy.[61] And another major evil was the lack of laws to regulate many matters where legislation was needed in order to protect important public interests.[62]

Sheppard advanced many specific practical suggestions for simplifying the intricacies of civil and criminal proceedings. Some of these have been adopted[63] during the years since he wrote, and some are still under discussion today.[64]

The revolt in 1970 of prisoners confined in the Tombs emphasizes the timeliness of Sheppard's demand "That Malefactors may come speedily to Tryal; and not lye long in Prison before Tryal."[65] Current controversy about sentencing echoes his criticism of the unreviewable power of a judge to impose excessive fines.[66] He proposed "To consider of a special Commission, and special Commissioners, to examine the injuries by unjust Sentences, and to give remedy as they shall see cause."[67] And his insistence "That there be enough of Courts of Justice; rather too many th[a]n too few: And that they be not overburdened with business"[68] strikes a responsive chord in the hearts of present-day litigants, lawyers, and judges struggling with court congestion and crowded calendars.

Improvements in the land law were also proposed by Sheppard. The use of simple forms of deed[69] and the establishment of a public registry for titles were favored.[70] That entails upon land are "inconvenient" is the final grievance enumerated in the book.[71]

But the proposals of Sheppard and of the Hale Commission were neglected, and reform of the legal system ceased to be a pressing issue, when royal rule was revived and the republican form of government was replaced by the restoration of Charles II.

In September, 1658, Cromwell died. His feeble son Richard, who succeeded him as protector, was evicted from office in May, 1659. Though it now seems clear that the forces making for restoration of the monarchy were irresistible, a new outburst of pamphlets advocating social reform (and law reform) appeared in 1659.[72] This agitation led to discussions in Parliament, but the elevation of Charles II to the throne soon put an end to any prospect for thoroughgoing law reform.[73]

Analysis of the bills considered by Parliament in 1653 shows that they dealt chiefly with the land law, criminal law, the chancery court, family relations formerly governed by ecclesiastical law, court procedure, and regulation of the legal profession.[74] Holdsworth's comment on the failure of the law reform movement to accomplish more significant results is perceptive. "Some few of the proposals in these long lists of projected law reforms were accepted, and became law either during the Commonwealth period, or during the latter years of the seventeenth century. But, for the acceptance of the majority of them, it has been necessary to wait till the nineteenth and twentieth centuries, and some are still unrealized."[75] Lack of stable government and opposition on the part of the legal profession are the reasons why so little was accomplished.[76]

"During the Commonwealth period abuses in the law were attracting much public attention, the party which ruled the state was not very favourably disposed to the lawyers, and it lent a sympathetic ear to proposals for the reform of the law. If so little was done under these favourable conditions, we can hardly expect that much would be attempted" after the Restoration changed the situation.[77]

Much routine legislation[78] enacted during the interregnum[79] displays a pattern of continuity with statutory law before and after that era.[80] At the Restoration the general principle was followed that only acts of the Long Parliament which had received the king's assent were valid, and that all other acts of pretended legislation[81] were null and void.[82] Parliament did not begin to claim the sovereign power of legislating without the king's participation until March 5, 1642, although it seems proper to date the breakdown of the monarchy from January 10, 1642, when Charles I fled from London with his family, and to date the beginning of the Civil War from August 22, 1642, when the king's standard was raised at Nottingham.[83] A chief cause of the Civil War was conflict over control of the militia. On March 5, 1642, Parliament asserted its autonomous authority by adopting an ordinance concerning the militia.[84] After the execution of the king, Parliament decided to abolish the kingly office, as well as the House of Lords.[85] On May 19, 1649, England was officially proclaimed to be a commonwealth. The term "Protectorate" was also used after Cromwell had been named "Lord Protector" by the Instrument of Government of December 16, 1653.[86]

One of the few significant reforms effected during the interregnum era was the abolition of military tenures.[87] This mode of holding land required the tenant to perform military duties in return for the grant of land to him. Such service was honorable and free in nature, but indefinite, uncertain, and contingent as to amount. For example, it might consist of "cornage," or the duty "to wind a horn whenever the Scots invaded the realm." Tenure by "socage," on the other hand, required services honorable and becoming a freeman, but which were definite and certain as to quantum or amount. Tenure by "copyhold" required services which, like knight service, were uncertain, but which in nature were base and suitable only to "villeins" or persons of lowly rank. Copyhold constituted an express exception in the commonwealth legislation which eliminated the undesirable incidents of knight service and transformed it into socage, which thereafter was the prevailing form of freehold tenure throughout England. ("Frankalmoin," or land held by religious services, and the purely honorary aspects of "grand serjeanty," such as the duty to be the king's champion at his coronation,[88] were likewise preserved, along with copyhold.)

150

Tenure by knight service had been a vital feature of the feudal system, but later a money payment called "scutage" was substituted for actual military service. Exorbitant demands made by King John in the guise of "scutage," along with other abuses of the incidents of feudal tenure, fomented the discontents which led to Magna Carta.[89]

The Restoration did not undo the modernization of land law embodied in the elimination of military tenures. Confirmation of this reform was one of the first measures adopted by Parliament under Charles II.[90] Later, from time to time, other legislation from the Puritan era was re-enacted. Thus the Restoration did not result in a complete return to the law as it had stood in 1640. "The changes made during 1640–60 had a permanent effect on the English legal system." The verdict of history has vindicated the Puritan law reformers in that they foresaw the path of the future. What they strove for ultimately came to pass.[91]

As summarized by a recent writer:

Counsel was allowed to the defence on a charge of treason in 1697 and of felony in 1738. Witnesses were allowed for the defence on charges of treason in 1695 and of felony in 1702. English was reintroduced as the legal language in 1731. The purchase of the office of jailer was forbidden in 1730. The *peine forte et dure* was abolished in 1772 and a refusal to plead was made equivalent to a plea of guilty; in 1827 such a refusal was treated as a plea of not guilty. The reduction of the number of capital offences started in 1808; by 1837 it had been reduced to fifteen and by 1861 it was confined to treason, murder, piracy with violence, and setting fire to dockyards and arsenals. Benefit of clergy was abolished in 1827 for all except peers, who had to wait until 1841. Fines and Recoveries were abolished in 1833. In the same year the law of inheritance was amended to permit the half-blood to succeed in default of heirs of the whole blood. County courts were established on a nation-wide basis in 1846, with a jurisdiction of up to £20. The Court of Common Pleas in 1847 gave the right of audience to all barristers.

The fatal Accidents Act 1846 enabled the personal representatives of a deceased's estate to sue for damages for the benefit of the deceased's family if the deceased had a right of action before he died. Judges and court officials were not salaried until the first half of the nineteenth century with the general abolition of sinecures and establishment of a modern civil service. Forfeiture for felony and treason were abolished in 1870. The drawing and quartering of persons condemned to death for treason was abolished in the same year. A Deeds Registry was opened in Middlesex in 1708, and in the three ridings of Yorkshire between 1703 and 1735. Land Registration was introduced in 1875, but only now is it being rapidly extended to cover the whole country on a compulsory basis. Between 1873 and 1875 the administration of law and equity was fused, court procedure unified, the rules of law and equity were assimilated, and it was provided that where common law and equity were in conflict, equity was to prevail. Law Commissioners with a permanent responsibility for keeping the law up to date were established only in 1965.[92]

The foregoing summary of Puritan proposals for law reform has disclosed their similarities to Jefferson's program. One of the foremost objectives of the commonwealth efforts was mitigation of the severity of the criminal law, by proportioning crimes and punishments and reducing the number of offenses calling for the death penalty.[93] This was likewise a principal feature of Jefferson's plan of law reform in Virginia.[94]

Another significant aim of the Puritan reformers was to facilitate transactions relating to land;[95] in particular to abolish primogeniture and entail.[96] This also was an outstanding feature of Jefferson's Virginia reforms.[97]

It may have been the result of Puritan influences, as well as of economic conditions in an area where labor was scarce, that primogeniture was abandoned in New England and Pennsylvania long before Jefferson's program of law reform in Virginia after the Revolution. In Plymouth, Massachusetts Bay, Connecticut, and Pennsylvania equal distribution among children was the rule from the seventeenth century on, except that the eldest son received a double portion in accordance with Biblical precedent (Deut. 21:17). Massachusetts abolished the double portion in 1789, Pennsylvania in 1794. The custom of equal division in Plymouth is mentioned as early as 1627; in Massachusetts Bay it was embodied in articles 81 and 82 of the Body of Liberties of 1641.[98] A Pennsylvania law of 1705 and a New Hampshire law of 1718 containing similar provisions seem to have been allowed to stand, although a New Hampshire act of 1693 and a Pennsylvania act of 1700 were disallowed by the English government as contrary to English law.[99] Pennsylvania doubtless adopted the New England practice because of its suitability to local conditions rather than because of Puritan sentiment. As Jefferson said: "It is in Pennsylvania that the two characters [New England and Southern] seem to meet & blend, & to form a people free from the extremes both of vice and virtue."[100]

The Puritans likewise emphasized their desire to popularize the law (hitherto the exclusive domain of an esoteric and unpopular profession) by making it intelligible to the ordinary citizen. They hoped to shorten and simplify the body of the law, to state it in clear and understandable terms (in the English language, rather than Latin and Norman French), to make legal proceedings less protracted and expensive (and especially to do away with the evils of the cumbersome chancery court).[101] Jefferson likewise favored simplification of the language used in statutes,[102] and introduced jury trial in equity cases.[103]

152

Besides a strong penchant for law reform, Jefferson and the Puritans held in common a number of basic principles regarding the nature of the legal system and its constitutional structure. Many important concepts which are characteristically Puritan will be recognized at once as also being characteristically Jeffersonian.

These include the tenets that by the law of nature all men are equal; that government is based upon a compact or covenant, and derives its just powers from the consent of the governed;[104] that the powers of government are established and limited by a fundamental law which is unalterable by the ordinary legislature but which the people may change at their pleasure;[105] and that pursuant to such fundamental law certain natural rights (especially those relating to freedom of conscience) are reserved to the people and excluded from the sphere of authority entrusted to the civil government.[106]

Particularly with respect to freedom of religion, Jefferson and the Puritans spoke in kindred tones. His labors for freedom of religion were regarded by Jefferson as one of the three major services to the public by which he wished to be remembered.[107] He held that the civil government had no power over the realm of conscience.[108] From his metaphor the Supreme Court derived the "wall of separation between Church and State" as a principle of constitutional law.[109] But English Puritans had long before spoken to the same effect. During the debates of Cromwell's officers at Whitehall on December 14, 1648,[110] Captain John Clarke declared forthrightly that "no man or magistrate on the earth hath power to meddle . . . as between God and man."[111] This statement has a true Jeffersonian ring. Cromwell himself in addressing Parliament on September 12, 1654, said: "Some things are fundamentals. . . . In every government there must be somewhat fundamental, somewhat like a *Magna Charta*, that should be standing and unalterable. . . . [I]s not liberty of conscience a fundamental? . . . Liberty of conscience is a natural right."[112]

In addition to the foregoing basic similarities, several minor resemblances between Jeffersonian and Puritan ways of thinking may be noted. Thus when Jefferson in the Declaration of Independence used the phrase "pursuit of happiness" rather than "property" in conjunction with "life" and "liberty" as "unalienable rights," he may have done so because he regarded property as a right derived from the state, whereas he was enumerating in the declaration only "natural" rights, and "it is a moot question whether the origin of any kind of property is derived from nature at all."[113] Similarly Cromwell's son-in-law Henry Ireton during the debates at Putney in October, 1647, among officers in the "New-Model" army asserted that "the Law of God doth not give me property, nor the Law of Nature, but property is of human constitution."[114]

153

Opposition to monopolies was another policy with respect to which Jefferson and the Puritans were in agreement.[115] The right of expatriation was also recognized in Jeffersonian and Puritan thinking.[116]

Another curious notion which Jefferson and Puritan political philosophers shared was the doctrine of the "Norman yoke."[117] This was "an idea generally held by the reformers" of the Puritan era.[118] According to this theory, Anglo-Saxon liberties had been extinguished under a yoke of feudal tyranny as a result of the Norman conquest.[119] To restore the ancient rights of the people revolutionary measures of law reform were required.[120]

Lilburne emphatically condemned the entire common-law system as being derived from the Norman conquest. In his pamphlet *The Just Man's Justification*[121] he complained of the requirement that his lawsuit be handled by lawyers, whom he did not know and therefore did not trust.[122] But

> the greatest mischiefe of all, and *the oppressing bondage of England* ever since the *Norman yoke*, is this, I must be tryed before you by a Law (called the Common Law) that I know not, nor I think no man else, neither do I know where to finde it, or reade it; and how can I in such a case be punished by it, I know not: For, my Lord, I have been with divers Lawyers about this businesse, I cannot find two of them of one mind, or that can plainly describe unto mee what is the way of your goings; so that I professe I am in the darke amongst briers and thornes, and fast in a trap by the heeles, and enemies round about me ready to destroy me, if I be not very wary with my tongue and which way to get out, or how, or to whom to call to for help I know not, for such an unfathomable gulfe have I by a little search found, the Law practises in Westminster Hall to be, that seriously I thinke there is neither end nor bottom of them, so many uncertainties, formalities, puntillo's, and that which is worse, all the entryes and proceedings in Latine, a language I understand not, nor one of a thousand of my native Country men, so that my Lord, when J read the Scripture, and the House of Commons late unparaleled Declaration, it makes me thinke that the practizes in the Courts at Westminster, flow not from God nor his Law, nor the law of Nature and reason, no nor yet from the understanding of any righteous, just or honest men, but from the Devill and the will of Tyrants.[123]

God gives law to men plainly in their own language, Lilburne continued,[124] "but if wee will but impartially read in English histories, wee shall clearly find, that the tedious, unknowne, and impossible to be understood, common law practises in *Westnmister* Hall, came in by the will of a Tyrant, namly *William* the Conqueror, who by his sword conquered this Kingdome, and professed he had it from none but God and his sword." William was a *"perjur'd Tyrant"* who violated oaths thrice sworn to restore the laws of Edward the Confessor. Lilburne insisted that "the main stream of our Common Law, with the practice thereof, flowed out of *Normandy*, . . . *and therefore I say it came from the* Will *of a Tyrant*."[125]

Lilburne's harsh judgment of the common law did not apply to statutes. He praised Magna Carta, the Petition of Right, and the act abolishing the court of Star Chamber as "gallant Lawes."[126] Yet Magna Carta "falles short of *Edward the Confessour's lawes*, which the conqueror rob'd England of, and in stead of them, set up the dictates of his own will, whose *Norman* rules, and practizes to this day yet remaines in the administrations of the *Common Law* at *Westminster Hall*, by reason of their tediousness, ambiguities, uncertainties, the entryes in Lattine (*as bad as* the French) because it is not our own tongue, their forcing men to plead by Lawyers, and not permitting themselves to plead their own causes, their compelling of persons to come from all places of the Kingdome, to seeke for justice at *Westminster*, which is such an iron *Norman* Yoke, with fangs and teeth in it, that if wee were free in every particular else, that our hearts can thinke of, yet were we slaves by this alone."[127]

A somewhat different view was taken by Lord Coke. "For Coke, English law was continuous; the common law stretched back into the past to Anglo-Saxon times; there had been no conquest by William I in 1066; he was a claimant to the throne under ancient law, who had vindicated his claim by trial of battle with Harold."[128] But Jefferson accepted without reservation the Leveller theory that prefeudal Anglo-Saxon institutions were the true criterion of English and American liberties.[129]

In view of the foregoing demonstration of significant resemblances between Jefferson's proposals for law reform and those of the English Puritans, it seems reasonable to claim for the Sage of Monticello, in addition to his other familiar appellations (Apostle of Americanism, World Citizen, Friend of France, Father of American Democracy, Man of Letters, Classical Scholar, Lawyer, Legislator, Librarian, Slippery Politician, Epicure of the White House, Patron of the Arts, Architect and Builder, Designer of Landscapes, Humanist, Scientist, Naturalist, Meteorologist, Paleontologist, Vaccinator, Geographer, Agriculturalist, Natural Philosopher, and the like)[130] the title of Virginia Puritan and Law Reformer.[131]

Like all who labor in the ranks of the legal profession, Jefferson could regard his achievements as an ample reward for the arduous pilgrimage. "So venerable, so majestic, is this living temple of justice, this immemorial and yet freshly growing fabric of the Common Law, that the least of us is happy who hereafter may point to so much as one stone thereof and say, the work of my hands is there."[132] But he saw clearly that his efforts to improve the law were not the final word. He was well aware that "new occasions teach new duties" and that law reform is a perennial, or more truly, a perpetual quest.

In a familiar statement of his attitude toward change, the septuagenarian statesman declared: "I am certainly not an advocate for frequent and untried changes in laws and constitutions. . . . But I know also, that laws and institutions must go hand in hand with the progress of the human mind. . . . Each generation is as independent as the one preceding, as that was of all which had gone before. It has then, like them, a right to choose for itself the form of government it believes most promotive of its own happiness."[133] The Declaration of Independence, as mankind well knew, had claimed for the people of America the right to alter or abolish their existing form of government, "and to institute new Government, laying its Foundation on such Principles, and organizing its Powers in such Form, as to them shall seem most likely to effect their Safety and Happiness." So too, this was the right of every people, and in every age.[134]

Notes

(In note 3 and hereafter the letter P. (preceded by volume number and followed by page number) is used as an abbreviation for *The Papers of Thomas Jefferson*, edited by Julian P. Boyd and associates. In footnote 8 the letter F. is used for P. L. Ford (ed.), *The Works of Thomas Jefferson*; and in footnote 9, M. stands for *The Writings of Thomas Jefferson*. edited by Andrew Lipscomb and Albert E. Bergh, Memorial Edition. For other abbreviations see the bibliography.)

INTRODUCTION

1. According to college records, Jefferson began to pay board on March 25, 1760 and continued to do so for two years and one month, up to April 25, 1762. Dumas Malone, *Jefferson the Virginian*, 50; Edward Dumbauld, *Thomas Jefferson, American Tourist*, 31–32; Marie Kimball, *Jefferson: The Road to Glory 1743 to 1776*, 44.

2. In 1766 he spent about three months on a trip to New York. Malone, *Virginian*, 98–100.

3. In 1787 Jefferson, writing to a Frenchman to discount reports of highway robbery in America, stated that he had never heard of a trial for that offense although "I attended the bar of the Supreme court of Virginia ten years as a student, and as a practitioner." To Lormerie, July 6, 1787, 11 P. 554. The first entry in his carefully kept Case Book (Huntington Library) is dated February 12, 1767. The last (No. 939) is dated November 9, 1774. It would thus appear that his practice continued for eight years. On August 11, 1774, he arranged for Edmund Randolph, later to be the first attorney general of the United States, to take over most of his business. In 1782 for a period of six months, after his retirement as governor of Virginia, during his wife's ill health before her death occasioned his irrevocable return to public life, he is known to have written six legal opinions for clients. John C. Wyllie, "The Second Mrs. Wayland, An Unpublished Jefferson Opinion on a Case in Equity," *American Journal of Legal History*, Vol. IX, No. 1 (January, 1965), 64.

4. As shown by the Case Book referred to in note 3, *supra*, he handled almost the "thousand cases, many of them upon trifling or transitory matters, to represent nearly half a lifetime" of which Justice Holmes spoke. Oliver Wendell Holmes, *Collected Legal Papers*, 245.

5. A rough breakdown shows that matters dealing with land ownership predominated, as was natural in that era (there were 146 petitions, and 283 caveats). There were 47 opinions rendered to clients, 8 deeds or other instruments drawn, 36 cases of slander, 49 of assault and battery, 65 "actions on the case" (including 4 of libel and 1 of trover), 32 actions of debt, 2 of covenant, 1 of replevin, 4 of account, 15 of trespass, 17 of ejectment, 24 actions at common law, 54 suits in chancery, 11 chancery appeals, 15

appeals at common law, 9 crown cases, 2 ecclesiastical cases, and 12 of detinue for slaves. In 3 actions which he brought for the freedom of slaves he charged no fee. He represented plaintiffs and defendants with approximately equal frequency. See also Henry S. Randall, *The Life of Thomas Jefferson*, I, 47.

6. Jefferson was employed on a general retainer by William Byrd, John Buchanan, Robert Carter, David Ross, T. M. Randolph, Kippen & Co., Richard Woods, and Alexander Banks (Case Book, Nos. 122, 130, 464, 500, 730, 732, 733, 737).

7. According to Jefferson's executor, his average annual profits from the practice of law reached $3,000. Randall, *Life of Jefferson*, I, 48; Malone, *Virginian*, 123. In Jefferson's Account Book for 1773 he calculates his total "profits" (receipts plus unpaid fees due) for 1767 as £293 4s. 5 3/4d.; for 1768, £304 8s. 5d.; for 1769, £370 11s.; for 1770, £521 5s. 10 1/2d.; for 1771, £280 12s.; and for 1772, £349 5s. 3d. For this and much other helpful assistance I am indebted to James A. Bear, Jr. Fees charged in 1773 and 1774 were not totaled by Jefferson, but apparently amount to £335 9s. 10d. and £60 1s. 3d., respectively, according to the Fee Book (HL:HM 836). Payments received in those years were £260 3s. 9d. and £78 14s. The uncollected balances assigned to Randolph came to £532 10s. 8 3/4d. A note in the 1774 Account Book says "by a rough estimate Mr. Randolph will have about 2/3 of the whole fees to receive," which were there stated as £519 3s. 1 3/4d.

8. Writing to a New England friend of long standing, Jefferson said with regard to the triumph of republicanism throughout the nation: "In your corner alone priestcraft and lawcraft are still able to throw dust into the eyes of the people." To Elbridge Gerry, August 18, 1802, 8 F. 393.

9. Thus he recognizes that "lawsuits must be always attended to by some person on the spot." To Thomas Barclay, August 3, 1787, 6 M. 216. Likewise he recommends methodical arrangement of material, and industriously pressing the lawyer's docket of court cases. To William Short, June 1, 1780, 15 P. 586; to Caesar Rodney, December 31, 1802, 9 F. 415. The neophyte beginning practice should argue a "judiciously selected" case in order to present himself favorably "to the view of clients." To John G. Jefferson, April 14, 1793, 19 M. 104. Jefferson recognizes that the profession is overcrowded, and discusses the comparative advantages of locating in the city or in the country. To Benjamin Austin, January 9, 1816, 11 F. 500; to James Monroe, February 8, 1798, 8 F. 365. He compares law with medicine, to the disadvantage of the former. To David Campbell, January 28, 1810, 12 M. 356-57. Comparing law and divinity he asks "which was it that crucified its Savior? Or were the two professions united among the Jews?" To Levi Lincoln, August 25, 1811, 13 M. 82. It is the trade of lawyers "to question everything, yield nothing, & talk by the hour." 1 F. 91. The "venality" of certain members of the profession "makes me ashamed that I was ever a lawyer." To John Taylor, February 13, 1821, 18 M. 312.

10. Randall, *Life of Jefferson*, I, 50. A Spanish diplomat, praising Jefferson's inaugural address as president of the United States, spoke of "your speech, which could not easily be heard in the room of the Senate." De Yrujo to Jefferson, March 13, 1801, HL:HM 5963. Various instances are recorded where Jefferson made important public speeches. On the occasion at St. John's Church in Richmond when Patrick Henry made his famous speech on liberty or death, Richard Henry Lee and Jefferson also spoke. Edmund Randolph recorded: "Jefferson was not silent. He argued closely, profoundly and warmly on the same side. . . . Washington was prominent, though silent." William W. Henry, *Patrick Henry*, I, 260. See also William N. Brigance, *A History and Criticism of American Public Address*, II, 590. In the Virginia House of Delegates, in 1781, he defended his

record as governor. Malone, *Virginian*, 366. In the Continental Congress he was spokesman for Virginia's position regarding her western lands. Merrill Jensen, *The Articles of Confederation*, 153, 155; Charles Francis Adams, *The Works of John Adams*, II, 492–94, 502; *Journals of the Continental Congress*, VI, 1083, 1077. As to other speeches probably made by Jefferson, see George Mason to Jefferson, April 3, 1779, 2 P. 249; 1 P. 529, 535–39.

11. "Edmund Randolph's Essay on the Revolutionary History of Virginia," *Virginia Magazine of History and Biography*, Vol. XLIII, No. 2 (April, 1935), 115, 122–23. Two of Jefferson's legal arguments are reported in his posthumous volume of law reports. See pages 82–85, *infra*.

12. Madison to Samuel H. Smith, November 4, 1826, Gaillard Hunt (ed.), *The Writings of James Madison*, IX, 260.

13. Isaac Jenkinson, *Aaron Burr, His Personal and Political Relations with Thomas Jefferson and Alexander Hamilton*, 261; Irwin S. Rhodes (ed.), *The Papers of John Marshall*, I, 93.

14. Woodrow Wilson. *A History of the American People*, III, 183–84; (2d ed.), VI, 69. This statement may have been meant as praise of Jefferson. Because Wilson himself "had been a failure as a lawyer," he came to "look with contempt upon lawyers as a class." Arthur S. Link, *Wilson: The Road to the White House*, 11. See also Saul K. Padover, *Jefferson*, 23; and Albert J. Nock, *Jefferson*, 37–41. Dumas Malone, reviewing Nock's book in *American Political Science Quarterly*, Vol. XX, No. 4 (November, 1926), 907, 908, says: "To him the real Jefferson is the 'man of science,' ill at ease in law and politics, the experimental farmer and inventor of mechanical devices, the enthusiastic architect and landscape gardener." See also Charles Warren, *Jacobin and Junto*, 180.

15. Jefferson's service as a Virginia legislator began on May 8, 1769. On June 21, 1775, he took his seat in the second Continental Congress. In the fall of 1776 he left Congress and initiated his program of law reform in the Virginia House of Delegates. On June 1, 1779, he was chosen as governor, and served for two years. On November 4, 1783, he resumed his seat in Congress. On May 7, 1784, he was appointed minister plenipotentiary to join John Adams and Benjamin Franklin in negotiating treaties of commerce with foreign nations. In 1785 he succeeded Franklin as minister to France.

16. The desire for legislative reform which inspired Jefferson's revisal of Virginia laws extended to the field of international law. In the course of negotiating a treaty he thus exhorted a Prussian diplomat: "Why should not this Law of Nations go on improving? Ages have intervened between its several steps; but as knowledge of late encreases rapidly, why should not those steps be quickened?" To de Thulemeier, November 10, 1784, 7 P. 491. Jefferson strove "while we are reforming the principles to reform also the language of treaties . . . by simplifying their style and structure." *Ibid.*, 463, 466, 476–77. On the desirability of simplicity and clearness in statutory language, see 1 F. 70; to George Wythe, November 1, 1778, 2 P. 230; to Joseph C. Cabell, September 9, 1817, 17 M. 417–18. He praised the plain and intelligible style of Edward Livingston's code for Louisiana. To Livingston, March 25, 1825, 16 M. 114. But Jefferson realized that "Law . . . has a language of its own." To Peter Wilson, January 20, 1816, 14 M. 403.

17. Autobiography, 1 F. 66–67. See page 132, *infra*.

18. George Wythe dealt with later English statutes, and Edmund Pendleton with Virginia legislation. Wythe and Jefferson later re-executed Pendleton's portion as he had merely copied the laws to be preserved, without reforming the language. See note 16, *supra*.

19. *Report of the Committee of Revisors Appointed by the General Assembly of Vir-*

159

ginia In MDCCLXXVI. Richmond. 1784. For a convenient reprinting with thorough editorial comment on the revisal, see 2 P. 305–665.

20. William Waller Hening, *The Statutes at Large* [of Virginia], XII, 84–86. For Jefferson's draft, which was amended in the legislature, see 2 F. 438–41. The bill on primogeniture was adopted at the October session, 1785. Malone, *Virginian,* 254.

21. Madison to Jefferson, January 22, 1786, 9 P. 195.

22. Cesare B. Beccaria, *Dei delitti e delle pene* was an influential treatise from which Jefferson copied extensive extracts in his Legal Commonplace Book. Edward Dumbauld, *The Constitution of the United States,* 283.

23. Malone, *Virginian,* 269–73; Madison to Jefferson, February 15, 1787, 11 P. 152. The bill for diffusion of knowledge was not pushed.

24. This bill, introduced on October 14, 1776, passed the House on October 23 and the Senate on November 1. Malone, *Virginian,* 251–54. Numerous bills drafted by Jefferson may be found in I and II, P. For comments on the nature of entails and their evil effects, see Blackstone, *Commentaries,* II, 112–16.

25. Autobiography, 1 F. 77.

26. H. R. McIlwaine (ed.), *Journals of the Council of State of Virginia,* I, 359. He had also served in that office in 1771 and perhaps earlier. Dewey, "Thomas Jefferson's Law Practice," *Virginia Magazine of History and Biography,* Vol. LXXXV, No. 3 (July, 1977), 300. He probably practiced little if at all in the County Courts, though he became eligible to do so in 1765. *Ibid.,* 300–301. For Jefferson's description of the County Courts, see page 25, *infra.* See also Malone, *Virginian,* 119. The County Court was an agency of local government, as in England. See William S. Holdsworth, *A History of English Law,* I, 286–93. The Council also, during Jefferson's wartime governorship, tried a case of disaffection to the United States. McIlwaine, *Journals of the Council of State of Virginia,* II, 314.

27. Pendleton to Jefferson, July 22, 1776, August 10, 1776, 1 P. 472, 489.

28. Letters to Hay during the Burr trial are given in 10 F. 394–409. Hay's law studies had been guided by Jefferson. Edmund Randolph to Jefferson, October 9, 1781, 6 P. 128.

29. "I do not know the method of drawing up an indictment against an whole people." Edmund Burke, speech on conciliation with America, March 22, 1775. The Declaration of Independence was itself a legal document based on lawyerlike study of English constitutional history. Edward Dumbauld, *The Declaration of Independence and What It Means Today,* 20–23, 56.

30. Autobiography, 1 F. 78; Charles Warren, *A History of the American Bar,* 343–46. According to Warren, Judge Tapping Reeve did not begin his law school at Lichfield, Connecticut until 1784, five years after Wythe's appointment. *Ibid.,* 357–58. Some have claimed priority for the New England school. For comments on Wythe's courses see to James Madison, July 26, 1780, 3 F. 33; to Ralph Izard, July 17, 1788, 13 P. 372. In 1810 Jefferson learned that a manuscript of Wythe's lectures existed. To John Tyler, November 25, 1810, 11 F. 158–59.

31. Perhaps the most detailed course of reading was that prepared "near 50. years ago" for Bernard Moore, a revised copy of which was sent in a letter to John Minor, August 30, 1814, 11 F. 420–26. Other significant advice was given to Marie Jean Hérault, July 5, 1787, 6 P. 547–48; to John Garland Jefferson, June 11, 1790, 6 F. 71–73; to Dr. Thomas Cooper, January 16, 1814, 16 M. 55–59; to Dabney Terrell, February 26, 1821, 15 M. 318–22; to Nicholas P. Trist, June 14, 1822, Worthington C. Ford (ed.), *Thomas Jefferson Correspondence Printed from the Originals in the Collections of William K. Bixby,* 272–73. He directed James Monroe's law study. Monroe

to Jefferson, September 9, 1780, 3 P. 622; Jefferson to Monroe, October 5, 1781, 6 P. 127.

32. Madison to Jefferson, December 10, 1783, 6 P. 377.

33. To John Tyler, May 26, 1810, 11 F. 142.

34. To Thaddeus Kosciusko, February 26, 1810, 12 M. 369–70.

35. He was desirous that Francis Walker Gilmer accept the professorship of law, but ill health prevented. Richard B. Davis, *Correspondence of Thomas Jefferson and Francis Walker Gilmer*, 118, 120, 125, 128, 145, 146, 147, 149, 153. The chair was not filled until after the university had been open for more than a year, when John T. Lomax accepted. Roy J. Honeywell, *The Educational Work of Thomas Jefferson*, 100–102, 105. To Madison, Jefferson wrote: "In the selection of our Law Professor, we must be rigorously attentive to his political principles." *Ibid.*, 122.

36. Honeywell, 121–22.

37. On moot courts see letters to Madison and Izard cited in note 30, *supra*.

38. 11 F. 423–24 (letter to Minor, with corrections from University of Pennsylvania copy, see note 31, *supra*, and note 10, chapter I, *infra*). Jefferson's own Commonplace Book (Library of Congress, Jefferson papers) contains 905 items and digests the reports of Andrews, Coke's third *Institute*, Salkeld, Lord Raymond, Peere Williams. These are followed by extracts from Lord Kames, *Historical Law-Tracts*, Dalrymple's *History of Feudal Property*, Hale's *History of the Common Law*, Croke's reports, Pelloutier's *Histoire des Celtes*, Stanyan's *Grecian History*, Spelman's *Law Terms*, Somner's *Gavelkind*, and material on the Dutch and Swiss confederations, the history of Sweden and Poland, Sullivan's *Historical Treatise on the Feudal Laws*, Montesquieu's *Esprit des Lois*, Beccaria's *Dei delitti e delle pene*, and Eden's *Principles of Penal Law*. Passages of Helvetius, Buffon, and Voltaire are also copied. Apparently at a later date Jefferson added abstracts from Blackstone's reports, Robinson's admiralty reports, and some criticisms on Hume, the latest bearing date of March 24, 1824. The book contains brief extracts from other sources. Gilbert Chinard, *The Commonplace Book of Thomas Jefferson*, prints only the titles of the earlier, purely legal items, but gives in full the political material (beginning with Pelloutier) which seems to have been written during the Revolution when establishment of a federal government for the United States was a matter of uppermost concern in Jefferson's mind. Kimball, *Road to Glory*, 87–89, undertakes to date the items upon grounds of handwriting and paper. She attributes the first 174 entries to 1766. In another commonplace book on equity, now in the Huntington Library, Jefferson digested (in 2018 items) chancery cases reported in Salkeld, Vernon, Peere Williams, Equity Cases Abridged, Lord Kames, *Principles of Equity*, Cases in Chancery, Freeman's Reports, Chancery Reports, Precedents in Chancery, Atkyns, and added a final item on statutory construction citing 11 Co. Rep., Fortescue, 1 Siderfin, and Lex. Parl.

39. Edward Dumbauld (ed.), *Political Writings of Thomas Jefferson*, xxiii–xxv, xxxvii; Dumbauld, "Thomas Jefferson and American Constitutional Law," *Journal of Public Law*, Vol. II, No. 2 (Fall, 1953), 370–71.

40. Published at Charlottesville, Virginia, 1829.

41. Hening's *Statutes* were printed in large part from manuscript material carefully collected and preserved by Jefferson. One of his manuscript laws was relied upon by a court in holding that certain litigants, claimed as slaves, were in fact free. Edward Dumbauld, "A Manuscript from Monticello," *American Bar Association Journal*, Vol. XXXVIII, No. 5 (May, 1952), 389–92, 446–47.

42. Randolph G. Adams, "Thomas Jefferson Librarian," in *Three Americanists*, 69–96.

43. To Francis Eppes, July 30, 1787, HL:HM 5590; to David Campbell, March 27, 1792, 6 F. 454; to Robert R. Livingston, May 31, 1801, 9 F. 257; to John Tyler, November 25, 1810, 11 F. 159; to W. H. Torrance, June 11, 1815, 11 F. 472; to Spencer Roane, October 12, 1815, 11 F. 488; to Philip S. Barziza, February 24, 1817.

44. To Mrs. Miller, August 2, 1825, Ford, *Jefferson Correspondence*, 297.

45. In the New Orleans batture controversy against Edward Livingston, he engaged William Wirt, George Hay, and Littleton W. Tazewell to represent him. On April 12, 1812, Jefferson paid $100 apiece to Wirt, Hay, and Tazewell. He also retained Wirt and Hay in another case. To William Wirt, April 12, 1812, 11 F. 227. In a case involving his father-in-law's estate, Jefferson paid Hay and Archibald Thweatt $74 on November 22, 1811. In a case involving David Michie he paid $20 to William T. Gordon on July 31, 1812, and the same amount on November 1, 1813. On the same date he paid Philip Barbour $20, and on November 7, 1813, the same amount to Chapman Johnson. In a suit brought against Jefferson by one Scott, he paid Hay $50 on July 26, 1813, and Wirt the same amount on August 1, 1813. On October 12, 1823, he paid Philip Barbour $10 for an opinion in a case involving Francis Eppes, and on the same date paid $50 to D. M. Randolph as a witness against the Hudsons in a suit concerning limestone lands.

46. In a letter to David Hartley, September 5, 1785, 4 F. 456, he recommended Hamilton as a New York lawyer "now very eminent at the bar, and much to be relied on."

47. He asked Burr to press claims of Dr. James Currie and Lewis Burwell of Richmond against Robert Morris. To Burr, May 20, 1798, 8 F. 421–22; February 11, 1799, 9 F. 38.

48. He complained that "an increasing stiffness in the wrist, the effect of age & ancient dislocation begins to render the use of the pen painful and slow." To Governor William C. Nicholas, October 9, 1816. William Short, who had been Jefferson's secretary in Paris when Jefferson's injury was sustained, wrote: "I recollect, as if it had taken place yesterday, the dislocation of the wrist you complain of, & the bungling manner in which the surgeon Louis, so much celebrated for his general skill, treated that particular case." William Short to Jefferson, December 17, 1822, MHS. To try the effect of the waters of Aix on his wrist was one of the reasons for Jefferson's tour of southern France. Dumbauld, *American Tourist*, 83. Regarding the occasion of this injury, which probably occurred on September 16, 1786, see Lyman H. Butterfield and Howard C. Rice, Jr., "Jefferson's Earliest Note to Maria Cosway with Some New Facts and Conjectures on his Broken Wrist," *William and Mary Quarterly* (3d series) Vol. V, No. 1 (January, 1948), 26, 30–31.

49. Declining to give an opinion regarding an invention dealing with the steam engine, he wrote: "I am grown old, and worn down with the drudgery of the writing table. Repose and tranquility are become necessities of life for me. . . . [N]o office I ever was in has been so laborious as my supposed retirement at Monticello. Unable to bear up longer against it, either in body or mind, I am obliged to declare myself in a *state of insurgency*, and to assume my right to live out the dregs of life at least, without being under the whip & spur from morning to night." To William A. Burwell, February 6, 1817.

50. When publication of Joseph Delaplaine's *Repository* began, Jefferson took advantage of the writer's request for comments to furnish for publication a letter praising the work, but at the same time imploring the public to relieve him from the intolerable burden of correspondence. To Joseph Delaplaine, December 25, 1816. In the letter of the same date for publication he wrote: "You know my aversion to the drudgery of the writing table. The great affliction of my present life is a too oppressive correspondence. It is wearing me down in body and mind; and leaves me scarcely a moment to attend to my affairs or to indulge in the luxury of reading and reflection." *Ibid.* See also letter cited in note 51, *infra.*

51. To John Adams, January 11, 1817, 12 F. 47.

52. To Stephen Kingston, September 25, 1816. See Edward Dumbauld, "Thomas Jefferson and Pennsylvania Courts," *Pennsylvania Bar Association Quarterly*, Vol. XXXVII, No. 3 (March, 1966), 240–41.

53. To John M. Goodenow, June 13, 1822, 15 M. 382.

54. To Benjamin Rush, August 17, 1811, 11 F. 212; to William Short, October 31, 1819, 15 M. 221.

55. To Roger C. Weightman, June 24, 1826, 12 F. 477. Jefferson's death (and that of John Adams) occurred on the Fourth of July, 1826. The passing of these two venerable patriarchs on that date seemed to awaken throughout the land a deeper sense of national destiny, as if that solemn moment marked the end of childhood and the beginning of maturity for the rising young republic. Lyman H. Butterfield, "The Jubilee of Independence," *Virginia Magazine of History and Biography*, Vol. LXI, No. 4 (April, 1953) 119.

56. To James Madison, August 30, 1823, 12 F. 309.

CHAPTER I

1. Jefferson's bill "for the more general diffusion of knowledge," probably prepared in 1778, was introduced in the Virginia legislature in 1780. 2 P. 526–35. Public education, in his view, was an essential feature of "a government truly republican." 1 F. 75, 77–78. In later life he took pride in his accomplishments as "Father of the University of Virginia." 12 F. 483. To a colleague in that enterprise he wrote: "A system of general instruction, which shall reach every description of our citizens from the richest to the poorest, as it was the earliest, so will it be the latest of all the public concerns in which I shall permit myself to take an interest." To Joseph C. Cabell, January 14, 1818, 12 F. 87. Regarding Jefferson's contributions to public education, see books by Arrowood, Cabell, Conant, Henderson, and Honeywell.

2. To John Harvie, January 14, 1760, 1 P. 3. Jefferson counselled his grandson to avoid "company as the bane of all progress." To T. J. Randolph, December 30, 1809, MHS.

3. To John Brazier, August 24, 1819, 15 M. 209. See also to Joseph Priestly, January 27, 1800, 9 F. 103: "I thank on my knees, him who directed my early education, for having put into my possession this rich source of delight."

4. Randall, *Life of Jefferson,* I, 11, 17–19; Malone, *Virginian,* 39–45. In a letter of introduction for "the son of the only class-mate I now have living," Jefferson wrote that "his father Mr. James Maury & myself were boys together at the school of his grandfather in this neighborhood." To John Brown, November 3, 1820, MHS.

5. 1 F. 5. Some indication of the scope of Jefferson's own reading as a student may be gained from the extracts he copied from classical writers and English authors. See Gilbert Chinard, *The Literary Bible of Thomas Jefferson,* 38–207. The Manuscript volume is in the Library of Congress. Jefferson believed that study of the Anglo-Saxon language was useful to law students as a means of understanding certain legal terms. 18 M. 363. See also Karl Lehmann, *Thomas Jefferson American Humanist,* 32–67, and page 237n. 15, *infra.*

6. To Thomas Jefferson Randolph, November 24, 1808, 11 F. 79–80. As to Small and Wythe see pages 4–5, *infra.* Peyton Randolph, among other public trusts, had been attorney general of the colony of Virginia, and president of the Continental Congress.

7. Dumbauld, *American Tourist,* 31–32.

8. *Ibid.,* 38–40.

9. 1 F. 5–6. Concerning Small, see Herbert L. Ganter, "William Small, Jefferson's

Beloved Teacher," *William and Mary Quarterly* (3d series), Vol. IV, No. 4 (October, 1947), 505–11.

10. To General John Minor, August 30, 1814, 11 F. 420–21. This letter contained a revised copy of a course of reading prepared "near 50. years ago" for Bernard Moore, which "formed a basis for the studies of others subsequently placed under my direction." For a copy of the original letter to Minor, I am indebted to the law school of the University of Pennsylvania. A facsimile with transcription and comment has now been published by Morris L. Cohen. See also LC 35940–35942.

11. To Rev. James Madison, December 29, 1811, 19 M. 183: "I have been for some time rubbing up my mathematics from the rust contracted by fifty years' pursuits of a different kind. And thanks to the good foundation laid at college by my old master and friend Small, I am doing it with a delight and success beyond my expectation." Jefferson advised his grandson that "Mathematics requires absolutely the assistance of a teacher," whereas in some other studies "the books will teach you . . . as well as any master can." To T. J. Randolph, December 30, 1809, MHS.

12. To William Duane, October 1, 1812, 11 F. 267–68.

13. To Benjamin Rush, August 17, 1811, 11 F. 212. See also David Eugene Smith, "Thomas Jefferson and Mathematics," in *The Poetry of Mathematics and Other Essays*, 49–70.

14. To William Short, October 31, 1819, 15 M. 221.

15. 11 F. 421 (Minor letter, see note 10, *supra*). Jefferson advised his grandson that "it is only by a methodical distribution of our hours, & a rigorous, inflexible observance of it that any steady progress can be made." To T. J. Randolph, December 30, 1809, MHS.

16. 11 F. 422. The plan prepared for Bernard Moore was copied in 1814 "without change, except as to the books recommended to be read; later publications enabling me in some of the departments of science to substitute better, for the less perfect publications which we then possessed. In this the modern student has great advantage." 11 F. 420. In 1824, in response to a request to furnish for "Col. Bowyer a list of the books proper to prepare his son for the bar" Jefferson enclosed "copies of two letters, written formerly, and on occasions which called on me for full and mature consideration of the subject. These will not only specify the books to be read, but also the reasons for their preference, and the course of other reading auxiliary to the accomplishment of a well prepared lawyer." He suggested that it "might be useful to some young students" if the list were printed as a pamphlet. To T. M. Randolph, January 4, 1824, MHS.

17. Jefferson advised his future son-in-law that "the study of the law . . . like history, is to be acquired from books. All the aid you will want will be a catalogue of the books to be read, and the order in which they are to be read. It being absolutely indifferent in what place you carry on this reading, I should propose your doing it in France . . . [where] you will at the same time acquire the habit of speaking French." 10 P. 307. He also stressed the importance of regular exercise, of which "walking is best," to be done in the evening "after the digestion of the dinner is pretty well over." *Ibid.*, 308; to John Garland Jefferson, June 11, 1790, 6 F. 72. See also to T. M. Randolph, Jr., July 6, 1787, 11 P. 557. In his opinion "ethics, history and Law, if you please, . . . can as well be acquired in his closet, as at an University." To J. W. Eppes, June 30, 1820, MHS.

18. To Thomas Turpin, February 5, 1796, 1 P. 23–24. Hence it would be advantageous for Turpin to provide his son with the books needed for carrying on his studies "without subjecting him to the inconvenience of expending his time for the emolument of another." They would be needed anyhow when he began practice "for a lawyer without books would be like a workman without tools." The same counsel against studying in a law office was

given to a son of Jefferson's cousin George. To John Garland Jefferson, June 11, 1790, 6 F. 71.

19. Autobiography, 1 F. 78. Among Wythe's students were John Marshall, Henry Clay, and St. George Tucker. Jefferson as governor signed Marshall's license to practice law. Alfred Z. Reed, *Training for the Public Profession of the Law*, 72, 116–19.

20. To Ralph Izard, July 17, 1788, 13 P. 372.

21. 11 F. 425–26 (Minor letter, see note 10, *supra*). On Jefferson as a public speaker, see page xi, *supra.*

22. 11 F. 422–23. With this conspectus of the development of English law should be compared the longer accounts given in letters to Thomas Cooper, January 16, 1814, 14 M. 54–59, and to Dabney Terrell, February 26, 1821, 15 M. 318–22. The latter is intended to outline a course of reading for a law student. In the Cooper letter Jefferson states that he has always considered "a translation and notes on Bracton . . . as one of the greatest desiderata in the law." 14 M. 55. This task is now being performed by Professor Samuel E. Thorne of the Harvard Law School.

23. 11 F. 423–24 (with corrections from University of Pennsylvania copy). Concerning Jefferson's own commonplace books on law and equity, see page 15, *supra.*

24. 11 F. 423.

25. *Ibid.* (with corrections from University of Pennsylvania copy). For other lists of law books compiled by Jefferson, see letter to Marie Jean Hérault, July 5, 1787, 11 P. 547–48; to John Garland Jefferson, June 11, 1790, 6 F. 72; to Nicholas P. Trist, June 14, 1822, in Ford, *Jefferson Correspondence*, 272–73.

26. 11 F. 423.

27. On this topic see Julian S. Waterman, "Thomas Jefferson and Blackstone's Commentaries," *Illinois Law Review*, Vol. XXVII, No. 6 (February, 1933), 629–59.

28. Jefferson thought that Lord Mansfield's innovations made the law more uncertain "under pretence of rendering it more reasonable." To Philip Mazzei, November [28], 1785, 9 P. 71. On Mansfield, see Holdsworth, *History*, XII, 465–560. On his preference for Blackstone over Coke, see John Campbell, *The Lives of the Chief Justices of England*, II, 327, 379.

29. To James Madison, February 17, 1826, 12 F. 456.

30. James Wilson, in his lectures on law, also said of Blackstone "I cannot consider him a zealous friend of republicanism"and cautioned that in matters of public law he should be "consulted with a cautious prudence." *Works of James Wilson* (ed. by Robert G. McCloskey), I, 79, 80.

31. To John Tyler, June 17, 1812, 13 M. 166–67.

32. To John Tyler, May 26, 1820, 11 F. 142. See also to Thomas Cooper, January 16, 1814, 14 M. 58. In the passage quoted from the Tyler letter the more reliable transcription in E. Millicent Sowerby, *Catalogue of the Library of Thomas Jefferson*, II, 228, reads "institutes, all, and reports." This indicates that Jefferson's pupils read all four parts of Coke's *Institutes*, not just Coke on Littleton or the second *Institute*, dealing with Magna Carta and other statutes of constitutional import, as suggested by A. E. Dick Howard, *The Road from Runnymede*, 130. When I was a law student and asked Dean Roscoe Pound whether he agreed with Jefferson's advice to read Coke he recommended reading the second *Institute*. See Roscoe Pound, *Jurisprudence*, II, 119; V, 384–91. I did read "all" of the *Institutes* but am not sure whether it was genuinely useful.

33. St. George Tucker's *Blackstone's Commentaries*, published in 1803, filled five volumes rather than the usual four. Appendices amounted to two-fifths as many pages as the original text. These "discussions of subjects which neither form a part of, nor even

bear any relation to, the laws of England" (such as the constitutions of the United States and Virginia), together with notes indicating whether Blackstone's statements were applicable in Virginia or had been modified or superseded by federal or state legislation, Tucker believed, would render Blackstone's "incomparable work a safe, as well as a delightful guide" to Virginia law students. Tucker's *Blackstone*, I, vi–vii. His views regarding the superficial learning of lawyers who neglected Coke for Blackstone coincided with those of Jefferson. *Ibid.*, I, iii–iv. For biographical data on St. George Tucker (with a portrait and a reproduction of the title page of his edition of *Blackstone*) see Howard, *Road from Runnymede*, 100–101, 268–69. For an extensive review, by Robert M. Cover, of a 1969 reprint of Tucker's *Blackstone*, see *Columbia Law Review*, Vol. LXX, No. 8 (December, 1970), 1475–94.

34. Cover (at page 1476 of book review cited in preceding note) states that Tucker's volumes "stand as a singular example of an attempt to translate Jeffersonian political theory into law."

35. Tucker's *Blackstone*, I, xiv. Jefferson avowed his attachment "to science, & freedom, the first-born daughter of science." To François d' Ivernois, February 6, 1795, 8 F. 103. It was his "conviction that science is important to the preservation of our republican government" and that "liberty . . . is the great parent of science and of virtue; and that a nation will be great in both, always in proportion as it is free." To ———, September 28, 1821, 15 M. 340; to Joseph Willard, March 24, 1789, 7 M. 329.

36. Tucker's *Blackstone*, I, xvii. Jefferson advised his future son-in-law: "Every political measure will for ever have an intimate connection with the laws of the land; and he who knows nothing of these will always be perplexed and often foiled by adversaries having the advantage of that knolege over him." To T. M. Randolph, Jr., July 6, 1787, 11 P. 557–58.

37. Tucker's *Blackstone*, I, 426; II, App. 90–97. For Jefferson's view, see Dumbauld, *Political Writings of Jefferson*, 17, 190, and page 18, *supra*.

38. Tucker's *Blackstone*, I, x; III, App. 3–32. Jefferson's bill abolishing estates tail was enacted in 1776 when he was himself in the legislature. Hening, *Statutes*, IX, 226; 1 P. 560–62. His bill abolishing primogeniture became law in 1785, through James Madison's efforts. *Ibid.*, XII, 138; 2 P. 391–93. See page xii, *supra*.

39. Tucker appends an abstract of Jefferson's bill for the more general diffusion of knowledge. Tucker's *Blackstone*, II, 86–89. See 2 P. 526–33.

40. Tucker's *Blackstone*, I, xi; II, App. 31–85; III, App. 73–97. See Dumbauld, *Declaration*, 146; Dumbauld, *Constitution*, 188–89; Dumbauld, *Political Writings of Jefferson*, 60–62; Autobiography, 1 F. 76–77.

41. Tucker's *Blackstone*, II, App. 3–30. See note 18, Chapter VII, *infra*.

42. What could be worse, Tucker inquires, than for the individual states to find that through the agency of the federal judiciary "the unwritten law of a foreign country, differing from them in the fundamental principles of government, is paramount to their own written laws, and even to those constitutions, which the people had sealed with their blood, and declared to be forever inviolable"? Tucker's *Blackstone*, I, 427. Only through adoption by the law-making authority of each state did the common law of England come into force in America. *Ibid.*, I, 432. This was Jefferson's view. Dumbauld, *Political Writings of Jefferson*, 82. It was not established until 1812 by Supreme Court decisions. *U.S.* v. *Hudson*, 7 Cr. 32 (1812); *U.S.* v. *Coolidge*, 1 Wheat. 415 (1816); *Wheaton* v. *Peters*, 8 Pet. 591, 658–60 (1834); Dumbauld, *Constitution*, 156, 335, 381.

43. For Jefferson's view, forcefully expressed in his *Notes on Virginia*, see pages 23–24, *infra*. See also Dumbauld, *Political Writings of Jefferson*, 104, 107–10, 118; Dumbauld, *Constitution*, 18–19. The Virginia courts, like Tucker, did not accept Jefferson's position.

Dumbauld, "Thomas Jefferson and American Constitutional Law," *Journal of Public Law*, Vol. II, No. 2 (Fall, 1953), 373; *Kamper* v. *Hawkins*, 1 Brockenbrough & Holmes 20, 37, 69 (1793). See page 23, *infra*.

44. Tucker's *Blackstone*, I, viii, 88. Tucker agrees with Jefferson as to the defects of the instrument (*ibid.*, I, 115), but believes it to be a valid constitution. *Ibid.*, I, 83.

45. Tucker's *Blackstone*, I, iv, xiii, 442. Jefferson was also a collector of rare statutory materials. See pages 121–25, *infra*.

46. The first volume of Sir William Blackstone, *Commentaries on the Laws of England* was published in 1765; Vol. II in 1766, Vol. III in 1768, and Vol. IV in 1769. Because a second and third edition of the first two volumes had appeared, what was in fact the second edition of the whole work, published in 1770, was called the fourth edition. David A. Lockmiller, *Sir William Blackstone*, 157. Jefferson's set of the 1770 edition came to the Library of Congress when he sold his books to the government in 1815. Sowerby, II, 228. The Tucker edition is also listed. *Ibid.*, II, 230.

47. Jefferson's name does not appear in the list of subscribers at the beginning of Vol. IV of Bell's edition, which includes other famous figures, such as John Adams, John Dickinson, John Jay, R. R. Livingston, Gouverneur Morris, John Page, Richard Peters, Caesar Rodney, Isaac Roosevelt, Richard Stockton, Roger Sherman, Edmund Pendleton, James Wilson, and Thomas Marshall (father of Chief Justice John Marshall).

48. Jefferson's note on page 148 of his copy of Coke (Sowerby #1783) reads: "See 1. HPC. 425. 1 Hawks. 75. Foster 281, & B1. 188 all of contrary opinion." [This quotation was supplied by courtesy of William Howard Adams of the National Gallery of Art while the volume was on display as item 48 of the Bicentennial exhibition "The Eye of Thomas Jefferson."] Blackstone (*Commentaries*, IV, 188) gives the same references to Hale, Hawkins, and Foster which Jefferson cites. However, Jefferson's annotations in his Blackstone [Sowerby #1806] chiefly deal with freedom of religion, and include a dozen references to Philip Furneaux's "most sensible observations" in his *Letters to the Honourable Mr. Justice Blackstone* [Sowerby #1712 and #2899]. On "presentment of Englishry" see Plucknett, *Concise History*, 86–87.

49. Quoted in Holdsworth, *History*, XII, 724, where a good discussion of Blackstone's *Commentaries* is given at pp. 702–37.

50. Upon the same model Hugo Grotius constructed his celebrated *Introduction to the Jurisprudence of Holland*, published in 1631, which enjoyed among Dutch lawyers a renown and authority similar to that of Blackstone in common-law countries. Edward Dumbauld, *The Life and Legal Writings of Hugo Grotius*, 67, 123, 165.

51. On the struggles of Daniel Webster, Joseph Story, John Quincy Adams, and others to master Coke, see Howard, *Road from Runnymede*, 267; and Warren, *History of the American Bar*, 173–77.

52. To Thomas Cooper, January 16, 1814, 14 M. 57; to John Page, December 25, 1762, 1 P. 5; to Dabney Terrell, February 26, 1821, 15 M. 319. For a grandson Jefferson imported a set of Thomas, costing $30.91, along with Bacon's *Abridgement* at $45.09. More than one dollar per volume of this price was caused by import duty. To J. W. Eppes, June 10, 1822; to Francis Eppes, June 12, 1822, MHS. Jefferson had protested against this tax on knowledge in a circular letter of September 28, 1821, 15 M. 337–40.

53. Littleton's book, written in law French, was printed in 1481 or 1482. There was a second edition in 1483, and there had been over seventy editions published before 1628, when Coke's commentary was published. Holdsworth, *History*, II, 574.

54. Holdsworth, *History*, V, 466. It was published in 1628. The second and third *Institutes* were finished at the same time, but not published until 1641, as was the

fourth *Institute*, which was completed in the later years of Coke's life. He died in 1634. His papers were seized by the Crown as seditious while he lay on his deathbed, but in 1641 the House of Commons directed their return to his heir. *Ibid.*, V, 454–55.

55. *Ibid.*, V, 467. A similar technique characterizes the *Florum Sparsio ad Jus Justinianeum*, a little-known work on Roman law by Hugo Grotius. Dumbauld, *Grotius*, 162–64.

56. Preface to 10 Rep. xv–xviii, quoted in Holdsworth, *History*, V, 466. See also *ibid.*, II, 573.

57. Altogether some thirty-nine statutes are commented on. See Holdsworth, *History*, V, 468–69.

58. For a good account of Coke's influence on constitutional law, see John Dickinson, *Administrative Justice and the Supremacy of Law in the United States*, 79–104. See also Howard, *Road from Runnymede*, 118–32; Pound, *Jurisprudence*, I, 217; II, 119; Charles F. Mullett, "Coke and the American Revolution," *Economica*, Vol. XII, No. 38 (November, 1932), 457–71. For a judicious appraisal of Coke by an eminent legal historian, see Samuel E. Thorne, *Sir Edward Coke 1552-1952*, a lecture to the Selden Society on March 17, 1952. See also the extensive treatment in Holdsworth, *History*, V, 424–93, particularly 489–93.

59. See Holdsworth, *History*, V, 469–70.

60. *Ibid.*, V, 470–71.

61. The king's central courts at Westminster were the courts of Exchequer, King's Bench and Common Pleas. The Exchequer in the twelfth century was the earliest department of government to be organized separately, and late in the thirteenth century the financial and judicial sides of the Exchequer were differentiated, and the Court of Exchequer became a recognized judicial tribunal. Holdsworth, *History*, I, 231–32. As early as 1178, Henry II ordered that some of his judges should sit permanently at the court, and in 1215 Magna Carta required the Court of Common Pleas to maintain a fixed seat, usually at Westminster, while the Court of King's Bench followed the sovereign "wheresoever we shall be in England." William S. McKechnie, *Magna Carta* 261, 267; Sir Frederick Pollock and Frederic W. Maitland, *The History of English Law before the Time of Edward I*, I, 198. The House of Lords, the Privy Council, and the Lord Chancellor also retained judicial authority.

62. Because English law after Henry II had become a homogeneous system of law enforced by the central government through the royal courts, Roman law was never received *en masse* in England, as it was in nations on the Continent. Frederic W. Maitland, *English Law and the Renaissance*, 35; William Stubbs, *Seventeen Lectures on the Study of Medieval and Modern History*, 157; Holdsworth, *History*, IV, 285–86.

63. Julius Goebel, "King's Law and Local Custom in Seventeenth Century New England," *Columbia Law Review*, Vol. XXXI, No. 3 (October, 1931), 416–48; Zechariah Chafee, "Colonial Courts and the Common Law," *Proceedings* of the Massachusetts Historical Society (1952), 132–59.

64. 3 *Inst.* 28–31; 4 *Inst.* 58–60.

65. See page xiii, *supra.* On the Reports, see J. H. Baker, "Coke's Note-books and the Sources of his Reports," *Cambridge Law Journal*, Vol. XXX, No. 1 (April, 1972), 59–86; Theodore F. T. Plucknett, "The Genesis of Coke's Reports," *Cornell Law Quarterly*, Vol. XXI, No. 2 (February, 1942), 190–213.

66. In the Continental or civil law systems based upon the Roman law tradition, primary importance is given to legislatively enacted codes. For an excellent discussion of the

role of the judiciary in various legal systems, see John P. Dawson, *The Oracles of the Law*, xiii *et passim*. As to England, see George W. Keeton, *English Law: The Judicial Contribution.*

67. On the doctrine of *stare decisis* in Anglo-American law, see Eugene Wambaugh, *The Study of Cases*, 15, 104–108; Holdsworth, *History*, XII, 146–62; and articles by Arthur L. Goodhart, T. Ellis Lewis, and Joseph H. Smith. Francis Bacon claimed credit for having secured, in 1617 while Lord Chancellor, the appointment of two paid reporters at £100 per year. Francis Bacon, *Works*, XIII, 69, 264–66. He believed that "great Judges [such as Dyer and Coke] are unfit persons to be reporters, for they have either too little leisure or too much authority." Dyer's work "is but a kind of note book," and Coke's reports "hold too much *de proprio.*" *Ibid.*, XII, 86.

68. Colonial courts before the Revolution often found themselves in this unsatisfactory situation. Julius Goebel, *History of the Supreme Court of the United States: Antecedents and Beginnings to 1801*, 112. The first substantial published volume of American law reports was that of Ephraim Kirby in 1789, covering cases in the Superior Court of Connecticut from 1785 to May, 1788. Francis Hopkinson's volume of judgments in the Admiralty of Pennsylvania seems to have preceded Kirby's by about a month, but contained only six cases filling only 131 pages. Kirby reported 201 cases in 456 pages, and patterned his work on English models. Frederick C. Hicks, *Materials and Methods of Legal Research* (3d ed.), 132; cf. Alan V. Briceland, "Ephraim Kirby: Pioneer of American Law Reporting, 1789," *The American Journal of Legal History*, Vol. XVI, No. 4 (October, 1972), 297, 307, 311, 315. In 1790 Alexander Dallas began his four-volume series of reports of cases by courts sitting in Philadelphia. J. C. Bancroft Davis, Appendix to 131 U.S. xv. Since then an avalanche of reports has overwhelmed the legal profession in this country.

69. The earliest cases begin with the twelfth year of the reign of Edward I in 1283; the last end with the twenty-seventh year of Henry VIII in 1535. The earliest printed Year Book is of the year 1292. For a good discussion of the Year Books, see Holdsworth, *History*, II, 525–56; and Dawson, *Oracles of the Law*, 50–65.

70. On the reporters, see Holdsworth, *History*, V, 355–74; VI, 551–73; XII, 102–46; XIII, 424–43; XV, 257–68; Dawson, *Oracles of the Law*, 65–80; Hicks, *Materials and Methods of Legal Research*, 114–29. For fuller treatment see John W. Wallace, *The Reporters*; W. T. S. Daniel, *The History and Origin of the Law Reports*; John C. Fox, *A Handbook of the English Law Reports*; Van Vechten Veeder, "The English Reports, 1587–1865" in *Select Essays in Anglo-American Legal History*, II, 123–68; William S. Holdsworth, *Sources and Literature of English Law;* Holdsworth, "The Named Reporters," *Anglo-American Legal History Series.*

71. Dawson, *Oracles of the Law*, 68. Before Coke, the pioneer was Edmund Plowden, the first of whose two volumes appeared in 1571. Then in 1585, three years after the death of Sir James Dyer, chief justice of the Court of Common Pleas, three volumes were published from notes of cases which he had prepared for his own use. *Ibid.*, 65–67. After Coke, numerous reports, of varying degrees of reliability and usefulness, were issued. The present Council of Law Reporting was established in 1865.

72. Warren, *History of the American Bar*, 160–64.

73. Jefferson acknowledged that he had not kept up with the reports appearing after Blackstone's time. See the letter to Terrell, note 22, *supra*. In a passage of that letter omitted at 15 M. 321 he refers to a case which should be turned to while reading Coke-Littleton on warranty. "It explains that subject easily which Coke makes difficult and too artificial." MHS. The case mentioned, *Gardner* v. *Sheldon*, Vaughan 259 (1669), does

not deal with warranty, but with the difference between a contingent remainder and an executory devise. Perhaps *Hayes* v. *Bickerstaff*, Vaughan 118 (1670), or *Bole* v. *Horton*, Vaughan 360 (1674), was meant.

74. The nominal author, Matthew Bacon, an Irish barrister, published the first edition anonymously as "By a gentleman of the Middle Temple." There were five volumes, appearing from 1736 to 1766. Bacon died before the work was completed; the material from the title "Sheriff" was furnished by Sayer and Ruffhead. Holdsworth, *History*, XII, 168–71.

75. Joseph Story, "Digests of the Common Law," in *The Miscellaneous Writings of Joseph Story*, 379, 386–87; Warren, *History of the American Bar*, 150, 170, 172; Howard, *Road from Runnymede*, 132; Goebel, *History of the Supreme Court*, 125, 637. In 1814, writing to Thomas Cooper, Jefferson said that the works of Coke, Matthew Bacon, and Blackstone "are possessed and understood by everyone." 14 M. 59, note 22, *supra*. A survey of 47 colonial libraries showed that 27 had Coke's works. In opinions of colonial courts before 1776, Coke was cited 294 times, and Bacon's *Abridgement* 172 times. Rodney L. Mott, *Due Process of Law*, 89. Eight American editions of Bacon have been published. Hicks, *Materials and Methods of Legal Research*, 289.

76. Story, *Miscellaneous Writings*, 387. See also *ibid.*, 394.

77. *Ibid.*, 386–87.

78. Hicks, *Materials and Methods of Legal Research*, 289.

79. In similar fashion the professorship at Harvard first held by Justice Joseph Story was founded in 1829 by Nathan Dane from proceeds of his nine-volume digest of American law published in 1823–29. Arthur E. Sutherland, *The Law at Harvard*, 95–99. On abridgments and digests, see Hicks, *Materials and Methods of Legal Research*, 282–94; Story, *Miscellaneous Writings*, 383–89; Holdsworth, *History*, II, 544–45; V, 375–78; XII, 162–69; and John D. Cowley, *A Bibliography of Abridgments, Digests, Dictionaries and Indexes of English Law to the Year 1800*.

80. Quoted in Holdsworth, *History*, V, 378. Roger North (1653–1734) gave similar advice. The decay of teaching in the Inns of Court made it important for students to assemble their own materials. *Ibid.*, VI, 494–96.

81. "This was no doubt an effective discipline but it was certainly laborious; many of these seventeenth-century commonplace books have come down to us in almost their original condition, that is to say almost completely blank." Some lawyers would take apart several such abridgments and reassemble them in one large alphabet. Plucknett, *Concise History*, 243.

82. There are 905 items in the Legal Commonplace Book, and 2018 in the Equity Commonplace Book.

83. Concerning a third similar compilation, containing items extracted by Jefferson from the writings of poets and philosophers, see note 5, *supra*.

84. The distinction between common law and equity was important until recent years because each was a separate system of rules applied by separate courts. Frederic W. Maitland, *Equity and the Forms of Action at Common Law*, 1. In early times the chancellor was usually an ecclesiastical dignitary and as "keeper of the king's conscience" undertook to mitigate the strictness of common law rules by an infusion of ethical and moral standards of equity and fairness. Likewise in Roman law the praetor acted *juris civilis adjuvandi aut supplendi aut corrigendi causa* to mitigate the rigor of the strict civil law. In Coke's day the chancery and common law courts were distinct and rival tribunals. Modern law seeks to amalgamate in a single body of law administered by a single tribunal the doctrines developed by both types of courts in the course of their history. Dumbauld, *Constitution*, 335.

A detailed explanation of equity is given by Jefferson in his letter of November [28], 1785, to Phillip Mazzei, 9 P. 67–72.

85.   Chinard, *Commonplace Book of Jefferson* contains an informative introduction describing the contents of the book, and prints those portions which are of political rather than strictly legal interest. The MS volume is in the Library of Congress. Chinard is skeptical regarding the possibility of dating the items with precision upon the dubious evidence of ink and handwriting. From the content he determines that items 1–550 were written when Jefferson was a law student or a young lawyer; that items 500–881 (on feudalism, federalism, Montesquieu, Beccaria, Voltaire, and the like) were written between 1774 and 1776; items 882–900 after 1781, and items 901–904 after 1801. Item 905 refers to a debate in the House of Commons on March 23, 1824. *Ibid.,* 13–14. Kimball, *Road to Glory,* 87–88, concludes from analysis of paper and handwriting that the first 174 items were written in 1766, and items 175–695 after August 1767.

86.   The MS volume is in the Huntington Library, Brock Collection, BR 13. Kimball, *Road to Glory,* 89, from analysis of the handwriting concludes that this book was begun in 1765 and that entries in it and the Legal Commonplace Book were made concurrently.

87.   William Salkeld [1671–1715], *Reports of Cases adjudged in the Court of King's Bench: with some special cases in the Courts of Chancery, Common Pleas, and Exchequer, alphabetically digested under proper heads: from the first year of K. William and Q. Mary to the tenth year of Q. Anne.* (This title from Sowerby #2073 describes the 6th edition of 1791.) The first two volumes were first published in 1717 under the supervision of Lord Hardwicke; Vol. III appeared in 1743. Wallace, *Reporters,* 400; Holdsworth, *History,* VI, 553. Items 79–241 of the Legal Commonplace Book, and items 1–21 of the Equity Commonplace Book are from Salkeld. The first 28 items of the Legal Commonplace Book are from *Reports of Cases argued and adjudged in the Court of King's Bench,* by George Andrews (fl. 1776), of the Middle Temple, published in 1754, covering the period 1737 to 1740. Sowerby #2080. On Andrews, see Veeder, *Select Essays,* II, 142. Items 29–77 are from Coke's *Institutes.* Item 78 involves statutes.

88.   Robert Raymond [1672–1733], *Reports of Cases argued and adjudged in the Courts of King's Bench and Common Pleas, in the Reigns of the late King William, Queen Anne, King George the First, and King George the Second.* Sowerby #2078. Lord Raymond became chief justice of the Court of King's Bench in 1724. His reports were published in 1743, and cover the period 1694–1732. Wallace, *Reporters,* 401–407; Holdsworth, *History,* XII, 437–42. Items 242–549 (except 485–87, 490, 504, and 527) in the Legal Commonplace Book are from Lord Raymond's reports.

89.   Of 905 items, 407 are from Salkeld or Lord Raymond. There are only 111 other abstracted cases from law reports (Nos. 588–693, 744, 899–903): the remainder of the compilation is composed of extracts from numerous authors, mainly on feudalism, federalism, and other political topics.

90.   Wallace, *Reporters,* 399; Holdsworth, *History,* VI, 555.

91.   Holdsworth, *History,* VI, 563. The third volume is considered to be of no authority, as it was printed from scattered papers not prepared for publication. Wallace, *Reporters,* 400; Holdsworth, *History,* VI, 558.

92.   Holdsworth, *History,* VI, 560; XII, 438; Wallace, *Reporters,* 401. Sir John Holt (1642–1710) was chief justice of the King's Bench from 1689 to 1710, and rendered notable decisions in the field of constitutional, criminal, and commercial law. William S. Holdsworth, *Some Makers of English Law,* 153–60; Holdsworth, *History,* VI, 264–72, 516–22.

93. See note 25, *supra*.

94. For a modern biography of Kames see Ian Ross, *Lord Kames (1696–1782) and the Scotland of his Day*. See also Holdsworth, *History*, XII, 583–84. Blackstone, *Commentaries*, III, 433, 441, referred to Kames as "a very ingenious writer in the other part of the island . . . whose works have given exquisite pleasure to every contemplative lawyer."

95. In the Library of Congress [Sowerby #1254] is a first edition of Henry Home, Lord Kames, *Essays on the Principles of Morality and Natural Religion* (1751) with marginal notes in Jefferson's hand. See Adrienne Koch, *The Philosophy of Thomas Jefferson*, 17–19, 45, 52. Jefferson also owned his *Introduction to the Art of Thinking* (2d ed. 1764, first published 1761) [Sowerby #1345], his *Elements of Criticism* (3d ed. 1765, first published 1762) [Sowerby #4699], his *Essays upon several subjects concerning British Antiquities* (3d ed. 1763, first published 1747) [Sowerby #2007]; his *The Gentleman Farmer* (2d ed. 1779, first published 1776) [Sowerby #710], as well as several of his works on legal subjects.

96. Published in 1760. Sowerby #1716. Items 1077–1131 in Jefferson's Equity Commonplace Book are from the first edition of Henry Home Kames, *Principles of Equity*. [Note that two items are numbered 1082.] Extracts from Kames, *Historical Law-Tracts* (first published anonymously in 1758) [Sowerby #2008] were included in Jefferson's Legal Commonplace Book (Nos. 557–568), printed in Chinard, *Commonplace Book of Jefferson*, 95–135.

97. Often called *Equity Cases Abridged*, the first part was first published in 1732, a second part in 1756. Sowerby #1755. See Holdsworth, *History*, XII, 171–72. Material from Peere Williams was used. See also Wallace, *Reporters*, 490. Items 1064–1076 of the Equity Commonplace Book are from "Abr. ca. eq."

98. Published from his manuscripts by his son, the first edition appearing in 1740, with a third volume in 1749. Sowerby #1750.

99. Cases from Peere Williams are digested in the Legal Commonplace Book (Nos. 485–87, 490, 504, 550–54) and marginal citations from Peere Williams added in other cases (for example, Nos. 128, 129, and 527). Items 619–1063 in the Equity Commonplace Book are from Peere Williams, with supplemental citations from Peere Williams inserted in prior cases (scattered, for example, from 550 to 617).

100. Holdsworth, *History*, XII, 140; Wallace, *Reporters*, 498–501. Lord Eldon thought the third volume less authentic than the first two. *Ibid.*, 499.

101. Henry Ballow (1707–1782) published his treatise anonymously in 1737. John de Grenier Fonblanque (1760–1837) brought the treatise up to date by inserting "voluminous notes." The first edition of the revised treatise appeared in 1793–94. Sowerby #1720.

102. Holdsworth, *History*, VI, 614. For John Selden's witticism see *The Table Talk of John Selden*, 61.

103. On the importance of Lord Hardwicke, see Holdsworth, *History*, XII, 237–97; and Holdsworth, *Makers of English Law*, 176–90. See also note 118, *infra*.

104. Dr. Johnson told Boswell (April 5, 1776) that all his knowledge of law was derived from Ballow. When Boswell wanted to know more about Ballow, Dr. Johnson exclaimed: "Sir, I have seen him but once these twenty years. The tide of life has driven us different ways." Quoted in Holdsworth, *History*, XII, 191.

105. The book thus served well to refresh the recollection of a practitioner familiar with the subject, but was of little utility to beginners. The owner of the copy in Lincoln's Inn library in 1781 inserted citations in his copy. Holdsworth, *History*, XII, 192.

106. *Ibid.*, 193. For a synopsis of Ballow's treatment of equity, see *ibid.*, 222–37.

107.　Warren, *History of the American Bar*, 150.

108.　On equity reports, see Holdsworth, *History*, VI, 616–19.

109.　See notes 87, 96, 97, 98–100, *supra*.

110.　*Cases argued and adjudged in the High Court of Chancery*.

111.　Holdsworth, *History*, VI, 617. See note 114, *infra*. Vernon covers the period 1681–1720. Wallace, *Reporters*, 493. His reports are brief and often inaccurate. Veeder, *Select Essays*, II, 150. Items 22–618 of the Equity Commonplace Book are from Vernon.

112.　These were *Reports of cases taken and adjudged in the Court of Chancery* [Sowerby # 1746], of which the first volume was published in 1693, the second in 1697, and the third in 1716; and *Cases argued and decreed in the High Court of Chancery* [Sowerby #1744], of which the first volume was published in 1697, the second between May 1700 and March 1701/1702, and the third in 1702. Holdsworth, *History,* VI, 616–17. According to Sowerby, II, 203: "These reports [Sowerby #1746] were published anonymously, but according to a manuscript note in the British Museum copy, were compiled from the papers of Sir Anthony Keck, 1630–1695, English lawyer, and commissioner of the great seal" in 1689. See note 114, *infra*. Wallace, *Reporters*, 480, considers *Cases . . . in . . . Chancery* to be of doubtful authority. On *Reports . . . in . . . Chancery*, see *ibid.*, 477–79. Veeder considers *Cases . . . in . . . Chancery* as "the best of the earlier reports." *Select Essays*, II, 149.

113.　He used only the first two volumes of each set of reports. Items 1587–1779 of the Equity Commonplace Book are from "1 Ch. Rep." and "2 Ch. Rep." while items 1132–1402 are from "1 Ca. Ch." and "2 Ca. Ch."

114.　Items 1403–1586 in the Equity Commonplace Book are from "Fr. C. R." Freeman (1646–1710) had been Lord Chancellor of Ireland. Keck's manuscripts were supposed to have been used for some part of the Chancery Reports and Chancery Cases (see note 112, *supra*) as well as for the reports of his son-in-law Freeman and possibly for those of his other son-in-law Vernon. See note 111, *supra*. Holdsworth, *History*, VI, 618–19.

115.　Items 1780–1999 of the Equity Commonplace Book are from "Pr. Ch." On this work see Wallace, *Reporters*, 497. Veeder rates it as fair, whereas Peere Williams is excellent. *Select Essays*, II, 151. The second edition, described in Sowerby #1748, was edited by Thomas Finch, 1756–1810, and usually known as Finch's Precedents. Sowerby gives the date of publication of the first edition, without Finch's notes, as 1747. Richard W. Bridgman, *A Short View of Legal Bibliography*, 264, gives 1733, as does Holdsworth.

116.　The manuscript was clandestinely stolen from Baron Gilbert (see pages 8, 14, *supra)* after his death and printed. The cases cover the period 1687 to 1722, and according to tradition those down to 1708 were supplied by Pooley, formerly supposed to be the author of the first volume of *A General Abridgment of Cases in Equity* (see note 97, *supra*). Holdsworth, *History*, VI, 618.

117.　The second edition of 1781 is described in Sowerby #1754.

118.　On the importance of Hardwicke, see note 103, *supra*. Not only did he systematize equity, but he decided cases promptly. "As I am satisfied what decree I ought to make, it is not proper to put it off, merely for the sake of putting my thoughts into better order and method." Holdsworth, *History*, XII, 295. But he considered giving reasons for a decision as the greatest of all securities for honesty on the part of judges, for "some persons would be ashamed to talk nonsense to the world in support of a judgment that they would suffer themselves to give silently." *Ibid.*, 250. "I always thought it a much greater reproach to a judge to continue in his error than to retract it." *Ibid.*, 261.

119.　Two subsequent volumes were issued in 1767 and 1768. On Atkyns see Wallace, *Reporters*, 510. Items 2000–2017 of the Equity Commonplace Book are from "1 Atk."

120. Item 2018. Authorities cited here, besides Coke's *Reports*, are Sir John Fortescue (1394?–1476?), *De Laudibus Legum Angliae*, a work written about 1470 for the instruction of Edward Prince of Wales in exile at Berri, first printed in 1567 and translated in 1737 [Sowerby #1775]; [George Petyt], *Lex Parliamentaria*, published in 1690 [Sowerby #2893]; and Sir Thomas Siderfin (fl. 1687) *Les Reports des divers special cases argue and adjudge en le Court del Bank le Roy*, published in 1683. A second volume was issued in 1683/84. Sowerby #2059. Siderfin is considered as inaccurate, and of small consequence. Wallace, *Reporters*, 33, 295; Veeder, *Select Essays*, II, 137.

121. "When I was a student of the law, now half a century ago, after getting through Coke Littleton, whose material cannot be abridged, I was in the habit of abridging and common-placing what I read meriting it, and of sometimes mixing my own reflections on the subject." To Thomas Cooper, Feb. 10, 1814, 14 M. 85.

122. Legal Commonplace Book, items 873 and 879; Chinard, *Commonplace Book of Jefferson*, 351–56, 359–63. The reference in the preceding note to law study "half a century ago" does not furnish a precise date for items 873 and 879. The first item contains a citation to the fourth volume of Blackstone, which was published in 1769. The second item cites David Houard's treatise on Anglo-Norman customs, published in 1776 [Sowerby #1774], and refers to Sir William Jones on bailments, published in 1781 [Sowerby #1982]. It is possible that Jefferson's interest in church law may have been aroused by his involvement in a case argued in 1771. See note 74, chapter 4, *infra*. His legislative activities in the fall of 1776 on behalf of religious freedom may also have stimulated his study of this subject. See 1 P. 525–58.

123. See note 27, chapter 4, *infra*.

124. See pages 76–82, chapter 4, *infra*. In two of the cases reported Jefferson himself participated as counsel.

CHAPTER II

1. Sowerby #3085. A manuscript version, collated with the printed pamphlet and with Jefferson's corrected copy in the Library of Congress, appears in 1 P. 121–37. For convenience I cite the facsimile edition by Thomas P. Abernethy (New York, 1943) of the copy in the John Carter Brown Library.

2. Dumbauld, *Declaration*, 21.

3. Peyton Randolph.

4. To John W. Campbell, September 3, 1809, 11 F. 115–16. In response to a proposition to publish "a complete edition of my different writings," Jefferson states in this letter that "no writings of mine, other than those merely official, have been published" [except the *Notes on Virginia*, the *Summary View*, and the *Parliamentary Manual*]. See also Autobiography, 1 F. 15 and 1 P. 669–76.

5. *Works of John Adams*, II, 511, 513–15.

6. As to Jefferson's emphasis on expatriation as a natural right, see notes 25 and 64, chapter 7, *infra*.

7. On consent of the governed, as proclaimed in the Declaration of Independence, see Dumbauld, *Declaration*, 69–71, 121.

8. On adoption of the common law, see *ibid.*, 33.

9. On the concept of connection through the crown, see *ibid.*, 121, 151–52.

10. *Summary View*, 6.

11. *Ibid.*, [7].

12. *Ibid.*, 11.

13. *Ibid.*, 16. In the Declaration of Independence, one of the charges against the king was that "he has combined with others to subject us to a Jurisdiction foreign to our Constitution, and unacknowledged by our Laws, giving his Assent to their Acts of pretended Legislation." Dumbauld, *Declaration*, 119–20.

14. *Summary View*, 16.

15. *Ibid.*, 16. Thus he had thwarted abolition of slavery. *Ibid.*, 16–17. A passage condemning the king for having "prostituted his negative" in this respect was eliminated by Congress from Jefferson's draft of the Declaration of Independence. Dumbauld, *Declaration*, 146.

16. *Ibid.,* 87.

17. *Ibid.*, 91; *Summary View*, 17.

18. Dumbauld, *Declaration*, 93–100; *Summary View*, 17–18.

19. Dumbauld, *Declaration*, 102–105; *Summary View*, 18–19. "From the nature of things, every society must at all times possess within itself the sovereign powers of legislation." *Ibid.*, 19.

20. *Summary View*, 19–21.

21. *Ibid.*, 20–21. Following Jefferson, I have changed "farmers," which appears in the printed text, to "laborers." 1 P. 137. Regarding the controversy in Virginia over the "pistole fee," see Dumbauld, *Declaration*, 105–108. Concerning Jefferson's view of Anglo-Saxon liberties and the "Norman Yoke," see note 15, chapter 7, *infra*.

22. *Summary View*, 21.

23. Dumbauld, *Declaration*, 117–18, 165.

24. This was a grievance asserted in the Declaration of Independence. Dumbauld, *Declaration*, 118–19.

25. *Summary View*, 22. I follow 1 P. 134, 137.

26. "*Ipse autem rex non debet esse sub homine sed sub deo et sub lege, quia lex facit regem.*" *Bracton on the Laws and Customs of England* (translated by Samuel E. Thorne), II, 33. See *ibid.*, 306: "*facit enim lex quod ipse sit rex.*" See also *ibid.*, 110.

27. *Summary View*, 22–23.

28. These queries are printed in 4 P. 166–67.

29. For Jefferson's account of the work, see Autobiography, 1 F. 93–95. His correspondence on the subject is collected in Sowerby #4167, IV, 301–30. On the 1800 appendix about Logan's speech, see *ibid.* #3225, III, 304–15 and #4051, IV, 224–27. For comment on the work, see Marie Kimball, *Jefferson: War and Peace*, 262–304; Malone, *Virginian*, 373–77 and *Rights of Man*, 93–106, 497, 505–506.

30. Dumbauld, *American Tourist*, 193; Malone, *Virginian*, 373–77. He had commenced gathering material for them late in 1780. To D'Anmours, November 30, 1780, 4 P. 168.

31. To Marbois, December 20, 1781, 6 P. 141–42. Because of delay in transmission, Marbois did not receive them until March or April of 1782.

32. To Chastellux, January 16, 1784, 6 P. 467: "I have lately had a little leisure to revise them. . . . They are swelled nearly to treble bulk."

33. To Charles Thomson, May 21, 1784, 7 P. 282.

34. The printing was finished on May 10, 1785. To Madison, May 11, 1785, 8 P. 147. The title page of this first edition of the *Notes* bears the date 1782. For this and other reasons the work is "one which bibliographers love." Adams, "Thomas Jefferson, Librarian," in *Three Americanists*, 78.

35. Alice H. Lerch, "Who Was the Printer of Jefferson's Notes?" in *Bookman's Holiday*, 44–56.

36. To John Vaughan, May 2, 1805, Sowerby, IV, 309. See also to M. L. and W. A. Davis, October 14, 1800, *ibid.*, 325: "The most correct edition is the one originally published in Paris. Stockdale's London edition is tolerably correct."

37. To C. W. F. Dumas, February 2, 1786, 9 P. 244; to Madison, February 8, 1786, 9 P. 265; to Edward Bancroft, February 26, 1786, 9 P. 299.

38. Jefferson prepared a seven-page list of "Errors in the Abbé Morellet's translation of the Notes on Virginia the correction of which is indispensable." 11 P. 37–38. Morellet felt obliged to soften some of the passages about religion for fear of censorship, and considered it a happy circumstance for Jefferson that he was a citizen of a free country and able to write as he wished. Kimball, *War and Peace*, 298. The "Advertisement" dated February 27, 1787, which is prefaced to Stockdale's London edition states that the writer "had a few copies printed, which he gave among his friends: and a translation of them has been lately published in France, but with such alterations as the laws of the press in that country rendered necessary. They are now offered to the public in their original form and language."

39. OBSERVATIONS SUR LA VIRGINIE, PAR M. J. * * *. TRADUITES DE L'ANGLOIS. A PARIS, Chez BARROIS, l'ainé, Libraire, rue du Hurepoix, près le pont Saint-Michel. 1786.

40. Publication by the middle of October, 1786, was anticipated when Jefferson sent a map to England to be engraved for use in the book. To Wm. S. Smith, August [10], 1786, 10 P. 212; Morellet to Jefferson, [August 1, 1786], 10 P. 182. The plate was sent to Jefferson by the engraver, Samuel J. Neele, on December 21, 1786, 10 P. 621–22. The letter was received on January 4, 1787, and the plate was made available to Morellet by March 24, 1787. William Short to Jefferson, March 26, 1787, 11 P. 240. Jefferson got it back from Barrois apparently on June 29, 1787. To Morellet, July 2, 1787, 11 P. 529–31. It is not clear whether Barrois had by then struck off enough maps to begin sale of Morellet's translation. The statement in note 38, *supra*, together with Jefferson's letter to Stockdale of February 1, 1787, that "a translation . . . is coming out" (11 P. 107) would indicate publication during February. Peden in the introduction to his edition (p. xviii) accepts this date, and July, 1787, as the date of publication by Stockdale (p. xix). Sowerby, IV, 319, also gives July as the date of publication by Stockdale. On August 3, 1787, Stockdale sent copies to Jefferson, which were at hand by August 14, 1787. *Ibid.*, 319–20. Malone, *Rights of Man*, 105, says: "The French edition of Barrois came out a few weeks earlier than the English edition of John Stockdale." Kimball, *War and Peace,* 298, infers that the map for Morellet's translation "was not yet printed" on July 2, 1787, when Jefferson had recovered the plate and sent it to Stockdale, and hence that "it was not until somewhat later that the book actually appeared."

41. To Madison, May 11, 1785, 8 P. 147–48; to Chastellux, June 7, 1785, 8 P. 184.

42. To George Wythe, August 13, 1786, 10 P. 243.

43. Madison to Jefferson, May 12, 1786, 9 P. 517.

44. As to the date of publication, see note 40, *supra*. Stockdale had earlier evinced an interest in publishing the *Notes*. Stockdale to Jefferson, August 8, 1786, 10 P. 201.

45. To Stockdale, February 1, 1787, 11 P. 107. The publisher agreed that Jefferson's text "shall be neatly and correctly Printed and Published, according to your desire, without one tittle of Alteration, tho' I know there is some bitter pills relative to our Country." He estimated that not over three weeks would be required for printing 500 copies. Stockdale to Jefferson, February 13, 1787, 11 P. 143.

46. To Stockdale, February 27, 1787, 11 P. 183. "They will require a very accurate

corrector of the press, because they are filled with tables, which will become absolutely useless if they are not printed with a perfect accuracy."

47. Sowerby #3225 and #4051.

48. In his *Notes,* 116–17, Jefferson had quoted as a specimen of Indian eloquence Logan's address popularized in McGuffey readers and frequently used for schoolboy declamations, in which he said "Col. Cresap, the last spring, in cold blood, and unprovoked, murdered all the relations of Logan, not sparing even my women and children. There runs not a drop of my blood in the veins of any living creature." *Ibid.*, 116. In 1797, a cantankerous Maryland lawyer, and militant Federalist, Luther Martin, whose deceased wife had been Cresap's daughter, charged, as a political maneuver, that Jefferson had fabricated the speech and libeled the family. Jefferson's appendix was a collection of affidavits to establish the authenticity of the speech and Cresap's participation in the incident. *Notes* (Peden ed.), 226–58, 298–301. The speech is contained in Jefferson's Account Book for 1775. HL.

49. This copy was acquired by the University of Virginia library in 1938. Joseph W. Randolph, publisher of the 1853 edition, was "third cousin once removed" of Jefferson's favorite grandson and executor. Peden edition, page xx.

50. This edition is the first ever to contain an index, which was prepared by Lester J. Cappon, and is the most convenient and accessible. However, I have cited the original Paris edition of 1785, because it was Jefferson's favorite edition, and was available to me. In the fullness of time, *Deo volente*, a new edition, copiously enriched by valuable editorial contributions, may be expected as part of Boyd's magnificent edition of the *Papers of Thomas Jefferson.* See 1 P. xv and 11 P. 38.

51. *Notes,* 193. In the original list submitted by Marbois, the first two items were: "1. The Charters of your State. 2. The present Constitution." 4 P. 166.

52. *Notes,* 193–200.

53. *Ibid.*, 201–205. This convention was accompanied by an act of indemnity. *Ibid.*, 206–207.

54. *Ibid.*, 202.

55. *Ibid.*, 207–208.

56. *Ibid.*, 208–209.

57. *Ibid.*, 209–10.

58. The Virginia constitution adopted by the convention of 1776 appears in 1 P. 377–86. The preamble (similar to charges against the king in the Declaration of Independence) was taken from a draft prepared by Jefferson and prefixed to the declaration of rights and frame of government prepared by George Mason. Dumbauld, *Declaration,* 21. Three versions of Jefferson's draft constitution exist. 1 P. 337–47; *ibid.*, 347–55; *ibid.*, 356–65. The third draft was taken by Wythe from Philadelphia to the convention. *Ibid.*, 336, 365, 377.

59. *Notes,* 211–28.

60. *Ibid.*, 211. Elsewhere in the *Notes* Jefferson urges extension of suffrage as a means of eliminating corruption by making it too expensive. *Ibid.*, 274–75. See also to Jeremiah Moor, August 14, 1800, 9 F. 142–43. Jefferson's policy regarding representation resembles the "one man one vote" rule adopted by the Supreme Court in *Reynolds* v. *Sims,* 377 U.S. 533, 561–68 (1964). In fact, Jefferson's views are cited in Chief Justice Warren's opinion in that case. *Ibid.,* 573.

61. *Notes,* 211–13.

62. The English constitution "relies on the house of commons for honesty and the lords for wisdom; which would be a rational reliance if honesty were to be bought with

money, and if wisdom were hereditary. . . . But with us, wealth and wisdom have equal chance for admission into both houses. We do not therefore derive from the separation of our legislature into two houses those benefits which a proper complication of principles is capable of producing, and those which alone can compensate the evils which may be produced by their dissentions." *Ibid.*, 213–14.

63. *Ibid.*, 214. Jefferson eloquently exclaimed: "An *elective despotism* was not the government we fought for; but one which should not only be founded on free principles, but in which the powers of government should be so divided and balanced among several bodies of magistracy as that no one could transcend their legal limits, without being effectually checked and restrained by the others." *Ibid.*, 214. The definition of despotism is from Montesquieu, *Esprit des Lois*, book XI, c. 6. See Dumbauld, *Constitution*, 320.

64. *Notes*, 217.

65. *Ibid.*, 226. On June 4, 1781, the House of Delegates "voted that, during the present dangerous invasion, forty members shall be a house to proceed to business. . . . But . . . danger could not authorize them to call that a house which was none." *Ibid.*, 226–27.

66. *Ibid.*, 227. Similar reasoning underlies the requirement that when a member of Parliament is charged with crime the case must first be laid before the house. Otherwise, the king, or even a private complainant, by fabricated accusations could "take any man from his service in the House; and so as many, one after another, as would make the House what he pleaseth." Jefferson's *Manual*, 25.

67. *Notes*, 227.

68. *Ibid.*, 234. Jefferson expatiates eloquently concerning proposals urged in December, 1776, and in June, 1781, to create a dictator. *Ibid.*, 228–35. On the first of these occasions, Archibald Cary won perennial renown by his threat to slay Patrick Henry if the eloquent orator were made dictator. Robert K. Brock, *Archibald Cary of Ampthill*, 65–66, 103–104. To Jefferson "The very thought alone was treason against the people; was treason against mankind." *Notes*, 231. Well-meaning advocates of the measure had been seduced by the example of Rome. *Ibid.*, 232–33. But Jefferson pertinently asks: "What clause in our constitution has substituted that of Rome, by way of residuary provision, for all cases not otherwise provided for?" *Ibid.*, 234.

69. Dumbauld, "Thomas Jefferson and American Constitutional Law," Emory University *Journal of Public Law*, Vol. II, No. 2 (Fall, 1953), 370–71, 373–74.

70. *Notes*, 225. See also Dumbauld, *Constitution*, 18. Jefferson's view was akin to doctrines of Locke and Vattel which were popular in the Colonies. *Ibid.*, 14, 16–17.

71. Answers to Démeunier, *circa* January 24, 1787, 10 P. 28–29. The same point is made in *Notes*, 219–21. He spoke in later life of the British constitution, which can be changed by any act passed by Parliament, as "no constitution at all." To Adamantios Coray, October 31, 1823, 15 M. 488.

72. Answers to Démeunier, January 24, 1786, 10 P. 18.

73. *Notes*, 234–35.

74. *Notes* (Stockdale ed.), 358. His 1783 draft expressly provided that "the general assembly shall not have power to infringe this constitution." *Ibid.*, 363.

75. *Notes* (Stockdale ed.), 357.

76. Answers to Démeunier, January 24, 1786, 10 P. 18. One of the purposes for which "I have long wished to see a convention called" was to make "our constitution paramount the powers of the ordinary legislature so that all acts contradictory to it may be adjudged null." To Edmund Pendleton, May 25, 1784, 7 P. 293.

77. *Notes*, 219–21. See also 2 F. 161: "he conceived them to be agents for the management of the war."

78. When the convention was elected, independence had not been declared. The convention itself on May 15, 1776, instructed the Virginia delegates in the Continental Congress to propose such a declaration; and on June 29, 1776, adopted a constitution, in the preamble to which Virginia declared its own independence before the Continental Congress acted. Hugh Blair Grigsby, *The Virginia Convention of 1776,* 17–18, 20. On May 6, 1776, when the convention met, the forty-five members of the House of Burgesses assembled at the Capitol disbanded, "thinking that the people could not be legally represented under the ancient constitution, which had been subverted by the king, lords and commons." Lord Dunmore, the royal governor, had abandoned his post more than a year previously. *Ibid.,* 8–9. See also James Brown Scott, *Sovereign States and Suits,* 10, 46, 56; Francis N. Thorpe, *Charters,* VII, 3812, 3814–15.

79. See notes 73 and 74, *supra.*

80. "Regardless of the manner of its adoption, that Constitution in actual practice was treated as a fundamental law, different in character and superior in authority to ordinary legislation." 6 P. 279. The ratification of the Fourteenth Amendment to the Constitution of the United States is another instance of validation by popular consent. Dumbauld, *Constitution,* 436.

81. *Kamper* v. *Hawkins,* 1 Brockenbrough and Holmes 20, 37, 69 (1793); Tucker's *Blackstone,* I (App.), 83–88.

82. *Notes,* 223–24. Did colonial acquiescence in British usurpations render them valid "and our present resistance wrong?" *Ibid.,* 224. See also to John H. Pleasants, April 19, 1824, 12 F. 352–53.

83. *Notes,* 221.

84. *Ibid.,* 222, 223.

85. *Ibid.* (Stockdale ed.), 356.

86. It was bound following the Appendix (pp. 367–390) consisting of Charles Thomson's "observations" commenting on Jefferson's material. After the draft constitution a four-page supplement contained the act for establishing religious freedom passed in 1786, and a sixteen-page supplement contained Jefferson's *Notes on the Establishment of a Money Unit, and of a Coinage for the United States.* The Stockdale edition includes all these items except the last. For thorough discussion of Jefferson's 1783 draft constitution, see 6 P. 178–317. The text of the draft appears at 6 P. 294–308.

87. Madison to A. B. Woodward, September 11, 1824, Hunt, *Writings of James Madison,* IX, 208.

88. 8 F. 159–62. Jefferson's letter of July 12, 1816, to Samuel Kercheval, 12 F. 3–17, may have been influential in bringing about the 1830 constitution. Grigsby, *Virginia Convention,* 181.

89. A single justice could try at any time and place a matter involving less than 4 1/6 dollars. *Notes,* 237.

90. *Ibid.,* 238.

91. A felony is a serious offense, which originally at common law occasioned forfeiture of land or goods. Blackstone, *Commentaries,* IV, 94; Holdsworth, *History,* II, 357–58.

92. *Notes,* 236–37.

93. *Ibid.,* 237. For Jefferson's views on the pardoning power, see page 236 n. 8, *infra.* For an interesting case involving exercise of the power in Virginia, see *Com.* v. *Caton,* 4 Call. 5, 8–9 (1782).

94. To John Taylor, May 28, July 16, 1816, 15 M. 20–21, 45; to Samuel Kercheval, July 12, 1816, *ibid.,* 34–35.

95. *Notes,* 238.

96. *Ibid.*, 238–39. There were five judges on the general court, and three on each of the other two courts. *Ibid.*, 238. This system was abandoned when the court of appeals was reorganized in 1788. See note 15, chapter 4, *infra.*

97. *Ibid.*, 239. Jefferson, in the *Notes* as elsewhere, eulogized jury trial. *Ibid.*, 236. See pages 152 and 250 n. 103, *infra.*

98. *Ibid., 239.*

99. See pages 18–19, *supra.*

100. Jefferson here apparently refers to the preamble to the laws of 1661/62, where the assembly professes to have endeavored "in all things (as neere as the capacity and constitution of this country would admitt") to adhere to "those excellent and often refined laws of England, to which we profess and acknowledge all due obedience and reverence." The laws made in Virginia are intended as brief memorials of "that which the capacity of our courts is utterly unabled to collect out of such vast volumes, though sometimes perhaps for the difference of our and their condition varying in small things, but far from the presumption of contradicting any thing therein conteyned." Hening, *Statutes*, II, 43.

101. *Notes,* 240–41. See page 166 n. 42, *infra.*

102. *Ibid.*, 241.

103. *Ibid.*, 241–42.

104. *Ibid.*, 242. He also describes the disadvantages of hospitals. *Ibid.,* 242–43. Cf. Dumbauld, *American Tourist*, 35.

105. *Notes,* 244.

106. *Ibid.*, 244–45.

107. *Ibid.,* 245. See pages xii, 140, 160 n. 24, *supra,* and 238 n. 24, *infra,* and note 24, chapter 7, *infra.*

108. *Ibid.*, 245.

109. *Ibid.*, 245.

110. *Ibid.*, 245–46.

111. *Ibid.*, 246–48.

112. *Ibid.*, 248.

113. *Ibid.*, 248–49. Jefferson's description of the mode of acquiring land was repeated in Tucker's *Blackstone,* III (App.), 3–10, 66–69.

114. Of 941 matters listed in Jefferson's case book, 283 were caveats. Representing petitioners for land (146) was the next most frequent type of business. See note 5, introduction, *supra.* As governor, Jefferson issued about 3000 patents for land, the first on October 23, 1779, and the last on April 10, 1781. Henry R. McIlwaine, *Official Letters of the Governors of the State of Virginia*, II, 4.

115. Tucker's *Blackstone,* III (App.), 67.

116. *Ibid.*, IV (App.), 32–34. According to Benjamin Watkins Leigh (ed.), *The Revised Code of the Laws of Virginia*, II (App. II), 340, "the proceeding by way of *caveat* (though, in its nature, strictly judicial,) was had before the Governor and Council, sitting as an executive body, not as judges sitting in the general court; nor was it 'till after the revolution, that cognizance of *caveats* was vested in the courts of justice."

117. *Notes,* 249–75.

118. *Ibid.*, 249.

119. See pages 132–43, *infra.*

120. See page 238 n. 23, *infra.*

121. Printed by Dixon and Holt, Richmond, 1784.

122. See pages 18–20 and 20–27, *supra.* In addition to the *Report* as a record of Jefferson's skill in drafting laws, it is fascinating to pursue his activities as a legislator through the pages of his own bound volume (in the Brock Collection at the Huntington Library) con-

taining the journals and legislation for the period 1776–81. Was he thinking of this volume when he told prospective publishers of his writings that they were mostly "of an official character, and are only to be found among the public documents of the times in which I have lived"? To Messrs. Parsons & Conley, February 14, 1823, MHS. See also to John W. Campbell, September 3, 1809, 12 M. 308.

123.   Adams to Timothy Pickering, August 6, 1822, Charles Francis Adams (ed.), *The Works of John Adams*, II, 513–14. "During the whole time I sat with him in Congress, I never heard him utter three sentences together." *Ibid.*, II, 511. Jefferson similarly remarked: "I served with General Washington in the legislature of Virginia before the revolution, and, during it, with Dr. Franklin in Congress. I never heard either of them speak ten minutes at a time, nor to any but the main point which was to decide the question. They laid their shoulders to the great points, knowing that the little ones would follow of themselves." Autobiography, 1 F. 90.

124.   Autobiography, 1 F. 90–91.

125.   For his attendance and election see *The Proceedings of the Convention of Delegates* . . . [held March 20, 1775], Williamsburg: Printed by Alexander Purdie, 1, 11; *The Proceedings of the Convention of Delegates* . . . [held July 17, 1775], Richmond: Ritchie, Truehart & Du-Val, Printers, 1816 (reprint), 12, 14.

126.   He first took his seat in Congress on June 21, 1775. Ford, *Journals of the Continental Congress*, II, 101. On October 10, 1776, Benjamin Harrison was chosen to replace him. *Journal of the House of Delegates of Virginia* (Session of October 7–December 21, 1776), 7–8. In Jefferson's bound volume labeled "Journals Legislature of Virginia 1776–1781," in Brock Collection, Huntington Library.

127.   See page 18, *supra.*

128.   *Journal of the House of Delegates of Virginia* (Session of May 3–June 26, 1779), 36. On June 12, 1781, Thomas Nelson, Jr., was elected to succeed Jefferson. *Journal* (Session of May 7–June 23, 1781), 21. Brock Collection.

129.   *Journals of the Continental Congress*, XXV, 803. On occasion Jefferson was chosen to preside over the Congress, in the absence of the president. *Journals*, XXVI, 133, 172. An important example of his achievement as a federal legislator is the Ordinance of April 23, 1784, for the temporary government of the western territory. 6 P. 613–15. This was a precursor of the better-known Ordinance of 1787. As reported by Jefferson for the committee of which he was chairman the ordinance would have prohibited slavery after 1800. That provision was deleted on a close vote, one New Jersey delegate being absent because of illness. *Ibid.*, 607–13. "Thus we see the fate of millions unborn hanging on the tongue of one man, and heaven was silent in that awful moment!" 10 P. 58. See also Jay A. Barrett, *Evolution of the Ordinance of 1787 With an Account of the Earlier Plans for the Government of the Northwest Territory*, 17–27.

130.   The first edition, printed in "Washington City" by Samuel Harrison Smith in 1801, is a pocket-size volume of 181 unnumbered pages preceded by a preface of five pages. A "SECOND EDITION. WITH THE LAST ADDITIONS OF THE AUTHOR. WASHINGTON: PUBLISHED BY WILLIAM COOPER; AND BY JOSEPH MILLIGAN, GEORGETOWN," was issued in 1812. For convenience, page references will be made to this edition. It contains at pages 11, 44, 75, 151, 152, 176, and 180 material not found in the first edition. These additions are not found in later editions issued during the lifetime of the author, namely, Lancaster: William Dickson, 1813; Berlin: Ferdinand Dümmler, 1819; Washington: Davis & Force, 1820; Washington: Gales & Seaton, 1822; Concord: George Hough & Jacob B. Moore, 1823.

131.   To John W. Campbell, September 3, 1809, 12 M. 308.

132. To George Wythe, January 22, 1797, 8 F. 274; February 28, 1800, 9 F. 115–17; April 7, 1800, 9 F. 117–18; to Edmund Pendleton, April 19, 1800, 9 F. 118–19.

133. Much of this book is written in pencil.

134. To George Wythe, February 28, 1800, 9 F. 116.

135. 9 F. 117–19.

136. Pendleton to Jefferson, June 17, 1800, LC 18305, 18470–72; Wythe to Jefferson, December 7, 1800, LC 18459 (Wythe's spelling and capitalization modernized). Pendleton and Jefferson had served together on a committee to prepare parliamentary rules for the Virginia House of Burgesses in 1769, soon after Jefferson became a member of that body. Kennedy, *Journals* (1766–69), 232, 323–25. For rules of order in the House in 1658 and 1663, see Hening, *Statutes*, I, 507–508; II, 206–207.

137. HM 5986. See also LC 41793–805.

138. The first reads: "Rules importance of. 107.110."
The second reads:
"All legislat. power ——H. of R. art. 1 § 1.
The Senators ——of U.S. art 1 § 6."
In the published text these references are expanded. What had been the first heading (Privilege) thus becomes the third in the printed book.

139. Item 23 in the Parliamentary Pocket-Book (MHS) says: "It is more material that there should be a rule to go by, than what that rule should be."

140. Nos. 2–14 (Legislature, Privilege, Election, Qualifications, Quorum, Call of the House, Absence, Speaker, Address, Committees, Committee of the whole, Examination before Committees, Arrangement of business).

141. Nos. 15–42.

142. Nos. 43–51 (Reconsideration, Papers sent to the other house, Amendments between the Houses, Conferences, Messages, Assent, Journals, Adjournment, Session).

143. Nos. 52 and 53.

144. *Manual*, 5–8. The situation in the Senate was regarded by Jefferson as an opportunity to eliminate the procedures of the Continental Congress, which were "so awkward & inconvenient that it was impossible sometimes to get at the true sense of the majority. . . . Parliamentary rules are the best known to us for managing the debates, & obtaining the sense of a deliberative body. I have therefore made them my rule of decision, rejecting those of the old Congress altogether; & it gives entire satisfaction to the Senate." To George Wythe, February 28, 1800, 9 F. 115–16.

145. *Manual*, 9–10. See note 139, *supra*. As Justice Brandeis said in *Di Santo* v. *Pennsylvania*, 273 U.S. 34, 42 (1927): "It is usually more important that a rule of law be settled, than that it be settled right."

146. Report of Conference Committee of Virginia House of Delegates, January 9, 1778, 2 F. 315. On parliamentary law as constitutional law, see also Leonidas Pitamic, *A Treatise on the State*, 122.

147. Report of Conference Committee, December 4, 1777, 2 F. 312. On adoption of English law, see pages 18–19 and 25, *supra* (note 11 and note 101).

148. No. 52, *Manual*, 168–74.

149. *Manual*, 168.

150. *Ibid.*, 171. Jefferson refers to the abrogation of the treaty of February 6, 1778, with France by the act of July 1, 1798, 1 St. 578, which contained recitals that there had been repeated violations on the part of France. See Dumbauld, *Constitution,* 291. Jefferson at one time believed that a treaty "was a law of superior order because it not only repeals

past laws, but cannot itself be repealed by future ones." *Ibid.*, 291; Opinion on Indian Trade, July 29, 1790, 6 F. 111.

151. *Manual*, 169–70. For a synopsis of current views, see Dumbauld, *Constitution*, 289; Louis Henkin, *Foreign Affairs and the Constitution*, 137–56. The Tenth Amendment, reserving to the states "powers not delegated to the United States," sheds no light on what powers are in fact granted to the federal government. Dumbauld, *Bill of Rights*, 65–66. Under present world conditions, most matters have an international impact and could properly be dealt with by treaty as "matters of international concern," to use the phrase of Charles Evans Hughes. Henkin, *Foreign Affairs*, 152. A possible example of a matter concerning which "the whole government is interdicted" by the Constitution from taking action would be an attempt to establish a religion, or prohibit free exercise of religion, in violation of the First Amendment. The whole federal government having no granted power in this area, a treaty or concordat with the Vatican to establish the Roman Catholic faith as the national religion would be void, even though the subject matter is one with respect to which other nations have entered into treaties, and would hence be a proper subject for international negotiation under Jefferson's first two criteria. But it would be prohibited by the third. Other examples of prohibited action (by treaty as well as otherwise) would be granting titles of nobility or depriving a state of its republican form of government. *Ibid.*, 140, 148. *Reid* v. *Covert*, 354 U.S. 1, 16–17 (1957), makes clear that the treaty power is subject to the constraints of the Constitution.

152. *Manual*, 170. If the fourth criterion means to exclude from the area of treaty-making any subject concerning which legislation by Congress (with the "participation" of the House) is permissible under the Constitution, it is obviously untenable. But the philosophy of "the less the better" may have appealed to Jefferson himself as a measure of policy. "On the subject of treaties, our system is to have none with any nation, as far as can be avoided." To Philip Mazzei, July 18, 1804, 11 M. 38–39.

153. Opponents of the Jay treaty relied on this criterion. Albert J. Beveridge, *The Life of John Marshall*, II, 119, 133–41. Advocates of the "Bricker Amendment" two decades ago vainly sought to undo the decision (*per* Holmes, J.) in *Missouri* v. *Holland*, 252 U.S. 416, 432 (1920), that under the "necessary and proper" clause Congress may enforce treaty provisions, even if they deal with a subject matter over which Congress would have no legislative authority in the absence of the treaty. See Henkin, *Foreign Affairs*, 147.

154. Dumbauld, "Thomas Jefferson and American Constitutional Law," Emory University *Journal of Public Law*, Vol. II, No. 2 (Fall, 1953), 379–80.

155. To Monroe, June 17, 1785, 4 F. 420–21.

156. The "Virginia Plan" contained such a provision. Farrand, *Records of the Federal Convention*, I, 21. For Madison's approval, see Brant, *James Madison*, III, 12, 24, 36, 38, 104–105, 126–29, 141.

157. Madison to Jefferson, March 18, 1787, Hunt, *Writings of James Madison*, II, 326.

158. To Madison, June 20, 1787, 5 F. 284.

159. *Ibid.*, 285.

160. Art. III, sec. 2, declaring that the federal judicial power shall extend to cases "arising under . . . Treaties," and Article VI, clause 2, that "all Treaties . . . shall be the Supreme Law of the Land; and the Judges . . . shall be bound thereby, any Thing in the Constitution or Laws of any State to the Contrary notwithstanding."

161. The letter of March 4, 1786, from Adams was referred by Congress to John Jay, secretary of foreign affairs, whose comprehensive report of October 16, 1786, reviewed

state legislation challenged by the British as violative of the treaty. *Journals of the Continental Congress*, XXXI, 781–84. The resolutions were adopted on March 21, 1787. *Ibid.*, XXXII, 124–25. They were accompanied by a circular letter to the states of April 13, 1787. *Ibid.*, 176–84.

162. *Ibid.*, XXXII, 183.

163. To George Hammond, May 29, 1792, 7 F. 3–98. His negotiations were hampered, however, by Alexander Hamilton's intrigues with British agents. Julian P. Boyd, *Number 7: Alexander Hamilton's Secret Attempts to Control American Foreign Policy*, 59, 85.

164. Report on Negotiations with Spain, March 18, 1792, 6 F. 414–45.

165. Opinion on the French Treaties, April 28, 1793, 7 F. 283–301.

166. *Ibid.*, 293. See Edward Dumbauld, "Independence under International Law," *American Journal of International Law*, Vol. LXX, No. 3 (July, 1976), 427–28.

167. On Jefferson's activities in the field of international law and foreign affairs, see John H. Latané, "Jefferson's Influence on American Foreign Policy," *University of Virginia Alumni Bulletin* (3d series), Vol. XVII, No. 3 (July-August, 1924), 245–69; Louis M. Sears, "Jefferson and the Law of Nations," *American Political Science Review*, Vol. XIII, No. 3 (August, 1919), 379–99; William K. Woolery, *The Relation of Thomas Jefferson to American Foreign Policy 1783–1793*; Charles M. Thomas, *American Neutrality in 1793*; Charles M. Wiltse, "Thomas Jefferson on the Law of Nations," *American Journal of International Law*, Vol. XXIX, No. 1 (January, 1935), 66–81.

168. See Louis M. Sears, *Jefferson and the Embargo*, 48–50; and Dumas Malone, *Jefferson the President, Second Term*, 469–90, 561–657.

169. "I love peace, and I am anxious that we should give the world still another useful lesson by showing to them other modes of punishing injuries than by war, which is as much a punishment to the punisher as to the sufferer. I love, therefore . . . [the] proposition of cutting off all communications with the nation which has conducted itself so atrociously." To Tench Coxe, May 1, 1794, Dumbauld, *Political Writings of Jefferson*, 182. "War is not the best engine for us to resort to. Nature has given us one in our commerce which, if properly managed, will be a better instrument for obliging the interested nations of Europe to treat us with justice." To Thomas Pinckney, May 29, 1797. *Ibid.*, 182–83. For numerous other references to the idea of peaceable coercion, see *ibid.*, 198.

170. *Ibid.*, 187.

171. No. 53, *Manual*, 174–83.

172. *Manual*, 67–167.

173. *Ibid.*, 174–75.

174. *Ibid.*, 175–83.

175. A case of a jury trial before a committee of Parliament, mentioned by Selden, is explained as not having been an impeachment by the Commons. *Ibid.*, 180. "The Commons, as the grand inquest of the nation, become suitors for penal justice." *Ibid.*, 176. The articles of impeachment take the place of an indictment. *Ibid.*, 177. The Commons are to be considered as performing the functions of a grand jury, rather than of a petty jury. *Ibid.*, 180–81.

176. The Commons must be present at the answer and judgment, as well as at examination of witnesses; but they must not be present while the Lords are deliberating on the judgment to be given. *Ibid.*, 181.

177. An impeachment is not discontinued by dissolution of Parliament, but may be resumed by the new Parliament. *Ibid.*, 183.

178. *Ibid.*, 182. This presumably means that in a case of treason, for example, the

gruesome incidents of the mode of execution cannot be eliminated. Cf. page 13, *supra.* The king's assent is required for a sentence of death. *Ibid.,* 183. But a pardon cannot be pleaded in bar of an impeachment. *Ibid.,* 179.

179. This conception of impeachment would make its function similar to the beneficial effects of the operation of the Court of Star Chamber against offenders too powerful to be dealt with by ordinary means. Joseph R. Tanner, *Tudor Constitutional Documents,* 285, 291–92.

180. *Manual,* 182.

181. *Impeachment: Selected Materials* (93d Cong., 1st. sess., House Doc. No. 93–7 [1973]) 94–96, 623, 628, 661, 668. (See also Dumbauld, *Constitution,* 317; and Raoul Berger, *Impeachment: the Constitutional Problems,* 56, 61–62, 67, 69–71, 74–75, 228, 268, 297.)

182. *Ibid.,* 626–28, 632, 692–95.

183. *Ibid.,* 619, 672–76, 682–88, 695–96. Since the scope of impeachment jurisdiction under Art. II, sec. 4 is the same for judges as for all other "civil Officers of the United States," a judge could not be impeached for lack of "good Behaviour" [see Art. III, sec. 1] unless such misconduct, though not criminal, fell within the category of "high Crimes and Misdemeanors."

184. Art. I, sec. 3, cl. 7, draws a clear distinction between impeachable and criminally punishable offenses by providing that: "Judgment in Cases of Impeachment shall not extend further than to removal from Office, and disqualification to hold and enjoy any Office of honor, Trust or Profit under the United States: but the Party convicted shall nevertheless be liable and subject to Indictment, Trial, Judgment and Punishment, according to Law." According to John W. Davis, in his final argument as one of the managers for the House on January 9, 1914, in the trial of Judge Robert W. Archbald, "this clause instead of being a declaration that impeachment and indictment occupy the same field, is a recognition of the fact that the field which they occupy may or may not be identical; and, recognizing this fact, it declares merely that when the field of impeachment and the field of indictment overlap there shall be no conflict between them, but that the same offense may be proceeded against in either forum or in both." *Ibid.,* 110. See also *ibid.,* 634.

185. A good example of impeachable conduct is afforded by the accusation in the reign of Charles II against Chief Justice Sir William Scroggs, that he "endeavored to subvert the fundamental laws, . . . and instead thereof to introduce . . . arbitrary and tyrannical government against law." *Ibid.,* 46. Scroggs escaped by reason of dissolution of Parliament. *Ibid.,* 630.

186. *Ibid.,* 56, 103–104, 635, 638.

187. Zechariah Chafee, *Three Human Rights in the Constitution of 1789,* 104. A criminal trial for treason was another available means. All three methods in England resulted in the death penalty. In early times it was hard to distinguish between impeachment and attainder. In the impeachment of Strafford, the Lords acted judicially and as the evidence of treason was unconvincing the Commons then proceeded by attainder. This required the king's assent, which he was reluctantly compelled to give. *Ibid.,* 105, 111–12. In America the Constitution limited the judgment in impeachment to removal and disqualification (Art. I, sec. 3, cl. 7); prohibited bills of attainder (Art. I, sec. 9, cl. 3); and defined treason (and the legal consequences thereof) strictly (Art. III, sec. 3).

188. *Ibid.,* 96. In the case of a peer, the criminal trial would have taken place in the House of Lords, until the Criminal Justice Act of 1948, 11 & 12 Geo. 6, c. 58, §30. *Ibid.,* 218. See page 12, *supra.*

189. To James Madison, February 15, 1798, 8 F. 369–70. At that time he considered

impeachment as a criminal prosecution, requiring jury trial under the Sixth Amendment. See also 12 P. 556-57.
190. To Joseph H. Nicholson, May 13, 1803, 10 M. 390.
191. To William B. Giles, April 20, 1807, 10 F. 387; to Spencer Roane, September 6, 1819, 12 F. 137; to Thomas Ritchie, December 25, 1820, 12 F. 177.

CHAPTER III

1. *Prepared for the Use of Counsel, by Thomas Jefferson.* On this book see Sowerby #3501. Jefferson's account book shows that on May 29, 1812, he paid Sargeant for printing $130, and on June 17, 1812, $21.50 more. On Jefferson's copy in the Library of Congress he notes: "The Errata in punctuation are too numerous to be corrected with the pen." The text is also available in John E. Hall's *American Law Journal,* Vol. V (1814), i–xii, 1–91; in Walter Lowrie and Walter S. Franklin, *American State Papers, Public Lands,* II, 76–102; and in 18 M. 1–132.
2. To Ezra Sargeant, February 3, 1812, 13 M. 132.
3. For Jefferson's praise of Livingston's code, see to Edward Livingston, March 25, 1825, 16 M. 114–15. Cordial relations between the two men had been previously restored. To James Monroe, March 7, 1824, 12 F. 346; to Edward Livingston, April 4, 1824, 12 F. 348. For Livingston's account of the reconciliation, see his argument in *New Orleans* v. *United States,* 10 Pet. 662, 691 (1836).
4. *Livingston* v. *Jefferson,* Fed. Cas. #8411 (1811); 1 Brockenbrough 203; 4 Hall's *L. J.* 78. On the rule established by this case, see Austin W. Scott and Robert B. Kent, *Cases and Other Materials on Civil Procedure,* 325–30. A Minnesota case in 1891 took the contrary position. *Ibid.,* 337.
5. To George Hay, December 28, 1811, in Sowerby, III, 404. Jefferson distributed copies of his book to every member of Congress. *Ibid.,* 404–406.
6. For a recent discussion of the batture controversy, see George Dargo, *Jefferson's Louisiana,* 74–101.
7. For a detailed account of this controversial incident, see New York *Times,* July 29, 1932. It is interesting to note that a question similar to the issue involved in the batture controversy was recently before the Supreme Court in *Nebraska* v. *Iowa,* 406 U.S. 117, 120–21, 123 (1972). In Iowa "private titles to riparian lands run only to the ordinary high-water mark on navigable streams and . . . the State is the owner of the beds of all [such] streams . . . and . . . of any islands that may form therein." *Ibid.,* 121. In Nebraska private titles extend to the *thalweg* or center of the main navigable channel. *Ibid.,* 123. A boundary was fixed by agreement in 1943. The court held that ownership of lands subsequently formed "should be determined under the law of the State in which they formed." *Ibid.,* 124–25. Hence areas formed in Iowa belong to the state.
8. Wickham to Jefferson, May 16, 1810, LC; Wickham to Livingston, May 16, 1810, Livingston Papers. The eminent Philadelphia lawyer Peter S. Duponceau, Livingston's friend and counsel, also wrote disapprovingly: "I shall say nothing of your late decision to sue Mr. Jefferson, tho' I candidly own I would not have advised it." Duponceau to Livingston, May 12, 1810, Livingston Papers.
9. To Wirt and Hay, May 19, 1810. For a recent sketch of Wirt, see Joseph C. Robert, "The Hon. William Wirt, The Many-Sided Attorney General," in Supreme Court Historical Society *Yearbook 1976,* 51–60. Wickham having evinced uncertainty whether he would take Livingston's case other than arranging for issuance of process, Jefferson "asked his

aid for myself," but Wickham declined. Wickham to Jefferson, May 22, 1810. He did continue to participate in the case on Livingston's behalf.

10.   Jefferson to Wirt, June 18, 1810; to Tazewell, June 28, 1810; Tazewell to Jefferson, July 5, 1810.

11.   *U.S.* v. *Burr*, Fed. Cas. #14693 (1807). For analysis of Marshall's opinion which led to Burr's acquittal, see Dumbauld, *Constitution*, 377–82. For a comprehensive and colorful account of the trial, see Beveridge, *Life of John Marshall*, III, 407–517. In the interval between Burr's commitment and trial, he was a guest at Wickham's house at a dinner which Marshall also attended. The incident, for which Marshall was criticized, was doubtless merely a normal expression of Virginia hospitality in that era, but nowadays would be considered improper judicial conduct. Beveridge, *Life of John Marshall*, III, 395–97.

12.   Beveridge, *Life of John Marshall*, III, 413.

13.   *Ibid.*, III, 433–47, 518–22.

14.   To George Hay, June 12, 1807, 10 F. 398.

15.   To Hay, June 17, 1807, 10 F. 400–401. Jefferson's formulation of "executive privilege" and Marshall's comments on the scope of judicial subpoena power in criminal trials were grist for the mill of lawyers, judges, and commentators concerned with *United States* v. *Nixon*, 418 U.S. 683 (1974). The Supreme Court's decision requiring production of the White House tapes was inevitable under the circumstances, and led to President Nixon's prompt resignation. But the opinion circumspectly left ample ground for denying disclosure where a trustworthy president makes a convincing case that military, diplomatic, or other compelling reasons genuinely require secrecy in the public interest. For comment on the case see article by Paul A. Freund and "Symposium: *United States* v. *Nixon*," *UCLA Law Review*, Vol. XXII, No. 1 (October, 1974), 1–140, especially (Gunther) 33–35, (Henkin) 45–46, and (Kurland) 70, 74. The best analysis of the Burr precedent is found in Malone, *President, Second Term*, 314–25, 333, 343–45; in the brief by Irwin S. Rhodes, and opinion of Judge Wilkey in the Court of Appeals in *Nixon* v. *Sirica*, 487 F.2d 700, 787–88 (C.A. D.C. 1973, No. 73–1962).

16.   *U.S.* v. *Burr*, Fed. Cas. #14692d (1807); David Robertson, *Reports of the Trials of Colonel Aaron Burr*, I, 177–89. The opinion was rendered on June 13, 1807.

17.   Beveridge, *Life of John Marshall*, III, 454.

18.   To Hay, June 20, 1807, 10 F. 404.

19.   *Ibid.*, 405. He concludes with a jibe that "it would be very different were we always on the road, or placed in the noisy & crowded taverns where courts are held." *Ibid.* Burr's preliminary hearing had been held before Marshall at the Eagle Tavern in Richmond. Beveridge, *Life of John Marshall*, III, 370.

20.   1 Cr. 137 (1803). Marshall's opinion in this case was "a political coup of the first magnitude." Edward S. Corwin, *John Marshall and the Constitution*, 66. See also Malone, *President, First Term*, 143–52; and Rhodes, *Marshall Papers*, I, 455.

21.   Charles Warren, *The Supreme Court in United States History*, I, 232, 244–45.

22.   James D. Richardson (ed.), *A Compilation of the Messages and Papers of the Presidents, 1789-1897*, I, 429. Beveridge interprets this language as an invitation to impeach Marshall. Beveridge, *Life of John Marshall*, III, 530. In commenting on the Burr trial Jefferson exclaimed: "we have no law but the will of the judge" (anticipating the quip of Charles Evans Hughes that "the Constitution is what the judges say it is"). In like vein an English judge said in 1345 that law "is the will of the justices," but a colleague retorted "No, law is reason" ("*Nanyl, ley est resoun*"). Margaret C. Klingelsmith, "Stonore

Said," *University of Pennsylvania Law Review,* Vol. LXI, No. 6 (April, 1913), 381. To William Thompson, September 26, 1807, 10 F. 501. Thomas P. Abernethy's *The Burr Conspiracy* is the most recent scholarly account of Burr's ambitious projects.

23. Jefferson's first impression, upon receiving Wickham's letter, was that the writ was one of "trespass on the case . . . in the Federal district court of this state." Hay promptly informed him that the action was trespass, not case, and in the circuit, not the district, court. Jefferson to Hay and Wirt, May 19, 1810; Hay to Jefferson, May 25, 1810. In the circuit court Marshall would sit with the ailing district judge Cyrus Griffin, whom Jefferson regarded as a "cypher." To Madison, May 25, 1810, 11 F. 140. In that letter he urged the appointment to Griffin's place of Governor John Tyler, a lifelong friend of Jefferson's and father of the president known by the slogan "Tippecanoe and Tyler too." Dumbauld, *American Tourist,* 32, 42–43. Griffin did die and Tyler was appointed in time to take part in the Livingston case. Griffin had served in 1780 and 1782 on the pre-Constitutional federal courts for admiralty appeals and for boundary disputes. 131 U.S. App. xxv–xxvi, lv.

24. Hay to Jefferson, May 25, 1810. After research this opinion was confirmed in Hay to Jefferson, June 1, 1810. Attorney General Caesar A. Rodney made the same point in his letter to Jefferson, June 17, 1810. Believing Livingston's object to be to obtain in circuitous fashion an opinion of the Supreme Court upholding his title to the batture, Rodney recommended a special plea of justification of the eviction, setting forth the title of the United States.

25. To Hay, June 18, 1810. Tazewell's proposal of a plea in abatement that Livingston was a resident of a territory and not of a state was rejected because it would require an affidavit and Jefferson could not swear that Livingston was not a resident of New York, "because I know nothing of the fact" although he had little doubt that "his assumed residence at N. York" was "merely temporary, and to qualify him to bring his action before his favorite judge." Tazewell to Jefferson, July 5, 1810; Hay to Jefferson, July 15, 1810; Hay to Jefferson, July 20, 1810; Jefferson to Hay, August 1, 1810; Jefferson to Tazewell, August 18, 1810.

26. To Rodney, September 25, 1810. "We must carefully claim a right of correcting every opinion he gives by carrying it to the Supreme court." To Hay, August 1, 1810.

27. To Gallatin, September 27, 1810, 11 F. 153. He urged the appointment of Levi Lincoln, of Massachusetts, to replace Cushing. *Ibid.,* 154. Lincoln declined, on account of impending blindness, Alexander Wolcott of Connecticut was rejected by the Senate, John Quincy Adams preferred to continue in his diplomatic post as minister to Russia, and there remained no choice but Joseph Story whom Jefferson distrusted. Beveridge, *Life of John Marshall,* IV, 109–110, 115.

28. To Hay, August 31, 1811.

29. To Hay, October 7, 1810; March 3, 1811.

30. To Hay, August 1, 1810; to Gallatin, August 16, 1810.

31. To W. C. C. Claiborne, June 11, 1810.

32. Hay to Jefferson, July 15, 1810. Hence the defense of lack of jurisdiction should be preserved and asserted by objections to evidence rather than by a preliminary plea.

33. Tazewell opposed a plea to the jurisdiction, since "it is highly desirable that *the merits* be settled, if that can be done without detriment to you personally." Tazewell to Jefferson, September 27, 1810.

34. Malone, *Virginian,* 257–59, 412, 419. It is perhaps significant that acquisition of territory (such as the Louisiana Purchase, about which Jefferson felt constitutional qualms) and the measures at New Orleans against Burr's conspiracy were viewed by Jefferson as

illustrations of the principle that "on great occasions, when the safety of the nation, or some of its very high interests are at stake" high officials have a duty beyond "strict observance of the written laws." To John B. Colvin, September 20, 1810, 11 F. 146–49. Another instance was Jefferson's military preparations at the time of the *Chesapeake* crisis, trusting that Congress would later appropriate the money. Message of October 27, 1808, Richardson, *Messages of the Presidents*, I, 428.

35.   To Claiborne, October 16, 1810. Jefferson informed Tazewell that he had suggested to Wirt and Hay, in addition to other defenses, pleading the general issue, which permits the title to the batture to be supported "which I have undertaken to the Governor to support." To Tazewell, November 22, 1810.

36.   Tazewell to Jefferson, December 29, 1810; Jefferson to Tazewell, March 23, 1811.

37.   To Hay, August 1, 1810.

38.   "I presume the government will take it off my hands." To Wirt and Hay, May 19, 1810. "I suppose I may expect that the government will leave nothing on me but the care of seeing the case fairly & fully laid before the court. . . . [I have written to Governor Claiborne as] I do not think his state will be, or ought to be inattentive to the case." To Hay, June 18, 1810. See also to Wirt, June 18, 1810; Rodney to Jefferson, June 17, 1810; Jefferson to Tazewell, June 28, 1810; Jefferson to Gallatin, August 16, 1810; Gallatin to Jefferson, September 10, 1810; and Jefferson to Gallatin, September 27, 1810.

39.   Tazewell to Jefferson, May 15, 1812.

40.   On the effect of this plea, see Benjamin J. Shipman, *Handbook of Common-Law Pleading*, 307–308. Justification must be specifically pleaded.

41.   The defense of immunity of an executive officer from tort liability to a private individual for official acts performed in good faith was upheld by the Supreme Court in *Spalding* v. *Vilas*, 161 U.S. 483, 498 (1896).

42.   For a synopsis of the pleadings, see 15 Fed. Cas. 660–61. The declaration was in eight counts. "The defendant demurred to the second, fifth, sixth, seventh, and eighth counts. He also pleaded the general issue, and four several pleas of justification." The third plea was the plea to the jurisdiction of the court, to which plaintiff replied that defendant resided in Virginia and was "not amenable to the jurisdiction of the courts of the territory of Orleans." Defendant demurred generally to this replication, and the plaintiff joined in demurrer. A question of law was thus presented to the court.

43.   To Hay, August 1, 1810.

44.   Hay to Jefferson, December 5, 1811. This letter states that "yesterday" the two judges overruled the replication to the plea of jurisdiction. A copy of the court's judgment (LC 34515), in which defendant's demurrer to the replication is "adjudged good," bears the date of Thursday, December 5, 1811. The memoir had finally been forwarded to counsel on November 11, 1810, with Jefferson's letter of that date to Hay.

45.   To Wirt and Hay, May 19, 1810. Hay reported on May 25, 1810, that an order had been put on record requiring security for costs. The declaration was forwarded to Jefferson with Hay's letter of July 20, 1810, received by Jefferson four days later.

46.   Hay to Jefferson, May 25, 1810. Likewise when enclosing to Jefferson for his approval a draft of the pleas to be filed by February 10, 1811, Hay said: "The time, it is true, has been prolonged by agreement to the 22d, yet I do not wish to avail myself of Mr. Wickham's indulgence, if we can be in readiness on the day first named." Jefferson did not receive Hay's letter until March 2, 1811. Hay to Jefferson, January 25, 1811; Jefferson to Hay, March 3, 1811.

47.   To Madison, May 30, 1810. Letters were written the same day to Secretary of State Robert Smith, to Secretary of War Dr. William Eustis, to Secretary of the Treasury Albert

Gallatin, and to Attorney General Caesar A. Rodney. In his book, *The Proceedings of the Government of the United States, in Maintaining the Public Right to the Beach of the Missisipi, Adjacent to New-Orleans, against the Intrusion of Edward Livingston,* 21, Jefferson stresses that the eviction of Livingston was pursuant to an opinion of the attorney general given on October 24, 1807, and consideration at a cabinet meeting on November 27, 1807. In the letter to Rodney of May 30, 1810, Jefferson says, "I believe you did not give me a written opinion; but you did furnish one to Congress." This was Rodney's opinion of June 12, 1809. *American State Papers, Public Lands,* II, 5. On February 28, 1810, Robert Smith produced a copy of Rodney's opinion of October 24, 1807. *Ibid.,* 12.

48. Eustis to Jefferson, June 4, 1810.

49. Robert Smith to Jefferson, June 4, 1810, June 6, 1810.

50. John Graham to Jefferson, June 11, 1810.

51. James Mather to Jefferson, November 29, 1810.

52. To Claiborne, June 11, 1810; James Mather to Claiborne, August 5, 1810; Claiborne to Jefferson, August 11, 1810, August 25, 1810; James Mather to Jefferson, November 30, 1810.

53. After this sentence, in a letter to Wirt of the same date, Jefferson adds: "When fully possessed of the materials, I shall state the points on which I consider myself justified, submit the matter to my counsel, recieve their advice, & concert with them the course of defence." To Wirt, June 18, 1810.

54. To Hay, June 18, 1810. See also to Madison, July 13, 1810.

55. To Madison, May 25, 1810, 11 F. 141; to Madison, July 26, 1810; to Gallatin, August 16, 1810; to Hay, October 7, 1810. In the letter to Hay, Jefferson says that after a "thorough revisal" using the suggestions made by Madison, Smith, Gallatin, and Rodney he will deposit his memoir with counsel. Only Gallatin and Rodney offered helpful suggestions for Jefferson's memoir. Gallatin to Jefferson, July 14, 1810, September 10, 1810; Rodney to Jefferson, June 17, 1810, October 6, 1810, October 18, 1810. Tazewell commented at length on September 27, 1810; and Wirt on August 9, 1810. See notes 57 and 58, *infra.* Revisions in the text were also forwarded for scrutiny by Madison, Rodney, Smith, and Gallatin, as "my wish is to take no ground which they would disapprove." To Rodney, January 20, 1811; Rodney to Jefferson, March 4, 1811.

56. Hay to Jefferson, July 20, 1810, November 5, 1810. They did not wish to have to apply to the court for permission to file late. See note 46, *supra.* He finally sent a complete copy for use of counsel on November 11, 1810. To Hay, November 11, 1810.

57. To Hay, August 1, 1810. Wirt returned it with comments on August 9, 1810, to which Jefferson replied on August 20, 1810. It was sent to Tazewell on August 18, 1810. In consequence of Wirt's criticism, Jefferson examined all the authors he possessed concerning the Nile, and prepared a long note on that subject (*Proceedings,* 51–52). To Madison, August 20, 1810; to Tazewell, November 22, 1810.

58. Gallatin to Jefferson, July 14, 1810 (received July 19) enclosing memorandum (LC 33888).

59. To Gallatin, August 16, 1810. These included the argument that the Superior Court of Orleans Territory lacked chancery powers (*Proceedings,* 73–76), and the point regarding the reasons why John Gravier took the batture property by purchase and inventory rather than as an heir of Bertrand Gravier (*ibid.,* 10). Further corrections (LC 34095–97) were suggested in Gallatin's letter of September 10, 1810 (LC 33957–58), to which Jefferson replied on September 27, 1810, 11 F. 152.

60. Louis Casimir Elisabeth Moreau de Lislet (1767–1832), a Louisiana jurist and politician, had been educated in France. His *Mémoire* (dated October 31, 1808), a docu-

ment of 136 pages in a handsome script on light blue paper, is in the National Archives (RG 59 E. 116; see bibliography, *infra*). It is discussed by Jefferson in a long note in *Proceedings*, 36–39.

61. To Madison, May 30, 1810, July 13, 1810; John Graham to Jefferson, June 11, 1810; to Gallatin, August 16, 1810; Gallatin to Jefferson, September 10, 1810; Jefferson to Rodney, September 25, 1810; to Claiborne, October 16, 1810; Rodney to Jefferson, October 18, 1810. Livingston and Attorney General Rodney also desired the benefit of Moreau's *Mémoire*. Livingston to Duponceau, November 20, 1808, February 20, 1809; Duponceau to Livingston, April 20, 1809; Livingston to Duponceau, May 6, 1809; Livingston Papers.

62. To Tazewell, November 22, 1810. Jefferson acknowledged being heavily indebted to Moreau, whose treatment was the ablest he had seen, when finally forwarding his statement of the case to counsel. To Hay, November 11, 1810.

63. To William Branch Giles, November 12, 1810; to John W. Eppes, November 12, 1810.

64. To Hay, August 1, 1810; to Gallatin, August 16, 1810.

65. See note 44, *supra*.

66. To Hay, December 28, 1811. The manuscript of the *Proceedings*, with a bold signature at the end dated July 31, 1810, is LC 34667–709. There are also revisions and additions (LC 34653–57) and maps (LC 34658–66). A mass of work papers have also been preserved, including a list of sources (LC 34073), a list of books needed (LC 34116 *verso*), a list of papers sent to counsel (LC 34106), an outline (LC 34079), a synopsis (LC 34081), an amplified outline (LC 34082–83), notes on Roman, French, and Spanish law (LC 34084–85), a summary of correspondence and documents numbered 1–110 (LC 34088–93), a rough draft (LC 34117–35), revisions suggested by Rodney (LC 38094) and Gallatin (LC 34095–97), additional revisions (LC 34108–16, 34142–47), and much other material.

67. Hay to Jefferson, January 29, 1812 (listing ten items of documents), May 5, 1812 (sends residue, "Wirt was the delinquent"). Jefferson returned "more than *all*" the documents borrowed from government archives (as he explained in his covering letter of May 26, 1812, to Secretary of State Monroe) "because I have annexed others procured from other quarters, which I have thought might as well go & remain with the rest, as belonging to the same subject, and making part of the justification of the Executive." These documents constitute the bound volume in NA (RG 59, E. 110). He placed the remaining materials returned by Hay under the heading "Louisiana tracts" in his library. They are now in the Rare Book Room of the Library of Congress. Sowerby, III, 396–414.

68. Published at Philadelphia by William Duane in 1811. Antoine Louis Claude Destutt de Tracy (1754–1836) was a French economist whom Jefferson had met in Paris at the salon of Mme. Helvétius. Because of political conditions he wished the work to appear in English without revealing the author's identity.

69. Jefferson to William Duane, September 16, 1810, Sowerby, III, 5. I cannot discern the superlative value which Jefferson detected in this work. Perhaps this is one of Jefferson's inexplicable enthusiasms, like the navy of ships on land.

70. In Jefferson's letter of this date he says he has, since his earlier letter of August 12, 1810, completed reading the entire French text in French handwriting.

71. Sowerby #2327, III, 3–11.

72. Jefferson to Destutt de Tracy, November 28, 1813. Sowerby, III, 9.

73. See note 56, *supra*.

74. To Hugh Nelson, December 28, 1811.

THOMAS JEFFERSON AND THE LAW

75.   See pages 52–53, *infra.* See also to Claiborne, June 11, 1810.

76.   Rodney to Jefferson, June 17, 1810.

77.   *Mostyn* v. *Fabrigas*, Cowp. 161 (K.B. 1775). For a fuller account, including the trial at common pleas, see 20 Howell's *State Trials* 81–238.

78.   20 *State Trials* 228, 230, 231. Mansfield recognized that "Whatever is a justification in the place where the thing is done, ought to be a justification where the case is tried." *Ibid.*, 232.

79.   20 *State Trials* 237–38. See also *ibid.*, 233.

80.   15 Fed. Cas. 664. In Mansfield's opinion, Marshall points out, he refers to "two cases decided by himself, in which an action was sustained for trespass on lands lying in the foreign dominions of his Britannic majesty; but both those decisions were at nisi prius. And though the overbearing influence of Lord Mansfield might have sustained them on a motion for a new trial, that motion never was made, and the principle did not obtain the sanction of the court. In a subsequent case, (Doulson v. Matthews [1792] 4 Durn. & E., 4 Term R. 503), these decisions are expressly referred to and overruled, and the old distinction is affirmed." *Ibid.* Wickham in his letter of May 16, 1810, to Livingston had cited the *Doulson* case as "decisive" and "in conformity to the general Rules of Law." See note 8, *supra.*

81.   15 Fed. Cas. 660. Even this count alleges entry on the land. The second count charges expulsion of plaintiff from the land, preventing him from making improvements, and receiving the rents and profits from the land. The third count charges entering on Livingston's canal, which was destroyed by the rising water of the river. The fourth count charges similar destruction of his levee on the northern part of the land. The remaining counts duplicate the first four, with the addition in each case that defendant "with his servants" did enter, etc. *Ibid.*, 660–61.

82.   Hay to Jefferson, July 20, 1810, received July 24, 1810.

83.   Jefferson to Hay, August 1, 1810.

84.   Opinion of Jared Ingersoll and William Rawle, August 3, 1808. *American State Papers, Public Lands,* II, 73. The opinion of Edward Tilghman and William Lewis, of August 16, 1808, pronounced that the order of eviction was invalid and "that those who issued it, the marshal who obeyed it, and all who had assisted in its execution, are joint trespassers, and answerable in damages to Mr. Livingston for the wrong and injury which he has sustained." *Ibid.,* II, 74. See page 61, *infra.*

85.   Sometimes spelled "D'Orgenoy." The court papers in this case (No. 375), and in a later suit (No. 414) against his successor as marshal, Michel Fortier, have been made available through the courtesy of Nelson B. Jones, clerk of the United States District Court for the Eastern District of Louisiana. Unless otherwise indicated, statements regarding the course of this litigation are based upon these records.

86.   *Livingston* v. *D'Orgenoy,* 108 Fed. 469, 470 (D. La. 1809). Reported also at 1 Martin (O.S.) 87, 89. [The correct date of this opinion is October 24, 1810.]

87.   The opinion does not appear in the court papers, but is printed in 108 Fed. 471. On November 14, 1810, the previous judgment was confirmed and it was ordered "that the proceedings in this Case be finally stayed." This ruling of the district court was taken to the Supreme Court by writ of error. Duponceau advised Livingston with respect to the appeal and called a meeting of his other Philadelphia counsel (Lewis, Tilghman, Rawle, and Ingersoll). However, none of them was able to go to Washington for the argument. Duponceau to Livingston, May 4, 1812, September 19, 1812, and January 20, 1813.

Livingston Papers. Two prominent Maryland lawyers, Philip Barton Key and Robert Goodloe Harper, argued for Livingston, according to the report in 7 Cr. 577, 579, 586.

88. *Livingston* v. *Dorgenois*, 7 Cr. 577, 589 (1813). The District of Orleans court papers contain the actual writ dated March 17, 1813. Judge Hall later became a dramatic figure in the history of the judiciary when he was arrested by order of the headstrong General Andrew Jackson for having issued a writ of habeas corpus. When the excitement had died down, Jackson paid a fine of $1,000 for contempt of court. Charles Gayarré, *History of Louisiana*, 591, 609, 625. For other instances of judicial courage, see Dumbauld, *Constitution*, 6.

89. United States District Court for the District of Louisiana, Minute Book No. 3 (1811-15), 227. The judgment also appears as an endorsement on the amended petition in the file papers. The date of the decision is given as August 4, 1813, in Livingston's *Answer to Mr. Jefferson's Justification*, 178. On August 5, 1813, reciting recovery of a judgment against D'Orgenois, Livingston covenanted with him not to demand any money damages from him. The Docket of Suits, page 187, shows:
writ of possession issued
August 17th 1813
marshals return on
giving Possession 19 Augt. 1813.

90. Judge Hall may have relied on reasoning similar to that in *Little* v. *Barreme*, 2 Cr. 170, 177-79 (1804), where Chief Justice Marshall held that instructions from President Adams to seize ships bound *to or from* French ports, when the statute authorized only seizure of ships bound *to* such ports, "cannot . . . legalize an act which, without those instructions, would have been a plain trespass." Similarly, in *Gilchrist* v. *Collector of Charleston*, Fed. Cas. #5420 (Circuit Ct. S.C. 1808), Justice William Johnson (a Jefferson appointee) held that the Embargo Act of April 25, 1808, 2 Stat. 501, permitted detention of a ship only if the *collector* believed that a false destination was being declared in order to evade the embargo, and that Jefferson's more inclusive instructions, unsupported by the statute, were no justification. Contrary to public opinion in New England, the constitutionality of the embargo was upheld in *U.S.* v. *The Brigantine William*, Fed. Cas. #16,700 (D. Mass. 1808).

91. In a speech to the New Orleans city council on August 9, 1813, Claiborne said that in his opinion only D'Orgenois could appeal, and that he would not do so. But an attempt would be made for the city council and governor to seek review of Judge Hall's ruling. Dunbar Rowland (ed.), *Official Letter Books of W. C. C. Claiborne*, VI, 254.

92. Claiborne to Jefferson, August 14, 1813, Rowland, *Official Letter Books*, VI, 258.

93. Clippings in NA, RG 59 E. 110, dated November 17, 1810.

94. Tully Robinson (United States attorney) to J. M. Fortier (marshal), November 19, 1810; James Mather to Jefferson, November 30, 1810; Thomas B. Robertson to Jefferson, December 7, 1810; Claiborne to Jefferson, December 24, 1810. See also Claiborne to James Monroe, February 14, 1812, Rowland, *Official Letter Books*, VI, 254.

95. See note 25, *supra*.

96. "I observe by the papers that Livingston's suit against the Marshal . . . came before the federal court of Orleans, on the 24th. of April, on the plea that he was not a citizen of New York . . . A jury found him to be a citizen of New York." Jefferson to John Tyler, June 17, 1812, Sowerby, III, 409.

97. In October, 1818, John R. Grymes was given leave to withdraw the plea of not guilty filed by him on behalf of the defendant, since "he had appeared in the . . . suit at

the instance of Governor Claiborne who had promised to cause his counsel's fee to be paid by the United States which had never been done." Minute Book No. 4 (1815–19), 343. It was United States Attorney Philip Grymes who had at first (on September 25, 1808) permitted the public to continue to dig earth on the batture after Livingston's eviction, but withdrew that permission upon instructions from Washington dated October 5, 1809. Jefferson wished to maintain the status quo without either permitting or prohibiting the customary use of the batture by the public. See page 60, *infra.*

98. See page 64, *infra.*

99. Regarding the court papers in this case (No. 414), see note 85, *supra.*

100. To Gallatin, September 27, 1810, 11 F. 152–55. Gallatin's memorandum (see note 58, *supra*) reads more like a lawyer's brief. It embraces three main points:

> I. The Law authorises the President to remove E. Livingston.
> II. The decree of the territorial Court in favour of Livingston did not preclude the President from the right of exercising the general powers vested in him.
> III. E. Livingston had no claim for damages because he had no title.

101. Rodney to Jefferson, October 6, 1810, LC; Wirt to Jefferson, April 15, 1812, Sowerby, III, 407.

102. *Proceedings*, 9. This is Gallatin's third point, concluding: "He [Livingston] now claims damages. If he had no title he received none." See note 100, *supra.*

103. This proposition is supported upon three grounds: (1) Thierry's view that alluvion accrues only to rustic, not urban, lands; (2) since the bank of the river had become part of the port, which is public domain, any alluvion added to it likewise was public property; (3) when Bertrand Gravier sold the front lots, he also sold the right of alluvion, which was incidental or accessory to the riparian land.

104. *Answer*, 10. "I am an intruder on the public, or he an invader of private rights. The only true enquiries were, Was the land in question the property of the United States? Had the president a right to seize it if it were?" *Ibid.*, 167.

105. In Roman law the distinction was between *ager arcifinius* (riparian land) and *ager limitatus* (delimited land). The rule was that *"in agris limitatis jus alluvionis locum non habere constat."* ("The right of alluvion does not appertain to delimited land.") Dig. 41.1.16.

106. *Proceedings*, 7, 8. Rodney regarded this idea as "new & conclusive. They are thus caught in their own net." See letter cited in note 101, *supra.* Livingston, *Answer*, 11, argues that the deeds from Gravier, by reference to a plan or map, can be seen to give only to an existing road, not to the water. This depends on whether the words *"todo conforme al plano"* ("all in conformity with the plan") apply to the front lots first described in the deed from Gravier, as well as to the lots in the rear, which are then described immediately preceding the reference to the plan. Livingston charges Jefferson with mistranslation for omitting the word "all" when quoting from the deed. Without examining the plan, I should think Jefferson's interpretation more plausible, especially since the grantor reserved a right to dig earth from the batture to make bricks. "Now if nothing was meant to be conveyed *beyond* the front line marked in the plan, why reserve a right to dig earth on the batture, which is *beyond* that line?" *Proceedings*, 8.

107. This point was suggested by Gallatin. See note 59, *supra*.

108. On this point see Livingston, *Answer*, 14. Livingston produced as a witness one of the appraisers, who said that he had walked on the batture to estimate its value, but that it had been omitted inadvertently. Jefferson pointed out that at the date of the appraisement the river was high and the batture was covered with water. He also stressed that the appraised value of $2470 would have been higher if the batture had been included. *Proceedings*, 11. Jefferson's contention was ultimately sustained in a suit brought by the other heirs of Bertrand Gravier. See page 70, *infra*.

109. *Proceedings*, 13. Livingston held a half-interest in the first purchase; on learning of the second he sued de la Bigarre to protect his interest. *Answer*, 17. Livingston contended that since Gravier had possession of the land, he could legally sell it even though other claims were outstanding (many tracts in Kentucky had been the subject of successive and conflicting grants by the land office) and it was prudent and proper for Gravier to retain title until paid and for the purchaser to condition his bargain upon obtaining good title as a result of the lawsuit. *Ibid.*, 18, 21. In any event de la Bigarre's champerty did not give the United States any title. *Ibid.*, 15.

110. He cited a provision of Roman law punishing those "who wickedly participate in another's lawsuit" (*"qui improbe coeunt in alienam litem"*). Dig. 47.8.6.

111. *Proceedings*, 14.

112. *American State Papers, Public Lands*, II, 22, 23. Regarding Moreau, see note 60, *supra*.

113. *Ibid.*, II, 14. Livingston claimed that this purchase was worth $80,000, plus an expense of $13,000 for improvements. Girod was probably one of Gravier's grantees where the batture was expressly mentioned in the deed. Livingston bought up those claims for $10,700 in addition to what he obtained from Gravier (probably, as Jefferson thought, as his fee). *Answer*, 12; Sowerby, III, 399. Senator William Branch Giles of Virginia was reported to have said that Livingston could not have acquired the batture so cheaply if the title were good. Duponceau to Livingston, June 4, 1809, Livingston Papers.

114. *American State Papers, Public Lands*, II, 23, 33. Prevost was intimate with Livingston, and lived in the same house with him. Claiborne to Jefferson, December 10, 1804. Clarence E. Carter (ed.), *The Territorial Papers of the United States*, IX, 348. On that date Claiborne administered the oath of office to Judge Dominic A. Hall. See note 88, *supra*.

115. *American State Papers, Public Lands*, II, 23. On June 2, 1806, a twelve-day trial had begun before judges Sprigg and Mathews.

116. *Ibid.*, 33. For text of the opinion, see *ibid.*, II, 13–14.

117. *Ibid.*, II, 13–14.

118. *Ibid.*, II, 14. Proceedings in the *Gravier* case are also printed in Livingston's *Address*, to be found in Jefferson's Louisiana Tracts in LC (see note 67, *supra*, and Sowerby #3493); and MS copies are part of the court papers in *Livingston* v. *D'Orgenoy* (see note 85, *supra*, and note 128, *infra*).

119. *Proceedings*, 16. See also Claiborne to Jefferson, May 20, 1807, NA (RG 59, E. 110), Carter, *Territorial Papers*, IX, 737.

120. *American State Papers, Public Lands*, II, 37–43. See also Hall's *American Law Journal*, Vol. II (1809), 282–306; James A. Padgett, "Some Documents Relating to the Batture Controversy," *The Louisiana Historical Quarterly*, Vol. XXIII, No. 3 (July, 1940), 679–732; and separate prints in French and English in Louisiana Tracts (LC). Pierre Auguste Charles Bourguignon Derbigny (1767–1829) left France in 1793 and became a

French colonial official in Louisiana. He was secretary of state of Louisiana from 1820 to 1827, and governor in 1828. He was counsel for the city of New Orleans in the suit brought by Jean Gravier. See note 112, *supra*.

121. *Proceedings*, 16.

122. *Ibid.*, 17.

123. *Ibid.*, 19.

124. *American State Papers, Public Lands*, II, 12. Rodney also had before him the opinion of the territorial court, and Jefferson read an article in the *Encyclopédie* cited by Derbigny in his opinion. Jefferson to Gallatin, November 4, 1807, Henry Adams, *The Writings of Albert Gallatin*, I, 366. Livingston believed (based upon his letter to Rodney of July 20, 1808, and Rodney's reply of July 25, 1808, *American State Papers, Public Lands*, II, 36–37) that Rodney had not seen the territorial court's decision when he gave his opinion. *Address*, xxvi. He told Rodney that "it is desirable that I should know to which the president has given the greatest credit, the solemn deliberate decision of three judges, appointed by himself, and sworn to do justice between the parties, or the *ex parte* statement of a lawyer, feed to maintain a contrary opinion."

125. 2 Stat. 445–46. The terms of this statute will be discussed in detail subsequently. See pages 66–68, *infra*.

126. *American State Papers, Public Lands*, II, 12. Rodney's opinion of October 24, 1807 (see note 47, *supra*), his letter of the same date to Madison in like vein, and most of the documentation underlying the account of events given in Jefferson's *Proceedings* are to be found in NA (RG 59, E. 110).

127. *Proceedings*, 72. Accordingly, a letter of the same date was written by the secretary of war to the commanding officer at New Orleans, but no military force was used. *Ibid.* Madison's instructions to the marshal (which are printed in 7 Cranch 578) were delivered to him on January 25, 1808, having been received by Claiborne the preceding day (a Sunday). Claiborne to Madison, January 29, 1808, NA (RG 59, E. 110).

128. *Proceedings*, 72–73. Later the river in its flood season destroyed the partially completed canal and levee. See note 81, *supra*. Copies of the court papers relating to the injunction granted by judges George Mathews, Jr. and Joshua Lewis of the territorial court are contained in the district court file of case No. 375 (*Livingston* v. *D'Orgenois*). See note 85, *supra*. The marshal's own account of what occurred is given in his report to Claiborne of January 27, 1807, in NA (RG 59, E. 110).

129. *Proceedings*, 76–77; Richardson, *Messages of the Presidents*, I, 442–43. Upon reading that message, Claiborne wrote that if the property belongs to the United States, "I sincerely hope it may be forthwith transfer'ed to the corporation, for the use thereof is essential to the growth and convenience of this City." Claiborne to Jefferson, April 26, 1808, NA (RG 59, E. 110). Four months earlier Gallatin had made, and Jefferson had approved, such a suggestion. Gallatin to Jefferson [December 23, 1807], LC 30654; Jefferson to Gallatin, December 24, 1807, LC 30655. Gallatin preferred this solution to the establishment of a special tribunal to hear the batture case. Jefferson to Gallatin, March 2, 1808, LC 31067, 12 M. 2 [with misprint "future" for "batture"]; Gallatin to Jefferson, March 2, 1808, LC 31071, Adams, *Writings of Gallatin*, I, 375: "I do not like much the idea of creating a special court for deciding the question of the bature. If we give our right to the corporation, they may afterwards fight it with the courts as they please."

130. *American State Papers, Public Lands*, II, 6–7.

131. *Ibid.*, II, 7–8.

132. Claiborne thought that Congress should provide for appeals from the territorial court either to the Supreme Court or to a special court of appeals. Claiborne to Madison,

September 16, 1807, NA (RG 59, E. 110). To settle the batture controversy he proposed "a special Board of Commissioners" to sit in Washington. Claiborne to Jefferson, April 16, 1808, *ibid.* Jefferson had already considered such a plan "that the claim to the batture given to the city should be decided by Special commissioners, to whom the evidence & arguments in writing shall be sent, without any necessity of their going there." Jefferson to Gallatin, December 24, 1807, LC 30655. See note 129, *supra.*

133. *American State Papers, Public Lands*, II, 5.

134. Duponceau to Livingston, April 15, 1809, Livingston Papers. On Peter S. Duponceau, *A Review of the Cause of the New Orleans Batture*, see note 141, *infra.* The idea of a second injunction had been mentioned earlier. Duponceau to Livingston, February 28, 1809, Livingston Papers. Regarding Rodney, see also Duponceau to Livingston, February 22, 1809; Livingston to Duponceau, April 17, 1809; Duponceau to Livingston, April 20, 1809; Livingston to Duponceau, May 6, 1809; Duponceau to Livingston, May 8, 1809 [No. 2], May 30, 1809, Livingston Papers.

"Impatient at the Delay of the Attorney General," Livingston had measures introduced in Congress to restore his possession of the batture and refer the question of title to commissioners. Livingston to Duponceau, June 2, 1809, June 3, 1809, June 26, 1809; Duponceau to Livingston, December 19, 1809, March 5, 1810, March 8, 1810, March 12, 1810, March 26, 1810, April 4, 1810, Livingston Papers. But Congress did not act. Livingston's hope in the Madison administration (Duponceau to Livingston, December 21, 1808, February 22, 1809, February 28, 1809; Livingston to Duponceau, April 13, 1809, April 17, 1809, Livingston Papers) was vain. Duponceau rightly feared "that you will have against you the party of the late President, & that [Rodney's] opinion will be their rallying point." Duponceau to Livingston, June 13, 1809, Livingston Papers.

135. *American State Papers, Public Lands*, II, 43–53. This was dated December 10, 1807. [Although it has separate pagination, I have not found it published except as one of the items annexed to Livingston's *Address* in 1808. See Sowerby #3484 and #3496. It is also printed in Hall's *American Law Journal*, Vol. II (1809), 307–358. It must have been issued separately, as Duponceau in his opinion of July 26, 1808, also annexed to the *Address*, refers to the *Examination* as "a printed pamphlet," and he did not see the *Address* until he received Livingston's letter of October 24, 1808. [See his reply of November 29, 1808, Livingston Papers.]

136. *American State Papers, Public Lands*, II, 69–72. [Livingston's questions and the opinions of counsel are also printed in Hall's *American Law Journal*, Vol. II (1809), 434–55.]

137. *American State Papers, Public Lands*, II, 72–73.

138. *Ibid.*, II, 73–74.

139. *Ibid.*, II, 59–69. [It is also printed in Hall's *American Law Journal*, Vol. II (1809), 392–433.] Peter Stephen Duponceau (1760–1844) was a French lawyer who came to the United States in 1777, as secretary to Baron Steuben. He became a citizen of Pennsylvania in 1781, and achieved eminence at the Philadelphia bar.

140. See note 120, *supra.* "Mr. Derbigny's arguments I answer seriously—Mr. Thiery's with the weapon of ridicule, which he really deserves." Duponceau to John R. Livingston, February 17, 1809, Livingston Papers. See also note 141, *infra.*

141. With philosophical amusement Duponceau dwelt upon the contradictions between the arguments of Thierry and Derbigny. Derbigny, he said, had been disavowed as spokesman of New Orleans, which had sponsored Thierry's pamphlet; while Derbigny viewed Thierry's concessions as disastrous. *Review*, 8, 10–12, 26, 39, 44. [Duponceau's *Review* is also printed in Hall's *American Law Journal*, Vol. IV (1813), 517–62.] For comments

on his *Review*, see Duponceau to John R. Livingston, February 17, 1809; Duponceau to Edward Livingston, February 22, 1809, February 28, 1809 [sends 3 copies, has sent copies to the president and heads of departments], March 8, 1809, March 29, 1809, Livingston Papers. For Livingston's comment on the quarrel between Derbigny and Thierry, see Livingston to Duponceau, November 20, 1808, Livingston Papers. For Duponceau's comment on Thierry's reply to his *Review*, see Duponceau to Livingston, July 22, 1809, September 27, 1809, Livingston Papers.

142. Jean Baptiste Simon Thierry (d. 1815), a French journalist, came to the United States in 1804 and printed a newspaper in New Orleans. His *Examen des Droits* was dated October 15, 1808.

143. See note 60, *supra*. Jefferson ventured to disagree with Moreau (*Proceedings*, 36–39) as well as with Thierry (*ibid.*, 32–33) where they made concessions which he considered unnecessary and damaging. Jefferson to Hay, November 11, 1810. See Livingston, *Answer*, 61–62. Derbigny had warned Jefferson that Thierry was a printer, "not versed in jurisprudence." Derbigny to Jefferson, November 14, 1808, Sowerby III, 402. Livingston described him as "a hireling printer, who has no legal reputation to lose." *Address*, xxix.

144. Julien de Lalande Poydras (1746–1824) arrived in Louisiana in 1768. After the Louisiana Purchase he became a friend of Governor Claiborne and held various public offices, including that of delegate from the Territory of Orleans to Congress. He published several pamphlets and speeches in support of the right of the public to the batture. See Sowerby #3485–89 and #3503–5.

145. Printed in *American State Papers, Public Lands*, II, 12–74. Livingston sent Duponceau 200 copies for members of Congress but Duponceau considered it "most impolitic" and refused to distribute it. Livingston to Duponceau, October 24, 1808; Duponceau to Livingston, November 29, 1808, December 6, 1808, December 21, 1808, Livingston Papers. Livingston replied that the address had already been made public in New Orleans, and that it had been sent to the president. Moreover, "you do not know as well as I do the malice and malignity of my enemies. . . . I am convinced that I have nothing to hope but from their fears. . . . I can write, and I have a strong case of wanton oppression which sooner or later will raise the indignation of the public." Livingston to Duponceau, January 22, 1809, Livingston Papers. Livingston did acquiesce in Duponceau's strategy (of preventing the batture controversy from being made a partisan conflict, which Livingston's forces could not win) to the extent of refusing to authorize a republication of the address. Livingston to Duponceau, April 17, 1809; Duponceau to Livingston, April 18, 1809, Livingston Papers. See page 60, *supra*.

146. When Duponceau first saw Jefferson's book, he said, "The work is well & skilfully written, but might be very easily refuted." Later he wrote, "Mr. Jefferson's printed instructions to his Counsel . . . will be best answered, I think, before the Supreme Court U.S. on the final hearing of your Cause." [See note 87, *supra*.] But subsequently he urged, "You owe it to yourself to publish an answer." Duponceau to Livingston, May 15, 1812, June 20, 1812, January 20, 1813, Livingston Papers. Duponceau carefully read proof and made corrections when Livingston's *Answer* was published. Duponceau to Livingston, January 20, 1813, Livingston Papers.

147. *Proceedings*, 21. See also to Madison, May 19, 1808, 12 M. 57–59; and Moreau, *Mémoire*, 83.

148. Hunter Miller, *Treaties and Other International Acts of the United States of America*, II, 508–509.

149. The Louisiana Purchase was effected by the treaty of April 30, 1803. *Ibid.*, II,

498–511. Acquisition of this "empire for liberty" is one of the major accomplishments of Jefferson's administration, though he himself entertained qualms as to its constitutionality. Dumbauld, *Political Writings of Thomas Jefferson*, 50, 144. On the topic generally, see Malone, *President, First Term*, 284–320.

150. "*Quod per alluvionem agro tuo flumen adjecit, jure gentium tibi adquiritur.*" *Inst.* 2.1.20.

151. Livingston, *Answer*, 29–33. Jefferson did not admit that French private law was superseded by Spanish, even after transfer of the province to Spain in 1769, in the absence of express action by the new sovereign. *Proceedings*, 21. This view is supported by Blackstone (*Commentaries*, I, 107) as well as by rulings of Chief Justice Holt in *Blankard* v. *Galdy*, 2 Salkeld 411 (K. B. 1693) and of Chief Justice Marshall in *U.S.* v. *Percheman*, 7 Pet. 51, 86–87 (1833). The former case was digested by Jefferson in his Legal Commonplace Book, item 175. See also *Anon.*, 2 P. Wms. 75 (1722).

152. *Proceedings*, 25. Roman law, says Jefferson, formed a subsidiary part of the custom of Paris. As to this, see Wirt to Jefferson, August 9, 1810, and Jefferson to Wirt, August 20, 1810.

153. *Proceedings*, 26. Guyot and Le Rasle agreed with Pothier, but other authorities disagreed. Tazewell to Jefferson, September 27, 1810. Duponceau refers to Le Rasle disparagingly as a person "of whom nothing is known but that he was hired by the booksellers to compile the legal section of the new encyclopaedia." *American State Papers, Public Lands*, II, 64–65. See note 124, *supra*. It was Duponceau's conclusion, in his opinion of July 26, 1808, that under French law alluvion belongs to the riparian owner. *Ibid.*, II, 69.

154. Livingston, *Answer*, 32, says that there was no evidence that any alluvion was formed between 1763 and 1769.This seems unlikely in view of the yearly inundation by the river. As Duponceau pointed out, if there was no alluvion before 1769 there would be nothing for French law to operate upon. *American State Papers, Public Lands*, II, 69. See also Duponceau to John R. Livingston, January 28, 1809, Livingston Papers. (Accretion between October 1, 1800, and April 30, 1803, would also have been governed by French law.) According to Gallatin's memorandum (see notes 58 and 100, *supra*), "It is uncertain when that batture, which is the subject matter of this controversy began to be noticed. It is however proved that a portion existed before the year 1763, and that it had increased considerably in 1788."

155. Article 2 of the treaty of Paris of April 30, 1803, included in the cession to the United States "all public lots Squares, vacant lands and all public buildings, fortifications, barracks and other edifices which are not private property." Miller, *Treaties*, II, 500. Article 3 protected private property. Livingston, *Answer,* 124, contended that the batture did not fall within the description of "vacant lands," but he invoked the benefit of Article 3.

156. *Proceedings*, 29. Livingston, *Answer*, 40–43, interpreted the edict differently.

157. Jefferson regarded *attérissement* (accumulation or addition) and *accroissement* (increment or accretion) as generic terms, of which *alluvion* was a species. *Proceedings*, 33. But it was Tazewell's opinion that land formed by the river which was not contiguous to the shore could not be *alluvion*, but was *accroissement*. Tazewell to Jefferson, May 15, 1812. In Duponceau's opinion (included in Livingston's *Address*, but separately paginated, xii) *accroissement* is defined as "land which is suddenly transported from one place to another by the violence of the waters of a river" and *attérissement* as "land which is left uncovered when a river suddenly changes its bed altogether, and opens to itself an entire new channel." In Derbigny's opinion (also included in the *Address*, but separately paginated, xix) *attérissement* is described as "a heap of sand and slime that the sea or the rivers transport from one place to another, which changes their bed and shores." Derbigny regards

accroissement as "a generical term" including *alluvion*. Livingston, *Answer*, 41, says the term *accroissement* includes some species of land formed by the river which are neither *attérissements* nor *alluvions*. The characteristic feature of alluvion (as distinguished from avulsion, a sudden shift of location by the river) is that it is "an addition to riparian land gradually and imperceptibly made by the water to which the land is contiguous." *County of St. Clair* v. *Lovingston*, 23 Wall. 46, 68 (1875). See also *Nebraska* v. *Iowa*, 143 U.S. 359, 360–62 (1892).

158. *Proceedings*, 28–29.

159. *American State Papers, Public Lands*, II, 60–61. This point had been referred to earlier in Livingston's *Examination*, 33–35.

160. See page 249 n. 89, *infra*.

161. *American State Papers, Public Lands*, II, 62. For Livingston's discussion of the Bordeaux case, see *Answer*, 56–61. He points out that the king yielded on July 28, 1786, while Jefferson was in France. *Ibid.*, 61. Duponceau had written to friends in France and procured rare documents regarding the Bordeaux case. Duponceau to Livingston, July 28, 1809, August 1, 1809, and August 11, 1809, Livingston Papers. Jefferson argues that this case simply proved that the Roman law rule was the custom of Bordeaux, "not that it was then the law of all France." *Proceedings*, 34. Gallatin in his suggested revisions noted that "The argument drawn by Livingston from the decree of Bordeaux does not seem to be fully answered." LC 34095.

162. *American State Papers, Public Lands*, II, 63–64. This point had been made earlier in Livingston's *Examination*, 22, 36–38.

163. *Proceedings*, 30–32. Moreau, *Mémoire*, 30, gave a shorter and better answer to Duponceau's point by showing that the king's rights in navigable rivers were a consequence of his sovereignty, not of his feudal dominion.

164. *Proceedings*, 30.

165. *Ibid.* Livingston replied, in language reminiscent of the Declaration of Independence, that "a separate property in lands as well as moveables may be reasonably supposed to have existed before the establishment of any civil government, and . . . civil government was resorted to, to secure and perpetuate those rights, but did not *create* them." *Answer*, 63. See page 153, *infra*.

166. *Proceedings*, 38–41.

167. See Jean Baptiste Thierry, *Examen des Droits des Etats-Unis*, 32–33. Concerning Thierry's legal ability, see note 143, *supra*.

168. *Proceedings*, 39. See note 105, *supra*.

169. Livingston, *Answer*, 67, citing Dig. 50.15.4.2: "*agrum in civitate*." The term "*area*" was not the only Latin word applicable to a city lot.

170. This argument was forcefully stated by Louis Moreau de Lislet: *Examen de la Sentence*, 21; *Mémoire*, 104–108, 113. He cited provisions in the Spanish code (*Partida* 3, title 28, law 9) referring to ports and sandy beaches (*arenales*) as public property. However, this contention had been rejected by the territorial court. See page 58, *supra*, and *American State Papers, Public Lands*, II, 26.

171. Gustavus Schmidt, "The Batture Question," *The Louisiana Law Journal*, Vol. I, No. 2 (August, 1841), 147–49. The same writer cites a French jurist, Charles Compte, *Traité de la Propriété* (Brussels, 1835), 95–117, as upholding Jefferson's view of French law. *Ibid.*, 100. According to Schmidt, the 1807 decision was wrong and is an instructive example of the "fatal consequences to which a single judicial error may lead." *Ibid.*, 149–50.

172. *Municipality No. 2* v. *Orleans Cotton Press*, 18 La. 122, 231–36 (1841). For Martin's comment, see *ibid.*, 262–63.

173. *Proceedings*, 42, 44.

174. Gallatin in his suggested revisions criticized the distinction between apposition and deposition as "more ingenious than solid." LC 34096. Rodney also commented on this point. LC 34094.

175. *Answer*, 80–81. "If they provoke a smile even from the man who has been ruined by their application, certainly no indifferent reader can peruse them without a broader expression of mirth." *Ibid.*, 83. However, see Moreau, *Mémoire*, 90–91; and Tazewell's concept of alluvion, note 157, *supra*. Claiborne also said the batture was really a "shoal" rather than alluvion, since it was covered by water during some months every year, and during that time is part of the bed of the river. Claiborne to Jefferson, October 24, 1808, Rowland, *Official Letter Books*, IV, 232. In *Morgan* v. *Livingston*, 6 Martin 19, 216 (1819), Judge Martin defined batture as "a bottom of sand, stone, or rock mixed together, rising towards the surface of the water," as "an elevation of the bed of a river, under the surface of the water." The term, however, is "sometimes used to denote the same elevation of the bank, when it has arisen above the surface of the water, or is as high as the land on the outside of the bank." Not until the gradually and imperceptibly formed deposit rises above water and can be reclaimed as dry land by advancing the levee farther towards the river, is it susceptible of becoming private property, belonging to the riparian owner. *Ibid.*, 217.

176. *Proceedings*, 44, 45–46.

177. *Ibid.*, 52, 53.

178. *Ibid.*, 49.

179. *Ibid.*, 49–50.

180. *Ibid.*, 50. Moreau, *Mémoire*, 85, takes the same view; as does Judge Martin for the Louisiana Supreme Court in *Morgan* v. *Livingston*, 6 Martin 19, 229 (1819).

181. A long note was added in response to Wirt's comments. See note 57, *supra*.

182. *Proceedings*, 47.

183. Livingston, *Answer*, 98, defines the bank as what contains the river in its natural state. He considers it anomalous that under Jefferson's definition the settlers along the shore are living in the bed of the river until they erect an effective levee. That would mean that the land could not be granted to them as private property until the construction of the levee. *Ibid.*, 96.

184. *Proceedings*, 9.

185. *Ibid.*, 5.

186. *Ibid.*, 55–58.

187. Enforcement procedures under Roman law are then also reviewed. *Ibid.*, 58–61.

188. *Ibid.*, 61–63. In *Henderson* v. *Mayor of New Orleans*, 5 La. 416, 423 (1832), the court held that consent by the jury of riparian proprietors could not be withheld "when the public safety is not endangered" or subjected to arbitrary conditions. In *Packwood* v. *Walden*, 7 Martin (N.S.) 81, 85–87 (1828), it had been held that the legislation of 1808 was abrogated by inconsistent provisions of a later statute enacted in 1813 giving the city council power to regulate the construction of roads and levees.

189. However, as Gallatin pointed out, this argument weakens the force of the contention that Livingston was properly removed as an intruder on public lands acquired by treaty (see Act of March 3, 1807, 2 Stat. 445, page 66, *infra*). "If Mr. Livingston was removed as an intruder of public lands, could the territorial legislature pass an act under which he might be re-instated [?]. May not therefore the admission of that power render

questionable the power exercised by the President, by considering the batture not as public lands absolutely, but as that species of public property which was under the controul of the local legislature [?] I have always feared that the strongest argument of Livingston would be to deny that the batture was public land, within the meaning of the act of 3 March 1807, and to insist that it was the bed or bank of the river. For that reason, merely as it relates to the suit agst. Mr. Jefferson, the whole of the argument against Livingston's claim which is derived from the batture being part of the bank or bed has appeared to me somewhat dangerous." LC 34096. For Jefferson's comment, see to Gallatin, September 27, 1810, 11 F. 152.

190. *Proceedings*, 76.

191. "Would he have done this? If he would, he deserves impeachment for his disregard of what he says is the right of the United States; if he would not, he deserves something worse for the unfounded assertion." *Answer*, 105.

192. *Proceedings*, 64.

193. *Answer*, 107, 109. In summarizing his pamphlet, Livingston says on this point: "The singular idea that the President of the United States is required or authorized to abate nuisances in the city of New Orleans, has been exposed to the derision it deserves." *Ibid.*, 170.

194. *Ibid.*, 110, 112, 170.

195. *Ibid.*, 110, 170.

196. *Proceedings*, 65.

197. *Proceedings*, 66–67. On this topic Livingston remarked that Jefferson "forgets that we have only a few fragments of those celebrated laws; but he is quite as well acquainted with the laws he has not read, as he appears to be with those which he has." *Answer*, 115.

198. *Proceedings*, 67, 68. Livingston disputes Jefferson's statements about the need for an inquest of office, but there is little difference between their statements of the English law of remedies against the crown. *Answer*, 118–20. Jefferson describes these formalities as "playing push-pin with judges and lawyers." *Proceedings*, 80.

199. *Proceedings*, 68–69.

200. *Answer*, 122–71.

201. *Ibid.*, 136. However, it seems clear that the action of the president in enforcing the Act of 1807 would fall within the rule that: "Whenever a statute gives a discretionary power to any person, to be exercised by him, upon his own opinion of certain facts, it is a sound rule of construction, that the statute constitutes him the sole and exclusive judge of the existence of those facts." *Martin* v. *Mott*, 12 Wheat. 19, 31–32 (1827). Livingston's eloquent assertion that the president "may take allegation for proof; suspicion for evidence, and substitute the suggestions of malice for the records of title" resembles Jefferson's denunciation of the Alien and Sedition Acts, under which the president "may himself be the accuser, counsel, judge & jury, whose suspicions may be the evidence, his order the sentence, his officer the executioner, & his breast the sole record of the transaction." *Address*, xxix; 8 F. 472.

202. See page 59, *supra*.

203. *Answer*, 140.

204. 2 Stat. 445. The right, title, and claim of offenders is forfeited by this section of the act to the United States "without any other or further proceedings: *Provided*, that nothing herein contained, shall be construed to affect the right, title, or claim, of any person to lands in the territories of Orleans or Louisiana, before the boards of commissioners established by the act [of March 2, 1805, 2 Stat. 324] shall have made their reports and the

decision of Congress been had thereon." Section 2 of the act relates to permission to be given to persons who had before the passing of the act settled on ceded lands and who on the date of the act did "actually inhabit and reside on such lands" to remain thereon as tenants at will under certain conditions. Section 3 relates to records to be kept of such permissions. Section 4 authorizes removal by the marshal, after January 1, 1808, of persons found on the land without such permission. Such settlers prior to passage of the act are to be given three months' notice. Nothing in section 4, according to a proviso, shall apply to persons whose claims shall have been filed with the proper commissioners before January 1, 1808. The time for filing claims under the Act of 1805 was extended from March 1, 1806, until January 1, 1807, by the Act of April 21, 1806, 2 Stat. 391–92, and until July 1, 1808, by the Act of March 3, 1807, 2 Stat. 441.

205. Livingston acquired the property after the territorial court's judgment of May 23, 1807. See page 58, *supra*. His works commenced in August. See page 59, *supra*. Moreau, *Mémoire*, 129, 135, points out that Livingston's possession could not have begun before the date of the judgment, because his grantor (as well as the defendants in the case) were bound by the preliminary injunction maintaining the status quo pending the final judgment. Livingston argued that his possession merely continued that of his predecessors in interest, which originated long before 1807; and that the statute applied only to *new* possession. *Answer*, 125–26.

206. "Previously" doubtless means before the intruder's entry on the land, rather than before the date of the act or of the treaty. Gallatin so interpreted the act in his memorandum. See notes 58 and 100, *supra*.

207. Moreau, *Mémoire*, 131–33, corroborates this contention of Gallatin's.

208. "If there is any impropriety in this provision, it attaches to the act of Congress, not to the act of the President. The object of the law is however obvious. The United States cannot permit that possession should be taken of the public lands under colour of claims not recognized by law. The whole of the public lands would otherwise be invaded & probably irretrievably lost. Nor can the United States be sued, or the Courts by indirection permitted to give possession so long as the lands continue to be public lands. . . . Such is the general intention of the land laws."

209. Regarding the extent of land litigation involving spurious titles, see Homer Cummings and Carl McFarland, *Federal Justice*, 120–24.

210. In the case of completed grants, "as aforesaid, it shall not be necessary for the claimant to have any other evidence of his claim recorded, except the original grant or patent, together with the warrant or order of survey, and the plat." Act of March 2, 1805, section 4, 2 Stat. 326–27. [Italics supplied.] See note 204, *supra*. For Livingston's comment on this provision, see *Answer*, 129.

211. There was a proviso "that nothing in this act contained, shall be construed so as to recognize any grant or incomplete title" bearing date subsequent to October 1, 1800, or to authorize the commission to make any decision thereon. Section 5, 2 Stat. 327.

212. The cession from France to the United States undoubtedly included all public property incident to sovereignty over the territory, even if it was not specifically included in Article 2 of the treaty. See note 155, *supra*. In *New Orleans* v. *De Armas*, 9 Pet. 224, 234 (1835), Chief Justice Marshall said that Article 2 comprehended in the cession "every right vested in France."

213. The effect of the proviso in section 1 of the Act of 1807 (see note 204, *supra*) is simply to prevent the removal of an intruder from affecting the decision of the commissioners (appointed under the Act of 1805, see note 211, *supra*) with respect to the merits of a claim made by him to the land from which he had been removed. In other words the

forfeiture under section 1 of the Act of 1807 would not preclude favorable action by the commissioners on the claim. Livingston's rhetorical question is plausible but not persuasive: "Does it not *affect* my *right* to lands, to give another the legal power to deprive me of their enjoyment?" *Answer*, 130. The claimant really has no *right* until it has been recognized by the commissioners.

214. Livingston claimed that the procedure provided in the act had not been followed. See page 66, *supra*.

215. That is to say, January 1, 1808. Livingston complains that Madison's letter of instructions was sent on November 30, 1807 (see note 127, *supra*). *Answer*, 134. But the actual removal did not take place until January 25, 1808 (see page 59, *supra*).

216. 2 Stat. 446. The Act of March 26, 1804, 2 St. 283–89, divided the land ceded by France into two territories, Orleans and Louisiana. Section 14 of that act (relating to *Louisiana*), which seems to have been the pattern for the broader removal provisions of sections 1 and 4 of the Act of 1807 pursuant to which Jefferson removed Livingston, provided that "it shall . . . be lawful for the President of the United States to employ such military force as he may judge necessary to remove from lands belonging to the United States" any citizen or other person who shall have made or attempted to make a settlement thereon. *Ibid.*, 289.

217. It will be remembered that such permission was to be granted, pursuant to section 2 of the act, only to persons actually residing on the land on March 3, 1807, and who had "taken possession of, occupied, or made a settlement" on it before that date. See note 204, *supra*. Livingston did not qualify under this category of claimant. *Proceedings*, 69. Only such early settlers were entitled under the first proviso in section 4 of the act to three months' notice before eviction by the marshal. A second proviso made section 4 inapplicable "to persons claiming lands . . . whose claim shall have been filed with the proper commissioners before [January 1, 1808]."

218. See note 127, *supra*. Cf. *Gelston* v. *Hoyt*, 3 Wheat. 246, 331 (1818).

219. The language is that it shall be lawful "for the President . . . to direct the marshal . . . in the manner herein after directed, and also to take such other measures, and to employ such military force as he may judge necessary and proper, to remove [the intruder]." See note 204, *supra*.

220. "*Provided* . . . that *nothing in this section* contained shall be construed to apply to any persons claiming lands . . . whose claims shall have been filed with the proper commissioners before the first day of *January* next." 2 Stat. 446. [Italics supplied.]

221. By the Act of March 3, 1807, 2 Stat. 441, c. 36. See note 204, *supra*. However such an extension was not made by the Act of March 3, 1807, 2 Stat. 445–46, c. 46 (apparently enacted later). The date expressly specified in the later act would supersede the date fixed in the earlier act, in case of contradiction between the two. Perhaps Congress inadvertently failed to insert the July date in the later act, but the words actually used are controlling.

222. *Answer*, 134.

223. That is to say, July 1, 1808. See note 221, *supra*.

224. See page 66, *supra*. Livingston, of course, had not filed any claim with the commissioners by January 1, 1808.

225. See page 59, *supra*.

226. See note 59, *supra*.

227. *Proceedings*, 73–76. He also regarded the injunction as "a nullity as to the United States" because the United States was not a party, and land in the hands of the United States is not subject to judicial cognizance. *Ibid.*, 76. See also *ibid.*, 16, 68.

228. The Act of March 2, 1805, 2 Stat. 322–23, for establishment of the government of Orleans Territory repealed so much of the earlier Act of March 26, 1804, 2 Stat. 283–89, as was repugnant thereto, and provided that "inhabitants of the territory of Orleans shall be entitled to and enjoy all the rights, privileges, and advantages [secured by the Northwest Ordinance of July 13, 1787, 1 Stat. 51–53], and now enjoyed by the people of the Mississippi territory." The Act of April 7, 1798, 1 Stat. 549–50, for establishing the latter territory provided that its government should be "in all respects similar to that now exercised in the territory northwest of the river Ohio [except for the last article forbidding slavery]." 1 Stat. 550. The Ordinance established a court "who shall have a common law jurisdiction" (1 Stat. 51), and in Article II of the articles of compact provided that "The inhabitants . . . shall always be entitled to the benefits of the writ of habeas corpus, and of the trial by jury; of a proportionate representation in the legislature, and of judicial proceedings according to the course of the common law." 1 Stat. 52.

229. Act of March 2, 1805, sec. 4, 2 Stat. 322; *Answer*, 157–61; *Proceedings*, 74. Akin to Gallatin's argument set forth in the following note, is the rule that federal courts in Louisiana, after its admission to the union, exercise the same equity powers as they would anywhere else, insofar as procedural and remedial questions are concerned. *Livingston* v. *Story*, 9 Pet. 632, 657–58 (1835). [This case, which continued until after Livingston's death, arose from his deed conveying a batture lot in 1822 as security for a debt, 11 Pet. at 353.] See also *Bein* v. *Heath*, 12 How. 168, 178–79 (1851); *U.S.* v. *Howland*, 4 Wheat. 108, 115 (1819) [Marshall, C. J.]; *U.S.* v. *King*, 7 How. 833, 844 (1849) [Taney, C. J.]; *Parsons* v. *Bedford*, 3 Pet. 433, 448 (1830) [Story, J.]. Since *Erie R.R.* v. *Tompkins*, 304 U.S. 64 (1938), federal equity courts follow state law as to questions of substantive law. *Guaranty Trust Co.* v. *York*, 326 U.S. 99, 105–112 (1945). Cases such as *Neves* v. *Scott*, 13 How. 268, 272 (1851), are now obsolete.

230. Gallatin's memorandum (see note 58, *supra*) says: "In all cases where the principles of the civil law differ from those of the common law, the judges of Orleans must also in their decisions be governed by the principles of the civil law which is the law of the land. But this does not extend the jurisdiction of the judges beyond the limits fixed by the technical words 'common law jurisdiction' [in the organic charter]." He points out that jury trial is itself "a most material encroachment on the civil law" but is unquestionably guaranteed to the inhabitants. In other words, Gallatin is arguing, quite persuasively, that the jurisdiction of tribunals for the administration of justice is a matter of public (rather than private) law, and hence that under the cases cited in note 151, *supra*, the institutions of the successor state would replace those of the former sovereign.

231. *Proceedings*, 79. See note 41, *supra*. For Livingston's comments, see *Answer*, 173. It is interesting to note that on an earlier occasion Jefferson was apprehensive of being sued personally on account of public transactions entered into while he was governor of Virginia. To Benjamin Harrison, September 22, 1782, 3 F. 302–303.

232. *Proceedings*, 79–80. Livingston comments that "if he really think his own conduct to have been legal and meritorious, his sense of right and wrong is entirely confounded, and his principles are even more dangerous than his practice. . . . That he should obstinately justify an invasion of private property, in a manner that puts it in the power of a president with impunity to commit acts of oppression, at which a king would tremble—That he should do all this, and still talk of conscious rectitude, must amaze all those who look only to the reputation he has enjoyed, and who do not consider the inconsistency of human nature, and the deplorable effects of an inordinate passion for popularity." *Answer*, 173, 177.

233. Dumbauld, *American Tourist*, 194–95.

234. See Malone, *Virginian*, 441–44.

235. For references to disputes and litigation, see to H. Skipwith, May 6, 1791, October 5, 1791; to N. Lewis, October 11, 1791; to T. M. Randolph, November 17, 1793; to Archibald Thweatt, May 23, 1810; James Pleasants to Jefferson, April 21, 1822, Huntington Library. See also case between T. Jefferson & J. Harvie, about land on Southwest Mountain [July 30, 1795 (?)]; copy of report in the Court of Chancery between Thomas Jefferson and William Bentley, administrator of William Ronald, July 10, 1797; to [Christopher] Clarke, August 5, 1794; to John Coalter, October 8, 1801; to George Hay, November 14, 1806; to Nicholas H. Lewis, May 30, 1819; to Robert Anderson, June 13, 1819; to Samuel Greenhow, April 21, 1820; to James Bowling, July 28, 1820; to Samuel Walkup, October 5, 1820; to Thomas E. Randolph, September 10, 1822; to Isaac Miller, September 14, 1822, Massachusetts Historical Society. See also page 215 n. 4, *supra.* Jefferson was executor for the Polish patriot General Kosciusko. To Wirt, January 5, 1818; June 27, 1819, 12 F. 79–81, 129–31; *Estho* v. *Lear*, 7 Pet. 129, 131 (1833). Jefferson's testimony was also used by other litigants. To Col. Van Ness and Judge Cranch, February 11, 1809, Ford, *Jefferson Correspondence*, 174–75; to Dabney Carr, April 12, 1815, HL:HM 5756; to W. B. Giles, August 29, 1813, 12 F. 305.

236. To William Wirt, April 12, 1812, 11 F. 227.

237. Gallatin to Jefferson, September 10, 1810.

238. Justice Holmes in *Compañia General de Tabacos* v. *Collector*, 275 U.S. 87, 100 (1927).

239. As Justice Brandeis observed in *Myers* v. *Bethlehem Shipbuilding Corp.*, 303 U.S. 41, 51–52 (1938): "Lawsuits . . . often prove to have been groundless; but no way has been discovered of relieving a defendant from the necessity of a trial to establish the fact."

240. John E. Hall's view [*American Law Journal*, Vol. V (1814), iv], that Livingston's *Answer* "is emphatically, *a réplique sans réponse*" is exaggerated. Schmidt, "The Batture Question," *Louisiana Law Journal*, Vol. I, No. 2 (August, 1841), 96. That the conflict was not one-sided is shown by the persistence of controversy over many years. *Ibid.*, 100, 134, 148–49. See note 241, *infra.*

241. In *Packwood* v. *Walden*, 7 Martin (N.S.) 81 (1828), the court said: "The batture . . . has been a most fruitful source of litigation during the last twenty-four years." In *Cochran* v. *Fort*, 7 Martin (N.S.) 622, 624 (1829), the record included "all the conflicting evidence which this seemingly never-failing source of litigation has produced for the last twenty-five years." The dispute was still raging a decade later. *Municipality No. 1* v. *Municipality No. 2*, 12 La. 49, 51, 55, 61–62, 64–65 (1838); *Municipality No. 2* v. *Orleans Cotton Press*, 18 La. 122, 222, 236, 263, 265 (1841).

242. *Gravier et al.* v. *Livingston et al.*, 6 Martin (O.S.) 281, 413 (1819).

243. *Ibid.*, at 409. See notes 59 and 108, *supra.* In Livingston's *Answer*, 125, he had asserted that the coheirs had ratified the purchase by John Gravier.

244. *Morgan* v. *Livingston*, 6 Martin (O.S.) 19 (1819). The opinion was written by the celebrated Judge François-Xavier Martin.

245. *Ibid.*, 120. The court held that this language made Poeyfarré a riparian owner. *Ibid.*, 224–26. See pages 56–57, 58, *supra.* Cf. *Cambre* v. *Kohn*, 8 Martin (N.S.) 572, 574, 578–80 (1830).

246. In *Municipality No. 2* v. *Orleans Cotton Press*, 18 La. 122, 263 (1841), Judge Martin observed that on the issue of dedication to the public Gravier won his case because his adversaries failed to offer adequate proof. See note 172, *supra.*

247. See page 58, *supra.* The same rule was applied in *Cochran* v. *Fort*, 7 Martin (N.S.) 622, 625 (1829), and the court made a similar finding, based upon the preponder-

ance of the evidence, in favor of a defendant deriving title from the heirs of Bertrand Gravier. *Ibid.*, 631. The court went on to say: "There is no positive evidence before us at what height batture may be reclaimed from the river, and appropriated to private use." The position of the deposit, the force of the stream, and other circumstances are relevant factors in the decision. *Ibid.*, 632. Being submerged by five feet during high water did not suffice, however, to negate susceptibility to reclamation. *Ibid.*, 633. The question is apparently one appropriate for determination by a finding of a jury. *Livingston* v. *Heerman*, 9 Martin (O.S.) 656, 712 (1821). See note 175, *supra.* Recent cases clarify the criterion: "When a batture . . . becomes visible above the surface of the water at its ordinary stage, in such a way as to give it an appearance of permanence, it then becomes susceptible of ownership" and becomes the property of the riparian owner, subject to the requirements of public use. *Maginnis Land & Improvement Co.* v. *Marcello*, 168 La. 997, 1003–1004 (1929); *State* v. *Richardson*, 140 La. 329, 350 (1916).

248.   6 Martin (O.S.) at 217, 226. The sales involved in the *Gravier* case were made in 1794 and 1795. *American State Papers, Public Lands*, II, 25.

249.   6 Martin (O.S.) at 227. The *Gravier* and *Morgan* cases were compared in *Packwood* v. *Walden*, 7 Martin (N.S.) 81, 83 (1828).

250.   6 Martin (O.S.) at 131.

251.   *Municipality No. 1* v. *Municipality No. 2*, 12 La. 49, 51–52, 61–62 (1838). Hence future alluvion would belong to the public, for the city would be the riparian owner. *Packwood* v. *Walden*, 7 Martin (N.S.) 81, 89 (1828); *Municipality No. 2* v. *Orleans Cotton Press*, 18 La. 122, 219, 276 (1841); *New Orleans* v. *United States*, 10 Pet. 662, 717 (1836).

252.   12 La. at 55, 57, 64–65. The terms of the compromise are summarized by counsel in *Remy* v. *Municipality No. 2*, 11 La. Ann. 148, 149–50 (1856); and by the court in *Heirs of Jourdan* v. *Heirs of Gravier*, 10 La. Ann. 804 (1855). Section 11 of the Act of March 8, 1836, forbade disposition of batture land by the city in violation of the terms of the compromise. This was repealed by the Act of March 21, 1850, which permitted sale of land no longer needed for public use, pursuant to agreement with the parties to the 1820 agreement, provided that one-third of the proceeds be applied to the debt of the old municipal corporation. Such an agreement was notarized on June 30, 1851, dividing the proceeds equally between the old corporation, Municipality No. 2, and parties to the 1820 agreement in proportion to their frontage. *Ibid.*, 806. See also *Municipality No. 2* v. *Orleans Cotton Press*, 18 La. 122, 232, 265 (1841); *Packwood* v. *Walden*, 7 Martin (N.S.) 81, 87, 91 (1828); Schmidt, "The Batture Question", *Louisiana Law Journal*, Vol. I, No. 2 (August, 1841), 102; William B. Hatcher, *Edward Livingston*, 167–69.

253.   *Livingston* v. *Heerman*, 9 Martin (O.S.) 656, 712 (1821). The court commented that the principal difference between the case at bar and the *Gravier* case was that the former was a suit for slander of title rather than for trespass. *Ibid.*, 736.

254.   See notes 245 and 248, *supra.*

255.   9 Martin (O.S.) at 686, 718–19.

256.   *Ibid.*, 711–12, 718–19.

257.   See pages 56–57, *supra.*

258.   Hatcher, *Edward Livingston*, 167–69. A lengthy litigation, lasting until after Livingston's death, arose from his deed of July 25, 1822, conveying a tract of batture land as security for a debt incurred to construct buildings. *Livingston* v. *Story*, 11 Pet. 351, 353 (1837). Louise Livingston was substituted as a party after her husband's death on May 23, 1836. *Ex Parte Story*, 12 Pet. 338, 343 (1838).

259.   Hatcher, *Edward Livingston*, 185. Regarding this debt, see page 36, *supra.* On

April 4, 1834, Livingston brought suit against G. R. Stringer in the federal court (E.D. La. No. 3409) to recover five lots on the North Street of the New Market "in the Faubourg St-Mary on that part commonly known as the Bature" detained by Stringer under title "by virtue of a forced alienation in favor of the United States at the suit of the said United States vs Your Petitioner." These were part of 54 lots claimed by Livingston, as shown on a plan of May 25, 1822, made by the surveyor of the City of New Orleans. The court papers show that on August 6, 1834, documents were withdrawn from the files by defendant's counsel "for the purpose of drawing up the Act of compromise between the Plff and defendant."

260. Hatcher, *Edward Livingston*, 189.

261. *New Orleans* v. *U.S.*, 10 Pet. 662 (1836).

262. Butler cited Livingston's *Answer* to show that the case was not one in equity for an injunction, but for a "prohibitory interdict" as in the *Gravier* case. 10 Pet. at 674–75. The tract was also cited with regard to ownership of alluvial deposits. *Ibid.*, 680. Livingston replied that "the same remedy was given by the territorial court, that would have been given by a court of equity, had the distinction been known to the laws of the country; but it was not known; therefore, the proceeding in that case was not a chancery proceeding, but one in the ordinary execution of the powers of the court. Here, on the contrary, the suit is brought in a court having chancery jurisdiction." *Ibid.*, 691. See notes 227–30, *supra*.

263. See notes 149, 155, and 212, *supra*.

264. Moreau (see note 60, *supra*) had also represented the city. He procured the maps of 1724 and 1728 from archives of the French navy department in Paris. 10 Pet. at 667, 670. The court found this proof conclusive on the issue of dedication to public use. See page 74, *infra*. Moreau had lost a case in the Supreme Court of Louisiana involving the same issues. *De Armas* v. *New-Orleans*, 5 La. 132 (1832). Judge Martin dissented. *Ibid.*, 185. The government relied strongly on this case, but the court did not follow it (10 Pet. at 719) as it would now be required to do under *Erie* principles. See note 229, *supra*. An attempt to secure Supreme Court review of the *De Armas* case failed for lack of federal jurisdiction. *New Orleans* v. *De Armas*, 9 Pet. 224, 234–36 (1835).

265. 10 Pet. at 689.

266. *Ibid.*, at 717.

267. See note 263, *supra*.

268. See note 264, *supra*.

269. 10 Pet. at 715, 718. See also *ibid.*, 703–704 (Livingston's argument).

270. *Ibid.*, 721, 724, 736–37.

271. *Ibid.*, 723.

272. *Ibid.,* 724. The court here relied on *Partida* 3, title 20, law 9, which Moreau had cited to good effect in the earlier controversy with Livingston. See note 170, *supra*.

273. Like streets and highways, *ibid.*, 720, 730.

274. *Ibid.*, 731. The latter type of property was known in Spanish law as *"propios."* *Ibid.*, 702. In *Packwood* v. *Walden*, 7 Martin (N.S.) 81, 91 (1828), the court uses the expression *"quae sunt propria civitatis et quae non sunt in usu publico."*

275. Job 31:35.

276. 10 Pet. at 691. See note 3, *supra*.

277. Rev. 14:13.

278. To James Madison, April 27, 1809, 12 M. 277.

CHAPTER IV

1. See page 8 at n. 24, *supra.*

2. See page 10 at n. 45, *supra.* Tucker regarded the lack of statutory materials as "one of the greatest difficulties attending the study of law in Virginia." Tucker's *Blackstone,* I, 442. Acts of Assembly were not regularly printed until 1733, ten years before Jefferson's birth. See pages 122, 131, 228 n. 7, *infra.*

3. The first printed Virginia report, *Decisions of Cases in Virginia, by the High Court of Chancery, with Remarks upon Decrees by the Court of Appeals, reversing some of those Decisions,* appeared in 1795. Sowerby #1759. It was the work of Jefferson's mentor George Wythe. Warren, *History of the American Bar,* 330. A second edition, by B. B. Minor, was issued in 1852.

4. Thomas Jefferson, *Reports of Cases Determined in the General Court of Virginia,* v–vi. See pages 25 and 43, *supra.*

5. Commonly cited as "Jeff." Published by F. Carr and Co., Charlottesville. The manuscript is in the Massachusetts Historical Society.

6. The early Virginia cases reported by Randolph and Barradall which Jefferson omitted were not published until Barton's *Virginia Colonial Decisions* appeared in 1909.

7. See note 3, *supra.*

8. See page 127, *infra.*

9. *Lawes* [1662], 11. The "monthlie" courts also became known as county courts in 1642, since they met only six times a year. Hening, *Statutes,* I, 272.

10. The 1679 instructions permitted appeals to the governor and council "and to no other court or judicature whatever." Previously an appeal lay to the General Assembly from the governor and council. This was expressly forbidden by more explicit instructions in 1682 (and the amount appealable to the privy council was then fixed at one hundred pounds, but was raised to three hundred pounds in 1685). Virginia's protests and efforts to retain the appeal to the assembly proved unavailing. Leonard Labaree, *Royal Instructions to British Colonial Governors 1670–1776,* I, 318, 320–21 (§§ 442, 446); Joseph H. Smith, *Appeals to the Privy Council from the American Plantations,* 80, 83; Henry Hartwell, James Blair, and Edward Chilton, *The Present State of Virginia, and the College* (Hunter D. Farish, ed.), 1940, 27–28, 46–47.

11. As reorganized after independence. Hening, *Statutes,* IX, 401–19. The court had five judges. Jefferson drafted the bills concerning the General Court, the High Court of Chancery, the Court of Admiralty, and the Court of Appeals. 1 P. 605–49.

12. Established after independence. There were three judges. Hening, *Statutes,* IX, 389–99.

13. Established after independence. There were three judges. *Ibid.,* IX, 202–206.

14. *Ibid.,* X, 89–92. For an earlier plan of 1778, which never became operative, see *ibid.,* IX, 522–23.

15. Act of December 22, 1788. *Ibid.,* XII, 764. At the same time legislation was adopted to reduce the High Court of Chancery to one chancellor as vacancies occur. *Ibid.,* 766. See also David J. Mays, *Edmund Pendleton,* II, 164, 273–75.

16. Francis H. McGuire, "The General Court of Virginia," *Report of the Seventh Annual Meeting of the Virginia State Bar Association* (1895) 197–229; Margaret V. Nelson, *A Study of Judicial Review in Virginia,* 13–16; Robert G. H. Kean, "Our Judicial System: Some of its History, and Some of its Defects," *Report of the First Annual Meeting of the Virginia State Bar Association* (1889) 139–59.

17. Likewise the unpublished General Court cases after 1826 before the new system took effect were reported in 5 and 6 Randolph. Nelson, *Study of Judicial Review*, 21–22.

18. See note 3, *supra*.

19. Sowerby #2090. A second volume appeared the following year. Washington (1762–1829) was a nephew of the first president and was a justice of the Supreme Court of the United States from 1798 to 1820, appointed by John Adams. For a sketch of Justice Washington, see Albert P. Blaustein and Roy M. Mersky, "Bushrod Washington," in Leon Friedman and Fred L. Israel (eds.), *The Justices of the United States Supreme Court*, I, 243–66.

20. Call (6 vols.) covers 1797 to 1818 [until 1833 when 4–6 Call were published, no reports were available for 1803 to 1806]. Hening and Munford (4 vols.) covers 1806–10. Munford (6 vols.) covers 1810–20. [5 Munford came down to April, 1817; three years elapsed before publication of Vol. VI, during which time the judges made their demand for an official reporter.] Nelson, *Study of Judicial Review*, 22. For a full account of early Virginia reporters see G. G., "American Reports and Reporters," *The American Jurist and Law Magazine*, Vol. XXII, No. 43 (October, 1839), 108–42, at 128–30; Wallace, *Reporters*, 590; and Conway Robinson's preface to 1 Robinson [40 Va.] iii–x.

21. Commencing with 75 Va. See 91 Va. xvii for list of numbers from 1 through 74 Va. assigned to reports published before 1880. See also Hicks, *Materials and Methods of Legal Research* (3rd ed.), 510.

22. Of 42 cases, 23 deal with slaves; 9 of these are included in the 11 cases reported by Jefferson himself. Six deal with land, four with procedure; two are suits against sheriffs for permitting escape of debtors from prison; there is one case in each of six other miscellaneous categories.

23. See note 4, *supra*. Accordingly, after the Revolution "uprooted the old land laws and Emancipation destroyed slavery the pronouncements of the General Court . . . were largely historical, with the result that Jefferson's reports have been cited by the Court of Appeals of Virginia only six times altogether, and only once in the last hundred years." Mays, *Edmund Pendleton*, I, 238.

24. Jeff., 137–42; reprinted in 1 F. 453–70.

25. Jeff., vi.

26. *Ibid.*, 142.

27. This material was derived from Jefferson's Legal Commonplace Book, items 873 and 879. Chinard, *Commonplace Book of Jefferson*, 351–56, 359–63. These were copied for Dr. Thomas Cooper in a letter of February 10, 1814, 14 M. 85–97. Jefferson repeats his thesis in letters to John Adams, January 24, 1814, 14 M. 72–75; to John Cartwright, June 5, 1824, 16 M. 48–51; to Edward Everett, October 15, 1824, 16 M. 80–84.

28. Discussed in Holdsworth, *History*, VIII, 407–10. Blackstone was among those asserting that Christianity "is part of the laws of England." Blackstone, *Commentaries*, IV, 59.

29. *Rex* v. *Taylor*, 1 Ventris 293; 3 Keble 607 (1675/76).

30. *Evans* v. *Chamberlain of London*, 2 Burns Eccl. Law 218; 16 Parl. Hist. 315 (1767). Likewise Lord Keble declared that "the law of God is the law of England." *The Trial of Lieutenant-Colonel John Lilburne for High Treason*, 4 State Trials 1269, 1307 (1649). On Lilburne's contribution to the development of constitutional rights, see page 245 n. 29, *infra*.

31. These authorities, Jefferson observes, all depend on Prisot or on nothing, "for they all quote Prisot, or one another, or nobody." Legal Commonplace Book #873. Prisot was "an expert lawyer who helped Littleton to write his *Tenures* and who in 1449 became Chief

Justice of the Common Pleas." Courtney Kenny, "The Evolution of the Law of Blasphemy," *The Cambridge Law Journal*, Vol. I, No. 2 (1922), 130.

32. *Humphrey Bohun* v. *John Broughton, Bishop of Lincoln*, Y.B. 34 Hen. VI Pasch. (1458), *Les Reports des Cases* (London, 1679) 38–41. The passage quoted by Jefferson [see note 41, *infra*] is on page 40 and is cited by Lord Sumner in *Bowman* v. *Secular Society*, [1917] A. C. 406, 455.

33. *Ratcliff's Case*, 3 Rep. 37a, 40a (1592).

34. *Caudrey's Case*, 5 Rep. 1, 7a (1595). The statute is the Act of Uniformity of 1559, 1 Eliz. c. 2 sec. 2. For further details, see Faith Thompson, *Magna Carta: Its Role in the Making of the English Constitution*, 206, 213. I take "34 H. 6.14" as a reference to *Bohun* v. *Broughton* since that would be an appropriate citation because of the similarity of subject matter, whereas the reference to "14" is meaningless. Professor Joseph H. Smith has suggested that "14" might be a misprint for "41."

35. *People* v. *Ruggles*, 8 Johnson 290, 294–97 (N. Y. 1811); *Updegraph* v. *Commonwealth*, 11 S. & R. 394, 400 (Pa. 1824); *State* v. *Chandler*, 2 Harrington 553, 555, 558–64 (Del. 1837); *Com.* v. *Kneeland*, 20 Pickering 206, 213, 216, 219–20 (Mass. 1838); *Vidal* v. *Girard's Exrs.*, 2 How. 127, 198–201 (U.S. 1844); *State* v. *Mockus,* 120 Maine 84, 91 (1921). In the *Chandler* case Jefferson's discussion of the subject was cited by counsel and commented on by the court. 2 Harr. at 554, 558–64.

36. 2 Harr. at 556–57. However, the United States Supreme Court in *Torcaso* v. *Watkins*, 367 U.S. 488, 495 (1961), held that Maryland could not exclude from public office persons refusing to declare their belief in the existence of God.

37. *McGowan* v. *Maryland*, 366 U.S. 420, 433–35 (1961).

38. William G. Brown, *The Life of Oliver Ellsworth*, 300–31.

39. Sir Frederick Pollock, *Essays in Jurisprudence and Ethics*, 290–94.

40. Blackstone, *Commentaries*, III, 242–48. See also 6 Rep. 49. The words *quare impedit* mean "wherefore does he obstruct."

41. Legal Commonplace Book #873. "It is proper for us to give credence to such laws as they of holy church have in ancient writing; for it is common law on which all kinds of laws are founded, and also, sir, we are obliged to recognize their law of holy church, and likewise they are obliged to recognize our law." For another translation, see Lester J. Cappon (ed.), *The Adams-Jefferson Letters*, II, 422. For an amplified version by Jefferson, see to Edward Everett, October 15, 1824, 16 M. 81. [It was Everett who brought Jefferson's view to Story's attention.] A good explanation of this passage and of the background of the case is given in Kenny, *loc. cit.*, note 31, *supra*, 130–31.

42. 16 M. 81-82. See note 48, *infra*.

43. *Law, or, a discourse thereof; in four books.* "Finch's Law, until the publication of Blackstone's Commentaries, was regarded as the best elementary law book." Sowerby, II, 216 (#1778).

44. Legal Commonplace Book #873. Continuing, Jefferson says that Finch "cites the above case and the words of Prisot in the margin. Finch's law. B. 1. c. 3. published 1613." According to Kenny, *loc. cit.* note 31, *supra*, 130: "Finch does give, in his margin, Prisot's actual words, but he misunderstands and mistranslates them. The misunderstanding was first detected, so far as I am aware, not by any English lawyer, but by an American one, less known to us indeed, as a lawyer, than as statesman—the acute and brilliant President Jefferson."

45. William W. Story, *Life and Letters of Joseph Story*, I, 430–33, II, 6–8. In his inaugural lecture as Dane Professor at Harvard Law School on August 25, 1829, he attacked Jefferson's position. Story, *Miscellaneous Writings*, 517. There is an article [dated

1824, perhaps a misprint for 1829] by J[oseph] S[tory], "Christianity A Part of the Common Law," in the *American Jurist and Law Magazine*, Vol. IX (April, 1833), 346–48. For a recent discussion of Story's position, see James McClellan, *Joseph Story and the American Constitution*, 118–26. See note 47, *infra*.

46. See note 27, *supra*. The letter had been published in Thomas J. Randolph's *Memoir, Correspondence and Miscellanies, from the Papers of Thomas Jefferson*, IV, 395.

47. Charles Francis Adams (ed.), *Memoirs of John Quincy Adams*, VIII, 291. Kenny, *loc. cit.*, note 31, *supra*, 127–42, gives an excellent account of the authorities and supports Jefferson's interpretation. Story, he says, treated the matter "with less than his usual fairness." *Ibid.*, 130. Story's real concern is one of policy: what becomes of the whole church establishment and legal rights growing out of it if Christianity is not part of the law? Holdsworth's position is similar: Finch's misunderstanding of Prisot does not disprove the existence of the doctrine, which is a consequence of the laws against religious nonconformity. Holdsworth, *History*, VIII, 403.

48. See note 42, *supra*.

49. John N. Figgis, *Studies of Political Thought from Gerson to Grotius*, 43; Holdsworth, *History*, VIII, 403.

50. This view, held by both Roman Catholic and Calvinist adherents, took its name from Hildebrand, who as Pope Gregory VII deposed Emperor Henry IV and compelled him to make homage at Canossa, barefooted in the snow. James Bryce, *The Holy Roman Empire*, 158–60; Sidney Z. Ehler and John B. Morrall, *Church and State Through the Centuries*, 39–43, 160. See also bull *Unam sanctam* of Pope Boniface VIII in 1302 in *ibid.*, 89–92.

51. So named for Thomas Erastus (1524–83), a German Swiss follower of Zwingli. See Helen M. Cam (ed.), *Selected Historical Essays of F. W. Maitland*, 207–208. The Act of Supremacy, 26 Henry VIII c. 1 (1534) by which that monarch assumed the station of "Supreme Head in earth of the Church of England" is the acme of Erastianism. The statute is printed in Tanner, *Tudor Constitutional Documents*, 46–48. Sir Thomas More, logically insisting that the king cannot make a priest, lost his life in 1535. Edward Dumbauld, "Judicial Interference with Litigation in Other Courts," *Dickinson Law Review*, Vol. LXXIV, No. 3 (Spring, 1970), 377.

52. The phrase "wall of separation" comes from Jefferson's letter to Danbury Baptist Association, January 1, 1802, 16 M. 281–82. See Dumbauld, *Bill of Rights*, 106–15.

53. Dumbauld, *Grotius*, 11, 99, 117–18. Grotius was Erastian and Arminian in his views, though sometimes erroneously said to be Calvinist. Dumbauld, "Some Modern Misunderstandings of Grotius," in *Volkenrechtelijke Opstellen ter ere van de Hoogleraren B. M. Telders, F. M. Baron van Asbeck en J. H. W. Verzijl*, 63.

54. Maitland's admonition is pertinent: "We shall have to think away distinctions which seem to us as clear as the sunshine; we must think ourselves back into twilight. This we must do, not in a haphazard fashion, but of set purpose, knowing what we are doing." Cam, *Essays of F. W. Maitland*, 10.

55. Professor Beale contends that in Massachusetts more of the common law was in force than had been supposed. Joseph H. Beale, "The Study of American Legal History," *West Virginia Law Quarterly*, Vol. XXXIX, No. 2 (February, 1933), 95–103. The explanation may be, as Goebel urges, that it was the law of the local tribunals rather than that of the central courts at Westminster which took root in the colonies. See note 63, chapter 1, *supra*.

56. Edward Dumbauld, "Pennsylvania's Contributions to the Law," in Homer T.

Rosenberger, *Pennsylvania's Contributions to the Professions*, 10–11.

57. To Albert Gallatin, September 27, 1810, 11 F. 154.

58. Mark DeWolfe Howe, *Readings in American Legal History*, 165–66; Warren, *History of the American Bar*, 63; George L. Haskins, *Law and Authority in Early Massachusetts*, 36. See also Max Farrand, *The Laws and Liberties of Massachusetts*, 1.

59. Warren, *History of the American Bar*, 63–65; Howe, *Readings in American Legal History*, 181–82, 185–86; R[alph] H. C[lover], "The Rule of Law in Colonial Massachusetts," *University of Pennsylvania Law Review*, Vol. CVIII, No. 7 (May, 1960), 1001–36, at 1014–16. The word of God was also the rule in force in Connecticut and Rhode Island. Warren, *History of the American Bar*, 128–29, 140; Haskins, *Law and Authority in Early Massachusetts*, 106, 124–26, 128–31, 141–62.

60. Haskins, *Law and Authority in Early Massachusetts*, 2, 37, 120, 136–40.

61. Holdsworth, *History*, I, 598–632. For example, church courts retained jurisdiction of divorce and probate until 1857. *Ibid.*, 624, 629. On the function of the Dean of the Arches and Doctors' Commons in maintaining the separate status of the church courts, strongly influenced by civil law doctrines, see *ibid.*, IV, 235–36. See also Anthony H. Manchester, "The Reform of the Ecclesiastical Courts," *American Journal of Legal History*, Vol. X, No. 1 (January, 1966), 75.

62. Dumbauld, "Judicial Interference with Litigation in Other Courts," *Dickinson Law Journal*, Vol. LXXIV, No. 3 (Spring, 1970), 375–78.

63. *History*, I, 614. These heads of jurisdiction are discussed in greater detail in *ibid.*, 615–32.

64. *Ibid.*, II, 179.

65. *Ibid.*, I, 329. By the end of the thirteenth century the king's courts had assumed jurisdiction over land held in frankalmoin as exclusive as over that held by any other free tenure. *Ibid.*, I, 630; III, 35. For early instances of writs of prohibition against church courts, see *ibid.*, II, 305. See also Samuel E. Thorne, "The Assize Utrum and Canon Law in England," *Columbia Law Review*, Vol. XXXIII, No. 3 (March, 1933), 430.

66. Translation in Ehler and Morrall (eds.), *Church and State Through the Centuries*, 56–60; Lee, *Source-Book*, 133–36.

67. Statute of Praemunire, 27 Edw. III st. 1, c. 1 (1353). This punished those who drew "any out of the Realm in Plea whereof the cognizance pertaineth to the king's court, or of things whereof judgments be given in the king's court, or which do sue in any other court to defeat or impeach the judgment given in the king's court." A later Statute of Praemunire, 16 Rich. II c. 5 (1392/93), was aimed at those who undertook proceedings in Rome or elsewhere to hinder the king's court's jurisdiction over presentments to benefices. Holdsworth, *History*, I, 587. See also *Premunire*, 12 Rep. 37, 39–41 (1606).

68. Holdsworth, *History*, I, 588–89.

69. *Ibid.*, I, 597.

70. See note 41, *supra*.

71. Great apprehension was caused among dissenters in America by rumors that an American episcopacy was contemplated. John Adams to Dr. J. Morse, Dec. 2, 1815, *Works of John Adams*, X, 185.

72. See pages 18–19, 25, 31, *supra* and Haskins, *Law and Authority in Early Massachusetts*, 4–6. In *Updegraph* v. *Commonwealth*, 11 S. & R. 394, 409 (Pa. 1824), the court said that the laws regarding establishment of the Church of England were not part of the common law received in Pennsylvania.

73. See page 132, *infra.* Relief of dissenters from paying tithes to maintain the

Anglican church was one of Jefferson's first pieces of legislation. 1 P. 525–58; Hening, *Statutes*, IX, 165. The thoroughgoing act for religious freedom came later. See note 40, chapter 7, *infra*.

74. *Godwin* v. *Lunan*, Jeff., 96 (October, 1771); 2 F. 16–35.

75. Jeff., 108; 2 F. 16.

76. Jeff., 97.

77. *Ibid.*, 97.

78. *Commentaries*, II, 22–23.

79. See note 40, *supra*.

80. See note 67, *supra*.

81. Jeff., 108.

82. See note 75, *supra*.

83. Jeff., 108.

84. *Howell* v. *Netherland*, Jeff., 90 (April, 1770); 1 F. 470–81.

85. Jeff., 92. The Roman jurists recognized that slavery arose under the *jus gentium* because it was generally practiced, whereas by the *jus naturale* all men are born free and equal. Dumbauld, *Declaration*, 43, 56–57.

86. In the political forum of mankind Jefferson's doctrine received a more favorable hearing when six years later in the Declaration of Independence he proclaimed that all men are created equal.

87. Jeff., 96.

88. Act of 1705, c. 49, s. 18. 1 F. 473; Baskett, *Acts of Assembly*, 309; Parks, *Collection*, 218; Hening, *Statutes*, III, 453.

89. Act of 1723, c. 4, s. 22. 1 F. 474; Parks, *Collection*, 339; Hening, *Statutes*, IV, 133.

90. Italics supplied.

91. Jeff., 96. The Latin quotation is from Vergil, *Aeneid*, III, 98.

92. To Madison, May 25, 1788, 13 P. 203. The observation was made in the context of the unwillingness of Congress to provide adequately for the expenses of diplomatic intercourse with foreign nations.

93. Mays, *Edmund Pendleton*, I, 226–31. The rivalry was renewed when Wythe became sole chancellor in 1789 but Pendleton moved to the court of appeals, which reversed many of Wythe's decisions. Wythe's indignant comments were embodied in his *Decisions*, the first volume of Virginia law reports ever published. *Ibid.*, II, 290–96. See note 3, *supra*.

94. Of the 11 cases reported by Jefferson, counsel are not named in two. Pendleton and Wythe were both involved in five, in three of which Pendleton defeated Wythe. In one they were both on the same side and lost. In one (*Brent* v. *Porter*, Jeff., 72), it is not clear who represented the victorious plaintiff. In one case Pendleton defeated Mason, in another Mason defeated Bland. In one case Jefferson opposed Wythe and lost; in another he and Wythe were together and were victorious over Attorney General John Randolph.

95. *Gwinn* v. *Bugg*, Jeff., 87 (October, 1769).

96. Jeff., 89.

97. *Ibid.*, 89. However, when Jefferson urged the same point in *Howell* v. *Netherland* in addition to the question whether defendant could be held in servitude at all under the Acts of 1705 and 1723, he had no success. See note 87, *supra*.

98. *Robin* v. *Hardaway*, Jeff., 109 (April, 1772).

99. See note 24, chapter 6, *infra*.

100. Act of 1682, c. 1, Purvis 282; Hening, *Statutes*, II, 490–91.

101. Dumbauld, *Declaration*, 3.

102.   Here he "cited 8 Co. 118.a. Bonham's case. Hob. 87.7 Co. 14a. Calvin's case." For references discussing this line of authorities, see Dumbauld, *Constitution*, 6.

103.   Jeff., 113–114.

104.   *Ibid.*, 113.

105.   Act of 1684, c.7. Hening, *Statutes*, III, 17–22.

106.   Act of 1691, c.9. Hening, *Statutes*, III, 69.

107.   Act of 1705, c. 49, sec. 4. Hening, *Statutes*, III, 447. This act provided that all servants brought in by sea or land who were not Christians in their native country should be slaves notwithstanding their conversion to Christianity afterwards. Another Act of 1705, c. 52, *ibid*. 464–69, re-enacts the Act of 1691, c. 9, *ibid*. 69, providing for free trade with all Indians whatsoever and repealing all former acts restraining such trade.

108.   Jeff., 116.

109.   *Ibid.*, 117.

110.   Jefferson had cited Samuel Pufendorf, *De Jure Naturae et Gentium*, Book VI, c. iii, §§ 4 and 9 in his argument in *Howell* v. *Netherland* two years earlier. See note 85, *supra*. The passage cited by Bland was § 10 of the same chapter. Mason in reply cited §§ 2, 4, and 5.

111.   Citing Blackstone, *Commentaries*, I, 91. Jeff., 118.

112.   Citing the passage mentioned in note 110, *supra*.

113.   Jeff., 122. He pointed out that Africans are slaves in their own land, only the chiefs being free. Hence they fit the description in the statute. The words "brought in by land" means from neighboring colonies, to which they had been shipped. *Ibid.*

114.   *Ibid.*, 123.

115.   The Act of 1705 was carried forward in the Revisal of 1748, c. 14. [Hunter 1752 ed. p. 285; cf. Parks ed. 1733, p. 218]. A note by Jefferson remarks that the 1748 Act (Hening, *Statutes*, V, 547) instead of the words "all servants imported" says "all persons who have been or shall be imported." This is "an alteration of few words indeed, but of most extensive barbarity." It makes slaves of many immigrants, and even many persons who were free inhabitants before enactment of the revised statute. Jeff., 112.

116.   See pages 123–25, *infra.*

117.   Hening, *Statutes*, III, 69.

CHAPTER V

1.   Malone, *Virginian*, 459. See also *ibid.*, 117–18. For location of the originals, see Dumbauld, *American Tourist*, 242.

2.   The last entry, on June 26, 1826, shows payment of $4.84 to "Isaacs for cheese."

3.   Dumbauld, *American Tourist*, 33, 94. Charitable gifts were often recorded: "towards building a Presbyterian church on F. Street" in Washington; or "for a college in Washington county" in Pennsylvania; or "toward rebuilding Princeton College" after the destruction of Nassau Hall by fire in 1802. More colorful items might note expenses "to see a ventriloquist" or a bear, or to note that he "measured a mule" in Marseilles; or that "Wild figs . . . grow out of the joints of the Pont du Gard. . . . The high hills of Languedoc are covered with snow."

4.   A number of such items are scattered through volumes 1 and 233 of the Jefferson Papers, Library of Congress. In the Massachusetts Historical Society, in addition to lists of cases and other miscellaneous material, there is a bound volume entitled "Law Treaties 1778–88," which includes a copy of Jefferson's comments on whether Christianity is part of the common law [see pages 76–82, *supra*], of the bill for proportioning crimes and punishments [see pages xii, 135–38, *infra*], and a comparison of the treaties of 1784 and 1788 with France.

5. To John Page, February 21, 1770, 1 P. 35.

6. Wyllie, "The Second Mrs. Wayland, An Unpublished Jefferson Opinion on a Case in Equity," *American Journal of Legal History,* Vol. IX, No. 1 (January, 1965), 64–68, reproduces, with valuable editorial comment, an opinion dated August 16, 1782. This was one of six opinions known (from account book entries) to have been written by Jefferson in 1782 after his governorship and before his wife's death. Those shown on February 17 and March 1, 1782, for James Dabney of Louisa County, and on July 25 and 29, 1782, for Charles Smith of Albemarle County, have not been found. Three opinions have been published by Boyd: one of January 16, 1782, for John Lyne (6 P. 143–44); one of February 15, 1782, for Mace Freeland (6 P. 151–58); and one for Thomas Watkins, in response to his letter of May 9, 1782 (6 P. 180–82). An opinion of November 21, 1777, on the much-disputed will of Carter Burwell is listed as item #30 in Constance E. Thurlow and Francis L. Berkeley, Jr., *The Jefferson Papers of the University of Virginia,* 5. See also LC 41708.

7. For example, to Alexander White, April 19, 1769, 1 P. 25–26.

8. Identified as HM 326. See page 157 n. 3, *supra.* Another volume in the Huntington Library, HM 836, known as Jefferson's Fee Book, is purely a financial journal. It contains 187 leaves of which 167 pages bear writing and 209 are blank. Fol. 2b–38a contain a record of legal fees from February 12, 1767, to December 28, 1774. Fol. 163a–186b are an index to the record of legal fees. Other data in the volume include a "statement of my debts when I went to Europe How and by whom paid," accounts with various individuals, of the estates of family members and of the Wine Company (April 1774–February 1778), an unsuccessful undertaking by Jefferson and Philip Mazzei to produce wine in America. See Malone, *Virginian,* 164–65, 289.

9. The correct total is 941. Cases #443 and 685 are subnumbered a and b.

10. Beginning in 1773 (case #784) Jefferson ceased to rule off the items, and beginning with the next page (at case #789) even the ruled margin was eliminated.

11. Randolph was active in the Constitutional Convention of 1787, and finally supported ratification by Virginia of the Constitution of the United States, although he was one of three delegates refusing to sign the document. (The others were George Mason and Elbridge Gerry.) Dumbauld, *Constitution,* 39, 41, 47, 51, 57, 270, 282, 453, 457.

12. Caveat proceedings began with issuance of a summons ("Sum."), and final judgment was in the form of an order in council ("ord. conc."). See page 27 and note 116, chapter 2, *supra.* "N.S." refers to a second or new summons.

13. The Case Book shows 47 opinions for clients. See also note 6, *supra.* In Henry Tucker's cases, Jefferson noted, "There are three distinct cases, two of them troublesome: so charge two fees." Case #416, May 23, 1770. (In extracts from the Case Book Jefferson's peculiarities of spelling, including omission of capital letters at the beginning of sentences, will be followed; although abbreviations that might be confusing will sometimes be expanded in brackets.)

14. The Case Book lists 283 cases of caveats, and 146 petitions. On the procedure regarding land grants, see page 26, *supra.* See also note in 4 Call 21–22, and the full text of a caveat at 4 Call 268–69. For examples of fraudulent grants see 4 Call 213, 253. In one petition prosecuted by Jefferson the adverse claimant for whom the land had been surveyed "ran away to Carolina & was hanged there" leaving no relatives. Presumably Jefferson's client obtained the land. Case #875, September 6, 1773.

15. Case #123, June 18, 1768. This was "one of G. W.'s caveats who put his docket into my hands."

16. Case #167, November 8, 1768: "qu. if pl. has not pd. fee to G. W.? if so, charge none."

17.   Case #783, December 29, 1772. This was "one of mr Wythe's caveats, which he desired me to finish June 18. 1768. . . . the reason of never entering this before was that I did not mean to charge any thing in those cases of G.W.'s unless the clients voluntarily offd. it." Similarly in *Goodwin* v. *Lunan* [a case included in Jefferson's *Reports*, see page 82, *supra*], he noted: "empld. by J. Blair for plts. charge no fee if he has recd." However, Jefferson received £5, but the case is marked "E.R. to finish." Case #510, February 14, 1771. See also case #509.

18.   Case #8, March 19, 1767.

19.   Case #182, December 11, 1768. Another action of slander was "for saying he saw the pl. who is a married man in bed with Elizabeth Burkin." Case #48, November 17, 1767. Jefferson also represented that client in cases #35 and 388. For another sex scandal (with no details) see cases #337 and 338. Jefferson handled 36 slander cases; in 18 he represented the plaintiff, and in 18 the defendant. He represented the husband in connection with an order "for present maintenance till suit for separate maintenance determd." Case #877, September 6, 1773. Case #295, June 13, 1769, is perhaps a slander action. Jefferson was defending Walter Coles "for words [illegible] in to committee of the H.B." Since there is a private plaintiff (Nathaniel Terry) it is obviously not a case of contempt against the dignity of the House of Burgesses.

20.   Case #20.

21.   Case #455, October 4, 1770. Francis Willis, Sr., was a fellow student and crony of Jefferson's at Williamsburg. Dumbauld, *American Tourist*, 32; 1 P. 8–9, 21.

22.   Case #558, May 7, 1771. Eppes was Jefferson's brother-in-law. His son in 1797 married Jefferson's younger daughter Mary. Malone, *Virginian*, 157, 162, 432.

23.   Case #912, January 3, 1774. Randolph's son in 1790 married Jefferson's elder daughter Martha.

24.   Case #938, October 9, 1774. Nothing is said about a fee in this case.

25.   See pages 83–85, *supra.*

26.   Case #345, October 10, 1769. The right-hand page is totally blank with respect to the disposition of the case. From the *Reports*, we know that Jefferson lost the case to Wythe. See page 84, *supra.*

27.   Case #708, September 10, 1772. See also cases #659 and 769, which remained for Randolph to finish. Cf. cases #697 and 698.

28.   Case #845, June 9, 1773.

29.   Replevin was an action to recover personal property or chattels wrongfully seized or taken by another party.

30.   Case #116, June 18, 1768. However, on May 23, 1771, he "recd. 2/6." See also case #51, November 19, 1767. This was one of three slander actions brought against different defendants. In 1771 the actions abated by reason of the plaintiff's death. "def. being poor I agreed to remit the fee in this suit, receiving them in the other suits No. 16. 17."

31.   Case #46, November 6, 1767: "the def. is dead so abates. charge no fee." See also case #51, note 30, *supra.*

32.   Case #13, May 18, 1767: "the caveat being dropped remit my fee." Case #188, February 17, 1769: "no suit brot, so remit fee." Case #732, October 14, 1772: "remit fee as it is dismis'd." See also cases #93, 286, 717, 719, 831.

33.   Case #855, July 22, 1773. (AB. refers to assault and battery, a type of case appearing frequently in Jefferson's practice.)

34.   Cases #670, 775, 935.

35.   Case #789, January 14, 1773. Apparently cases #791, 792, 795, 796, met the same fate. Likewise in cases #916 and 917 the notation appears: "patd. so make no charge."

36. There are also a number of instances where there is no reason evident why Jefferson decided to forego his fee. See cases #525, 534, 563, 642, 643, 865.

37. Case #163, October 28, 1768. In another case, *Samuel Meredith* v. *John Aylett*, Jefferson noted: "1772, Oct. 14. retire from the cause and remit fee." Case #544, April 18, 1771. The reason for his withdrawal is not stated. It may have been conflict of interest.

38. Regarding Randolph Jefferson see Bernard Mayo, *Thomas Jefferson and his Unknown Brother Randolph*.

39. Case #433, June 21, 1770: "with mr J. Nicholas's approbation therefore I brot this suit some time ago and did not enter it. . . . charge no fee." It was Nicholas who had employed Jefferson to represent Bates in case #163. On one occasion he could not remember who had employed him to obtain a judgment on behalf of the king. "I somehow omitted to enter it in Mm book, so have forgotten, who emploied me." Case #858.

40. Procuring issuance of summons was a clerical or ministerial act, which a party himself might perform without a lawyer. Jefferson on another occasion furnished that service for a party he was unable to represent: "Banks [in a case against William Byrd, whom Jefferson, as we shall see (note 56, *infra*) represented on a general retainer] desires me to issue writ in [trespass on the] Case. Dam[ages]. £100. I wrote him I would do it, but that I must appear for def. who retained me first." Case #803, March 25, 1773. In a similar situation involving David Ross [see case #500] "appear for pl. under general retainer. note I refused a fee of def. who offered it to me." Case #905, November 3, 1773. John Buchanan had also retained Jefferson in all his caveat business [Case #130], and in a case of that nature "J. Bowyer applied to me for defs, but refused, being retained by Buchanan." Case #197, March 24, 1769.

41. Case #361, November 10, 1769. Jefferson represented White in a caveat proceeding against Mary and James Wood involving adjacent land. Case #140, August 18, 1768.

42. Case #892, October 9, 1773.

43. Case #891, October 9, 1773.

44. Ejectment was the complex and cumbersome action at common law to recover possession of land, brought by a party out of possession.

45. Case #493, January 7, 1771. Jefferson withdrew at the same time from a companion case, #494, involving lands surveyed "about 1746. by Thos. Jefferson who becoming a lunatic did not make out the works." This individual was evidently not President Jefferson's great-grandfather or grandfather, as the latter died in 1715. Malone, *Virginian*, 427.

46. Case #868, August 17, 1773. For earlier cases where Jefferson represented Turk, see cases #564 and 690. Another of Jefferson's clients was named James Turk. Case #579.

47. Case #21, June 10, 1767. In another case he wrote, "remit the rest as I gave a rec[eip]t in full." Case #419, June 8, 1770. The case was one where "I was sometime ago emploied . . . and omitted to enter it here." For other belated entries, see, for example, cases 194, 198, 216, 217, 286, 433 [note 39, *supra*], 937. Case #936 is entirely blank except for the number and caption in the margin.

48. Case #27, August 18, 1767. See also case #150.

49. Case #120, May 12, 1768. "note the pl. talks of giving me £30 in that case, but qu? ——1773. Oct 14. . . . so remit fee." In case #743 the defendant "promises me £5 if we succeed." Only 25/6 was received by Jefferson. In case #354 he noted, "I shall remit the fees if unsuccessful." He received £7 7s.6d. with instructions to dismiss the case and two other connected cases.

50. Case #571, June 29, 1771. Two horses, valued at £55, were accepted by Jefferson "to be applied as a satisfaction for my . . . very great trouble in these matters" handled for

William Waterson. Two separate books were required for the documents relating to this client. There were some five petitions and 50 caveats. See cases #211-15, 223-32, 246-85. On another occasion Jefferson credited a client £3 for "2. gross of bottles." Case #760.

51.   Case #28, August 18, 1767. Jefferson received £1-10, but Randolph was to "finish & receive bal[an]ce. £1-2-6."

52.   Trespass lies for direct injuries, case for indirect (including negligence). See Shipman, *Handbook of Common-Law Pleading*, 72, 83–93.

53.   Case #65, November 19, 1767. See also cases #66–68. Conversely, in case #452 he dismissed a writ in case and issued one in trespass instead.

54.   Case #80, March 17, 1768.

55.   Case #203, April 4, 1769. The strategy was successful. In April, 1774, the suit abated by death of plaintiff. See also cases #189, 190, 242, and 396.

56.   Case #122. However, Jefferson brought suit for wages against a lead mine in which Byrd was a partner. Cases #135–37. On March 23, 1770, he "wrote to pl. to endeavor to get new vouchers, those he had left with me having been burned in the house, with my other papers." See note 5, *supra*. For other general retainers (cases #130, 464, 500, 730, 732, 733, 737) see note 6, Introduction, *supra*.

57.   Cases #244, 728, 734, 784, 785, 803.

58.   Case #612, October 31, 1771.

59.   Case #860, August 9, 1773: "obtd verd[ict]. last April court & jdmt for £21-2"; #861, 862 [judgment for £109 7s.3d. sterling]; 863. Both Robert Carter Nicholas and John Blair were eminent lawyers. Mays, *Edmund Pendleton*, I, 231–32. On Blair see also note 17, *supra*.

60.   Case #492, December 12, 1770. The plaintiffs were from Antigua. On behalf of a London merchant Jefferson drew a bill in chancery against numerous prominent Virginia merchants (including Thomas Adams, who had employed Jefferson to draw the bill). Case #897, October 22, 1772.

61.   Case #244, May 21, 1769.

62.   On the Robinson affair, see Mays, *Edmund Pendleton*, I, 174–223. Administration of the Robinson estate "was to prove the longest and most tedious undertaking of Pendleton's life." *Ibid.*, 331. By "a lucky operation of paper money" Pendleton paid off the debt to Virginia in 1781. *Ibid.*, 223. The affairs of the estate were not finally settled until 1832, by a decree of Chief Justice John Marshall, long after Pendleton's death in 1803. *Ibid.*, 340.

63.   *Ibid.*, 181.

64.   Case #421, June 12, 1770.

65.   Case #723, October 8, 1772.

66.   See note 46, *supra*.

67.   Case #690, August 18, 1772. In view of the importance of land grants at that time, the reliability of the surveyor's work was of serious concern to property holders.

68.   Case #907, November 29, 1773.

69.   Case #616, November 2, 1771.

70.   Case #751, October 19, 1772.

71.   Case #889, October 11, 1773.

72.   Case #898, October 25, 1773.

73.   Case #767, October 29, 1772. In case #910, on December 3, 1772, Jefferson notes that "William Herbert (Fincastle) desires me to appear before council for him," but the nature of the proceeding is not stated.

74.   Case #747, October 16, 1772. For an interesting account of instances where John

W. Davis defended a fellow attorney, see William H. Harbaugh, *Lawyer's Lawyer: The Life of John W. Davis*, 298–317.

75.   See page 213 n. 73, *supra.*

76.   Case #204, April 8, 1769.

77.   Malone, *Virginian*, 43; Robert D. Meade, *Patrick Henry*, I, 118–34; Smith, *Appeals to the Privy Council*, 607–26.

78.   As was the case in *Goodwin* v. *Lunan*. See note 79, *infra.*

79.   Case #510, February 14, 1771. See note 17, *supra.*

80.   See pages 82–83, *supra.*

81.   Case #489.

82.   BR 2. The MS contains 120 leaves, and is in Jefferson's handwriting except for 56 leaves in the handwriting of Anderson Bryant. [A note by Jefferson on fol. 65 verso, the last page of the second argument for plaintiff, says: "This elegant hand writing is by Anderson Bryant of Albemarle."] The arguments have separate pagination, some in Jefferson's hand. In 1975 a uniform pagination, continuing through the whole volume was given to the MS by the Huntington Library, and is used in references hereinafter. The arguments will be cited as "Arg."

83.   Arg. 1–2. This is in Jefferson's handwriting. It is a synopsis of the plaintiff's bill in equity and of defendant's answer and of the depositions of two witnesses.

84.   Arg. 4–13. This is in Jefferson's handwriting, and comprises 13 pages, according to Jefferson's numbering on the margin. Since often two such numbers appear on the same page of the manuscript, he has evidently copied this argument, perhaps from an original in Wythe's large handwriting.

85.   In his own hand. Arg. 16–76. This extends for 61 pages, using Jefferson's numbers in the upper left-hand corners.

86.   *Wankford* v. *Wankford*, 1 Salkeld 299 (K.B. 1703), abstracted in Jefferson's Legal Commonplace Book in item #147. The transcript is in the hand of Anderson Bryant. Arg. 78–90.

87.   Arg. 74. In a marginal note he adds: "since transcribed and to be found at pa. 63."

88.   Arg. 92–127. In Bryant's hand. It also seems to be a copy, for the same reason as stated in note 84, *supra.* Presumably the argument was by Wythe, though this is not indicated as was done in the opening argument. On internal considerations, there are many short paragraphs in this argument, and it is not so certainly attributable to Wythe on stylistic grounds as is the concluding argument or reply for plaintiff.

89.   For Jefferson's second argument, see Arg. 128–176. Plaintiff's concluding reply [Arg. 178–239], in Bryant's hand, fills 62 pages of the book. On the left margins there are numbers, often two per page, totaling 80. These are explained as follows at the end of the argument: "The plaintiff's counsel had made it a question whether the emblements before the act of assembly, would have passed by a devise of the land on which they grew. Afterwards finding the point settled by authorities he suppressed his first argument, the material parts of which, as to the other points, were transcribed, with additions, into the second, the figures in the margins of this refer, those on the right hand to the pages of that, and those on the left hand to the pages of the second argument of the defendant's counsel." Arg. 239.

90.   Because of Jefferson's habitual facility (and felicity) with the pen, it may be safe to assume that he probably also drafted the two-page statement of facts, to the satisfaction of his adversary. See note 83, *supra.*

91.   "Bolling of Virginia," *Virginia Magazine of History and Biography,* Vol. XXII No. 2 (April, 1914), 215–17; No. 3 (July, 1914), 332–33. See also Wyndham Robertson, *Pocahontas . . . and her Descendants,* 32, 61–63. However, for the death of John Bolling

I have accepted the date of September 5 (rather than 6) given in Lemay, "Robert Bolling and the Bailment of Colonel Chiswell," *Early American Literature,* Vol. VI, No. 2 (Fall, 1971), 125; and for the death of Edward Bolling the date of August 18 (rather than 10) given in Jefferson's argument (Arg. 1, 8, 17); and for the dates of Robert and Archibald Bolling those furnished in letters of December 30, 1974, and February 15, 1978, by Waverly K. Winfree of the Virginia Historical Society. Lemay's article describes a controversy in 1766 (important for the growth of freedom of the press in Virginia) in which Jefferson's preceptor George Wythe, his future father-in-law John Wayles, and his future clients Robert Bolling and William Byrd III were involved.

92.   It should perhaps be explained that in lawyer's language a gift of land by will is a devise, while a gift of chattels or personal property by will is called a bequest or legacy. The recipients of such gifts are "devisees" or "legatees," as the case may be. The appropriate verbs are "devise" and "bequeath," respectively. A person to whom land descends by operation of law in the absence of a will is an "heir." Personal property goes at death not to the testator's heir but to his "next of kin" or "distributee" after his "personal representative" ("executor," if appointed by will, or "administrator" if appointed by a court, to administer the estate) has collected receivables, paid debts and legacies, and proceeds to distribute the surplus, if any, remaining in his hands.

93. The entire will is quoted at the beginning of Jefferson's first argument. Arg. 16–17. It was probated October 1, 1770, and Robert Bolling qualified as executor on November 5, 1770. Amherst County Will Book I (1761–80), 184–86. Virginia State Library, reel 17.

94.   In other words there was no contention by plaintiff that defendant was an officious intruder or wrongful intermeddler known as an "*executor de son tort.*" Blackstone, *Commentaries,* II, 507.

95.   The dispute was solely with regard to crops *which had not been harvested* at the time of the testator's death. It was conceded by defendant that the crops which had already been severed from the soil before Edward Bolling's death constituted personal property and (if not needed to pay debts or pecuniary legacies) should pass as part of the residue.

96.   Blackstone, *Commentaries,* II, 122–23, 146, 404.

97.   Matthew L. Davis, *Memoirs of Aaron Burr,* II, 14. Possibly this was an oral argument. Jefferson captions it "G. Wythe's argum' verbal." But it is evidently copied from another paper, and not notes taken during argument. See note 84, *supra.*

98.   "Yea they are in law, before they be severed, mobilia . . . mere personal chattels following the sower, the consequence is, that they will not pass with land by a devise." Arg. 4.

99.   Arg. 8. Wythe's initial superficiality may indicate an attitude similar to that of John W. Davis, whereas Jefferson's resembled that of Charles Evans Hughes. "Hughes knew 'all there was to know about the case, Davis all he needed to know.' " William H. Harbaugh, *Lawyer's Lawyer,* 408.

100.   Arg. 4–7. Godbolt was particularly criticized: "I cannot allow such a book as this to deserve much credit." Arg. 7.

101.   22 Geo. 2, c. 3, sec. 30 [October, 1748, Hening, *Statutes,* V, 464].

102.   Arg. 9. The act applies where the owner dies between March 1 and December 25.

103.   Arg. 11. That rule was also argued to be inapplicable because there were particular legacies given to the executor. Arg. 12.

104.   He who bears the burden should also have the benefit.

105.   Arg. 12.

106.   This item is not argued at length by Jefferson, as it was conceded by plaintiff. Arg. 56.

107. Arg. 18.

108. Arg. 18. "Whatever is planted in the soil belongs to the soil."

109. Pufendorf, *De Jure Naturae et Gentium*, Bk. IV, cap. 7, sec. 2; Inst. Lib. II, tit. 1, sec. 31.

110. Arg. 19.

111. Including the case in Godbolt, case 219, as Wythe had anticipated. Jefferson says it is identical with the case at bar except that there the grant was by deed, not by will. Arg. 21. See note 100, *supra*.

112. Arg. 23–26. That is why a devise will not pass after-acquired lands, whereas all personal property owned at the time of death will pass by will. With much erudition Jefferson traces the history of English land law with regard to alienation of interests in land.

113. Arg. 27.

114. Similar to the baseball player's counsel to "keep your eye on the ball" and "bunch your hits." Jefferson again resorts to this technique in postponing discussion of the meaning of "assets" in the Virginia statute. See Arg. 49.

115. Arg. 27.

116. Arg. 7.

117. A marginal note here states "they have license."

118. Arg. 28.

119. Arg. 28–29.

120. Arg. 29.

121. See notes 100 and 111, *supra*.

122. He points out that Lord Raymond's reports are explicitly on the title page described as "taken and collected" by him.

123. Perhaps the best-known instance of Jefferson's mathematical mode of argumentation is his statistical computation designed to allay alarm over the Shays Rebellion in Massachusetts. "We have had 13. states independant 11. years. There has been one rebellion. That comes to one rebellion in a century and a half for each state. What country before ever existed a century and a half without a rebellion? . . . What signify a few lives lost in a century or two. The tree of liberty must be refreshed from time to time with the blood of patriots and tyrants. It is it's natural manure." To W. S. Smith, November 13, 1787, 12 P. 356.

124. Leonard covers 58 years, Anderson 71, Dyer 72, Noy 91, Benloe 94, Moore 132, and Jenkins 408.

125. Arg. 30.

126. Arg. 30.

127. Cro. Eliz. 61 [1587].

128. Arg. 23. *Knevett* v. *Poole*, Cro. Eliz. 463 [1594]. See also 5 Rep. 85 [1596]. Jefferson points out that a passage in that case ("but he who sowed the land") quoted by Wythe does not appear in the book. Arg. 34. The case in Cro. Eliz. 61 [1587] was also cited in *Grantham* v. *Hawley*, Hobart 132 [1615]. The fifth edition of Hobart's *Reports* (London, 1724) was apparently used. In the London edition of 1641 the case is #171 at pages 185–86.

129. Thomas Wentworth, *The Office and Duty of Executors*, 59. [First published in 1641; the London edition of 1728 may have been used.]

130. Arg. 7.

131. Arg. 37–38.

132. The reference to Coke and Blackstone is at Arg. 43; the passage on *stare decisis*

at Arg. 38. Jefferson then proceeds to quote Lord Mansfield in *Windham* v. *Chetwynd*, 1 Burr. 414, 423 (1757), and Blackstone, *Commentaries*, I, 69.

133. Arg. 46.

134. Second argument for plaintiff, Arg. 94; reply for plaintiff, Arg. 193. See also Arg. 128 and 239, quoted in note 89, *supra*. [Sir Geoffrey Gilbert], *The Law of Evidence*, 250, was the decisive authority. This had been cited by Jefferson at Arg. 22.

135. Act of 9 Anne, c. 2, sec. 17, October, 1711; Hening, *Statutes*, IV, 21–22.

136. Act of 3 & 4 Geo. 2, c. 8, secs. 10 and 11, May, 1730; Hening, *Statutes*, IV, 283–84.

137. Act of 22 Geo. 2, c. 5, secs. 30 and 31, October, 1748; Hening, *Statutes*, V, 464–65. According to Jefferson this act [in sec. 31] merely provided that when the slaves are turned over to the heir or legatees by the executor or administrator they must be *clothed*. It did not alter the prior law at all in any other respect. Arg. 41. Sec. 30 of the Act of 1748 is substantially identical with sec. 11 of the Act of 1730.

138. See page 97, *supra*.

139. Arg. 46–47.

140. Arg. 47. To the argument that it is unjust for the owner of the emblements to receive the benefit of the labor of slaves belonging to other persons (the legatees of such slaves) Jefferson responds that it would be even more unjust to give that labor to the residuary legatee. Arg. 56.

141. Arg. 48.

142. Arg. 49.

143. Arg. 51.

144. Act of October, 1705, 4 Anne, c. 23, sec. 4; Hening, *Statutes*, III, 334.

145. Act of Parliament, 5 Geo. 2, c. 7, sec. 4.

146. Act of 29 Car. 2, c. 3 (statute of frauds).

147. Act of 29 Car. 2, c. 3, sec. 12. Jefferson cites *Oldham* v. *Pickering*, 2 Salkeld 464 (K.B. 1696), to show that this type of estate, though made "assets" by the statute, when not needed to pay debts, remains a freehold estate and is not to be distributed as goods and chattels in accordance with the statute of distributions, 22 & 23 Car. 2.

148. Arg. 56–57. Jefferson concludes his discussion of point I by recapitulating the propositions he has covered in the body of the argument.

149. Arg. 58. For the full text of this provision of the will, see note 93, *supra*.

150. In this argument Jefferson contended that the testator's intent to give defendant a beneficial legacy "will appear on the *Face* of the will" and also "from *Parol Proof* dehors of the will." Arg. 59, 68. He later conceded that parole evidence was not admissible and that "upon the will alone therefore that question is to rest." Arg. 167. For plaintiff's convincing argument, see Arg. 111–13.

151. Arg. 59, 73.

152. Arg. 216. For Jefferson's use of that expression, see Arg. 157.

153. Arg. 60–61.

154. Arg. 222.

155. Arg. 62–63. Jefferson is here invoking the canon of construction known as *noscitur a sociis*. For amusing comment by Judge Herbert Goodrich on the small benefit to be gained from using maxims such as *noscitur a sociis* and *ejusdem generis*, see *Keystone Automobile Club* v. *Commissioner*, 181 F.2d 402, 404–405 (C.A. 3, 1950).

156. Arg. 63. Wythe contended that the clause is merely an appointment of Robert Bolling as executor, by circumlocution; but that "will not warrant us to ramble into the

field of conjecture to find another meaning. . . . And why is the clause to be thus tortured, perverted, interpolated, when it is intelligible, it is satisfied, by being considered as the appointment of an executor." Arg. 108, 110. In his second argument Jefferson denied interpolation, saying his words were only a paraphrase. Arg. 165. Wythe wittily withdrew the offensive epithet, but characterized Jefferson's "paraphrase" as "commentitious." Arg. 227. The two illustrious adversaries behave like present-day justices of the United States Supreme Court accusing each other of "judicial legislation" instead of legitimate interpretation of the language being construed.

157. Here Jefferson adds parenthetically: "And here I must beg the will may be turned to, and read over; having inserted it verbatim in the state of the case for this purpose principally." See note 93, *supra*. This is perhaps one of Jefferson's strongest and most lawyerlike arguments in support of his interpretation of the clause. The sixth reason is likewise a strong ground, and the cumulative effect of all six arguments is impressive.

158. Arg. 64–65. Both Jefferson and Wythe displayed admirably "the subtle reasonings of the law" throughout this case.

159. Arg. 65.

160. Arg. 65–66.

161. "The rest of my estate, negroes, horses, clothes, and every other part of my estate not already given I give and bequeath to my brother Archibald Bolling."

162. This rule limits general terms in a series of things to those of the same nature as those previously named. See note 155, *supra*.

163. Arg. 67–68.

164. Arg. 68.

165. Arg. 68. See note 150, *supra*.

166. Arg. 69.

167. *Ibid.* Plaintiff conceded that the sale was a revocation of the devise to Archibald Bolling. Arg. 228. Apparently plaintiff also conceded that if defendant received the outstanding debts as a beneficial legacy the £500 from Buchanan was included. It was also conceded that defendant would not be liable to pay the legacy to Sarah Tazewell. Arg. 163. Jefferson argued that the £100 legacy to her was "already given" by the will and hence did not comprise part of the residuary bequest to plaintiff. Arg. 72–73.

168. Arg. 70.

169. Arg. 17. See also Arg. 123–35 and 229. Jefferson computed each brother's share as £400 sterling and £40 currency. Wythe estimated between £500 and £600.

170. Arg. 70.

171. *Ibid.*

172. Arg. 71. On the rule of *ejusdem generis* see note 162, *supra*.

173. Arg. 71.

174. *Ibid.* In any event, Jefferson contends, "the award would only be that the father's debts should be paid with the testator's own debts out of the Credits *so far as they should go:* that their excess might not make this bequest of the Book a charge on Rob. Boll." Arg.72.

175. See note 87, *supra*.

176. John Locke, *Two Treatises of Government* (1963 ed.), 329–41 [Bk. II, §§27–44].

177. Arg. 94. See page 102, *supra*. See also Arg. 193.

178. Arg. 96–97. But does the statute suspend the devisee's right to the *land*, or merely require him to permit the slaves to finish the *crops* for another person?

179. Arg. 105–106.

180. Arg. 109–110.

181. Arg. 117. See page 96, *supra*. *Wankford* v. *Wankford,* upon which Jefferson

relied, is criticized as "an extrajudicial opinion" [that is, dictum, dealing with a point not involved in the question before the court.] Arg. 118.

182. Arg. 120-21, citing Lord Hardwicke in *Carter* v. *Carter*, 1 Vesey, Sr. 168, 169 (1748), to the effect that the will as a whole must be looked at.

183. Arg. 123.

184. Arg. 127. See also Arg. 109. Jefferson answers that this argument carries no weight, since new purchases were made of other properties, creating debts owed by the testator greater in amount than the proceeds of the Pocahontas sale. Arg. 166.

185. Arg. 132.

186. Arg. 134. In the case at bar the erudite discussion of accession was only academic and pertinent with respect to the effect of the Virginia legislation; for no crop was in fact planted after the testator's death: "[We claimed] only those growing at the time of his death . . . and say that had any been planted after (tho' in truth none were) they would have been ours as an Accession to our soil, in like manner included in the devise of the land." Arg. 145.

187. See page 109, *supra.*

188. Arg. 137. For Wythe's reply, see Arg. 188-89 and page 114, *infra.*

189. Arg. 139. See also Arg. 144.

190. Arg. 140. He also urges that plaintiff's argument proves too much, for it would include slaves (which are liable to debts) among the personal estate to be distributed; but slaves are not so distributable. Arg. 141.

191. Arg. 146. See page 104, *supra.*

192. 2 Salk. 464; Holt 503; 3 Salk. 137.

193. It will be remembered that the church courts handled probate and distribution of personal property; and that the common law courts used the writ of prohibition to confine the church courts to their appropriate jurisdiction. See pages 81 and 213 n. 61.

194. Arg. 149.

195. Arg. 149-50.

196. Arg. 151-52.

197. Arg. 153. Jefferson then shows that *Oldham* v. *Pickering* was not weakened by a later case, *Witter* v. *Witter*, 3 P.W. 99, 102 (1730), cited by plaintiff. There the court of equity itself subjected to distribution a new lease which had been obtained by an executor in violation of fiduciary duty. Arg. 153-55. He also points out that in *Manwood* v. *Turner*, 3 P.W. 163 (1732), cited by plaintiff, no questions as to the rights of distributees were involved. Arg. 156.

198. 14 Geo. 2, c. 20.

199. Arg. 158. For plaintiff's point, see Arg. 102. In his reply Wythe said he was "so thoroughly convinced that the case proves nothing at all material in the present dispute, he will admit it to be law." Arg. 218.

200. Arg. 158-59.

201. Arg. 159-62.

202. See pages 104-107, *supra.*

203. Arg. 163.

204. Arg. 108. For Jefferson's case, see Arg. 60.

205. Arg. 163-64. Wythe reiterated that he still thought his idea "a very good one, wherever 'picked up.' " Arg. 222.

206. Arg. 164. For plaintiff's point, see Arg. 109, page 109, *supra.* Wythe warmly replied that Jefferson's admission properly amounted to a concession that the executor was accountable to the residuary legatee (since on the assumption that Robert Bolling was

collecting for the testator and not himself, there was no legacy to him, and the proceeds fell into the residue). Arg. 225–26.

207. Arg. 168–69. See note 175, *supra*.

208. See note 182, *supra*.

209. Arg. 172.

210. Arg. 121, citing Ca. temp. Talbot 242.

211. Jefferson is here by implication deriding Wythe's earlier attempts to question the authority of precedents cited by defendant. See pages 98–101, *supra*.

212. Arg. 172–73. On Talbot, see Holdsworth, *History*, XII, 214–18. Jefferson is evidently here referring to Justice Powell in *Wankford* v. *Wankford*. He also cites Blackstone as in agreement. See Arg. 76.

213. *Fox* v. *Fox*, 1 Atk. 463 (1737), cited at Arg. 122. Jefferson considered this case merely an instance of marshaling assets. Arg. 173.

214. Arg. 174.

215. Arg. 175.

216. Arg. 176.

217. *Ibid.*

218. The exchange of thrusts regarding "interpolation" has already been mentioned. See note 156, *supra*.

219. See notes 185 and 186, *supra*.

220. Arg. 182, 186.

221. See page 109, *supra*.

222. Arg. 188–89.

223. Arg. 187. Wythe is here referring to the extracts from Pufendorf, Justinian's *Institutes*, Bracton, and Blackstone quoted by Jefferson. See notes 109 and 185, *supra*.

224. Arg. 189–90. See also Arg. 207.

225. Arg. 176, see page 114, *supra*.

226. Arg. 192.

227. Arg. 196.

228. Arg. 196–97.

229. Arg. 193. See also Arg. 219. Wythe points out that at common law emblements were liable for debts; so the legislation accomplished little if all it did was to make them liable for debts only, as Jefferson contends. Arg. 194.

230. Arg. 203–205.

231. Arg. 207–18. See page 110, *supra*. Wythe furnishes a table comparing the status of slaves and emblements, "that what they agree and what they differ in may be more easily perceptible; from whence perhaps the defendant's counsel himself may see the matter in a different light from what he hath hitherto done." Arg. 209–10.

232. Arg. 214–15.

233. Arg. 224.

234. Arg. 230.

235. See pages 107–108, *supra*.

236. Arg. 231. See note 156, *supra*.

237. Arg. 229.

238. Arg. 232. See page 112, *supra*.

239. *Ibid.*

240. See page 116, *supra.*

241. Arg. 74. See note 175, *supra.* Jefferson's statement of the law is in accordance with the opinion of Justice Powell in the *Wankford* case. Arg. 83; 1 Salkeld at 303. See note 244, *infra.*

242. Justice Gould thus stated the question. Arg. 79; 1 Salkeld at 300.

243. The plaintiff was the widow of the debtor, and sued as administrator of her father the testator. She had refused to prove her father's will and serve as his executor in her capacity as her husband's executor.

244. Arg. 83; 1 Salkeld at 303.

245. Arg. 85, 86–87; 1 Salkeld at 305, 306.

246. Arg. 117–21.

247. That is, not joined in by his colleagues on the bench.

248. Arg. 168–69.

249. Arg. 169.

250. Arg. 250 (Jefferson's concession); Arg. 121 (plaintiff's question).

251. Arg. 233, 234. Wythe then quotes the passage from Holt set forth above, see page 117.

252. Arg. 234–35. Wythe correctly interprets Holt; but does not all this show that Powell's view is preferable? If the executor is always accountable for the amount of his debts as assets, what is left of the rule that appointing a debtor as executor works a *forgiveness* of the debt, when it is not bequeathed or needed as assets?

253. Arg. 235–36.

254. *Brown* v. *Selwin*, Talbot 240 (1734). See Arg. 113–15. For Jefferson's comment on that case, see Arg. 75–76, and 169–71. This is the case where Talbot's "inclination" to regard such a debt as assets for the payment of legacies generally was expressed. See note 210, *supra.*

255. Talbot 242.

256. Arg. 74, 176.

257. Arg. 237. Ascribing to Jefferson the opinion that there is a general rule "that where a debtor is appointed executor the debt is *released* if it be not particularly described and bequeathed away," Wythe asks "where he found and how he proves the rule? It is not to be 'picked up' even in Powell's argument, nor is it contained in terms of the like import in the case of Brown v. Selwin." Arg. 238. Wythe here retaliates for Jefferson's earlier use of the same expression (see pages 112, 225 n. 205, *supra),* but Jefferson's position is supported by Powell. See notes 241 and 244, *supra.*

258. Arg. 239.

259. Both Jefferson and Wythe had obviously complied with the "threefold imperative" prescribed by Justice Frankfurter: "(1) Read the statute; (2) read the statute; (3) read the statute!" Henry J. Friendly, *Benchmarks,* 202.

260. These traditional handmaidens of the law are discussed in the familiar lectures of Justice Benjamin N. Cardozo, *The Nature of the Judicial Process,* 30–31.

261. However, throughout the *Bolling* case, Wythe refrained from indulging in quotations from classical writers. This "engaging pedantry" characterized his judicial opinions. "Greek and Latin maxims, long dead names from old anthologies, allusions to figures of history and literature, snatches of scientific truths, and algebraic equations, follow each other across the pages of his decisions." It was said of him that "he could hardly refrain from giving a line of Horace the force of an act of Assembly." Mays, *Edmund Pendleton,*

II, 292. Wythe became one of three judges of the Court of Chancery in 1778, and from 1789 (see note 15, chapter 4, *supra*) was sole chancellor of Virginia. Reversals of his decrees by his rival Pendleton (then on the Court of Appeals) aroused his resentment. (See notes 3 and 93, chapter 4, *supra*.) When in 1802 additional chancery courts were erected in Williamsburg and Staunton, Wythe remained as Chancellor of the Richmond court until his death in 1806.

CHAPTER VI

1. He estimated that four folio volumes would suffice for the purpose, whereas those who wished to possess as many of the laws as were then available in print would have to buy six folio volumes "to wit, Purvis & those [revisals] of 1732, 1748, 1768, 1783 & 1794, and in all of them possess not one half of what they wish." To George Wythe, January 16, 1796, 8 F. 214–17; also printed in Hening, *Statutes*, I, viii–ix (where it is wrongly dated 1795). On Purvis and the revisals, see pages 128; 130–31; 235 n. 112; 235 n. 115; 137, 238 n. 34; 139, 240 n. 55, *infra*. In later life Jefferson spoke of "the lubberly volumes of the law." To Isaac McPherson, August 13, 1813, 13 M. 336. He likewise avowed that "I am now too old to read books solidly unless they promise present amusement or future benefit. To me books of law offer neither." To John M. Goodenow, June 13, 1822, 15 M. 382.

2. To St. George Tucker, May 9, 1798; to Ebenezer Hazard, February 18, 1791. Hazard's *Historical Collections* was published in Philadelphia, in two volumes, 1792–94. Regarding four MS volumes of state papers collected by Jefferson, which he hoped W. W. Hening might edit after completing *The Statutes at Large*, see to Hening, September 28, 1820; May 8, 1822. A recent publication from manuscripts owned by Jefferson is Susan M. Kingsbury (ed.), *The Records of the Virginia Company of London*. See Sowerby #1831. Jefferson also assembled a valuable collection of newspapers and pamphlets. To Hening, June 13, 1822. Of particular interest was a curious collection of scurrilous partisan writings attacking his administration and containing personal abuse. Samuel Harrison Smith, *Memoir of the Life, Character, and Writings of Thomas Jefferson*, 23.

3. To T. M. Randolph, January 12, 1796; to George Wythe, January 12, 1796; to Wythe, May 29, 1799.

4. See note 1, *supra*. Jefferson enclosed "A statement of the Volumes of the Laws of Virginia, Manuscript & Printed in my possession." Item 17010, dated January 13, 1796, LC.

5. Wythe to Jefferson, July 27, 1796. A copy of the broadside is preserved in LC.

6. Hening, *Statutes*, I, vii–xi. The first of Hening's thirteen volumes appeared in 1809, the last in 1823 (three years before Jefferson's death). See page 123, *infra*.

7. Hening, *Statutes*, I, v, 127. According to Barton, *Virginia Colonial Decisions*, I, 193, session acts were not printed in Virginia until William Parks began to do so after publication in 1733 of his *Collection*, which was the first law book printed in Virginia. See page 131, *infra*.

8. To John Daly Burk, June 1, 1805, 10 F. 148. Burk's *The History of Virginia, from its First Settlement to the Present Day* was published in four volumes, 1804–16. The author used material supplied by Jefferson. On Purvis, see note 78, *infra*.

9. Vol. I was "Purvis's collection 1662–1682," Vols. II–IV the Revisals of 1733, 1748, and 1768, containing laws from 1662 to the dates thereof; and Vols. VI–VIII were of dates subsequent to 1772. [10 F. 148; Sowerby, II, 246 (#1837–62)]. Concerning the various revisals of the Virginia laws, see William E. Ross, "History of Virginia Codification," *Virginia Law Register*, Vol. XI, No. 2 (June, 1905), 79–101. See also note 58, *infra*.

10. To John Daly Burk, June 1, 1805, 10 F. 148–49.

11. To John D. Burk, Feb. 21, 1803. See also to W. W. Hening, July 25, 1809.

12. Hening (1767–1828) was clerk of the Richmond Chancery Court. See *Com.* v. *Hening*, 1 Brockenbrough & Holmes 324 (1814). See also notes 28 and 31, *infra*.

13. See page 121, *supra.* The General Assembly by Act of February 5, 1808, authorized publication and subscribed for 150 copies for the state. For the Act of 1808 and subsequent legislation regarding publication of the laws, see Leigh, *Revised Code*, II, 330–32. Jefferson's correspondence with Hening concerning the project is given in Sowerby, II, 256–60 (#1863).

14. "I have now the pleasure of presenting to you the first volume of my Statutes at Large, which was published on yesterday only." Hening to Jefferson, Oct. 22, 1809. In acknowledging the volume, Jefferson commented by way of testimonial: "The opinion I entertain of the importance of the work may be justly inferred from the trouble & expence I incurred during the earlier part of my life, to save such remains of our antient laws as were then still in existence. The compilation appears to be correctly and judiciously made and gives us exactly what I had so long considered as a desideratum for our country. It sheds a new light on our early history, and furnishes additional security to the tenure ot our rights & property." To Hening, December 1, 1809.

15. All volumes of the first edition were published in Richmond, except volume XIII which was published in Philadelphia. Jefferson had repeatedly commented on the inferior paper and typography of local printers in Virginia. See note 13, *supra,* and page 125, *infra.* Of the set which I used and cite (in the Department of Justice library in Washington) the first four volumes are of the second edition.

16. William H. Martin, "Hening and the Statutes at Large," *Virginia Law Register*, Vol. XIII (new series), No. 1 (May, 1927), 25–37; Hening to Jefferson, September 23, 1816.

17. Hening, *Statutes*, I, xxiii. Jefferson furnished the list of governors of Virginia printed by Hening. *Ibid.*, I, 3–5.

18. To Hening, July 25, 1809.

19. To Hening, August 28, 1809. On September 4, 1809, Hening wrote to Jefferson that he had received the volume from George Jefferson. The book had been sent to Richmond in 1805 when Burk was writing his history of Virginia. See note 8, *supra.* See also Sowerby #1841.

20. After the sale, Jefferson wrote to Hening requesting return of the volume; but he acceded to Hening's wish to keep it until completion of volume VIII of *The Statutes at Large*. To Hening, March 11, 1815; March 25, 1815.

21. Sowerby #1841 speaks as if the volume had been received by the Library of Congress in 1820, although it is now missing, but cites no evidence (nor have I found any) later than Hening's letter to Jefferson of August 19, 1820, stating his intention of returning it to the Library of Congress after completing volume VIII.

22. *Pallas* v. *Hill*, 2 Hen. & Munf. 149 (1808). There were in fact six cases pending which involved the same question. Hening to Jefferson, February 7, 1808.

23. The case is discussed in detail in Dumbauld, "A Manuscript from Monticello," *American Bar Association Journal*, Vol. XXVIII, No. 5 (May, 1952), 389.

24. *Ibid.*, 390. Apparently the form of action used in a suit for freedom was trespass for assault and battery or false imprisonment. The restraints and chastisements inflicted upon slaves undoubtedly constituted adequate grounds for such an action, in the absence of the privilege which the status of slavery afforded to the master of a slave. If the person held in servitude were not a slave, he could recover against a wrongdoer who unlawfully

deprived him of the liberty enjoyed by free men. Cf. the medieval writ *de libertate probanda.* Holdsworth, *History*, III, 497.

25.   4 Anne c. 2, Session of October 23, 1705. Hening, *Statutes*, III, 464–69.

26.   *Coleman* v. *Dick & Pat*, 1 Wash. 233, 239 (1793).

27.   *Hudgins* v. *Wrights*, 1 Hen. & Munf. 134, 138–39 (1806).

28.   3 W. & M. c. 9, Session of April 16, 1691. Hening, *Statutes*, III, 69. Hening was already at work on his publication of the laws, in which he relied heavily on the MS from Northumberland. See note 72, *infra.*

29.   2 Hen. & Munf. at 151, 159.

30.   *Id.,* at 150.

31.   Hening to Jefferson, February 7, 1808.

32.   Jefferson to Hening, January 14, 1807. See also page 122, *supra.*

33.   See note 31, *supra.*

34.   Jefferson to Hening, February 26, 1808.

35.   2 Hen. & Munf. 157–58.

36.   See note 31, *supra.*

letter to Wythe which had been printed. See note 5, *supra.*

37.   See note 34, *supra.* For the contents of Jefferson's collection, he referred to the

38.   See page 123, *supra.*

39.   See page 122, *supra,* regarding the practice of using handwritten copies of legislative enactments.

40.   Designated respectively as A, 43, F, a MS copied by Jefferson himself, a MS from Charles City, B, a MS from Rosewell, a second Charles City MS containing the laws of 1705. These are described by Sowerby, in items numbered 1822, 1823, 1824, 1826, 1827, 1828, 1830, 1829, respectively.

41.   Dated June 7, 1808. LC 31529, printed in Sowerby, II, 258 (#1863).

42.   Items 2, 3, 4, 5, 7, and 8 of the list of June 7, 1808, were returned by Hening, and acknowledged in Jefferson's letter of April 8, 1815, to Hening. LC 36225. Item 6 is apparently nowhere mentioned, but is in the Library of Congress. Sowerby #1828. Jefferson noted that item 1 (MS A) and MS D were missing. The former turned up years later after a strange odyssey and was returned in 1820. Jefferson to George Watterston, September 1, 1820; Jefferson to Hening, September 3, 1820. "In 1810, it seems, Colo. Croghan found it in possession of mr. Lyttleton Tazewell of Williamsburg among some neglected papers, and carried it into the Western country." Noting an endorsement in Jefferson's handwriting, "he conjectured it might be mine, took care of it, & having occasion lately to come to Virginia, and to pass through this neighborhood, he left it for me with a friend, and I have recieved and returned it to the librarian of Congress."

43.   Designated as D and a "MS. appendix to a copy of Pervis's collection from the Westover library given by the late Colo. W. Byrd to mr. Wayles, whose library came to my hands." These are items 1825 and 1832 in Sowerby. The Byrd MS was not sent to Hening.

44.   LC 17010, dated January 13, 1796. See note 4, *supra.*

45.   No. 5 on the Hening list, the Charles City MS.

46.   "I found it in Lorton's tavern, brought in to be used for waste paper. Much had already been cut off for thread papers and other uses. Debnam, the then clerk, very readily gave it to me, as also another hereafter mentioned. It still contains from chap. 31 of the session of 1661/2 to 1702." LC 17010. The date Jefferson thus acquired the Charles City manuscripts is not stated. His account book shows payments for entertainment at that tavern on October 6, 1770, and December 10, 1770. But he traveled that route often while

courting the future Mrs. Jefferson at The Forest, in Charles City County. They were married on January 1, 1772. Dumbauld, *American Tourist*, 37.

47. This was MS D. See notes 42 and 43, *supra*.

48. Sowerby #1825. On August 19, 1820, Hening informed Jefferson that he had returned this manuscript to the Librarian of Congress, in accordance with Jefferson's instructions. Hening to Jefferson, September 23, 1816; Jefferson to Hening, October 12, 1816; Hening to Jefferson, August 19, 1820.

49. On Randolph, see [Edmund Randolph], *A Vindication of Mr. Randolph's Resignation*; Moncure D. Conway, *Omitted Chapters of History Disclosed in the Life and Papers of Edmund Randolph*; and Dumas Malone, *Jefferson and the Ordeal of Liberty*, 85, 161–62, 263–64.

50. Hening, *Statutes*, I, 238, *et passim;* Hening to Jefferson, April 15, 1815. MS D was not included on the list of June 7, 1808, of materials sent to Hening [see notes 40, 41, and 42, *supra*], as Jefferson acknowledged in his letter to Hening of April 25, 1815. See note 52, *infra*.

51. Jefferson to Hening, September 3, 1820; Hening to Jefferson, September 9, 1820; Hening, *Statutes*, I, xxiii–xxiv, 238. Hening now described the manuscript as one "received from Edmund Randolph, Esq. which was once the property of Sir John Randolph, who transmitted it to his son Peyton Randolph, Esq. after whose death, it was purchased, with his library, by Thomas Jefferson, Esq., from whom it was borrowed by Edmund Randolph, Esq."

52. Jefferson to Hening, April 25, 1815.

53. *Report of the Committee of Revisors Appointed by the General Assembly of Virginia In MDCCLXXVI*, Richmond, 1784. Sowerby #1864. For a convenient reprinting with thorough editorial comment, see 2 P. 305–665. See pages 132–39, *supra*.

54. 1 F. 66–67.

55. See note 1, *supra*. Regarding early publications of Virginia statutes, see John Stewart Bryan, "Report of Committee on Library and Legal Literature" [delivered on July 6, 1898] in *Report of the Tenth Annual Meeting of the Virginia State Bar Association*, 55–70; and articles by Ross and Martin. See also Leigh, *Revised Code*, II, 324–33; and Conway Robinson, preface to *The Code of Virginia* (1849), iii–x [Swem attributes this to George W. Munford]; as well as "A Complete Library of Virginia Statute Law," *Virginia Law Register*, Vol. XI (April, 1906), 1048–52. The foregoing will be cited hereinafter simply by the author's name.

56. Thomas J. Wertenbaker, *Virginia under the Stuarts*, 19, 22–24, 27, 35–37. For the charters, see Francis N. Thorpe, *The Federal and State Constitutions, Colonial Charters, and Other Organic Laws*, VII, 3783–89, 3790–3802, 3802–10.

57. FOR The Colony in Virgine[a] BRITTANIA. Lavves Diuine, Morall and Martiall, &c. Printed at London for *Walter Burre*. 1612. (Library Company of Philadelphia copy.) The volume was compiled by William Strachey. A convenient paperback edition by David H. Flaherty, containing an informative introduction, was issued by the University Press of Virginia in 1969. The Dale code thus being now readily available, I have abridged my account of it, but without changing the page references or quotations taken from the 1612 edition.

58. Martin, 15, 17; Bryan, 55–58. Hening (*Statutes*, I, vi) and most writers regard the revision of September 4, 1632 (printed in Hening, *Statutes*, I, 178–209) as the first revisal, that of March 2, 1642/43 (Hening, I, 238–82) as the second, and that of March 13, 1657/58 (Hening, I, 429–95) as the third. Until printed by Hening these three revisals

existed only in manuscript (preserved by Jefferson). Martin, 17–18; Leigh, II, 333. There is considerable hairsplitting among Virginia writers as to the precise meaning of the term "revisal." It is to be distinguished from a "compilation" or "consolidation" which merely reproduces existing law in a more coherent and convenient form. In its strictest sense it implies a printed revision made pursuant to the report of a committee officially authorized by the General Assembly to propose desirable changes in existing law as well as to restate the whole in orderly form. See Martin, 17, 198, 279, 281, 321, 324–25, 385–86, 389, 396; Ross, 87, 90. Under the strict definition the only pre-Hening revisals were those of 1661/2, 1752, and 1792. Martin, 396.

59.   An attempt to identify the new matter attributable to Dale is made in the excellent discussion of Dale's code by Walter F. Prince, "The First Criminal Code of Virginia," in *Annual Report* of the American Historical Association for 1899 (1900), I, 309–63.

60.   *Lavves*, 2–19.

61.   *Ibid.,* 20. The religious, civil, and political laws are embodied in 37 articles.

62.   These include blasphemy, treason, unreverent demeanor towards ministers, sodomy, incest, theft, murder, false witness, murmuring, intemperate railings, "base unmanly speeches," and the like.

63.   These are summarized in 51 articles (*Lavves*, 20–34), and subsequently specified in 47 articles (*ibid.*, 42–46). Military behavior is prescribed in special instructions directed to personnel of various ranks. *Ibid.*, 34–41, 47–89. These precepts contain much advice and exhortation, somewhat after the fashion of Benjamin Franklin's worldly wisdom (for example, *ibid.*, 55, 81).

64.   *Ibid.*, 10, 12–13.

65.   *Ibid.*, 13–14, 17–19.

66.   See *ibid.*, 3–7, 10, 12–14, 16–19 for instances of these punishments (other than death, as to which see note 67, *infra*).

67.   Among offenses punishable by death were failure to attend church services or slander, calumny, or utterance of "unseemly and unfitting speeches" (third offense) [*ibid.*, 3, 6]; false witness [*ibid.*, 6]; stealing [*ibid.*, 7–8]; slaughtering animals or poultry without permission from the General [*ibid.*, 10–12]; plucking a flower from a garden or stealing ears of growing corn [*ibid.*, 14–15]; private trading with mariners or Indians [*ibid.*, 17, 31–32]; and numerous military offenses such as cowardice, desertion, feigning sickness in time of battle, disobedience, selling or otherwise disposing of weapons, noise during a maneuver requiring stealth, failure to retreat when the signal is given, and the like [*ibid.*, 29–32].

68.   *Ibid.*, 22–23. Thus one who displays cowardice or surrenders "without hauing performed, first the part of a good souldier, and an honest man, shall suffer death with the arms which he carrieth." *Ibid.*, 30.

69.   *Ibid.*, 16.

70.   Martin, 74.

71.   From the Huntington Library copy, with bookplate of E. D. Church. For another copy with a "manuscript continuation of 84 pages, to October 1677, which differs in some essential particulars from the text printed by Hening," see [Charles R. Hildeburn], *The Charlemagne Tower Collection of Laws* (privately printed for the Historical Society of Pennsylvania, 1890) 253 (#903). The Tower copy, omitting the printer's name and address, is believed to be earlier. Martin, 74.

72.   Printed in Hening, *Statutes*, II, 41–148. He used the Northumberland MS as standard, together with Jefferson's Charles City MS and the printed text of Purvis, which

he considered to be full of errors, as well as the 1733 edition printed by Parks. *Ibid.*, 42. See notes 7, 28, and 46, *supra*, and notes 78, and 101, *infra*.

73.   *The Lawes of Virginia Now in Force*, 1. For the act authorizing the printing of this volume, see Hening, *Statutes*, II, 147–48.

74.   Robinson, iii–iv. This was the first copyrighted book in America. Martin, 75.

75.   Bryan, 60; Ross, 85; Martin, 76. It was also unknown as late as 1819 to so learned a scholar as B. W. Leigh. Leigh, II, 324.

76.   On Purvis, see note 78, *infra*.

77.   Bryan, 86; Martin, 75. See also Hening, *Statutes*, III, 9, 14.

78.   From Jefferson's copy (with a continuation of MS laws for over 100 pages, see note 43, *supra*) in the Library of Congress. Another copy there lacks title page and dedication, but has a title page supplied in Jefferson's handwriting and a note that he received the book from John Page of Rosewell. See Sowerby #1832 and #1837; and *Charlemagne Tower Collection* #904 (copy of Robert Beverly, the historian).

79.   Leigh, II, 324; Bryan, 62; Ross, 86. This is probably an inference from the dedication. Sowerby, II, 245, says: "The date of printing of this compilation is not known but was probably between 1683 and 1687, the dates of the governorship of Lord Howard of Effingham, to whom, in that office, the book is dedicated by *J. P.* [John Purvis]."

80.   Martin, 78–80.

81.   Henry R. McIlwaine (ed.), *Journals of the House of Burgesses of Virginia 1659/60 –1693*, xlvii–xlviii, 201–202.

82.   *Ibid.*, 203.

83.   *Ibid.*, 201–202.

84.   See note 74, *supra*. See also Martin, 80, 144, 149.

85.   Bryan, 62. On the "plant-cutting" see also Hening, *Statutes*, III, 542.

86.   The next official revisal (Hening's fifth, existing only in manuscript until he printed it in *Statutes*, III, 229–481) was that of October 23, 1705. Martin, 148–50; McIlwaine, *Journals of the House of Burgesses of Virginia 1702 . . . 1712*, xxviii–xxix. See note 58, *supra*.

87.   AN ABRIDGEMENT OF THE LAWS In Force and Use in *Her Majesty's Plantations*; (*Viz.*) Of VIRGINIA, JAMAICA, BARBADOES, MARYLAND, NEW-ENGLAND, NEW-YORK, CAROLINA, &c. Digested under proper Heads in the Method of Mr. *Wingate*, and Mr. *Washington's Abridgements*. LONDON, . . . 1704.

88.   Bryan and Ross do not mention the "Plantation Laws" as it was unofficial, incomplete, and inaccurate. Only 82 pages dealt with Virginia. It omitted acts from 1682 to 1704; included laws repealed during that period but omitted laws in force, and copied many of the errors of Purvis. Martin, 148. Incautious bibliographers sometimes list this book as if "Farewell" were the editor's name, as that word ("farewell") ends the preface.

89.   Or, indeed, in any of the colonies except for Cotton's abstract of the laws of New England [Ward's Body of Liberties?] published in 1641. Martin, 147.

90.   His name is written once on the title page. This might indicate ownership rather than authorship. Nothing else is in his handwriting. The work seems to be that of a competent lawyer, and Ludwell was not a lawyer. It may well have been compiled under his direction or supervision. Martin, 146.

91.   *An Abridgment of the Laws of Virginia, Compiled in 1694*, reprinted in 1903 in Richmond from the *Virginia Magazine of History and Biography*. The title page reads: "An alphabeticall Abridgment of the Laws of Virginia Under certaine heads containing ye Title of ye law, an abstract of ye matter, ye year Wn [when] made, ye year of ye Kings

Reign, who was then Governr and ye number of ye acts made each Assembly. God Save ye Queen." *Ibid.*, 3.

92. *Ibid.,* 4. This is a reference to Morrison's *Lawes* of 1662. See pages 127–28, *supra.*

93. There is uncertainty whether the work is by Robert Beverley, the historian, or his son William, or even by Peter Beverley, a prominent figure in public life. Martin, 194–97. In the Huntington Library copy (which I used) the words "by William Beverley" have been written in ink on the title page. However, a similar inscription in the 1728 edition in the Library of Congress is in Jefferson's handwriting, and this adds authority to the attribution. Sowerby, II, 164 (#1870). It should be noted, however, that in Robert Beverley's copy of Purvis he added in manuscript "an index and numerous legal forms." *Charlemagne Tower Collection,* 254.

94. *An Abridgement of the Publick Laws of Virginia, In Force and Use, June 10, 1720.* London, 1722. An edition practically identical was issued in 1728. See note 93, *supra.*

95. The "larger Volume" here anticipated is doubtless Baskett's edition of 1727. Martin, 198–99. See note 97, *infra.*

96. Hening, *Statutes,* III, 9. See note 7, *supra.* This shows that Hening must have been unfamiliar with the volumes of Dale, Morrison, the "Plantation Laws," and Baskett. Martin, 282. See notes 57, 70, 88, *supra,* and note 97, *infra.*

97. The second volume was never published. Both editions (the second bearing the signature of Joseph Hopkinson) were consulted in the Library Company of Philadelphia. See Martin, 201, and *Charlemagne Tower Collection* #905. Baskett in 1716 had printed the "Vinegar" Bible, which derives its name from the misprint in the headline of Luke, chapter 20, referring to the "parable of the vinegar" instead of the "parable of the vineyard." On account of its many errors this edition is often called the "Basketfull of Errors." Josiah H. Penniman, *A Book About the English Bible,* 400; Newton, *The Greatest Book in the World,* 25.

98. Since Morrison's "printed laws" of 1662. See note 70, *supra.*

99. Martin, 198. Swem, "A Bibliography of Virginia Part III. The Acts and the Journals of the General Assembly of the Colony," [Bulletin of the Virginia State Library, Vol. XII, Nos. 1 and 2 (January, April, 1919) 36 (#22502)], argues rather convincingly, that if Hening had known Baskett he would have copied the full text of the acts of the May, 1702, session rather than merely printing the titles.

100. Martin, 199–202.

101. Huntington Library copy. See also Sowerby #1833. Listed in Jefferson's letter to Wythe. See notes 1, 4, and 9, *supra.*

102. "This is not a revisal, but a collection as the title says." It is the first collection of Virginia laws published in Virginia. Swem, "A Bibliography of Virginia, Part III," 39 (#33517). It was the first private annotated codification of Virginia laws under legislative sanction. Martin, 279, 281. Ross, 88, considers it a private enterprise. Jefferson called it a revisal. See notes 9 and 58, *supra.*

103. Webb (1682–1758) was author of a well-known manual *The Office and Authority of a Justice of Peace,* also printed by William Parks, at Williamsburg in 1736 [Sowerby #1970], in which he refers constantly to the 1733 compilation of laws.

104. Some of the presswork may have been done in Annapolis, where Parks had been printing. The type, similar to Caslon, may have been made in Holland. Martin, 279–81.

105. On Parks, see Lawrence C. Wroth, *The Colonial Printer,* 41–45, 68, 271, 273; and Wroth, *William Parks Printer and Journalist of England and Colonial America,* 11, 26, 49–50.

106. See page 123, *supra.*

107. As in Jefferson's copy. Sowerby #1833.

108. An Exact ABRIDGMENT Of all the Public Acts of Assembly, of *VIRGINIA,* In Force and Use. By John Mercer, Gent. Williamsburg: Printed by William Parks. M,DCC,XXXVII.

109. John Mercer (1704–68) was an Irish immigrant. Mercer's *Abridgment* was printed by Parks, but very poorly. The second edition of 1759 was printed in Glasgow. I used the Huntington Library copies, as well as Jefferson's copies in the Library of Congress. Sowerby #1871 and #1872. For another copy of the edition of 1737, see *Charlemagne Tower Collection* #906. *A Continuation of the Abridgment Of all the Public Acts of Assembly of Virginia In Force and Use* was published by Mercer in 1739, also printed by Parks. Martin, 286–87.

110. Martin, 288.

111. Kimball, *Road to Glory,* 86, says that the characteristics of this specimen of Jefferson's handwriting show that it belongs in the year 1764. However, an annotation on the interleaf opposite page 19 cites a statute of 1766, and one opposite page 25 cites one of 1765. Similar references appear opposite pages 44, 59, 71, 98, 101, 119, 137, 140, 147, 161, 175, 185, and on 251. There are no acts cited later than 1766. The ornate formal hand used in items 444–554 of the Legal Commonplace Book and in items 619–1076 of the Equity Commonplace Book appears opposite pages 43, 82, 91, 161, and 198 of Mercer's *Abridgment.* The signature of a former owner, John Robinson, dated 1759, appears at the front of the book.

112. *The Acts of Assembly, Now in Force, in the Colony of Virginia. . . . Publish'd pursuant to an Order of the General Assembly.* From Huntington Library copy, with inscription by Edmund Pendleton: "This Book does not belong to the County but is the property of Edmd. Pendleton." George Wythe is named in the list of subscribers. The acts of the session of February 27, 1752, are bound with the volume. See also Sowerby #1839.

113. Printed in Hening, *Statutes,* V, 408–558; VI, iii, 1–215. Listed in Jefferson's letter to Wythe; see note 9, *supra.*

114. Martin, 324–25. See note 58, *supra.* For the act of assembly authorizing the revisal, see Hening, *Statutes,* V, 321–24. Benjamin Waller was a member of the committee.

115. *The Acts of Assembly, Now in Force, in the Colony of Virginia. . . . Published by Order of the General Assembly. Charlemagne Tower Collection* #921; Sowerby #1840. Listed in Jefferson's letter to Wythe; see note 9, *supra.* This volume embodied the revisal of March 31, 1768. It was the last printed collection of laws which appeared during the colonial era. Hening considered it a compilation rather than a revisal. It corrected errors in the 1752 edition and omitted the repealed acts. He had in his possession the very copy of the 1752 edition from which that of 1769 was printed. Martin, 329; Hening, *Statutes,* V, v.

116. As distinguished from the "Chancellor's revisal" of 1783 and the revised code contained in the editions of 1794, 1803, and 1814. Hening, *Statutes,* VI, iii; Martin, 330. See pages 137, 238 n. 34, and 240 n. 56, *infra.*

117. Martin, 325; Hening, *Statutes,* V, 432, 567–68.

118. *Acts of Assembly, Now in Force, in Virginia. Occasioned by the Repeal of Sundry Acts made in the Twenty Second Year of his Majesty's Reign, and in the Year of our Lord 1748.* Probably published in 1753, though no date is shown on the volume. [On November 27, 1753, the House of Burgesses awarded Hunter 60£ for his work. McIlwaine, *Journals of the House of Burgesses of Virginia 1752-1755, 1756-1758,* 138.] The Huntington Library copy, which I used, formerly belonged to Benjamin Waller and St. George Tucker,

according to a note by R. A. Brock in 1868. The acts of the session of February 25, 1752, are bound with the volume. A note by one of the former owners reads: "April 8. 1752. Govr. Dinwiddie inform'd the General Assembly that he had just recieved his Majestys order in Council *repealing Ten Acts* passed at the Session of the General Assembly in October 1748. See Journals April 8, 1752. See also the Revisal of 1748. which contains the acts thus repealed. . . . The Laws thus *repeal'd* are omitted in the acts of the Session of 1748. in the Edition of 1769."

CHAPTER VII

1. See page xii, *supra.*

2. On October 12, 1776, Jefferson and two others were appointed as a committee to bring in a bill for that purpose, which was reported to the House of Delegates on October 15 and passed on October 17. The act in its final form became law when the Senate passed it on October 26, 1776. 1 P. 562–63; Hening, *Statutes,* IX, 175–77.

3. 2 P. 314.

4. 2 P. 325–28. Also printed in Mays, *Edmund Pendleton,* II, 373–76.

5. The first period ended with the reign of Henry VIII; the second at the [English?] Revolution; the third "to the present Day." The fourth part included the rest of the Virginia laws, together with the criminal law and land law. This was assigned to Mason, "but if he finds it too much, the other Gentlemen will take off his Hands any Part he pleases." The fifth part, assigned to Lee, dealt with "Regulation of Property in Slaves, and their Condition, and also the Examination of the Laws of the other Colonies." Jefferson was "to undertake the first Part, with the Law of Descents;" Pendleton the second, and Wythe the third. 2 P. 328. See also 2 P. 316.

6. 2 P. 325.

7. Cf. the modern notion that criminal penalties for narcotics addiction constitute cruel and unusual punishment. *Robinson* v. *California,* 370 U.S. 660, 666 (1962).

8. Jefferson held a theoretical view (based upon a passage from Beccaria which he copied in his Legal Commonplace Book) that in a republic the laws should be merciful, but their execution inexorable; the pardoning power was therefore superfluous. Dumbauld, *Constitution,* 283. See also I P. 359, 505.

9. "Mr. Pendleton wished to preserve the right of primogeniture, but seeing at once that that could not prevail, he proposed we should adopt the Hebrew principle and give a double portion to the elder son. I observed that if the eldest son could eat twice as much, or do double work, it might be a natural evidence of his right to a double portion; but being on a par in his powers & wants, with his brothers and sisters, he should be on a par also in the partition of the patrimony, and such was the decision of the other members." Autobiography, 1 F. 69.

10. This may have been directed at the cumbersome and circuitous action of ejectment. The land law was made the subject of earlier separate treatment and was not included in the report of the revisers. 2 P. 133–67, 328.

11. Autobiography, 1 F. 67–68. In this account Jefferson says: "The common law and statutes to the 4. James I. (when our separate legislature was established) were assigned to me; the British statutes from that period to the present day to Mr. Wythe, and the Virginia laws to Mr. Pendleton." Under Pendleton's proposal "we should have retained the same chaos of law-lore from which we wished to be emancipated, added to the evils of the uncertainty which a new text and new phrases would have generated." To John Tyler, June 17, 1812, 13 M. 167.

12. For Jefferson's criticism of legalistic verbiage, see also Autobiography, 1 F. 70; to George Wythe November 1, 1778, 2 P. 230 [transmitting draft of bill for proportioning crime and punishment]; to J. C. Cabell, September 9, 1817, 17 M. 417–18.

13. "In the execution of my part, I thought it material not to vary the diction of the antient statutes by modernizing it, nor to give rise to new questions by new expressions. The text of these statutes had been so fully explained and defined by numerous adjudications, as scarcely ever now to produce a question in our courts." Autobiography, 1 F. 69–70.

14. To Skelton Jones, July 28, 1809, 12 M. 298–300. The late David J. Mays, biographer of Pendleton, has pointed out that Pendleton was not present when the revisers conferred in Williamsburg in February, 1779. 2 P. 317. Jefferson's Account Book shows that he was in Williamsburg February 18–27, 1779. It is tempting to suppose that the revisers were at work on the twenty-third when he "pd for paper at Purdie's 8/." As to the number of bills prepared by the revisers, see note 23, *infra*. As to the scope of Jefferson's assignment, see notes 5 and 11, *supra*. His share doubtless increased when other members failed to perform the tasks originally assigned to them. See 2 P. 316.

15. This illustrates Jefferson's belief in the Whig doctrine of a Utopian Saxon free government before imposition of the "Norman yoke" of feudalism by William the Conqueror. See pages 154, 245 n. 24, 251 n. 117, and 252 n. 129, *infra*. In like vein he urged that students should learn Anglo-Saxon, because they "will imbibe with the language their free principles of government." Chinard, *Commonplace Book of Jefferson*, 56–62, 188–93; Blackstone, *Commentaries*, II, 48–52. See also H. Trevor Colbourn, *The Lamp of Experience*, 162, 180–84. Lord Kames shared this belief in Saxon virtues, as did Bishop William Stubbs, Henry Adams, and others in the nineteenth century. *Ibid.*, 29, 196. As a corollary Jefferson wished land tenure to be allodial. Edmund Pendleton, a shrewd and successful practitioner of law and politics alike, feared Jefferson's proposal was visionary. Jefferson to Pendleton, August 13, 1776, 1 P. 491–93; Pendleton to Jefferson, August 26, 1776, 1 P. 507. See pages 19–20, *infra*.

16. Lengthy extracts from Montesquieu fill items 775 to 802 of the Legal Commonplace Book; extracts from Beccaria, items 806–31; and extracts from William Eden, *Principles of Penal Law*, items 838–45. Eden's book echoed the sentiments of Montesquieu and Beccaria. Chinard, *Commonplace Book of Jefferson*, 45. These items were probably written between 1774 and 1776 (thus before the revisal). *Ibid.*, 14. Beccaria and Montesquieu are cited in Jefferson's notes to the bill.

17. Malone, *Virginian*, 269–70. The document is LC 42052-58. Another ornate exemplar of the bill is in Massachusetts Historical Society, Coolidge Collection. For a full printed version see 2 P. 492–507. It is Bill No. 64 in the *Report of the Revisors*, 46–47, where Jefferson's notes and comments are omitted.

18. Malone, *Virginian*, 273. He directed that he be described on his tombstone as "Author of the Declaration of American Independence of the Statute of Virginia for Religious Freedom, and Father of the University of Virginia." 12 F. 483.

19. 2 P. 310. See also *ibid.*, 505. It was also ironical that the bill on crime and punishment proved to be the stumbling block which frustrated Madison's efforts to complete the enactment of the revisal. 2 P. 322, 505–506. The bill was defeated in the House by a single vote. "The rage against Horse stealers had a great influence on the fate of the Bill." Madison to Jefferson, February 15, 1787, 11 P. 152.

20. Recognition of the fact that capital punishment irrevocably and irreversibly "exterminates" the culprit, together with the fact that "people whose innocence is later convincingly established" are often convicted by fallible fact-finders, constitutes the strongest argument advanced by modern opponents of the death penalty. *Furman* v. *Georgia*, 408 U.S. 238, 366 (1972).

21.   2 P. 492–93. See also *ibid.*, 506. Jefferson's comments on his bill did not mention the analogy of chapter 20 of Magna Carta (1215) forbidding excessive amercements (pecuniary penalties, discretionary in amount, exacted by the king): "*Liber homo non amercietur pro parvo delicto, nisi secundum modum delicti; et pro magno delicto amercietur secundum magnitudinem delicti, salvo contenemento suo*" ("A free man shall not be amerced for a trivial offense, except in accordance with the degree of the offense; and for a serious offense he shall be amerced according to its gravity, saving his livelihood"). McKechnie, *Magna Carta*, 284–99; J. C. Holt, *Magna Carta*, 322–23; Thompson, *Magna Carta*, 44–46, 63, 185, 237, 275.

22.   *Report of the Revisors*, 3; Hening, *Statutes*, IX, 175–76; 2 P. 301–302.

23.   Originally there were 128 bills. One "for regulating the inspection of tobacco" was deleted before Jefferson numbered them from 1 to 127. Then No. 13 "for establishing a loan office" was deleted, and those remaining renumbered from 13 to 126. 2 P. 318, 334. The text of No. 15, concerning enlistment of troops (2 P. 378–81) was omitted in *Report of the Revisors*, 12, as temporary wartime legislation, already enacted and expired. For the catalogue of titles, see *Report of the Revisors*, 405; 2 P. 329–35.

24.   Nos. 8, 9, 10, 15, 24, 55, 65, 93, 98, and 119. Some others (such as 5, 6, 59, 78, and 96) were acted on separately after 1779. 2 P. 321. Several (for example, nos. 5, 6, and 92) were introduced but failed of passage. 2 P. 311. Nor should the reforms be forgotten which Jefferson himself had introduced separately, before the revision of the laws as a whole was undertaken. 1 P. 306. His bill on entail was introduced on October 14, 1776, passed the House on October 23, and the Senate on November 1. 1 P. 560–62. His bills for establishing courts of justice also became law. 1 P. 605–49. See also page 213 n. 73.

25.   No. 55, 2 P. 476–79. Jefferson considered this a notable piece of legislation. See note 64, *infra*.

26.   In his *Notes*, 249–50, Jefferson observed that the revisal had been reported "but probably will not be taken up till a restoration of peace shall leave to the legislature leisure to go through such a work." See also Martin, 391.

27.   *Report of the Revisors*, 6.

28.   2 P. 309.

29.   Printed by Dixon and Holt, Richmond, 1784. Cited hereinabove and hereafter as "*Report of the Revisors*." I used the copy in the Department of Justice Library, Washington, D.C.

30.   2 P. 305–665.

31.   2 P. 308–13.

32.   2 P. 309.

33.   Resolution of June 16, 1783. Martin, 389–90; 2 P. 321, citing *Journals of the House of Delegates*, May 1783 (1828 reprint) 53.

34.   A COLLECTION OF ALL SUCH PUBLIC ACTS OF THE GENERAL ASSEMBLY, AND ORDINANCES OF THE CONVENTIONS OF *VIRGINIA*, Passed since the year 1768, as are now in force; with a TABLE OF THE PRINCIPAL MATTERS. *Published under inspection of the* JUDGES *of the* HIGH COURT *of* CHANCERY, *by a resolution of* GENERAL ASSEMBLY, the 16th day of June 1783. RICHMOND: *Printed by* THOMAS NICHOLSON *and* WILLIAM PRENTIS. M,DCC,LXXXV. Sowerby #1861.

35.   On November 24, 1783, the chancellors reported that they had not yet completed their work. Hening, *Statutes*, XI, 547–48. Ross, 90–91, seems to confuse Jefferson's revisal and the chancellors' revisal. See Martin, 390.

36. See Hening, *Statutes*, XII, 84–86, 120–98, 330–58.

37. *Journal of the House of Delegates*, October 17, 1785–January 21, 1786, 10–11. The list of printed bills was read twice and committed to a committee of the whole. Boyd states that there were 118 bills introduced (Nos. 7, 8, 9, 15, 16, 18, 30, and 36 having been eliminated as expired, repealed, or of temporary nature). 2 P. 322.

38. Boyd's annotations show that the bills passed at the 1785 session were Nos. 2, 3, 12, 14, 17, 20–22, 24, 25, 27–29, 32, 35, 37, 39–42, 45, 46, 48, 49, 51–54, 56–58, 60–63. See Hening, *Statutes*, XII, 84–198.

39. Hening, *Statutes,* XII, 138–40; Bill No. 20, 2 P. 391–93 (passed by the House on November 22, 1785, and by the Senate on November 30, 1785).

40. Hening, *Statutes,* XII, 84–86; Bill No. 82, 2 P. 545–53; 2 F. 438–41. For Madison's account of the legislative maneuvers leading to passage of this law which "in this country extinguished for ever the ambitious hope of making laws for the human mind," see Madison to Jefferson January 22, 1786, 9 P. 195–96.

41. Nos. 66, 69, 71–76, 84, 87, 97, 103–106, 108–15. (Nos. 100, 121, and 122 were passed in 1789.) 2 P. 322; Hening, *Statutes,* XII, 330–58.

42. Madison to Jefferson, January 22, 1786, 9 P. 195; Madison to George Washington, November 11, 1785, Hunt, *Writings of Madison,* II, 192: "The present temper promises an adoption of it in substance. The greatest danger arises from its length compared with the patience of the members."

43. Madison to Jefferson, January 22, 1786, 9 P. 195.

44. *Ibid.*; Madison to Washington, December 9, 1785, Hunt, *Writings of Madison,* II, 199. See note 40, *supra.*

45. *Journal of the House of Delegates*, October 16, 1786–January 11, 1787 (1828 reprint), 16–17.

46. Madison to Pendleton, January 9, 1787, Hunt, *Writings of Madison,* II, 304: "The advance of the Session, the coldness of a great many, and the dislike of some to the subject, required that it should be pressed more gently than could be reconciled with a prosecution of the work to the end."

47. Madison to Jefferson, December 4, 1786, 10 P. 575.

48. Madison to Jefferson, February 15, 1787, 11 P. 152.

49. Observations for Démeunier, finished June 22, 1786, 10 P. 47–48. The same idea is expressed in a note to the bill for proportioning crimes and punishments itself. 2 P. 500. Moreover, an act "to encourage the apprehending of horse stealers" by offering a reward to unimplicated captors was passed as part of Jefferson's revisal. Hening, *Statutes,* XII, 331; Bill No. 69, 2 P. 515–16. Jefferson as secretary of state questioned the desirability of an extradition treaty with a nation where the punishment would be "immensely disproportionate to the crime;" for example, in England and probably in Canada, "to steal a horse is death, the first offence." March 22, 1792, 8 M. 332.

50. Madison to Jefferson, February 15, 1787, 11 P. 153. Patrick Henry was to be a member at the next session. Only the twenty-three acts passed at the 1786 session were suspended until July 1, 1787, those passed at the preceding session left "to commence as then determined." Madison to Pendleton, January 9, 1787, Hunt, *Writings of Madison,* II, 304–305. For the act of January 2, 1787, for completing the revision of the laws, see Hening, *Statutes*, XII, 409–11. See also 2 P. 323.

51. 2 P. 323–24; Martin, 393; Robinson, v. Likewise nothing came of an act of November 18, 1789, concerning a new edition of the laws. Hening, *Statutes*, XIII, 8–9.

52. On November 7, 1786, Madison was chosen as a Virginia delegate to Congress

and was already in New York serving in that capacity when he wrote to Jefferson that the bill on crime and punishment had been defeated. See note 48, *supra*. In 1787 the Constitutional Convention met in Philadelphia.

53. By the Act of December 23, 1790. Hening, *Statutes,* XIII, 130.

54. By the Act of December 28, 1792, "providing for the republication of the Laws of this Commonwealth." Hening, *Statutes*, XIII, 531. See Martin, 395–96.

55. *A Collection of all such Acts of the General Assembly of Virginia, of a Public and Permanent Nature, as are now in Force, with a Table of the Principal Matters. . . . Richmond: Printed by Augustine Davis, Printer for the Commonwealth, 1794.* Sowerby #1862.

56. Although this was in fact merely a compilation of existing laws [Ross, 91], the revisers were authorized to prepare bills, and Martin, 396, considers it as a "revisal." See note 58, chapter 6, *supra*. It was supplemented by volumes issued by Samuel Pleasants, Jr., and Henry Pace in 1803, and by Pleasants in 1808, 1812, and 1814. In 1819 *The Revised Code of the Laws of Virginia*, under authority of an act of 1817 appointing revisers, was published by Benjamin Watkins Leigh, who considers his edition as the ninth revisal of the laws of Virginia. Leigh, II, 325. Leigh's code made no radical revisions. Ross, 93. Hening's first volume appeared in 1809 and the thirteenth in 1823.

57. Martin, 396.

58. *Notes*, 250–51, 265–68, 275. The *Notes* were written in 1781 and 1782. Jefferson began gathering material for them late in 1780. 4 P. 166–68. Thus they were his next major project of scholarly productivity after the revisal.

59. It should be remembered that the *Notes* were written in response to inquiries from a French diplomat. Another Frenchman was given in 1786 a brief and lucid description of the revisal: "Virginia thought it might be necessary to examine the whole code of law, to reform such parts of it as had been calculated to produce a devotion to monarchy, and to reduce into smaller volume such useful parts as had become too diffuse. A Committee was appointed to do this work; they did it; and the assembly began in Octob. 1785. the examination of it, in order to change such parts of the report as might not meet their approbation and to establish what they should approve. We may expect to hear the result of their deliberations about the last of February next." Answers to Démeunier's First Queries, January 24, 1786, 10 P. 12. [It was June 23, 1786, when Jefferson received Madison's letter of January 22, 1786, reporting the progress of the revisal. 9 P. 202. See notes 40 and 42, *supra*.]

60. For a Pennsylvania lawyer today it is hard to see why treating slaves as personal rather than real property was a noteworthy reform. Logically, it might be thought desirable that an adequate labor force should pass with the land, in order that it might be profitably worked. But perhaps the point is that until abolition of primogeniture and entail, to increase the amount of personalty in a decedent's estate would encourage the possibility of equal distribution among the "next of kin" or legatees, and thereby perhaps diminish the amount of property automatically passing to the common law "heir" (defined by Blackstone as "he upon whom the law casts the estate [in land] immediately upon the death of the ancestor." *Commentaries*, II, 201). An act of 1748 (Hening, *Statutes*, V, 432–43) making slaves personalty was repealed by the Order in Council of October 31, 1751. Virginians may have felt this interference by the English government as a grievance. In *Blackwell* v. *Wilkinson*, Jeff., 73 [Oct. 1768] it was held that slaves could not be entailed without being annexed to lands.

61. This may refer to No. 31, A Bill for Levying County Rates, 2 P. 418–19, which does not appear to be a particularly notable example of taxation according to "ability to pay."

62. "No such provision is comprized in the Road bill reported and printed. If it be any

where in existence I wish you could put me on the means of getting a sight of it. I conceive such a reform to be essential and that the Legislature would adopt it, if presented in a well digested form." Madison to Jefferson, June 19, 1786, 9 P. 661. No. 46, A bill concerning Public Roads, does provide that where a *bridge* or causeway is necessary, "and the surveyor with his assistants cannot make or maintain the same, the court of the county are impowered and required to contract for the building and repairing such bridge or causeway." 2 P. 451. With respect to roads, the bill provides that they are to be "cleared and kept in good repair" by the labor of male inhabitants over sixteen years of age (as an obligation of citizenship, like serving on a jury or in the militia). 2 P. 449–50.

63. It was hardly an innovation in 1779 to require just compensation to the owner for property taken for a public use. See Dumbauld, *Bill of Rights*, 53.

64. The natural right of expatriation was always emphasized by Jefferson. Dumbauld, *Declaration*, 51, 59. His *Summary View of the Rights of British America*, published in 1774, proclaimed the doctrine. See also to John Manners, June 12, 1817, 12 F. 66; and 1 P. 344, 558–59. He regarded it as a basic principle that "the rights of man do not depend on the geography of his birth." To Joseph C. Cabell, January 1, 1817. [Cabell], *Early History of the University of Virginia*, 70.

65. The principles established by this legislation have become a basic feature of American polity, recognized by the First Amendment to the United States Constitution and Supreme Court decisions explanatory thereof. See Dumbauld, *Bill of Rights*, 103–15.

66. *Notes*, 251. At this point Jefferson explains that this revolutionary proposal was not contained in the revisal as reported but was to be introduced as an amendment. He then devotes a long excursus to the question whether "the blacks . . . are inferior to the whites in the endowments both of body and mind." *Ibid.*, 251–65.

67. *Ibid.*, 265. In connection with criminal law, Jefferson adds: "Pardon and privilege of clergy are proposed to be abolished; but if the verdict be against the defendant, the court in their discretion, may allow a new trial. No attainder to cause a corruption of blood, or forfeiture of dower. Slaves guilty of offences punishable in others by labour, to be transported to Africa, or elsewhere, as the circumstances of the time admit, there to be continued in slavery. A rigorous regimen proposed for those condemnèd to labour." *Ibid.*, 268.

68. *Ibid.* A lengthy explanation of his proposed system of public education then follows. *Ibid.*, 268–75. "The general objects of this law are to provide an education adapted to the years, to the capacity, and the condition of every one, and directed to their freedom and happiness." *Ibid.*, 270. He emphasizes the political utility of education. It will render "the people the safe, as they are the ultimate, guardians of their own liberty. . . . The influence over government must be shared among all the people." *Ibid.*, 273, 274. To accomplish these ends the study of history and of foreign languages should be begun at an early age. *Ibid.*, 270–73.

69. *Ibid.*, 275. See also 2 P. 544–45.

70. He continued: "Had it been a digest of all our laws, it would not have been comprehensible or instructive but to a native. But it is still less so, as it digests only the British statutes and our own acts of assembly, which are but a supplementory part of our law. The great basis of it is anterior to the date of the Magna charta, which is the oldest statute extant. The only merit of this work is that it may remove from our shelves about twenty folio volumes of statutes, retaining all the parts of them which either their own merit or the established system of laws required." To G. K. van Hogendorp, October 13, 1785, 8 P. 632, replying to van Hogendorp's statement of September 8, 1785, 8 P. 503. See also 8 P. 324. On van Hogendorp, see Willem J. M. van Eysinga, *Sparsa Collecta,*

238-50; and 7 P. 52, 80-83, 207-209. Like the queries from Marbois which led to the *Notes*, van Hogendorp posed questions about America (8 P. 296-98) which Jefferson himself revised and used (2 P. 324-26) in order to obtain information on the economic conditions of the eastern states on his way to embark for Europe as an envoy to negotiate treaties of commerce. Dumbauld, *American Tourist*, 57-58. See also 10 P. 190, 297-300.

71. See notes 24 and 39, *supra*.

72. See notes 25 and 64, *supra*.

73. See notes 17, 20, 43, 48, and 67, *supra*.

74. See notes 68, *supra*, and 78-97, *infra*.

75. See notes 18, 40, and 44, *supra*.

76. Autobiography, 1 F. 77-78.

77. Two were enacted as part of the revisal, through Madison's efforts; one had been adopted while Jefferson was himself a member of the Assembly. See notes 24, 39, and 40, *supra*.

78. See note 18, *supra*.

79. Jefferson to Joseph Coolidge, Jr., April 12, 1825, 18 M. 337. Jefferson died on July 4, 1826.

80. To Joseph C. Cabell, January 14, 1818, 12 F. 87.

81. No. 79, 2 P. 526-34.

82. See note 68, *supra*. Boyd says: "The exalted declaration of purpose in the preamble remains one of the classic statements of the responsibility of the state in matters of education." 2 P. 534. That public education is a state responsibility was an innovation put forward in Plato's *Republic*. Werner Jaeger, *Paideia*, II, 210; III, 245, 253-54. For Jefferson's opinion of Plato's "whimsies, puerilities, and unintelligible jargon," see to John Adams, July 5, 1814, 11 F. 396.

83. 2 P. 527.

84. Honeywell, *Educational Work of Jefferson*, 10-11. Not until 1796 did Virginia enact a law providing for elementary public schools. 2 P. 535.

85. No. 80, 2 P. 535-43.

86. No. 81, 2 P. 544-45.

87. *Dartmouth College* v. *Woodward*, 4 Wheat. 517, 629-30, 650, 652 (1819). Timothy Farrar, *Report of the Case of the Trustees of Dartmouth College against William H. Woodward* [1819] contains the arguments of counsel and court opinions both in the state and United States Supreme Courts. Regarding the Massachusetts act of February 29, 1812, concerning Harvard College (which was repealed after protest by the college), see *ibid.*, 397-98.

88. *Bracken* v. *William & Mary College*, 3 Call (Va. 1790) 573, 579, 599.

89. Honeywell, *Educational Work of Jefferson*, 64, 71.

90. *Ibid.*, 233-43; Cabell, *Early History*, 413-27.

91. Honeywell, *Educational Work of Jefferson*, 65-66.

92. *Ibid.*, 71-76. It is said that Jefferson prepared a list of octogenarians in Albemarle County as evidence of its healthful climate. *Ibid.*, 73. For the report of the commissioners, see *ibid.*, 248-60; and Cabell, *Early History*, 432-47.

93. By the Act of February 14, 1816. Cabell, *Early History*, xxiv, 391-93.

94. *Ibid.*, xxiii.

95. On January 6, 1818, the visitors of Central College offered to transfer it if the university were established. *Ibid.*, 403. See also Honeywell, *Educational Work of Jefferson*, 45, 70-71.

96. *Ibid.*, 77-78. For the act, see Cabell, *Early History*, 447-50. On the circumstances of its passage, see Joseph C. Cabell to Jefferson, January 25, 1819, *ibid.*, 153.

97. To James Breckinridge, April 9, 1822, 15 M. 363; to J. W. Eppes, June 30, 1820, MHS. See note 79, *supra*. On Jefferson's architectural designs for the university, see Fiske Kimball, *Thomas Jefferson Architect*, 74-80. On recruiting professors, see Davis, *Correspondence of Jefferson and Gilmer*, 18, 81. On choice of law professor and textbooks, see notes 35 and 36, introduction, *supra*.

98. First in the list, however, was his promoting navigation of the Rivanna River; next was mentioned the Declaration of Independence. 9 F. 163. Malone, *Virginian,* 280, dates this memorandum (LC 39161) in September, 1800.

99. Clarence R. Keim, "Influence of Primogeniture and Entail in the Development of Virginia," *Abstracts of Theses*, University of Chicago, Humanistic Series, Vol. V (1928), 289-92, emphasizes that primogeniture applied only in the event of intestacy, whereas deeds of gift and wills were ordinarily in fee simple. Entails were exceptional; even in the Tidewater they were not as prevalent as commonly supposed. Land held for speculation had to be fee simple. Economic necessities, rather than legislation, brought about disintegration of large estates. See also Keim, "Primogeniture and Entail in Colonial Virginia," *Wm. & Mary Quarterly* (3d series), Vol. XXV, No. 4 (October, 1968), 545-86.

100. 9 F. 164. Continuing, Jefferson refers to his importation of olive plants from Marseilles, and of upland rice from Africa. "The greatest service which can be rendered any country is, to add an useful plant to its culture; especially a bread grain; next in value to bread is oil." *Ibid.*, 165.

101. For the purpose of justifying his request to the legislature to permit sale of his property by means of a lottery, to pay his debts, in view of the depressed market for real estate. "Thoughts on Lotteries," [February, 1826], 12 F. 435-50.

102. And omits reference to the bill for proportioning crimes and punishments, as well as to the expatriation act. 1 F. 444-47.

CHAPTER VIII

1. An excellent treatment of the Puritan proposals is found in Donald Veall, *The Popular Movement for Law Reform 1640-1660,* hereinafter cited as Veall, *Law Reform.* See also Holdsworth, *History*, VI, 412-29; Stuart E. Prall, *The Agitation for Law Reform during the Puritan Revolution 1640-1660;* G. B. Nourse, "Law Reform under the Commonwealth and Protectorate," *Law Quarterly Review,* Vol. LXXV, No. 300 (October, 1959), 512-29; Goldwin Smith, "The Reform of the Laws of England 1640-1660," *University of Toronto Quarterly,* Vol. X, No. 4 (July, 1941), 469-81; Frederick A. Inderwick, *The Interregnum,* 201-245; Edward Jenks, *The Constitutional Experiments of the Commonwealth,* 54, 82, 129; and R. Robinson, "Anticipations under the Commonwealth of Changes in the Law," in *Select Essays in Anglo-American Legal History*, I, 467-91.

2. Dumbauld, *Declaration*, 22. John Rushworth's *Historical Collections*, covering the period from 1618 to the execution of Charles I in 1649, was first published in London 1659-1701. The 1721-22 edition belonging to Jefferson is now in the Library of Congress. Sowerby #2723. When in 1786 Jefferson and John Adams visited Edgehill and Worcester, "where freemen had fought for their rights" against the royalist troops, Jefferson doubtless shared the sentiments concerning the civil wars put forth by Adams in a stirring exhortation to the populace. Dumbauld, *American Tourist*, 80.

3. For a good account of Puritan political thought, see A. S. P. Woodhouse, *Puritanism*

and Liberty; William Haller, *The Rise of Puritanism*; Joseph Frank, *The Levellers*; Margaret James and Maureen Weinstock (eds.), *England during the Interregnum.*

4. To Henry Lee, May 8, 1825, 12 F. 409. Algernon Sidney's *Discourses concerning Government* [described by Jefferson as "a rich treasure of republican principles," Sowerby #2330]; and James Burgh's *Political Disquisitions* [Sowerby #2720] were political treatises congenial to Jefferson's thinking. See Bernard Bailyn, *The Ideological Origins of the American Revolution*, 41, 132.

5. George Thomason, a London bookseller, tried to collect a copy of every item published, noting the date of acquisition, which was usually the date of publication. During the period 1640–61 he assembled some 22,255 pamphlets, now in the British Museum. Modern writers rely heavily on analysis of the Thomason Tracts (to which Fortescue's *Catalogue* is a useful guide) and of published collections such as the *Harleian Miscellany* and *Somers Tracts*. See Veall, *Law Reform*, xii, 73, 247; Haller, *The Rise of Puritanism*, 326–27. Other useful collections are William Haller, *Tracts on Liberty in the Puritan Revolution 1638-1647*; William Haller and Godfrey Davis (eds.), *The Leveller Tracts 1647-1653*; and Don M. Wolfe, *Leveller Manifestoes of the Puritan Revolution*. Jefferson's program of law reform in 1776 was undoubtedly formulated without use of these sources.

6. John W. Allen, *A History of Political Thought in the Sixteenth Century*, 214; Holdsworth, *History*, IV, 47–48; VI, 122–24; Cam, *Essays of F. W. Maitland*, 201. On the Elizabethan settlement see Maitland's account, *ibid.*, 152–246.

7. Woodhouse, *Puritanism and Liberty*, [14–19].

8. *Ibid.*, [36–37], [43–44].

9. *Ibid.*, [15, 19].

10. Joseph R. Tanner, *English Constitutional Conflicts of the Seventeenth Century, 1603-1689*, 121–22; Samuel R. Gardiner, *The Constitutional Documents of the Puritan Revolution*, 267–71; Samuel R. Gardiner, *History of the Great Civil War*, III, 11–12.

11. Charles H. Firth and Robert S. Rait, *Acts and Ordinances of the Interregnum, 1642-1660*, I, 582–607; William A. Shaw, *A History of the English Church during the Civil Wars and under the Commonwealth*, I, 336, 353, 356; Gardiner, *Great Civil War*, II, 51–52. On August 26, 1645, another ordinance was adopted for the more effectual putting in execution of the directory of worship. Firth and Rait, *Acts and Ordinances*, I, 755–57.

12. Firth and Rait, *Acts and Ordinances*, I, 749–54; Shaw, *History*, I, 196; Daniel Neal, *The History of the Puritans or Protestant Non-Conformists*, II, 199.

13. Shaw, *History*, I, 199; II, 2, 4, 12.

14. Firth and Rait, *Acts and Ordinances*, I, 852–55; Shaw, *History*, I, 297 (gives date as June 9); Neal, *History*, II, 198–200 (gives date as June 6). See also an earlier ordinance of March 14, 1646, on the same subject. Firth and Rait, *Acts and Ordinances*, I, 833–38.

15. Neal, *History*, II, 201. Later, "being resolved speedily and more effectually to settle the Presbyterial government," Parliament enacted another ordinance of January 29, 1648. Firth and Rait, *Acts and Ordinances*, I, 1062; Shaw, *History*, II, 16–17. This was followed by a comprehensive ordinance of August 29, 1648, prescribing the form of church government to be used in the churches of England. Firth and Rait, *Acts and Ordinances*, I, 1188–1215. It directed that elders were to be chosen forthwith. *Ibid.*, 1189. This was the last official action of Parliament on behalf of the establishment of Presbyterianism. Shaw, *History*, II, 18–19. Presbyterian dominance was undermined by the sentiment for toleration among the Independents and other sects in Cromwell's army. The Instrument of Government in 1653 proclaimed toleration; and the Restoration re-established Anglicanism with a measure of toleration for dissenters. *Ibid.*, 85, 117, 125.

16. Woodhouse, *Puritanism and Liberty* [16–17].

17. Allen, *History of Political Thought*, 220, 225–29.

18. Woodhouse, *Puritanism and Liberty*, [17–18].

19. *Ibid.*, [90]. "Freeborn John" Lilburne was one of the prominent Levellers. Gardiner, *Great Civil War*, III, 216, 526–29. See note 29, *infra*.

20. Gardiner, *Commonwealth and Protectorate*, I, 33.

21. *Ibid.*, I, 47. The Diggers were so named because in April, 1649, they assembled at St. George's Hill in Surrey, near Oatlands, and planted parsnips, carrots, and beans on the uncultivated land. They were soon dispersed. *Ibid.*, I, 47–49; James and Weinstock, *England during the Interregnum*, 211–13. They believed that they were entitled to common use of the land as a result of the popular victory over Charles I, the successor of the Norman oppressor William the Conqueror. Their leaders were William Everard and Gerard Winstanley. Woodhouse, *Puritanism and Liberty*, 379–86; Veall, *Law Reform*, 106.

22. The name was derived from their belief that the monarchies of Assyria, Persia, Greece, and Rome had fallen and that the monarchy of Christ was imminent. Louise F. Brown, *The Political Activities of the Baptists and Fifth Monarchy Men In England During the Interregnum*, 12–13.

23. Gardiner, *Commonwealth and Protectorate*, I, 32.

24. *Ibid.*, II, 265–66. Among the things demanded by Fifth Monarchy sermons and pamphlets was "the abolition of the existing laws of England as a remnant of the Norman yoke, and the substitution for them of the laws of God as laid down in the Scriptures." Brown, *Political Activities of Baptists and Fifth Monarchy Men,* 35. The seventh chapter of Daniel and the book of Revelation were a favorite source of texts. *Ibid.*, 22–23. See Daniel, 7:8, 18, 22, and 27.

25. Riots in London took place in 1657 and 1661 as a result of attempts by Fifth Monarchy men to establish the reign of Jesus. Brown, *Political Activities of Baptists and Fifth Monarchy Men*, 117; Robert S. Bosher, *The Making of the Restoration Settlement*, 205.

26. Daniel 7:18 declares that "the saints of the most High shall take the kingdom, and possess the kingdom for ever, even for ever and ever." See page 145, *supra*.

27. Woodhouse, *Puritanism and Liberty*, [43–45].

28. "The Levellers had the clearest programme of law reform and knew very much what they wanted." Veall, *Law Reform*, 234.

29. How the sufferings and pertinacity of cantankerous John Lilburne led to the establishment of the principle prohibiting self-incrimination now embodied in the Fifth Amendment to the United States Constitution has often been recounted. Dumbauld, *Bill of Rights*, 77–82; Zechariah Chafee, *The Blessings of Liberty*, 197–206; Leonard Levy, *Origins of the Fifth Amendment*, 196, 266–332; Pauline Gregg, *Free-born John*, 52–85. Other procedural innovations were won by his stubbornness as a defendant at his four famous trials. Veall, *Law Reform*, 162–66.

30. "The most active periods for law reform pamphlets were 1646–9, the time of Leveller ascendancy; 1653, the year of the Barebones Parliament; and 1659, after Cromwell's death." Veall, *Law Reform*, 74. See also *ibid.*, 74–79, 98–126, 234.

31. The Rump Parliament in 1649 set up a committee composed of members of the House of Commons, which made no real progress. In January, 1652, it established another committee, of nonmembers, under the chairmanship of Matthew Hale (who later became chief justice of the Court of King's Bench). *Ibid.*, 79.

32. Holdsworth, *History*, VI, 415. See note 37, *infra*. It is noteworthy also that Francis Bacon manifested a lifelong interest in law reform, desiring to restate common

and statute law so as to eliminate obsolete, repetitious, and unclear provisions, as well as to supply what was lacking and to mitigate the excessive severity of many criminal penalties. Francis Bacon, *Works*, XIII, 57–71. See also *ibid.*, VII, 302–303, 315–16, 325–87; VIII, 213–14, 339–40; IX, 77, 79, 336; XII, 41, 84–86; XIV, 242, 358–64. Pursuant to his urging, the Commons in 1620 chose seven lawyers (including Coke) "to draw all the statutes concerning one matter into one plain and perfect law; and to consider which were fit to be repealed, which in force, and which fit to be continued." Nothing came of this project or Bacon's many other proposals in like vein. *Ibid.*, XIV, 181.

33. Veall, *Law Reform*, 79–85. The historian John Rushworth was a member of the Hale commission. *Ibid.*, 81. See note 2, *supra*. Hale was "the greatest common lawyer who had arisen since Coke." Holdsworth, *History*, VI, 594.

34. The "Several Draughts of Acts heretofore prepared by Persons appointed to consider of the Inconvenience, Delay, Charge, and Irregularity in the Proceedings of the Law. Printed by the Order of Parliament of the 12th of July 1653, for the Members of the House" are available in Sir Walter Scott (ed.), *A Collection of Scarce and Valuable Tracts* [commonly called Somers Tracts], VI, 177–245. The bills are summarized in Holdsworth, *History*, VI, 415–21.

35. Veall, *Law Reform*, 86–88.

36. Arthur E. Sutherland, *Constitutionalism in America*, 78–87.

37. For Cromwell's speech of September 4, 1654, at the opening of the first Parliament under the Protectorate, see Wilbur C. Abbott (ed.), *The Writings and Speeches of Oliver Cromwell*, III, 439. At the opening of Parliament on September 17, 1656, he thought it "abominable . . . to hang a man . . . for a trifle and pardon murder." *Ibid.*, IV, 274. On April 21, 1657, he expressed disappointment at the slow progress made, due to technicalities: "We were more than three months and could not get over the word 'incumbrances' and then we thought there was little hope of regulating the Law. . . . But surely the laws need to be regulated. . . . I confess, I do not know how. . . . I have heard talk of 'demurrers' and such like things as I scarce know, . . . but I say certainly, that the people are greatly suffering." *Ibid.*, IV, 493.

38. Veall, *Law Reform*, 92.

39. *Ibid.*, 92; Holdsworth, *History*, VI, 421–22. It was a quasi-official project. Nancy M. Arnson, *William Sheppard (1595–1674): Law Reformer*, 49–52. For analysis of the book (of which sixteen copies are known to exist [*ibid.*, 185]), see *ibid.*, 128–60. For biographical data on the author, see *ibid.*, 25–60. Sheppard's preface to the reader is dated October 1, 1656. The title page of the volume shows publication in 1657. Admonishing his brethren at the bar not to oppose desirable reforms, he has "but this word to say, that . . . to take away the weeds, will not hurt the wheat." He reminds Parliament that "much speech hath been of Reformation, little done."

40. *Touch-stone of Common Assurances.*

41. An interesting resemblance may be noted to the unfilled commonplace books of seventeenth century law students. See note 81, chapter 1, *supra*.

42. *Englands Balme*, 203 [British Museum copy, shelf-mark 517a 13]. See also *ibid.*, 201: "Whether to make any change, and what change to make herein." See also *ibid.*, 209, 210, 214.

43. Thus in response to the complaint that idle persons, rogues, and vagabonds are not punished, the remedy proposed is "that the Laws already made as to this, may be put in execution." *Englands Balme*, 164. See also, *ibid.*, 167.

44. *Ibid.*, 138.

45. *Ibid.*, 139.

46. *Ibid.*, 78.

47. *Ibid.*, 49. Another remedy is that if the judges dislike the verdict they may certify the matter to judges of appeal who shall hear the witnesses and may fine the jurors and order damages to the party aggrieved. *Ibid.*, 50–51.

48. *Ibid.*, 30. So since perjury is common, it should be more easily punishable. *Ibid.*, 150. See also *ibid.*, 51–53. However, as a remedy for the evil that solemn oaths are so common that men become senseless of their sanctity, it is proposed that an engagement in writing be equally effective. *Ibid.*, 210–11. The United States internal revenue laws in 1949 adopted this suggestion, and eliminated the requirement of verifying tax returns by oath, substituting instead a written declaration subject to the penalties of perjury for a false return. Act of August 27, 1949, 63 Stat. 667.

49. *Englands Balme*, 35.

50. *Ibid.*, 20. See also *ibid.*, 100.

51. *Ibid.*, 23. Sheppard also proposed "to give reward to them that are industrious in Prosecution of Malefactors." *Ibid.*, 23.

52. *Ibid.*, 45. Moreover, to monitor the action of the judges Sheppard recommended that "some honest godly man, though no Lawyer, have an allowance to sit with them when he will, to see and report the manner and justice of their proceedings, to the Lord Protector." *Ibid.*, 45–46. The demand for good judges is an established tradition. Bracton said: "*Sedem quidem judicandi, quae est quasi thronus dei, non praesumat quis ascendere insipiensis et indoctus*" ("Let no one, unwise and unlearned, presume to ascend the seat of judgment, which is like unto the throne of God"). Samuel E. Thorne (trans.), *Bracton On the Laws and Customs of England*, II, 21. See also *ibid.*, II, 307. Magna Carta, cap. 45, reads: "*Nos non faciemus justiciarios . . . nisi de talibus qui sciant legem regni et eam bene velint observare*" ("We will not make justices . . . except of those who know the law of the land and mean to observe it well"). Holt, *Magna Carta,* 328–29.

53. *Englands Balme*, 50.

54. *Ibid.*, 37.

55. *Ibid.*, 41.

56. *Ibid.*, 4.

57. *Ibid.*, 5. He proposed to bring "all the Laws about one thing into one Law, and to make that Law as short and cleer as may be; and to have that which is in Latine and French, Englished." *Ibid.*, 18–19. Sheppard himself undertook to make such an alphabetical digest: AN EPITOME OF ALL THE Common & Statute LAWS OF THIS NATION, *Now in force . . .* LONDON, . . . 1656 [British Museum copy, shelf-mark 507g 7].

58. *Englands Balme*, 7–8. See also *ibid.*, 129.

59. *Ibid.*, 14. See also *ibid.*, 191, 195–96. On the other hand, some offenses are punished too leniently, as corruption in judges and extortion on the part of public officers. Burning in the hand for murder was another instance of too little punishment for a serious offense. *Ibid.*, 17. That was the penalty where benefit of clergy was allowed. A series of statutes, beginning in 1497, took away benefit of clergy for various types of wilful murder. Plucknett, *Concise History,* 395–96. See note 60, *infra.*

60. *Englands Balme*, 16. In general, benefit of clergy was accorded to anyone who could read (this requirement was abolished in 1707 by Anne, c. 9). The "neck verse" often used in the reading test (Ps. 51:1) could be memorized by a defendant beforehand. After 1490 (by 4 Hen. 7, c. 13) one not a genuine cleric who claimed the privilege was branded on the left thumb so as not to be able to claim it a second time. After 1576 (by 18 Eliz., c. 7) in addition to branding, imprisonment up to one year could be imposed at the discretion of the court. Later laws added other punishments, and took away benefit of clergy in

many cases. It was abolished in 1827 by 7 & 8 Geo. 4, c. 28. It was a clumsy and complicated means of mitigating the harshness of the criminal law and establishing a gradation of punishments. Plucknett, *Concise History*, 390–91. See also Tanner, *Tudor Constitutional Documents*, 14–15; Holdsworth, *History*, III, 294–302; Blackstone, *Commentaries*, IV, 360–64; Veall, *Law Reform*, 4–5. On *peine forte et dure* see *ibid.*, 27–28. For a description of the customary mode of punishment for treason, see *ibid.*, 6; *State Trials*, II, 184, 884; Coke, third *Institute,* 210. See also page 13, *supra.*

61. *Englands Balme*, 19.

62. *Ibid.*, 135. Sheppard complains "that there is no Law against lascivious gestures, . . . whorish attire, . . . bare shoulders, powdering . . . the Face, curling and shearing of the Hair; excess of Apparel in Servants and mean people." *Ibid.*, 162.

63. Thus consolidation of law and equity (*ibid.*, 64–65) is a reform which was not adopted in United States courts until the Federal Rules of Civil Procedure took effect on September 1, 1938. (It had been favored in the eighteenth century by two eminent Scottish jurists, Lord Kames and Lord Mansfield, but disapproved by Lord Hardwicke and most practitioners. Holdsworth, *History*, XII, 330, 583–84, 600). That proceedings should begin by summons rather than by arrest or capias (*Englands Balme*, 68–94) is a similar simple but long-delayed reform.

64. His proposal that counsel in capital cases should be permitted (*ibid.*, 80) bore fruit when in 1695 counsel was allowed in England to persons charged with treason, and in 1837 to persons charged with felony. Holdsworth, *History*, IX, 235. For later developments, see William M. Beaney, *The Right to Counsel in American Courts.*

65. *Englands Balme*, 23.

66. *Ibid.*, 197. The remedy proposed was to require reasons to be stated. *Ibid.*, 198.

67. *Ibid.*, 84.

68. *Ibid.*, 20.

69. *Ibid.*, 112–13.

70. *Ibid.*, 152. Confirmation of defective marriages, and registration of births and deaths, were also proposed. *Ibid.*, 155, 156.

71. *Ibid.*, 215. Abolition of entails was one of the first of Jefferson's reforms to be enacted. See page xii, *supra.*

72. The reforms most insistently called for were a registration system of titles to land, abolition of copyhold tenure, abolition of primogeniture, simplification and codification of the law, limitation of use of the death penalty, and local administration of justice. Distrust of the legal profession was strongly evinced in these proposals. Veall, *Law Reform*, 95.

73. *Ibid.*, 94–96.

74. Holdsworth, *History*, VI, 416–21. See note 72, *supra.*

75. Holdsworth, *History*, VI, 422. See also Veall, *Law Reform*, 235–36.

76. Holdsworth, *History*, VI, 422–23. See also Veall, *Law Reform*, 228–35.

77. Holdsworth, *History*, VI, 427.

78. Legislation enacted without the royal assent is collected in Firth and Rait, *Acts and Ordinances.* It is summarized in Holdsworth, *History,* VI, 423–28. See also *ibid.*, I, 429–34.

79. The interregnum technically began with the execution of Charles I on January 30, 1649, and ended with the restoration of Charles II by the Convention Parliament, which convened on April 25, 1660. On May 1, 1660, it declared that "according to the ancient and fundamental laws of this kingdom, the government is and ought to be by king, lords, and commons." The king arrived in London on May 29, 1660. Lee, *Source-Book*, 396–97.

80. Holdsworth, *History*, VI, 424.

81. To borrow a phrase from the American Declaration of Independence. See Dumbauld, *Declaration*, 119.

82. Holdsworth, *History*, VI, 165–66.

83. Samuel R. Gardiner, *The Fall of the Monarchy of Charles I*, II, 484–86; James and Weinstock, *England during the Interregnum*, 1.

84. Samuel R. Gardiner, *The Constitutional Documents of the Puritan Revolution*, 245. The validity of this ordinance was the subject of controversy with the king. See the proclamation of May 27, 1642, by Charles I (*ibid.*, 248–49) forbidding obedience to the ordinance and Parliament's declaration of June 6, 1642 (*ibid.*, 254–58) declaring the king's proclamation void, and metaphysically arguing that the king's will is manifested through Parliament in "a more . . . obligatory manner" than "by personal act . . . of his own." *Ibid.*, 257. The collection of Firth and Rait (see note 78, *supra*) begins with the militia ordinance. Firth and Rait, *Acts and Ordinances*, I, 1–5.

85. The vote to abolish the House of Lords was taken on February 6, 1649, and to abolish monarchy on the following day. Samuel R. Gardiner, *History of the Commonwealth and Protectorate*, I, 3. On March 17, 1649, the act to abolish monarchy was adopted; on March 19, 1649, the act to abolish the House of Lords. On May 19, 1649, the act declaring England to be a commonwealth was enacted. Firth and Rait, *Acts and Ordinances*, II, 18–20, 24, 122; Gardiner, *Constitutional Documents*, 384–87, 387–88, 388. See also Gardiner, *Commonwealth and Protectorate*, I, 64.

86. Firth and Rait, *Acts and Ordinances*, II, 813–22; Gardiner, *Constitutional Documents*, 405–17. This term is used by historians for chronological convenience, as the Instrument of Government itself still speaks of the "Commonwealth."

87. Act of February 24, 1645/46, Firth and Rait, *Acts and Ordinances*, I, 833; Act of November 27, 1656, *ibid.*, II, 1043. The Court of Wards and Liveries, which had been established in 1540 to deal with incidents of such tenure, was simultaneously abolished. Holdsworth, *History*, I, 431. Further reform was demanded since these measures did not remedy the grievances of the common people who as tenants by copyhold remained subject to the caprice of landlords. Veall, *Law Reform*, 52–54, 213.

88. G. Woods Wallaston, *Coronation Claims*, 16–19.

89. McKechnie, *Magna Carta*, 57–76. See also Blackstone, *Commentaries*, II, 60–62, 78, 90, 98; Holdsworth, *History*, III, 37–46, 51–53. The need of Charles I for revenue likewise led him to exploit the incidents of tenure by reviving the dormant obligation of holders of land worth £40 a year to assume the honor of knighthood or be mulcted for failure to do so. J. P. Kenyon, *The Stuart Constitution*, 88, 201; Samuel R. Gardiner, *The Personal Government of Charles I*, I, 204–205; Tanner, *English Constitutional Conflicts*, 74, 99. This abuse was abolished by the Act of August 10, 1641, 17 Car. 1, c. 20. Gardiner, *Constitutional Documents*, 196–97.

90. Act of 12 Car. 2, c. 24.

91. Veall, *Law Reform*, 227, 235–40. See page 149, *supra*.

92. *Ibid.*, 235–36. Likewise impetus was given during the Puritan era to the rule that judges should hold office during good behavior rather than at the pleasure of the executive. Firth and Rait, *Acts and Ordinances*, I, 1226–27. The use of the English language in court proceedings was also ordained during that period by the Act of November 22, 1650. *Ibid.*, II, 455–56. After the Restoration this obvious reform did not prevail until 1731. 4 Geo. 2, c. 26. Holdsworth, *History*, VI, 571–72.

93. Woodhouse, *Puritanism and Liberty*, 322; Veall, *Law Reform*, 88, 127–41, 152–66. See also pages 146, 148, 246 n. 37, 248 n. 72, *supra*. Prison reform and abolition of imprisonment for debt were also sought. *Ibid.*, 142–51.

94. Jefferson was interested in improving prisons. Autobiography, 1 F. 73–74; to Skelton Jones, July 28, 1809, 12 M. 301. See Howard C. Rice, Jr., "A French Source of Jefferson's Plan for the Prison at Richmond," *Journal of the Society of Architectural Historians,* Vol. XII (December, 1953), 28–30. See pages 135–38, *supra.*

95. Veall, *Law Reform,* 212–24.

96. *Ibid.,* 95, 217. During the Putney debates among the officers of Cromwell's army in 1647 one Nicholas Cowling demanded "whether the younger son have not as much right to the inheritance as the eldest." Woodhouse, *Puritanism and Liberty,* 64.

97. See pages xii, 137, 166 n. 38, *supra.*

98. George L. Haskins, "The Beginnings of Partible Inheritance in the American Colonies," *Yale Law Journal,* Vol. LI (June, 1942), 1280–81.

99. Concerning litigation before the Privy Council attacking the Connecticut and Massachusetts statutes, see Smith, *Appeals to the Privy Council,* 537–77.

100. To Chastellux, September 2, 1785. Sowerby, IV, 202.

101. Veall, *Law Reform,* 77, 87–89, 94, 95, 104, 107, 112; Woodhouse, *Puritanism and Liberty,* 321–22, 364–66. Parliament on June 26, 1657, passed an act regulating the Court of Chancery. Firth and Rait, *Acts and Ordinances,* II, 949–67. Cromwell had also attempted reform of the chancery court by an ordinance of August 21, 1654. Veall, *Law Reform,* 178–83; Holdsworth, *History,* I, 431–34.

102. See pages 134, 159 n. 16, 237 n. 12, *supra.*

103. Hening, *Statutes at Large,* IX, 394; for Jefferson's draft see 1 P. 615. "But this being found inconvenient the act was repealed, October, 1783, c. 26." Tucker's *Blackstone,* III (App.), 56. Jefferson favored the jury system in order "to introduce the people into every department of government as far as they are capable of exercising it." Dumbauld, *Political Writings of Jefferson,* 88–90.

104. Colonel Thomas Rainborough in the course of the Putney debates among the officers of Cromwell's army in October, 1647, urging universal suffrage, declared "really I think that the poorest he that is in England hath a life to live, as the greatest he; and therefore . . . every man that is to live under a government ought first by his own consent to put himself under that government; and I do think that the poorest man in England is not at all bound . . . to that government that he hath not had a voice to put himself under." Woodhouse, *Puritanism and Liberty,* 53. See also *ibid.,* 66, 201, 206, 327, 370, 433–34. On Jefferson's immortal exposition of the American philosophy of government, see Dumbauld, *Declaration,* 52–74.

105. Woodhouse, *Puritanism and Liberty,* 80, 433, 446. For Jefferson's views see Dumbauld, *Political Writings of Jefferson,* 102–28; Dumbauld, *Constitution,* 18–19; Dumbauld, "Thomas Jefferson and American Constitutional Law," Emory University *Journal of Public Law,* Vol. II, No. 2 (Fall, 1953), 373–74.

106. Dumbauld, *Political Writings of Jefferson,* 55, 57; Dumbauld, *Bill of Rights,* 145–46.

107. See page 237 n. 18, *supra.*

108. Dumbauld, *Bill of Rights,* 111.

109. *Ibid.,* 106–107.

110. The questions debated were: "Whether the magistrate have, or ought to have, any compulsive and restrictive power in matters of religion?" and "Whether to have [in the Agreement of the People] any reserve to except religious things or only to give power in natural and civil things and say nothing of religion?" Woodhouse, *Puritanism and Liberty,*

125. In like vein are articles 35–38 of Cromwell's Instrument of Government of December 16, 1653, quoted in Sutherland, *Constitutionalism in America*, 86.

111. Woodhouse, *Puritanism and Liberty*, 141. Yet "he hath in all ages usurped it," the speaker went on to say. For Jefferson's similar comment see note 106, *supra.*

112. Abbott, *Writings and Speeches of Oliver Cromwell*, III, 458–59. See also Clifford K. Shipton, "The Locus of Authority in Colonial Massachusetts," in George A. Billias (ed.), *Law and Authority in Colonial America*, 142–43, regarding the principle in New England.

113. Dumbauld, *Declaration,* 61. See page 62, *supra.* This idea goes back to St. Augustine and recurs in the sixteenth century dialogue *Doctor and Student.* Theodore Plucknett and J. L. Barton (eds.), *St. German's Doctor and Student*, xxiv, 19, 29, 57, 135, 183, 209.

114. Woodhouse, *Puritanism and Liberty*, 69.

115. Dumbauld, *Political Writings of Jefferson*, 138, 140, 141; Woodhouse, *Puritanism and Liberty*, 319, 429, 435.

116. Dumbauld, *Declaration*, 51, 59; Woodhouse, *Puritanism and Liberty*, 67.

117. On this subject see Christopher Hill, *Puritanism and Revolution*, 50–122. Levellers, such as Lilburne, and Diggers used the phrase. *Ibid.*, 76, 84. See note 15, chapter 7 and note 24, *supra.*

118. Holdsworth, *History*, VI, 414. See also Frank, *The Levellers*, 83–84; and Gregg, *Free-born John*, 143, 208–10.

119. Woodhouse, *Puritanism and Liberty*, [96–97], 65–66, 388.

120. Veall, *Law Reform*, 105–108, 212, 214.

121. THE IVST MANS IVSTIFICATION: OR A letter by way of Plea in Barre; written by L. COL. JOHN LILBURNE, to the Honourable Justice Reeves, . . . [Signed by Lilburne June 6, 1646; the date in ink, presumably of Thomason's purchase, June 10, 1646. I used British Museum copy, shelf-mark E 340 (12)].

122. *Ibid.*, 11. Lilburne had spent six months in Newgate prison after his arrest upon an action of trespass at the suit of Colonel Edward King, whom Lilburne charged with cowardice and treason.

123. *Ibid.*, 11. The reference is to the declaration of the House of Commons of April 17, 1646, that the end of government is the safety and weal of the people. Lilburne's complaint is similar to William Penn's observation: "Certainly, if the common law be so hard to be understood, it is far from being very common." *The Trial of William Penn and William Mead*, 6 *State Trials* 951, 959 (1670).

124. *The Just Man's Justification*, 12.

125. *Ibid.*, 13. In a later pamphlet, *The Legall Fundamentall Liberties of the People of England Revived, Asserted, and Vindicated*, 44, Lilburne repeats that the liberties of England were subdued "by the Bastard Norman Conqueror." This pamphlet struck principally at the evil of "an everlasting Parliament" which was "ten thousand times worse than no Parliament at all." *Ibid.*, 46. Deposition of the king has resulted in "a meer changing of persons" not in setting "the Nation free from Tyranny" itself. *Ibid.*, 42. He was then in prison by order of the House of Lords, which was not, he points out, like an act of Parliament, a law. *Ibid.*, 11 [British Museum copy, shelf-mark 1104 b 14].

126. *The Just Man's Justification*, 14. See Dumbauld, *Constitution*, 4–5, 7–9; Dumbauld, *Bill of Rights*, 78–81.

127. *The Just Man's Justification*, 15. He called upon Parliament "forever to annihilate this Norman innovation," and to provide for monthly trial of all cases by jury in the County

or Hundred where they arose, with no appeal except to Parliament, as well as for establishment of a public office to record land titles. *Ibid.*, 15.

128. Veall, *Law Reform*, 66. "We would derive from the Conqueror as little as we could." 3 Inst. pref. See Holdsworth, *History*, V, 475; J. G. A. Pocock, *The Ancient Constitution and the Feudal Law*, 53, 126.

129. *Summary View*, 1 P. 121, 132–33; to John Cartwright, June 5, 1824, 16 M. 42, 43. See also page 154, and note 15, chapter 7, *supra,* and Harold Trevor Colbourn, "The Saxon Heritage: Thomas Jefferson Looks at English History" (typewritten thesis, Johns Hopkins University, 1953).

130. For these characterizations of Jefferson, see the titles of works cited in the bibliography of Dumbauld, *American Tourist.*

131. A prominent historian speaks of Jefferson as "this typically Puritan revolutionary." Bernard Bailyn, "Boyd's Jefferson: Notes for a Sketch," *The New England Quarterly*, Vol. XXXIII, No. 3 (September, 1960), 386.

132. Sir Frederick Pollock, *Oxford Lectures and Other Discourses*, 111.

133. To Samuel Kercheval, July 12, 1816, 12 F. 11–12, 13. See also Dumbauld, *Declaration*, 59, 74–82.

134. "We surely cannot deny to any nation that right whereon our own government is founded, that every one may govern itself under whatever forms it pleases, and change these forms at it's own will." To Gouverneur Morris, November 7, 1792, 7 F. 198.

Bibliography

BIBLIOGRAPHICAL MATERIAL

For general bibliography on Jefferson, see the bibliography in Edward Dumbauld, *Thomas Jefferson, American Tourist,* 241–60, and in each volume of Dumas Malone, *Thomas Jefferson and His Time* (5 vols., 1948 to date). (Frequently cited works are often referred to by short titles or abbreviations in brackets.)

The following books on Jefferson are frequently cited:

Dumbauld, Edward. *The Bill of Rights and What It Means Today.* Norman, 1957. [*Bill of Rights*]
——. *The Constitution of the United States.* Norman, 1964. [*Constitution*]
——. *The Declaration of Independence and What It Means Today.* Norman, 1950. [*Declaration*]
——. *The Life and Legal Writings of Hugo Grotius.* Norman, 1969. [*Grotius*]
——. *Thomas Jefferson, American Tourist.* Norman, 1946. [*American Tourist*]
Kimball, Marie. *Jefferson: The Road to Glory 1743 to 1776.* New York, 1943. [*Road to Glory*]
——. *Jefferson: War and Peace 1776 to 1784.* New York, 1947. [*War and Peace*]
——. *Jefferson: The Scene of Europe 1784 to 1789.* New York, 1950. [*Scene*]
Malone, Dumas. *Jefferson and His Time.* 5 vols. to date, as follows:
——. *Jefferson the Virginian.* Boston, 1948. [*Virginian*]
——. *Jefferson and the Rights of Man.* Boston, 1951. [*Rights of Man*]
——. *Jefferson and the Ordeal of Liberty.* Boston, 1962. [*Ordeal*]
——. *Jefferson the President First Term, 1801–1805.* Boston, 1970. [*President, First Term*]
——. *Jefferson the President Second Term, 1805–1809.* Boston, 1974. [*President, Second Term*] (This is the standard biography of Jefferson, superseding Randall.)
Peterson, Merrill D. *Thomas Jefferson and the New Nation.* New York, 1970. (The best single-volume biography of Jefferson.)
Randall, Henry S. *The Life of Thomas Jefferson.* 3 vols. New York, 1858.
Sowerby, E. Millicent, *Catalogue of the Library of Thomas Jefferson.* 5 vols. Washington, 1952–59. (Cited by author's name and item number or volume

and page. Indispensable for information about law books and other volumes owned by Jefferson.)

On Jefferson and the law, very few studies have been published:

Bowers, Claude G. "Thomas Jefferson and the Courts," *Proceedings* of the North Carolina Bar Association, Vol. XXIX (1927), 26–45.

Caldwell, Lynton K. "The Jurisprudence of Thomas Jefferson," *Indiana Law Journal,* Vol. XVIII, No. 3 (April, 1943), 193–213.

Cohen, Morris L. "Thomas Jefferson Recommends a Course of Law Study," *University of Pennsylvania Law Review,* Vol. CXIX, No. 5 (April, 1971), 823–44.

Davis, John W. "Thomas Jefferson, Attorney at Law," *Proceedings* of the Virginia State Bar Association, Vol. XXXVIII (1926), 361–77.

Dewey, Frank L. "Thomas Jefferson's Law Practice," *Virginia Magazine of History and Biography,* Vol. LXXXV, No. 3 (July, 1977), 289–301.

Didier, Eugene L. "Thomas Jefferson as a Lawyer," *Green Bag,* Vol. XV, No. 4 (April, 1903), 153–59.

Dumbauld, Edward. "A Manuscript from Monticello," *American Bar Association Journal,* Vol. XXXVIII, No. 5 (May, 1952), 389–92, 446–47.

———. "Thomas Jefferson and American Constitutional Law," Emory University *Journal of Public Law,* Vol. II, No. 2 (Fall, 1953), 370–89.

———. "Thomas Jefferson and Pennsylvania Courts," *Pennsylvania Bar Association Quarterly,* Vol. XXXVII, No. 3 (March, 1966), 236–47.

Eaton, Clement. "A Mirror of the Southern Colonial Lawyer," *William and Mary Quarterly* (3d series), Vol. VIII, No. 4 (October, 1951), 521–34.

Finkelnburg, Gustavus A. "Thomas Jefferson as a Lawyer," *American Law Review,* Vol. XXXIX (May–June, 1905), 321–29.

Ireton, Robert E. "Jefferson and the Supreme Court," *Boston University Law Review,* Vol. XVII, No. 1 (January, 1937), 81–89.

Kean, Robert G. "Thomas Jefferson as a Legislator," *Virginia Law Journal,* Vol. XI (December, 1887), 705–24.

Killian, James R. "Thomas Jefferson, The Lawyer and Citizen," *Colorado Bar Association Reports,* Vol. XIII (1910), 121–39.

Lathrop, Mary F. "Jefferson's Contribution to the Law of the West," *Pennsylvania Bar Association Reports,* Vol. XXXIII (1927), 297–307.

Morris, Roland S. "Jefferson as a Lawyer," *Proceedings* of the American Philosophical Society, Vol. LXXXVII, No. 3 (July, 1943), 211–15.

Patterson, C. Perry. "Jefferson and Judicial Review," *American Bar Association Journal,* Vol. XXX, No. 8 (August, 1944), 443–51.

Sears, Louis M. "Jefferson and the Law of Nations," *American Political Science Review,* Vol. XIII, No. 3 (August, 1919), 379–99.

Thomas, Charles S. "Jefferson and the Judiciary," *Colorado Bar Association Reports,* Vol. XXVIII (1925), 172–84; *The Constitutional Review,* Vol. X, No. 2 (April, 1926), 67–76.

Wiltse, Charles M. "Thomas Jefferson on the Law of Nations," *American Journal of International Law,* Vol. XXIX, No. 1 (January, 1935), 66–81.

Wyllie, John Cooke. "The Second Mrs. Wayland, An Unpublished Jefferson Opinion on a Case in Equity," *American Journal of Legal History,* Vol. IX, No. 1 (January, 1965), 64–68.

On legal bibliography in general, with special reference to English and colonial Virginia law, the following are helpful:

"American Reports and Reporters," *The American Jurist and Law Magazine,* Vol. XXII, No. 43 (October, 1839), 108–42.

Beale, Joseph H. *A Bibliography of Early English Law Books.* Cambridge, Mass., 1926.

Bemis, Samuel F., and Grace G. Griffin. *Guide to the Diplomatic History of the United States.* Washington, 1935.

"Bibliography of Virginia and West Virginia Legal Publications in Library of College of Law, West Virginia University," *West Virginia Law Quarterly,* Vol. XXVI, No. 1 (November, 1919), 43–57.

Bridgman, Richard W. *A Short View of Legal Bibliography.* London, 1807.

Budd, Henry. "Reports and Some Reporters," *The American Law Review,* Vol. XLVII (July–August, 1913), 481–517.

Butterworth, J. *A General Catalogue of Law Books.* London, 1801.

Catalogue of the Library of the United States to Which is Annexed A Copious Index, Alphabetically Arranged. Washington, 1815.

A Catalogue of the Library of the University of Virginia. Charlottesville, Va., 1828.

Clarke, John. *A Catalogue of Modern Law Books.* London, 1808.

———. *Clarke's Bibliotheca Legum; or, Complete Catalogue of the Common and Statute Law-Books of the United Kingdom.* New edition. London, 1819.

"A Complete Bibliography of Virginia Statute Law," *Virginia Law Register,* Vol. XI (April, 1906), 1048–50, 1052.

Cowley, John D. *A Bibliography of Abridgments, Digests, Dictionaries and Indexes of English Law to the Year 1800.* London, 1932.

Daniel, W. T. S. *The History and Origin of the Law Reports.* London, 1884.

Dooley, Dennis A. *Index to State Bar Association Reports and Proceedings.* New York, 1942.

Eller, Catherine Spicer. *The William Blackstone Collection in the Yale Law Library.* New Haven, 1938.

Ford, Paul Leicester. *Bibliography and Reference List of the History and Literature relating to the Adoption of the Constitution of the United States, 1787–8.* Brooklyn, N.Y., 1888.

Fox, John C. *A Handbook of English Law Reports.* London, 1913.

Friend, William L. *Anglo-American Legal Bibliographies.* Washington, 1944.

Hicks, Frederick C. *Materials and Methods of Legal Research.* 2d ed. Rochester,

N.Y., 1933; 3d ed. Rochester, N.Y., 1942. (Contains convenient listing of English and Virginia reports.)

――――. *Men and Books Famous in the Law.* Rochester, N.Y., 1921.

[Hildeburn, Charles R.] *The Charlemagne Tower Collection of American Colonial Laws.* Privately printed for the Historical Society of Pennsylvania, Philadelphia, 1900. [*Charlemagne Tower Collection*]

Holdsworth, William S. "The Named Reporters," *Anglo-American Legal History Series,* New York University School of Law, Series 1, No. 8, New York, 1943.

――――. *Some Makers of English Law.* Cambridge, Eng., 1938.

――――. *Sources and Literature of English Law.* Oxford, 1925.

James, Eldon R. "A List of Legal Treatises Printed in the British Colonies and the American States before 1801," *Harvard Legal Essays,* Cambridge, Mass., 1934, 159–211.

Keitt, Lawrence. *An Annotated Bibliography of Bibliographies of Statutory Materials of the United States.* Cambridge, Mass., 1934.

Macdonald, Grace E. *Check-List of Legislative Journals of States of the United States of America.* Providence, R.I., 1938.

――――. *Check-List of Statutes of States of the United States of America.* Providence, R.I., 1937.

Martin, John H. *Bench and Bar of Philadelphia.* Philadelphia, 1883.

Marvin, John G. *Legal Bibliography.* Philadelphia, 1847.

Maxwell, W. Harold. *A Bibliography of English Law to 1650.* London, 1925. (Vol. II, from 1651 to 1800, by Leslie F. Maxwell, London, 1931; Vol. III, from 1801 to June, 1932, by Leslie F. Maxwell, London, 1933.)

Peden, William. "Some Notes Concerning Thomas Jefferson's Libraries," *William and Mary Quarterly* (3d series), Vol. I, No. 3 (July, 1944), 265–72.

[Poor, Nathaniel P.] *Catalogue. President Jefferson's Library.* Washington, 1829.

Soule, Charles C. *The Lawyer's Reference Manual.* Boston, 1884.

Swem, Earl G. *A Bibliography of the Conventions and Constitutions of Virginia.* Richmond, 1910.

――――. *A Bibliography of Virginia.* In four parts. Richmond, 1902–19.

Torrence, William C. *A Trial Bibliography of Colonial Virginia.* Richmond, 1908–10.

Tucker, Chas. Cowles. *A Chronological List of English and American Reports.* Washington, 1907.

Veeder, Van Vechten. "The English Reports 1297–1865," *Harvard Law Review,* Vol. XV, No. 1 (May, 1901), 1–25; No. 2 (June, 1901), 109–17.

――――. "The English Reports, 1587–1865," in *Select Essays in Anglo-American Legal History.* 3 vols. Boston, 1908. Vol. II, 123–68.

Wallace, John W. *The Reporters.* 4th ed. Boston, 1882.

Waters, Willard O. *Check List of American Laws, Charters and Constitutions of the 17th and 18th Centuries in the Huntington Library.* San Marino, Calif., 1936.

Winfield, Percy H. *The Chief Sources of English Legal History.* Cambridge, Mass., 1925.

Worral, John. *Bibliotheca Legum.* New edition. London, 1765.

On the history of Law, the following are often cited:

Holdsworth, William S. *A History of English Law.* 16 vols. Boston and London, 1923–66. [*History*] (This invaluable work was published and revised over a period of many years. Vols. XIII–XVI were edited after the author's death by A. L. Goodhart and H. G. Hanbury. The dates of each volume in my set follow: I [4th ed. Boston, 1931]; II [3d ed. Boston, 1923]; III [3d ed. Boston, 1927]; IV [Boston, 1924]; V [Boston, 1927]; VI [Boston, 1927]; VII [Boston, 1926]; VIII [Boston, 1926]; IX [Boston, 1926]; X [London, 1938]; XI [London, 1938]; XII [London, 1938]; XIII [London, 1952]; XIV [London, 1964]; XV [London, 1965]; XVI [London, 1966]. See F. B. Wiener, "Holdsworth's History Finally Completed," *American Bar Association Journal,* Vol. LIII, No. 4 [April, 1967], 321–24.)

Plucknett, Theodore, F. T. *A Concise History of the Common Law.* 3d ed. London, 1940. [*Concise History*]

Pollock, Sir Frederick, and Frederic W. Maitland. *The History of English Law before the Time of Edward I.* 2d ed. 2 vols. Cambridge, Mass., 1898. [*History*]

Veall, Donald. *The Popular Movement for Law Reform 1640–1660.* Oxford, 1970. [*Law Reform*]

MANUSCRIPT MATERIALS

The following collections of Jefferson papers have been used in connection with this book:

Library of Congress, Washington, D.C. Manuscripts Division, Jefferson Papers. [LC] (This is one of the principal collections of Jefferson papers. In this book, when a letter is cited by date only, with no other identification, it is from this collection.)

Henry E. Huntington Library, San Marino, California. [HL] (This collection is particularly useful for materials relating to Jefferson's law practice. In addition to items hereinafter specified, there are many letters and memoranda on legal matters, such as HM 5593 [Notes on title to 483 acres of land].)

Massachusetts Historical Society, Boston, Massachusetts. [MHS] (This collection is likewise particularly useful for the topics treated in this book.)

Princeton University Library, The Jefferson Papers. Princeton, N.J. (In connection with the ongoing publication of *The Papers of Thomas Jefferson,* under the editorship of Professor Julian P. Boyd, copies of the Jefferson holdings of other institutions have been assembled, along with various useful research aids.)

University of Virginia Library, Charlottesville, Va. (Here too, in addition to valuable items in its own holdings, conveniently available copies of other materials make this an important center for Jefferson research.)

In addition to Jefferson's correspondence and account books (as to which see Dumbauld, Thomas Jefferson, American Tourist, 242) the following volumes in Jefferson's handwriting relate directly to his law practice, and are more fully described and discussed in the text, supra:

Legal Commonplace Book. LC. (Contains notes on judicial decisions and other authorities compiled by Jefferson as a law student. Published in part by Gilbert Chinard.)

Equity Commonplace Book. HL: Brock Collection, BR 13. (A similar compilation of material on equity, as distinguished from common law, subjects.)

Case Book. HL: HM 326. (A volume in which Jefferson recorded cases during his law practice, covering the period from February 12, 1767, to November 9, 1774.)

Fee Book. HL: HM 836. (A financial record [1764–94] including legal fees from February 12, 1767, to December 28, 1774.)

Arguments in *Bolling* v. *Bolling.* HL: BR 2. (Written arguments in a chancery case submitted to arbitration.)

Parliamentary Pocket-Book. MHS. (A notebook of 145 items on parliamentary law, used by Jefferson in preparing his published *Manual of Parliamentary Practice, q. v. infra.* Many other valuable materials relating to legal matters, including correspondence and dockets, are to be found in the Massachusetts Historical Society. A later MS draft of the *Manual* is HM 5986 at the Huntington Library.)

National Archives [NA], Record Group 59, E. 116 is a bound volume entitled *Examination of the Claim of the United States and of the Pretensions of Edward Livingston to the Batture in front of the Suburb St. Mary's.* (It contains material procured by Jefferson from government departments, and returned (with additional items) under cover of his letter of May 26, 1812, to Secretary of State James Monroe. It comprises 457 handwritten pages, together with 97 printed pages, and 3 maps. Of special interest is the *Mémoire* of Moreau de Lislet, listed for convenience under the author's name in the bibliography.)

Livingston Papers. An extensive collection of papers of Edward Livingston and other members of his family, copies of material from which were courteously furnished by John W. Delafield, Esquire, of the New York Bar.

JEFFERSON'S PUBLISHED WRITINGS

The following books of Jefferson's authorship have been published separately, and are more fully described in chapters 2 and 3 of the text, supra:

Jefferson, Thomas. *A Manual of Parliamentary Practice. For the Use of the Senate of the United States.* Washington City. Printed by Samuel Harrison

Smith. MDCCCI (1801). (No pagination. References are to the second edition, 1812.) [*Manual*]

——. *Notes on the State of Virginia;* . . . [Paris], MDCCLXXXII (actually printed in 1785). [*Notes*]

——. *Observations sur la Virginie.* Par M. J. Paris, 1786.

——. *Notes on the State of Virginia. Written by Thomas Jefferson.* London: Printed for John Stockdale, opposite Burlington-House, Piccadilly. M.DCC.-LXXXVII (1787) [*Notes* (Stockdale ed.)]

——. *Notes on the State of Virginia.* Edited by William Peden. Chapel Hill, N.C., 1954. [*Notes* (Peden ed.)]

——. *The Proceedings of the Government of the United States, in Maintaining the Public Right to the Beach of the Missisipi* [sic], *Adjacent to New-Orleans, against the Intrusion of Edward Livingston. Prepared for the Use of Counsel, by Thomas Jefferson.* New–York: Published by Ezra Sargent, No. 86 Broadway, 1812. [*Proceedings*]

——. *Report of the Committee of Revisors Appointed by the General Assembly of Virginia In MDCCLXXVI.* Printed by Dixon and Holt, Richmond, 1784.

——. *Reports of Cases Determined in the General Court of Virginia. From 1730, to 1740; and from 1768, to 1772. By Thomas Jefferson.* Charlottesville. Published by F. Carr and Co., 1829. [Jeff.]

——. *A Summary View of the Rights of British America.* Williamsburg: Printed by Clementina Rind (1774). (For an account of other editions of this pamphlet, see the facsimile edition from the copy in the John Carter Brown Library, by Thomas P. Abernethy, New York, 1943, xi.)

The following publications of Jefferson's correspondence and other papers are cited in this book:

Boyd, Julian P. (ed.). *The Papers of Thomas Jefferson.* 19 vols. to date. Princeton, 1950–. [P.]

[Cabell, Nathaniel F. (ed.)]. *Early History of the University of Virginia as Contained in the Letters of Thomas Jefferson and Joseph C. Cabell.* Richmond, 1856.

Cappon, Lester J. (ed.). *The Adams-Jefferson Letters.* 2 vols. Chapel Hill, N.C., 1959.

Chinard, Gilbert. *The Commonplace Book of Thomas Jefferson.* Baltimore, 1926. (See Legal Commonplace Book under Manuscript Materials, *supra.*)

——. *The Literary Bible of Thomas Jefferson.* Baltimore, 1928. (This is Jefferson's commonplace book of quotations from philosophers and poets.)

Dumbauld, Edward (ed.). *The Political Writings of Thomas Jefferson.* New York, 1955.

Ford, Paul Leicester (ed.). *The Works of Thomas Jefferson.* Federal Edition. 12 vols. New York, 1904. [F.]

Ford, Worthington Chauncey (ed.). *Thomas Jefferson Correspondence Printed from the Originals in the Collections of William K. Bixby.* Boston, 1916.

Lipscomb, Andrew A., and A. Ellery Bergh (eds.). *The Writings of Thomas Jefferson.* Memorial Edition. 20 vols. Washington, 1903. [M.]

McIlwaine, Henry R. (ed.). *Official Letters of the Governors of the State of Virginia,* Vol. II, *Letters of Thomas Jefferson.* Richmond, 1928.

Randolph, Thomas J. (ed.). *Memoir, Correspondence and Miscellanies, from the Papers of Thomas Jefferson.* 4 vols. Charlottesville, Va. 1829.

    (The editions of Boyd, Ford, and Lipscomb and Bergh are cited as "P.," "F.," and "M.," respectively, preceded by volume number and followed by page number. For other publications of Jefferson letters see bibliography in Dumbauld, *Thomas Jefferson, American Tourist,* 242–44.)

PUBLIC RECORDS

ACTS OF PARLIAMENT

Pickering, Danby (ed.). *The Statutes at Large.* 46 vols. Cambridge, Eng., 1762–1807. (This edition of the English statutes has been used, in accordance with the customary practice of citing them by regnal years and chapter instead of by volume and page.)

For interregnum legislation:

Firth, Charles H., and Robert S. Rait. *Acts and Ordinances of the Interregnum, 1642–1660.* 3 vols. London, 1911.

Also useful are:

Adams, George B., and H. M. Stephens. *Select Documents of English Constitutional History.* New York, 1901.

Ehler, Sidney Z., and John B. Morrall (eds.). *Church and State Through the Centuries.* Westminster, Md., 1954.

Gardiner, Samuel R. *The Constitutional Documents of the Puritan Revolution 1625–1660.* 3d ed. Oxford, 1906.

Kenyon, J. P. *The Stuart Constitution 1603–1688.* Cambridge, Eng., 1966.

Lee, Guy Carleton. *Source-Book of English History.* 2d ed. New York, 1900.

Tanner, Joseph R. *Constitutional Documents of the Reign of James I, A.D. 1603–1625.* Cambridge, Eng., 1930.

———. *Tudor Constitutional Documents, A.D. 1485–1603.* 2d ed. Cambridge, Eng., 1930.

ACTS OF CONGRESS

    These are cited from the official *Statutes at Large* [cited "St." or "Stat." preceded by volume number and followed by page number] or from the West Publishing Company's convenient *United States Code Annotated* [cited USCA preceded by title number and followed by section number].

CONSTITUTIONS

These are conveniently found in:

Thorpe, Francis N. *The Federal and State Constitutions, Colonial Charters, and Other Organic Laws.* 7 vols. Washington, 1909. [*Charters*]

VIRGINIA STATUTES

These are ordinarily cited from:

Hening, William Waller (ed.). *The Statutes at Large: Being a Collection of All the Laws of Virginia, from the First Session of the Legislature in the Year 1619.* 13 vols. Richmond and Philadelphia, 1809–23. [*Statutes*]

[Acts of Assembly, unavailable to Hening.] *The following seven items contain early laws which came to light after publication of Hening's collection:*

"Proceedings of the First Assembly of Virginia, 1619," *Collections of the New-York Historical Society* (2d series), Vol. III, Part I (1857), 329–58. (Contributed by George Bancroft, from British records.)

"The Virginia Assembly of 1641. A List of Members and Some of the Acts," *Virginia Magazine of History and Biography,* Vol. IX, No. 1 (July, 1910), 50–59. (From Charles City Court House, preserved by a Massachusetts soldier when McClellan's troops were using the records there as fuel for their coffee.)

"Acts, Orders and Resolutions of the General Assembly of Virginia at Sessions of March, 1643–1646," *Virginia Magazine of History and Biography,* Vol. XXIII, No. 3 (July, 1915), 225–55. (From a manuscript volume in the Norfolk County Clerk's office, Portsmouth, Va.)

"Acts of the General Assembly, Jan. 6, 1639–40," *William and Mary Quarterly* (2d series), Vol. IV, No. 1 (January, 1924), 16–35; No. 3 (July, 1924), 145–62. (Copied by Conway Robinson from a book burned in 1865.)

Winfree, Waverly K. (ed.). *The Laws of Virginia Being a Supplement to Hening's The Statutes at Large. 1700–1750.* Richmond, 1971.

Billings, Warren M. (ed.). "Some Acts not in Hening's *Statutes:* The Acts of Assembly, April 1652, November 1652, and July 1653," *Virginia Magazine of History and Biography,* Vol. LXXXIII, No. 1 (January, 1975), 22–76.

Kukla, Jon (ed.). "Some Acts not in Hening's *Statutes:* The Acts of Assembly, October 1660," *Virginia Magazine of History and Biography,* Vol. LXXXIII, No. 1 (January, 1975), 77–97.

Occasionally, Virginia laws are quoted from the following other collections, described and discussed in chapter 6 of the text, supra:

An Abridgement of the Laws in Force and Use in Her Majesty's Plantations; (Viz.) Of Virginia, Jamaica, Barbadoes, Maryland, New-England, New-York, Carolina, &c. Digested under proper Heads in the Method of Mr. Wingate, and Mr. Washington's Abridgements. London, 1704. ("Farewel" at end of preface.)

An Abridgment of the Laws of Virginia, Compiled in 1694. Richmond, 1903. (Compiled in 1694, probably by Philip Ludwell.)

An Abridgement of the Publick Laws of Virginia, In Force and Use, June 10, 1720. London, 1722. (Attributed to William Beverley.)

An Abridgment of the Publick Laws of Virginia, in Force and Use, June 10. 1720. London, 1728. (Identical with 1722 edition except in the title page.)

The Acts of Assembly, Now in Force, in the Colony of Virginia. . . . Publish'd pursuant to an Order of the General Assembly. Williamsburg: Printed by William Hunter. MDCCLII [1752]. [Edmund Pendleton's copy, in Huntington Library. George Wythe's name appears in the list of subscribers. Containing acts to which the Crown did not assent, this collection was superseded by the edition of 1769.]

Acts of Assembly, Now in Force, in Virginia. Occasioned by the Repeal of Sundry Acts Made in the Twenty Second Year of His Majesty's Reign, and in the Year of Our Lord 1748. Williamsburg, printed by William Hunter, 1753.

Acts of Assembly, Passed in the Colony of Virginia, From 1662, to 1715. Volume I. London: Printed by John Baskett, Printer to the King's most Excellent Majesty, MDCCXXVII [1727]. [No second volume was published; the 1728 edition is identical except in the title page.]

Acts of Assembly, Passed in the Colony of Virginia, from the Year 1662. London: Printed by Order of the Lords Commissioners of Trade and Plantations, by John Baskett, Printer to the King's Most Excellent Majesty, and sold by Edward Symon in Cornhill, MDCCXXVIII [1728].

The Acts of Assembly, Now in Force, in the Colony of Virginia. With An Exact Table to the Whole. Published by Order of the General Assembly. Williamsburg: Printed by W. Rind, A. Purdie, and J. Dixon. MDCCLXIX [1769]. (The last edition of Virginia laws before the Revolution, this collection is often cited as the "old Body of Laws.")

The Code of Virginia. Richmond, 1849. (Published pursuant to Act of August 15, 1849, under the superintendence of John M. Patton and Conway Robinson. The unsigned preface [pp. iii–x] describing prior publications of Virginia laws is generally attributed to Conway Robinson, though Swem credits it to George W. Munford. William H. Martin, "Some Virginia Law Books in a Virginia Law Office," *Virginia Law Register* [new series], Vol. XIII, 485.)

A Collection of All the Acts of Assembly, Now in force, in the Colony of Virginia. . . . Publish'd, pursuant to an Order of the General Assembly, held at Williamsburg, in the Year M, DCC, XXVII. Williamsburg: Printed by William Parks. M,DCC, XXXIII. (One of the earliest Virginia imprints.)

A Collection of All Such Public Acts of the General Assembly, and Ordinances of the Conventions of Virginia, Passed since the year 1768, as are now in force; With a Table of the Principal Matters. Published under inspection of the Judges of the High Court of Chancery, by a resolution of General Assembly, the 16th day of June 1783. Richmond: Printed by Thomas Nicolson and William Prentis. M,DCC,LXXXV (1785). (This edition is generally called "The Chancellors' Revisal.")

A Collection of All Such Acts of the General Assembly of Virginia, of a Public and Permanent Nature, As Are Now in Force; with a Table of the Principal Matters. . . . Richmond: Printed by Augustine Davis, Printer for the Commonwealth, 1794. (The last folio edition of Virginia laws. It embodies what was enacted of Jefferson's Revisal printed in 1784.)

A Complete Collection of All the Lavvs of Virginia Now in Force. Carefully Copied from the Assembly Records. To which is Annexed an Alphabetical Table. London: Printed by *T. J.* for *J. P.* and are to be sold by Tho. Mercer at the Sign of the *Half Moon* the Corner Shop of the *Royal-Exchange* in *Cornhil.* (Compiled by John Purvis and probably printed in 1684. The most widely used source for early Virginia legislation.)

Leigh, Benjamin Watkins (ed.). *The Revised Code of the Laws of Virginia.* 2 vols. Richmond, 1819. [*Revised Code*]

Mercer, John (ed.). *An Exact Abridgment Of All the Public Acts of Assembly, of Virginia, In Force and Use. Together with Sundry Precedents, adapted thereto. And Proper Tables. By John Mercer, Gent.* Williamsburg: Printed by William Parks. M,DCC, XXXVII (1737).

————. *An Exact Abridgement of All the Public Acts of Assembly of Virginia, in Force and Use. January 1, 1758. Together with a Proper Table. By John Mercer, Gent.* Glasgow: Printed by John Bryce and David Paterson. MDCC-LIX (1759).

Moryson, Francis (ed.). *The Lawes of Virginia Now in Force. Collected out of the Assembly Records, and Digested into one Volume. Revised and Confirmed by the Grand Assembly held at James-City, by Prorogation, the 23d of March, 1661. in the 13th. Year of the Reign of our Soveraign Lord King Charles the II.* London: Printed by E. Cotes for A. Seile over against St. *Dunstans Church in Fleet-street.* M.DC.LXII (1662). (This edition, not Purvis, is meant by references in statutes to the "printed" laws.)

LEGISLATIVE JOURNALS

CONTINENTAL CONGRESS

Journals of the Continental Congress. Edited by Worthington C. Ford, Gaillard Hunt, and others. 34 vols. Washington, 1904–37. (Vols. II–VI, and XXV–XXVI cover the period of Jefferson's attendance.)

VIRGINIA

Colonial Legislature

Kennedy, John P. (ed.). *Journals of the House of Burgesses of Virginia 1766–1769.* Richmond, 1906.

―――. *Journals of the House of Burgesses of Virginia 1770–1772.* Richmond, 1906.

―――. *Journals of the House of Burgesses of Virginia 1773–1776.* Richmond, 1905.

McIlwaine, Henry R. (ed.). *Journals of the House of Burgesses of Virginia 1659/60–1693.* Richmond, 1914.

―――. *Journals of the House of Burgesses of Virginia 1695–1696, 1696–1697, 1698, 1699, 1700–1702.* Richmond, 1913.

―――. *Journals of the House of Burgesses of Virginia 1702/3–1705, 1705–1706, 1706–1712.* Richmond, 1912.

―――. *Journals of the Council of State of Virginia.* 2 vols. Richmond, 1931–32.

―――. *Legislative Journals of the Council of Colonial Virginia.* 3 vols. Richmond, 1918–19.

Revolutionary Conventions

The Proceedings of the Convention of Delegates for the Counties and Corporations In the Colony of Virginia, Held at Richmond town, in the county of Henrico, On the 20th of March 1775. Williamsburg: Printed by Alexander Purdie (1775?).

The Proceedings of the Convention of Delegates For the Counties and Corporations In the colony of Virginia, Held at Richmond town, in the county of Henrico, On Monday the 17th of July, 1775. Williamsburg: Printed by Alexander Purdie (1775).

The Proceedings of the Convention of Delegates, Held at the Town of Richmond, in the Colony of Virginia, on Friday the 1st of December, 1775, and afterwards, By Adjournment, in the City of Williamsburg. Williamsburg: Printed by Alexander Purdie (1776?).

The Proceedings of the Convention of Delegates, Held at the Capitol, in the City of Williamsburg, in the Colony of Virginia, on Monday the 6th of May, 1776. Williamsburg: Printed by Alexander Purdie, Printer to the Commonwealth (1776).

Commonwealth Assembly

(Session of October 7–December 21, 1776)

Journal of the House of Delegates of Virginia. Anno Domini, 1776. Williamsburg: Printed by Alexander Purdie, Printer to the Commonwealth (1776?).

Journal of the Senate. Anno Domini, 1776. Williamsburg: Printed by Alexander Purdie, Printer to the Commonwealth (1776?).

(Session of May 5–June 28, 1777)

Journal of the House of Delegates of Virginia. Anno Domino, 1777. Williamsburg: Printed by Alexander Purdie, Printer to the Commonwealth (1777).

Journal of the Senate of Virginia. Williamsburg: Printed by John Dixon and

William Hunter, Printers to the Commonwealth (1777). (No title page in copy in New York Public Library; title from Swem 7047.)

(Session of October 20, 1777–January 24, 1778)
Journal of the House of Delegates of Virginia. Anno Domini, 1778. Williamsburg: Printed by Alexander Purdie, Printer to the Commonwealth (1778).
Journal of the Senate. Williamsburg: Printed by John Dixon & William Hunter. MDCCLXXVII (1778?).

(Session of May 4–June 1, 1778)
Journal of the House of Delegates of Virginia. May 4th, Anno Domini 1778. Williamsburg: Printed by Alexander Purdie, Printer to the Commonwealth (1778).
Journal of the Senate. Williamsburg: Printed by John Dixon & William Hunter. MDCCLXXVIII (1778).

(Session of October 5–December 19, 1778)
Journal of the House of Delegates of the Commonwealth of Virginia; Begun and Held at the Capitol, in the City of Williamsburg, on Monday, the Fifth Day of October, in the Year of Our Lord One Thousand Seven Hundred and Seventy-Eight. Richmond: Printed by Thomas W. White, Opposite the Bell-Tavern. 1827. (Except in the reprint by White there is no known copy of this session's journal.)
Journal of the Senate. Williamsburg. Printed by J. Dixon & T. Nicolson. M,DCC,-LXXIX (1779).

(Session of May 3–June 26, 1779)
Journal of the House of Delegates of Virginia. Anno Domini, 1779. Williamsburg: Printed by John Clarkson and Augustine Davis, Printers to the Commonwealth (1779).
Journal of the Senate. Williamsburg: Printed by J. Dixon & T. Nicolson. M,DCC,-LXXIX (1779).

(Session of October 4–December 24, 1779)
Journal of the House of Delegates of Virginia. Anno Domini, 1779. Williamsburg: Printed by John Clarkson and Augustine Davis, Printers to the Commonwealth (1780?).
Journal of the Senate. Anno Domini, 1779. Williamsburg: Printed by John Clarkson and Augustine Davis, Printers to the Commonwealth (1780?).

(Session of May 1–July 14, 1780)
Journal of the House of Delegates of Virginia. Anno Domini, 1780. Richmond: Printed by J. Dixon & T. Nicolson (1780).

(Session of October 16, 1780–January 2, 1781)
Journal of the House of Delegates of Virginia. Anno Domini, 1780. Richmond: Printed by John Dixon and Thomas Nicolson (1781). (Copies in Library of Congress are incomplete. The reprint by White [Richmond, 1827] is complete.)

(Session of March 1–22, 1781)

Journal of the House of Delegates of Virginia March 1781 Session. Bulletin of the Virginia State Library, Vol. XVII, No. 1 (January, 1928), 3–54.

(Session of May 7–June 23, 1781)

Journal of the House of Delegates of Virginia. Charlottesville: Printed by John Dunlap and James Hayes, Printers to the Commonwealth. n.d.

(Session of October 1, 1781–January 5, 1782)

Journal of the House of Delegates of the Commonwealth of Virginia; Begun and Held in the Town of Richmond, in the County of Henrico, on Monday the First Day of October, in the Year of Our Lord One Thousand Seven Hundred and Eighty-one. Richmond: Printed by Thomas W. White, Opposite the Bell-Tavern. 1828. (Except in the reprint by White there is no known copy of this session's journal.)

(Session of May 5–June 28, 1783)

Journal of the House of Delegates of the Commonwealth of Virginia; Begun and Holden in the City of Richmond, In the County of Henrico, on Monday, the Fifth Day of May, in the Year of Our Lord One Thousand Seven Hundred and Eighty Three. Richmond: Printed by Thomas W. White, Opposite the Bell-Tavern. 1828.

(Session of October 17, 1785–January 21, 1786)

Journal of the House of Delegates of the Commonwealth of Virginia; Begun and Holden in the City of Richmond, In the County of Henrico, on Monday, the Seventeenth Day of October, in the Year of Our Lord One Thousand Seven Hundred and Eighty Five. Richmond: Printed by Thomas W. White, Opposite the Bell-Tavern. 1828.

(Session of October 16, 1786–January 11, 1787)

Journal of the House of Delegates of the Commonwealth of Virginia; Begun and Holden in the City of Richmond, In the County of Henrico, on Monday, the Sixteenth Day of October, in the Year of Our Lord One Thousand Seven Hundred and Eighty Six. Richmond: Printed by Thomas W. White, Opposite the Bell-Tavern. 1828.

JUDICIAL DECISIONS

The English reports and Virginia reports are described and discussed in the text, and in works listed in the section of this bibliography dealing with legal bibliography in general, *supra.* The most often cited are:

English

Coke, Sir Edward. *The Reports.* 13 vols. 4th ed. London, 1738. (When a lawyer cites simply "the Reports" [or more briefly, "Rep."] the reference is to Coke's *Reports.* When any other reports are cited, the name of the reporter, or of the jurisdiction referred to, must be given. In citing law reports, the name is preceded by the volume number and followed by the page number.)

Howell, Thomas B. *A Complete Collection of State Trials and Proceedings for High Crimes and Misdemeanors from the Earliest Times to the Year 1783.* 21 vols. London, 1816. [*State Trials*]

American

Federal Cases. (Cited "Fed. Cas.," with case number. Contains alphabetically cases from inferior federal courts through 1879.)

Federal Reporter and Federal Supplement. (Cited "Fed." or "F. [2d]" or "F. Supp.," preceded by volume number and followed by page number. After October 1, 1932, cases from district courts (and the Court of Claims) are reported separately in the *Federal Supplement,* while the second series of the *Federal Reporter* contains cases from the circuit courts of appeals.)

Reports of the Supreme Court of the United States. (Cited "U.S." preceded by volume number and followed by page number. For the period prior to 91 U.S., these reports are cited by the abbreviated names of the reporters—Dallas, Cranch, Wheaton, Peters, Howard, Black, and Wallace.)

Virginia Reports. (Described in text, *supra.* For early cases before the continuing series begins, see [in addition to Jefferson's *Reports*] Barton, Robert T. [ed.]. *Virginia Colonial Decisions.* 2 vols. Boston, 1909.)

ARTICLES AND BAR ASSOCIATION PROCEEDINGS

Adair, Douglass. "The New Thomas Jefferson," *William and Mary Quarterly* (3d series), Vol. III, No. 1 (January, 1946), 123–33.

Adams, Randolph G. "Thomas Jefferson, Librarian," in *Three Americanists,* Philadelphia, 1939, 69–96.

Anderson, Frank M. "Contemporary Opinion of the Virginia and Kentucky Resolutions," *American Historical Review,* Vol. V, No. 1 (October, 1899), 45–63; No. 2 (January, 1900), 225–52.

———. "The Enforcement of the Alien and Sedition Laws," *Annual Report of the American Historical Association for 1912,* 115–26.

Andrews, Charles M. "The Royal Disallowance," *Proceedings of the American Antiquarian Society,* (new series), Vol. XXIV, part 2 (October, 1914), 342–62.

Bailyn, Bernard. "Boyd's Jefferson: Notes for a Sketch," *The New England Quarterly,* Vol. XXXIII, No. 3 (September, 1960), 380–400.

Baker, J. H. "Coke's Note-books and the Sources of his Reports," *Cambridge Law Journal,* Vol. XXX, No. 1 (April, 1972), 59–86.

Balch, Thomas W. "The United States and the Expansion of the Law between Nations," *University of Pennsylvania Law Review,* Vol. LXIV, No. 2 (December, 1916), 113–40.

Beale, Joseph H. "The Study of American Legal History," *West Virginia Law Quarterly,* Vol. XXXIX, No. 2 (February, 1933), 95–103.

"Bolling of Virginia," *Virginia Magazine of History and Biography,* Vol. XXII, No. 1 (January, 1914), 103–107; No. 2 (April, 1914), 215–17; No. 3 (July, 1914), 331–33.

"Books in Colonial Virginia," *Virginia Magazine of History and Biography,* Vol. X, No. 4 (April, 1903), 389–405.

Briceland, Alan V. "Ephraim Kirby: Pioneer of American Law Reporting, 1789," *The American Journal of Legal History,* Vol. XVI, No. 4 (October, 1972), 297–319.

Brown, Elizabeth G. "Law and Government in the 'Louisiana Purchase': 1803–1804," *Wayne Law Review,* Vol. II, No. 3 (Summer, 1956), 169–89.

Bryan, John Stewart. "Report of Committee on Library and Legal Literature," in *Report of the Tenth Annual Meeting of the Virginia State Bar Association,* Richmond, 1898, 55–70.

Burdick, Francis M. "Can A Statute Be Well Written in English?" *New York State Bar Association Reports,* Vol. VI (1883), 130–34.

Burnett, Edmund C. "Note on American Negotiations for Commercial Treaties, 1776–1786," *American Historical Review,* Vol. XVI, No. 3 (April, 1911), 579–87.

Burns, Francis P. "The Graviers and the Faubourg Ste. Marie," *The Louisiana Historical Quarterly,* Vol. XXII, No. 2 (April, 1939), 385–427.

Butterfield, Lyman H. "The Jefferson-Adams Correspondence in The Adams Manuscript Trust," *The Library of Congress Quarterly Journal of Acquisitions,* Vol. V, No. 2 (February, 1948), 3–6.

———. "The Jubilee of Independence," *Virginia Magazine of History and Biography,* Vol. LXI, No. 4 (April, 1953), 119–40.

———, and Howard C. Rice, Jr. "Jefferson's Earliest Note to Maria Cosway with Some New Facts and Conjectures on his Broken Wrist," *William and Mary Quarterly* (3d series), Vol. V, No. 1 (January, 1948), 26–33.

Cabell, James Alston, "The Trial of Aaron Burr," *Proceedings of the New York State Bar Association,* Vol. XXIII (1900), 56–87.

Carpenter, William S. "Repeal of the Judiciary Act of 1801," *American Political Science Review,* Vol. IX, No. 3 (August, 1915), 519–28.

Chafee, Zechariah, Jr. "Colonial Courts and the Common Law," *Proceedings* of the Massachusetts Historical Society (1952) 132–59.

C[lover], R[alph] H. "The Rule of Law in Colonial Massachusetts," *University of Pennsylvania Law Review,* Vol. CVIII, No. 7 (May, 1969), 1001–36.

Coles, Harry L., Jr. "The Confirmation of Foreign Land Titles in Louisiana," *The Louisiana Historical Quarterly,* Vol. XXXVIII, No. 4 (October, 1955), 1–22.

Cooley, Thomas M. "The Acquisition of Louisiana," *Indiana Historical Society Publications,* Vol. II, No. 3 (1887), 65–93.

Cotterell, Mary. "Interregnum Law Reform: The Hale Commission of 1652,"

English Historical Review, Vol. LXXXIII, No. 329 (October, 1968), 689–704.

Cover, Robert M. Book Review, *Columbia Law Review,* Vol. LXX, No. 8 (December, 1970), 1475–94.

Crumrine, Boyd. "The Boundary Controversy between Pennsylvania and Virginia; 1748–1785," *Annals of the Carnegie Museum,* Vol. I, No. 4 (September, 1902), 505–24.

Dumbauld, Edward. "Independence under International Law," *American Journal of International Law,* Vol. LXX, No. 3 (July, 1976), 425–31.

———. "Judicial Interference with Litigation in Other Courts," *Dickinson Law Review,* Vol. LXXIV, No. 3 (Spring, 1970), 369–88.

———. "Pennsylvania's Contributions to the Law," in Homer T. Rosenberger (ed.), *Pennsylvania's Contributions to the Professions,* Gettysburg, Pa., 1964, 9–22.

———. "Some Modern Misunderstandings of Grotius," in *Volkenrechtelijke Opstellen ter ere van de Hoogleraren B. M. Telders, F. M. Baron van Asbeck en J. H. W. Verzijl,* Zwolle, 1957, 62–68.

Foster, Robert H. "Virginia Claims to Lands in Western Pennsylvania," *Pennsylvania Archives* (3d series), Vol. III (1896), 485–504.

Freund, Paul A. "On Presidential Privilege," *Harvard Law Review,* Vol. LXXXVIII, No. 1 (November, 1974), 13–39.

Ganter, Herbert L. "William Small, Jefferson's Beloved Teacher," *William and Mary Quarterly* (3d series), Vol. IV, No. 4 (October, 1947), 505–11.

Goebel, Julius. "King's Law and Local Custom in Seventeenth Century New England," *Columbia Law Review,* Vol. XXXI, No. 3 (March, 1931), 416–48.

Goodell, A. C., Jr. "An Early Constitutional Case in Massachusetts," *Harvard Law Review,* Vol. VII, No. 7 (February, 1894), 415–24.

Goodhart, Arthur L. "Precedent in English and Continental Law," *Law Quarterly Review,* Vol. L, No. 197 (January, 1934), 40–65.

Hall, Ford W. "The Common Law: An Account of Its Reception in the United States," *Vanderbilt Law Review,* Vol. IV, No. 4 (June, 1951), 791–825.

Hardy, Sally E. M. "Some Virginia Lawyers of the Past and Present," *Green Bag,* Vol. X, No. 1 (January, 1898), 12–25; No. 2 (February, 1898), 57–68; No. 3 (March, 1898), 109–21; No. 4 (April, 1898), 149–61.

Haskins, George L. "The Beginnings of Partible Inheritance in the American Colonies," *Yale Law Journal,* Vol. LI, No. 8 (June, 1942), 1280–1315.

Kean, Richard G. H. "Our Judicial System: Some of its History, and Some of its Defects," *Report of the First Annual Meeting of the Virginia State Bar Association* (1889), 139–59.

Keim, Clarence R. "Influence of Primogeniture and Entail in the Development of Virginia," *Abstracts of Theses,* University of Chicago, Humanistic Series, Vol. V (1928), 289–92.

———. "Primogeniture and Entail in Colonial Virginia," *William and Mary Quarterly* (3d series), Vol. XXV, No. 4 (October, 1968), 545–86.

Kenny, Courtney. "The Evolution of the Law of Blasphemy," *The Cambridge Law Journal,* Vol. I, No. 2 (1922), 127–42.

Klingelsmith, Margaret C. "Stonore Said," *University of Pennsylvania Law Review,* Vol. LXI, No. 6 (April, 1913), 381–96.

Latané, John H. "Jefferson's Influence on American Foreign Policy," *University of Virginia Alumni Bulletin* (3d series), Vol. XVII, No. 3 (July–August, 1924), 245–69.

Lemay, J. A. Leo. "Robert Bolling and the Bailment of Colonel Chiswell." *Early American Literature,* Vol. VI, No. 2 (Fall, 1971), 99–142.

Lerch, Alice H. "Who Was the Printer of Jefferson's Notes?" in Deoch Fulton (ed.), *Bookman's Holiday,* New York, 1943, 44–56.

Lewis, T. Ellis. "The History of Judicial Precedent," *Law Quarterly Review,* Vol. XLVI, No. 182 (April, 1930), 207–24; No. 183 (July, 1930), 341–60; Vol. XLVII, No. 187 (July, 1931), 411–27; Vol. XLVIII, No. 190 (April, 1932), 230–47.

McGuire, Francis H. "The General Court of Virginia," *Report of the Seventh Annual Meeting of the Virginia State Bar Association* (1895), 197–229.

Malone, Dumas. Book Review, *American Political Science Quarterly,* Vol. XX, No. 4 (November, 1926), 907–908.

Manchester, Anthony H. "The Reform of the Ecclesiastical Courts," *American Journal of Legal History,* Vol. X, No. 1 (January, 1966), 51–75.

Marraro, Howard R. (ed.). "Jefferson Letters Concerning the Settlement of Mazzei's Virginia Estate," *Mississippi Valley Historical Review,* Vol. XXX, No. 2 (September, 1943), 235–42.

———. "Unpublished Mazzei Letters to Jefferson," *William and Mary Quarterly* (3d series), Vol. I, No. 4 (October, 1944), 374–96.

Martin, William H. "Hening and the Statutes at Large," *Virginia Law Register,* Vol. XIII (new series), No. 1 (May, 1927), 25–37.

———. "Some Virginia Law Books in a Virginia Law Office," *Virginia Law Register* (new series), Vol. XII, No. 1 (May, 1926), 13–19; No. 2 (June, 1926), 74–84; No. 3 (July, 1926), 141–51; No. 4 (August, 1926), 193–202; No. 5 (September, 1926), 279–89; No. 6 (October, 1926), 321–30; No. 7 (November, 1926), 385–400; No. 8 (December, 1926), 478–90. [Cited by author's name]

Merriam, John M. "The Legislative History of the Ordinance of 1787," *Proceedings of the American Antiquarian Society,* Vol. V, No. 2 (April, 1888), 303–42.

Mullett, Charles F. "Coke and the American Revolution," *Economica,* Vol. XII, No. 38 (November, 1932), 457–71.

Nelson, Margaret V. "The Cases of the Judges: Fact or Fiction?" *Virginia Law Review,* Vol. XXXI, No. 1 (December, 1944), 243–55.

[Nixon, Richard M.]. "Symposium: *United States v. Nixon,*" *UCLA Law Review,* Vol. XXII, No. 1 (October, 1974), 1–140.

Nourse, G. B. "Law Reform under the Commonwealth and Protectorate," *Law Quarterly Review,* Vol. LXXV, No. 4 (October, 1959), 512–29.

Nussbaum, Frederick L. "American Tobacco and French Politics 1783–1789," *Political Science Quarterly,* Vol. XL, No. 4 (December, 1925), 561–93.

Padgett, James A. (ed.). "Some Documents Relating to the Batture Controversy," *The Louisiana Historical Quarterly,* Vol. XXIII, No. 3 (July, 1940), 679–732.

Pargellis, Stanley M. "The Procedure of the Virginia House of Burgesses," *William and Mary Quarterly* (2d series), Vol. VII, No. 2 (April, 1927), 83–86; No. 3 (July, 1927), 143–57.

Plucknett, Theodore F. T. "The Genesis of Coke's Reports," *Cornell Law Quarterly,* Vol. XXI, No. 2 (February, 1942), 190–213.

Prince, Walter F. "The First Criminal Code of Virginia," in *Annual Report* of the American Historical Association for 1899 (Washington, 1900), I, 309–63.

Proctor, Lucien B. "Jefferson and Marshall," *Albany Law Journal,* Vol. LIX (March 25, 1899), 289–93.

Randolph, Edmund. "Edmund Randolph's Essay on the Revolutionary History of Virginia (1774–1782)," *Virginia Magazine of History and Biography,* Vol. XLIII, No. 2 (April, 1935), 113–38; No. 3 (July, 1935), 209–32; No. 4 (October, 1935), 294–315; Vol. XLIV, No. 1 (January, 1936), 35–50; No. 2 (April, 1936), 105–15; No. 3 (July, 1936), 222–31; No. 4 (October, 1936), 312–22; Vol. XLV, No. 1 (January, 1937), 46–47.

Rhodes, Irwin S. "What Really Happened to the Jefferson Subpoenas?" *American Bar Association Journal,* Vol. LX, No. 1 (January, 1974), 52–54.

Rice, Howard C., Jr. "A French Source of Jefferson's Plan for the Prison at Richmond," *Journal of the Society of Architectural Historians,* Vol. XII (December, 1953), 28–30.

Robert, Joseph C. "The Hon. William Wirt, The Many-Sided Attorney General," in Supreme Court Historical Society *Yearbook 1976,* 51–60.

Robinson, R. "Anticipations under the Commonwealth of Changes in the Law," in Ernst Freund, William E. Mikell, and John H. Wigmore (eds.), *Select Essays in Anglo-American Legal History,* 3 vols., Boston, 1907–1909, I, 467–91.

Rose, U. M. "The Case between Jefferson and Marshall," *Colorado Bar Association Reports,* Vol. IV (1901), 123–56.

Ross, William E. "History of Virginia Codification," *Virginia Law Register,* Vol. XI, No. 2 (June, 1905), 79–101.

Schmidt, Gustavus. "The Batture Question," *The Louisiana Law Journal,* Vol. I, No. 2 (August, 1841), 85–151.

Shipton, Clifford K. "The Locus of Authority in Colonial Massachusetts," in George A. Billias (ed.), *Law and Authority in Colonial America,* Barre, Vt., 1953, 136–48.

Smith, David Eugene. "Thomas Jefferson and Mathematics," in *The Poetry of Mathematics and Other Essays,* New York, 1934, 49–70.

Smith, Eugene. "Edward Livingston and the Louisiana Codes," *Columbia Law Review,* Vol. II, No. 1 (January, 1902), 24–36.

Smith, Goldwin. "The Reform of the Laws of England 1640–1660," *University of Toronto Quarterly,* Vol. X, No. 4 (July, 1941), 469–81.

Smith, Joseph H. "New Light on the doctrine of judicial precedent in early America: 1607–1776," in John N. Hazard and Wenceslas J. Wagner (eds.), *Legal Thought in the United States of America Under Contemporary Pressure,* Brussels, 1970, 9–39.

Staples, Waller R. "History of the Old County Court System of Virginia, as It Existed before the Late War between the States," *Virginia State Bar Association Reports,* Vol. VII (1894), 127–56.

Stone, Frederick D. "The Ordinance of 1787," *Pennsylvania Magazine of History and Biography,* Vol. XIII, No. 3 (October, 1889), 309–40.

[Story, Joseph]. "Christianity a Part of the Common Law," *American Jurist and Law Magazine,* Vol. IX (April, 1833), 346–48.

Thompson, D. P. "A Talk with Jefferson," *Harper's Magazine,* Vol. XXVI, No. 156 (May, 1863), 833–35.

Thorne, Samuel E. "The Assize Utrum and Canon Law in England," *Columbia Law Review,* Vol. XXXIII, No. 3 (March, 1933), 428–36.

Trent, W. P. "The Case of Josiah Philips," *American Historical Review,* Vol. I, No. 3 (April, 1896), 444–54.

Turner, Jesse. "A Phantom Precedent," *American Law Review,* Vol. XLVIII (May–June, 1914), 321–44.

Turner, Kathryn [Conway]. "The Midnight Judges," *University of Pennsylvania Law Review,* Vol. CIX, No. 4 (February, 1961), 494–523.

Warren, Charles. "The Mississippi River and the Treaty Clause of the Constitution," *George Washington Law Review,* Vol. II, No. 3 (March, 1934), 271–302.

Waterman, Julian S. "Mansfield and Blackstone's Commentaries," *University of Chicago Law Review,* Vol. I, No. 4 (March, 1934), 549–71.

———. "Thomas Jefferson and Blackstone's Commentaries," *Illinois Law Review,* Vol. XXVII, No. 6 (February, 1933), 629–59.

Wiltse, Charles M. "Thomas Jefferson on the Law of Nations," *American Journal of International Law,* Vol. XXIX, No. 1 (January, 1935), 66–81.

BOOKS

Abernethy, Thomas P. *The Burr Conspiracy.* New York, 1954.

———. *Western Lands and the American Revolution.* New York, 1937.

Abbott, Wilbur C. (ed.). *The Writings and Speeches of Oliver Cromwell.* 4 vols. Cambridge, Mass., 1938–47.

Adams, Charles Francis (ed.). *The Works of John Adams.* 10 vols. Boston, 1850–56.

——. *Memoirs of John Quincy Adams.* 12 vols. Philadelphia, 1874–77.

Adams, Henry. *A History of the United States during the Administration of Thomas Jefferson.* 4 vols. New York, 1889–90.

——. *The Writings of Albert Gallatin.* 3 vols. Philadelphia, 1879.

Adams, John. *A Defence of the Constitutions of Government of the United States of America.* 3 vols. London, 1787–88.

Alien and Sedition Laws. Debates in the House of Delegates of Virginia in December, 1798, on Resolutions before the House on the Acts of Congress Called the Alien and Sedition Laws (62d Cong., 2d sess., S. Doc. No. 875). Washington, 1912.

Allen, John W. *English Political Thought 1603–1660.* Vol. I, 1603–44. London, 1938.

——. *A History of Political Thought in the Sixteenth Century.* New York, 1928.

Arnson, Nancy M. "William Sheppard (1595–1674): Law Reformer." (M.A. thesis, University of Maryland, 1974.)

Arrowood, Charles F. *Thomas Jefferson and Education in a Republic.* New York, 1930.

Austin, Benjamin. *Observations on the Pernicious Practice of the Law.* Boston, 1786.

Bacon, Francis. *Works.* Collected and edited by James Spedding, Robert Leslie Ellis, and Douglas Denon Heath. 14 vols. London, 1858.

Bailyn, Bernard. *The Ideological Origins of the American Revolution.* Cambridge, Mass., 1967.

Ballagh, James C. (ed.). *The Letters of Richard Henry Lee.* 2 vols. New York, 1911–14.

Bancroft, George. *History of the Formation of the Constitution of the United States of America.* 2 vols. New York, 1882.

Barrett, Jay A. *Evolution of the Ordinance of 1787 with an Account of the Earlier Plans for the Government of the Northwest Territory.* New York, 1891.

Beaney, William M. *The Right to Counsel in American Courts.* Ann Arbor, Mich., 1955.

Beccaria, Cesare B. *Dei delitti e delle pene.* [Leghorn, 1764].

Bemis, Samuel F. *The American Secretaries of State and their Diplomacy.* 10 vols. New York, 1927–29.

Bentham, Jeremy. *A Comment on the Commentaries: A Criticism of William Blackstone's Commentaries on the Laws of England.* Oxford, 1928.

Berger, Raoul. *Impeachment: the Constitutional Problems.* Cambridge, Mass., 1973.

Beveridge, Albert J. *The Life of John Marshall.* 4 vols. Boston, 1916–19.

[Beverley, Robert]. *The History and Present State of Virginia, in Four Parts. By a Native and Inhabitant of the Place.* London, 1705; 2d ed. London, 1722.

Blackstone, Sir William. *Commentaries on the Laws of England.* 4 vols. Oxford, 1765–69; Philadelphia, 1771–72. (Jefferson's set of the Oxford, 1770, edition is in the Library of Congress. This is the edition cited in this book unless otherwise noted.)

Bosher, Robert S. *The Making of the Restoration Settlement*. New York, 1951.

Boyd, Julian P. *The Declaration of Independence*. Washington, 1943; 2d ed. Princeton, 1945.

———. *Number 7: Alexander Hamilton's Secret Attempts to Control American Foreign Policy*. Princeton, 1964.

Bracton on the Laws and Customs of England. Translated by Samuel E. Thorne. 4 vols. to date. Cambridge, Mass., 1968–77.

Brady, Joseph P. *The Trial of Aaron Burr*. New York, 1913.

Brant, Irving. *James Madison*. 6 vols. Indianapolis, 1941–61.

Brigance, William N. *A History and Criticism of American Public Address*. 2 vols. New York, 1943.

Brock, Robert K. *Archibald Cary of Ampthill*. Richmond, 1937.

Brown, David Paul. *The Forum; or Forty Years Full Practice at the Philadelphia Bar*. 2 vols. Philadelphia, 1856.

Brown, Everett S. *The Constitutional History of the Louisiana Purchase 1803–1812*. Berkeley, Calif., 1920.

——— (ed.). *William Plumer's Memorandum of Proceedings in the United States Senate 1803–1807*. New York, 1923.

Brown, Louise F. *The Political Activities of the Baptists and Fifth Monarchy Men In England During the Interregnum*. Washington, 1912.

Brown, William G. *The Life of Oliver Ellsworth*. New York, 1905.

Bruce, Philip Alexander. *Institutional History of Virginia in the Seventeenth Century*. 2 vols. New York, 1910.

Bryce, James. *The Holy Roman Empire*. 5th ed. London, 1904.

Burgh, James. *Political Disquisitions*. 3 vols. Philadelphia, 1775.

Burk, John D. *The History of Virginia, from its First Settlement to the Present Day*. 4 vols. Petersburg, Va., 1804–16.

Burnett, Edmund C. (ed.). *Letters of Members of the Continental Congress*. 8 vols. Washington, 1921–36.

Caldwell, Lynton K. *The Administrative Theories of Hamilton and Jefferson*. Chicago, 1944.

Cam, Helen M. (ed.). *Selected Historical Essays of F. W. Maitland*. Cambridge, Eng., 1957.

Campbell, John. *The Lives of the Chief Justices of England*. 2 vols. London, 1849.

Cardozo, Benjamin N. *The Nature of the Judicial Process*. New Haven, 1921.

Carter, Clarence E. (ed.). *The Territorial Papers of the United States*. Vol. IX, *The Territory of Orleans 1803–1812*. Washington, 1940.

Chafee, Zechariah, Jr. *The Blessings of Liberty*. Philadelphia, 1956.

———. *Three Human Rights in the Constitution of 1787*. Lawrence, Kan., 1956.

Chitwood, Oliver. *Justice in Colonial Virginia*. Baltimore, 1905.

Chumbley, George L. *Colonial Justice in Virginia*. Richmond, 1938.

Clark, Charles. *A Summary of Colonial Law*. London, 1834.

Cobb, Sanford H. *The Rise of Religious Liberty in America.* New York, 1902.

Colbourn, Harold Trevor. *The Lamp of Experience.* Chapel Hill, N.C., 1965.

———. "The Saxon Heritage: Thomas Jefferson Looks at English History." (Typewritten thesis, Johns Hopkins University, 1953.)

Coles, Edward. *History of the Ordinance of 1787.* Philadelphia, 1856.

Conant, James B. *Thomas Jefferson and the Development of American Public Education.* Berkeley, 1963.

Conway, Moncure D. *Omitted Chapters of History Disclosed in the Life and Papers of Edmund Randolph.* New York, 1888.

The Correspondence between Citizen Genet, Minister of the French Republic, to the United States of North America, and the Officers of the Federal Government. Philadelphia, 1793.

Corwin, Edward S. *John Marshall and the Constitution.* New Haven, 1919.

Cotton, Joseph P., Jr. *The Constitutional Decisions of John Marshall.* 2 vols. New York, 1905.

Coxe, Brinton. *An Essay on Judicial Power and Unconstitutional Legislation, Being a Commentary on Parts of the Constitution of the United States.* Philadelphia, 1893.

Cummings, Homer S., and Carl McFarland. *Federal Justice.* New York, 1937.

Cutler, William P., and Julia P. *Life Journals and Correspondence of Rev. Manasseh Cutler, LL.D.* 2 vols. Cincinnati, 1888.

Dallas, George M. *Life and Writings of Alexander James Dallas.* Philadelphia, 1871.

Dargo, George. *Jefferson's Louisiana: Politics and the Clash of Legal Traditions.* Cambridge, Mass., 1975.

Daveiss, J. H. *View of the President's Conduct Concerning the Conspiracy of 1806.* Frankfort, Ky., 1807.

Davis, J. C. Bancroft. *Appendix to the Reports of the Decisions of the Supreme Court of the United States from September 24, 1789, to the End of October Term, 1888.* New York, 1902.

Davis, Matthew L. *Memoirs of Aaron Burr.* 2 vols. New York, 1836–37.

Davis, Richard B. *Correspondence of Thomas Jefferson and Francis Walker Gilmer 1814–1826.* Columbia, S.C., 1946.

Dawson, John P. *The Oracles of the Law.* Ann Arbor, Mich., 1968.

Debates and Other Proceedings of the Convention of Virginia, Convened at Richmond, on Monday the 2d Day of June, 1788, for the Purpose of Deliberating on the Constitution Recommended by the Grand Federal Convention. 3 vols. Petersburg, Va., 1788–89.

Debates in the Congress of the United States, on the Bill for Repealing the Law "For the More Convenient Organization of the Courts of the United States"; during the First Session of the Seventh Congress. And a List of the Yeas and Nays on that Interesting Subject. Albany, 1802.

The Defence of Young and Minns, Printers to the State, before the Committee of the House of Representatives. Boston, 1805.

275

Derbigny, Pierre Auguste Charles Bourguignon. *Case laid before Counsel for their Opinion, on the Claim to the Batture, situated in front of the Suburb St. Mary.* New Orleans, 1807. (Dated August 21, 1807. LC; Sowerby #3495.)

————. *Mémoire à Consulter, sur la Réclamation de la Batture, située en face du Faubourg Sainte-Marie de la Nouvelle-Orleans.* New Orleans, 1807. (English version on right hand pages.)

————. *Réfutation du Mémoire en forme de Consultation, Redigé par Mr. Duponceau.* New Orleans, 1808.

Dickinson, John. *Administrative Justice and the Supremacy of Law in the United States.* Cambridge, Mass., 1927.

Documentary History of the Constitution of the United States of America. 5 vols. Washington, 1894–1905.

[Douglas, D.]. *The Biographical History of Sir William Blackstone.* London, 1782.

Duponceau, Peter S. *Mémoire en forme de Consultation, en réponse à celle de M. Derbigny, au sujet des Prétentions du Gouvernement des Etats-Unis sur l'Alluvion du fleuve Mississipi, au devant du Faubourg Sainte-Marie, près la Nouvelle-Orléans, communément appelée La Batture des Jesuites.* New Orleans, 1808. (Dated July 26, 1808. LC; NA. Sowerby #3494.)

————. *A Review of the Cause of the New Orleans Batture and of the Discussions that have taken place respecting it; containing Answers to the late Publications of Messrs. Thierry & Derbigny on that subject.* Philadelphia, 1809. (Preface dated February 27, 1809.) [*Review*]

Eckenrode, Hamilton J. *The Randolphs.* Indianapolis, 1946.

————. *The Revolution in Virginia.* Boston, 1916.

Eden, William. *Principles of Penal Law.* London, 1772.

Elliot, Jonathan (ed.). *The Debates in the Several State Conventions on the Adoption of the Federal Constitution.* 5 vols. Washington, 1827–45.

Evans, Charles. *Report of the Trial of the Honorable Samuel Chase.* Baltimore, 1805.

Eysinga, Willem J. M. van. *Sparsa Collecta.* Leiden, 1958.

Farrand, Max. (ed.) *The Laws and Liberties of Massachusetts.* Cambridge, Mass., 1929. (Reprinted from the copy of the 1648 edition in the Henry E. Huntington Library.)

————. *The Legislation of Congress for the Government of the Organized Territories of the United States. 1789–1895.* Newark, N.J., 1896.

————. *The Records of the Federal Convention of 1787.* 4 vols. New Haven, 1911–37.

Farrar, Timothy. *Report of the Case of the Trustees of Dartmouth College against William H. Woodward.* Portsmouth, N.H., 1819.

Fifoot, Cecil H. S. *Lord Mansfield.* Oxford, 1936.

Figgis, John N. *Studies of Political Thought from Gerson to Grotius.* 2d ed. Cambridge, Eng., 1916.

Findley, William. *History of the Insurrection in the Four Western Counties of Pennsylvania.* Philadelphia, 1796.

Flaherty, David H. (ed.). *Essays in the History of Early American Law*. Chapel Hill, N.C., 1969.

Flippin, Percy S. *The Royal Government in Virginia*. New York, 1919.

Ford, Worthington C. *The Controversy between Lieutenant-Governor Spotswood, and his Council and the House of Burgesses, on the appointment of Judges on Commissions of Oyer and Terminer. 1718.* Brooklyn, N.Y., 1891.

Fortescue, G. K. (ed.). *Catalogue of the Pamphlets, Books, Newspapers, and Manuscripts relating to the Civil War, the Commonwealth and Restoration, Collected by George Thomason, 1640-1661.* 2 vols. London, 1908.

Frank, Joseph. *The Levellers*. Cambridge, Mass., 1955.

Friedman, Leon, and Fred L. Israel (eds.). *The Justices of the United States Supreme Court 1789-1969 Their Lives and Major Opinions*. New York, 1969.

Friendly, Henry J. *Benchmarks*. Chicago, 1967.

Gardiner, Samuel R. *The Fall of the Monarchy of Charles I.* 2 vols. London, 1882.

———. *History of the Commonwealth and Protectorate*. 3 vols. London, 1897–1903.

———. *History of the Great Civil War*. London, 1886–91.

———. *The Personal Government of Charles I.* 2 vols. London, 1877.

Gayarré, Charles. *History of Louisiana: The American Domination*. New York, 1866.

Giesecke, Albert A. *American Commercial Legislation before 1789*. New York, 1910.

[Gilbert, Sir Geoffrey]. *The Law of Evidence*. 2d. ed. London, 1760.

Goebel, Julius. *History of the Supreme Court of the United States: Antecedents and Beginnings to 1801*. New York, 1971.

Gregg, Pauline. *Free-born John*. London, 1961.

Grigsby, Hugh Blair. *Discourse on the Life and Character of the Honorable Littleton Waller Tazewell*. Norfolk, 1860.

———. *The History of the Virginia Federal Convention of 1788, with Some Account of the Eminent Virginians of That Era Who Were Members of the Body*. 2 vols. Richmond, 1890–91. (Originally delivered February 28, 1858; amplified by the author and edited by R. A. Brock.)

———. *The Virginia Convention of 1776*. Richmond, 1855.

Hale, Sir Matthew. *The History of the Common Law*. 4th ed. London, 1779.

Haller, William. *The Rise of Puritanism*. New York, 1938.

——— (ed.). *Tracts on Liberty in the Puritan Revolution 1638-1647*. 3 vols. New York, 1934.

———, and Godfrey Davis (eds.). *The Leveller Tracts 1647-1653*. New York, 1944.

Hamlin, Paul M. *Legal Education in Colonial New York*. New York, 1939.

Harbaugh, William H. *Lawyer's Lawyer: The Life of John W. Davis*. New York, 1973.

The Harleian Miscellany; or, a Collection of Scarce, Curious, and Entertaining Tracts, as well in Manuscript as in Print, Found in the Late Earl of Oxford's Library. 12 vols. London, 1808–11. (First published, 8 vols. 1744–46).

[Harrington, James]. *Common-Wealth of Oceana.* London, 1757. (Jefferson's copy in Library of Congress.)

[Harrison, Fairfax]. *Virginia Land Grants.* Richmond, 1925.

Hartwell [Henry], [James] Blair, and [Edward] Chilton. *The Present State of Virginia, and the College.* London, 1727; Williamsburg, 1940 (Hunter D. Farish, ed.).

Harvey, Alexander M. *Jefferson and the American Constitution.* Topeka, 1926.

Haskins, George L. *Law and Authority in Early Massachusetts.* New York, 1960.

Hatcher, William B. *Edward Livingston.* University, La., 1940.

Hazelton, John H. *The Declaration of Independence: Its History.* New York, 1906.

Henderson, John C. *Thomas Jefferson's Views on Public Education.* New York, 1890.

Hening, William Waller. *The New Virginia Justice.* Richmond, 1795.

Henkin, Louis. *Foreign Affairs and the Constitution.* Mineola, N.Y., 1972.

Henry, William W. *Patrick Henry Life, Correspondence and Speeches.* 3 vols. New York, 1891.

Hill, Christopher. *Puritanism and Revolution.* London, 1958.

Hill, Helen. *George Mason, Constitutionalist.* Cambridge, Mass., 1938.

Hobart, Henry. *The Reports of . . . Henry Hobart. . . .* 5th ed. London, 1724.

Holmes, Oliver Wendell, Jr. *Collected Legal Papers.* New York, 1920.

Holt, J. C. *Magna Carta.* Cambridge, Eng., 1965.

Honeywell, Roy J. *The Educational Work of Thomas Jefferson.* Cambridge, Mass., 1931.

Howard, A. E. Dick. *The Road from Runnymede.* Charlottesville, Va., 1968.

Howe, Mark DeWolfe. *Readings in American Legal History.* Cambridge, Mass., 1949.

Hunt, Charles H. *Life of Edward Livingston.* New York, 1864.

Hunt, Gaillard (ed.). *The Writings of James Madison.* 9 vols. New York, 1900–10.

Hutchinson, John A. *Land Titles in Virginia and West Virginia.* Cincinnati, 1887.

Impeachment: Selected Materials. (93d Cong., 1st sess., House Doc. No. 93–7), Washington, 1973.

Inderwick, Frederick A. *The Interregnum.* London, 1891.

Jaeger, Werner. *Paideia: the Ideals of Greek Culture.* Translated by Gilbert Highet. 3 vols. New York, 1943–45.

James, Margaret, and Maureen Weinstock (eds.), *England during the Interregnum.* London, 1935.

Jenkinson, Isaac, *Aaron Burr, His Personal and Political Relations with Thomas Jefferson and Alexander Hamilton.* Richmond, Ind., 1902.

Jenks, Edward. *The Constitutional Experiments of the Commonwealth.* Cambridge, Eng., 1890.

Jensen, Merrill. *The Articles of Confederation.* Madison, 1940; 2d ed., 1948.

Johnson, Samuel. *Taxation no Tyranny; an Answer to the Resolutions and Address of the American Congress.* London, 1775.

Johnston, Henry P. (ed.). *Correspondence and Public Papers of John Jay.* 4 vols. New York, 1890–93.

Jones, E. Alfred. *American Members of the Inns of Court.* London, 1924.

Justinian. *Corpus Juris Civilis.* Edited by Theodor Mommsen, Paul Krieger, Rudolf Schoell, and Wilhelm Kroll. 3 vols. 15th ed. Berlin, 1928.

Kames, Henry Home. *Historical Law-Tracts.* 2 vols. Edinburgh, 1758; 2d ed., 1776.

———. *Principles of Equity.* London and Edinburgh, 1760.

Keeton, George W. *English Law: The Judicial Contribution.* Newton Abbot [England], 1974.

Kimball, Fiske. *Thomas Jefferson Architect.* Boston, 1916.

Kingsbury, Susan M. (ed.). *The Records of the Virginia Company of London.* 4 vols. Washington, 1906–35.

Koch, Adrienne. *The Philosophy of Thomas Jefferson.* New York, 1943.

Labaree, Leonard. *Royal Instructions to British Colonial Governors 1670–1776.* 2 vols. New York, 1935.

Lawson, John D. (ed.). *American State Trials.* 16 vols. St. Louis, 1914–28.

Lehmann, Karl. *Thomas Jefferson, American Humanist.* New York, 1947.

Levy, Leonard. *Origins of the Fifth Amendment: The Right against Self-Incrimination.* New York, 1968.

Lilburne, John. *The Ivst Mans Ivstification.* [London, 1646.]

———. *The Legall Fundamentall Liberties of the People of England Revived, Asserted, and Vindicated.* [London, 1649.]

Link, Arthur S. *Wilson: The Road to the White House.* Princeton, 1947.

Livingston, Edward. *Address to the People of the United States, on the Measures Pursued by the Executive with respect to the Batture at New Orleans.* New Orleans, 1808. [*Address*]

———. *An Answer to Mr. Jefferson's Justification of his Conduct in the Case of the New Orleans Batture.* Philadelphia, 1813. [*Answer*]

———. *Examination of the Title of the United States to the Land Called the Batture.* (Dated December 10, 1807, and annexed to Livingston's *Address.*)

Locke, John. *Two Treatises of Government.* Edited by Peter Laslett. 2d ed. Cambridge, Eng., 1963. (First published London, 1690.)

Lockmiller, David A. *Sir William Blackstone.* Chapel Hill, N.C., 1938.

Lowrie, Walter, and Matthew S. Clarke (eds.). *American State Papers. Foreign Relations.* 4 vols. Washington, 1832.

———, and Walter S. Franklin (eds.). *American State Papers. Miscellaneous.* Vol. I. Washington, 1834.

———, and Walter S. Franklin (eds.). *American State Papers. Public Lands.* 2 vols. Washington, 1834.

McCaleb, Walter F. *The Aaron Burr Conspiracy.* 2d ed. New York, 1936.

McClellan, James. *Joseph Story and the American Constitution.* Norman, 1971.

Macdonald, George A. *How Successful Lawyers Were Educated*. New York, 1896.

McKechnie, William S. *Magna Carta*. 2d ed. Glasgow, 1914.

McRee, Griffith J. *Life and Correspondence of James Iredell*. 2 vols. New York, 1857–58.

Maestro, Marcello T. *Cesare Beccaria and the Origins of Penal Reform*. Philadelphia, 1973.

Maitland, Frederic W. *English Law and the Renaissance*. Cambridge, Eng., 1901.

———. *Equity and the Forms of Action at Common Law*. Cambridge, Eng., 1909.

Mayo, Bernard. *Thomas Jefferson and his Unknown Brother Randolph*. Charlottesville, Va., 1942.

Mays, David J. *Edmund Pendleton*. 2 vols. Cambridge, Mass., 1952.

Meade, Robert D. *Patrick Henry*. 2 vols. Philadelphia, 1957, 1969.

Meigs, William M. *The Growth of the Constitution in the Federal Convention of 1787*. Philadelphia, 1900.

Miller, Elmer I. *The Legislature of the Province of Virginia and Its Internal Development*. New York, 1907.

Miller, Hunter. *Treaties and Other International Acts of the United States of America*. Vols. I and II. Washington, 1931. [Treaties]

Minor, Berkeley, and James F. Minor (eds.). *Legislative History of the University of Virginia as set forth in the Acts of the General Assembly of Virginia 1803–1927*. Charlottesville, Va., 1938.

Minot, George R. *The History of the Insurrections, in Massachusetts, In the Year MDCCLXXXVI, and the Rebellion Consequent Thereon*. Worcester, Mass., 1788.

Montesquieu, Charles Louis de. *L'Esprit des Lois*. 2 vols. Paris, 1748.

Moreau de Lislet, Louis Casimir Elisabeth. *Examen de la Sentence rendue dans la Cause entre Jean Gravier et la Ville de la Nouvelle-Orléans*. New Orleans, 1807.

———. *Examination of the Judgment Rendered in the Cause between Jean Gravier and the City of New Orleans*. Washington, 1809.

———. *Mémoire au soutien des droits des Etats-unis à la Batture du Faubourg Ste. Marie*. (Dated and signed, New Orleans, October 31, 1808. MS in National Archives, RG 59 E. 116.) [*Mémoire*]

Mott, Rodney D. *Due Process of Law*. Indianapolis, 1926.

Mullett, Charles F. *Fundamental Law and the American Revolution*. New York, 1933.

Neal, Daniel. *The History of the Puritans or Protestant Non-Conformists*. 2 vols. London, 1754.

Nelson, Margaret V. *A Study of Judicial Review in Virginia 1789–1928*. New York, 1947.

Newton, A. Edward. *The Greatest Book in the World and Other Papers*. Boston, 1925.

Nock, Albert Jay. *Jefferson*. New York, 1926.

Nugent, Nell M. *Cavaliers and Pioneers. Abstracts of Virginia Land Patents and Grants 1623–1800.* Richmond, 1934.

Oster, John E. *The Political and Economic Doctrines of John Marshall.* New York, 1914.

Padover, Saul K. *Jefferson.* New York, 1942.

Palmer, William P. (ed.). *Calendar of Virginia State Papers and Other Manuscripts.* Vols. I and II. Richmond, 1875–1881.

Penniman, Josiah H. *A Book about the English Bible.* New York, 1919.

Pitamic, Leonidas. *A Treatise on the State.* Baltimore, 1933.

Plucknett, Theodore F. T., and J. L. Barton (eds.). *St. German's Doctor and Student.* (Selden Society Publications, No. 91.) London, 1975.

Pocock, J. G. A. *The Ancient Constitution and the Feudal Law.* 2d ed. New York, 1967.

Pollock, Sir Frederick. *Essays in Jurisprudence and Ethics.* London, 1882.

———. *Essays in the Law.* London, 1922.

———. *Oxford Lectures and Other Discourses.* London, 1890.

Pound, Roscoe. *Jurisprudence.* 5 vols. St. Paul, 1956.

Prall, Stuart E. *The Agitation for Law Reform During the Puritan Revolution 1640–1660.* The Hague, 1966.

[Priestley, Joseph]. *An Essay on the First Principles of Government and on the Nature of Political, Civil, and Religious Liberty.* 2d ed. London, 1771.

Pufendorf, Samuel. *De Jure Naturae et Gentium Libri Octo.* 2 vols. Oxford, 1934. (First published at Lund, Sweden, in 1672.)

Randolph, Edmund J. *A Letter of His Excellency Edmund Randolph, Esquire, on the Federal Constitution.* [Richmond, 1787.]

———. *Political Truth: or Animadversions on the Past and Present State of Public Affairs; with an Inquiry into the Truth of the Charges Preferred against Mr. Randolph.* Philadelphia, 1796.

———. *A Vindication of Mr. Randolph's Resignation.* Philadelphia, 1795.

Rankin, Hugh F. *Criminal Trial Proceedings in the General Court of Colonial Virginia.* Charlottesville, 1965.

Reed, Alfred Z. *Training for the Public Profession of the Law.* New York, 1921.

Reeves, John. *History of English Law.* 2 vols. London, 1784–85.

Rhodes, Irwin S. *Brief on True Rulings of Chief Justice Marshall in the Case of the United States v. Aaron Burr.* Washington, 1973. (Duplicated copy of brief filed with Court of Appeals for the District of Columbia in *Nixon* v. *Sirica*, No. 73–1962.)

——— (ed.). *The Papers of John Marshall.* 2 vols. Norman, 1969. [*Marshall Papers*]

Richardson, James D. (ed.). *A Compilation of the Messages and Papers of the Presidents 1789–1897.* Vol. I. Washington, 1896. [*Messages of the Presidents*]

Robb, Arthur. "The Founding of Washington City." Washington, 1936. (Typewritten manuscript in Department of Justice Library.)

Robertson, David. *Reports of the Trials of Colonel Aaron Burr, (Late Vice President of the United States,) for Treason, and for a Misdemeanor.* 2 vols. Philadelphia, 1808.

Robertson, James A. *Louisiana under the Rule of Spain, France, and the United States 1785–1807.* 2 vols. Cleveland, 1911.

Robertson, Wyndham [and R. A. Brock]. *Pocahontas . . . and her Descendants.* Richmond, 1887.

Ross, Ian. *Lord Kames (1696–1782) and the Scotland of his Day.* Oxford, 1972.

Rowland, Dunbar (ed.). *Official Letter Books of W. C. C. Claiborne.* 6 vols. Jackson, Miss., 1917.

Rushworth, John. *Historical Collections.* 8 vols. London, 1721–22. (This edition, belonging to Jefferson, is in the Library of Congress. First published 1659–1701.)

Scott, Arthur P. *Criminal Law in Colonial Virginia.* Chicago, 1930.

Scott, Austin W. *Fundamentals of Procedure in Actions at Law.* New York, 1922.

———, and Robert B. Kent. *Cases and Other Materials on Civil Procedure.* Boston, 1967.

Scott, James Brown. *Sovereign States and Suits before Arbitral Tribunals and Courts of Justice.* New York, 1925.

Scott, Sir Walter (ed.). *A Collection of Scarce and Valuable Tracts. . . .* 2d ed. 13 vols. London, 1809–15. [Somers Tracts]

Sears, Louis M. *Jefferson and the Embargo.* Durham, N.C., 1927.

Selden, John. *The Table Talk of John Selden.* Edited by Samuel H. Reynolds. Oxford, 1892.

Setzler, Edwin B., Edwin L., and Hubert H. *The Jefferson Anglo-Saxon Grammar and Reader.* New York, 1938.

Shaw, William A. *A History of the English Church during the Civil Wars and under the Commonwealth.* London, 1900.

Sheppard, William. *Englands Balme.* London, 1657.

———. *An Epitome of All the Common & Statute Laws of this Nation, Now in Force.* London, 1656.

———. *Touch-stone of Common Assurances.* 6th ed. by Edward Hilliard. London, 1791.

Shipman, Benjamin J. *Handbook of Common-Law Pleading.* 3d ed. St. Paul, 1923.

Shirley, John M. *The Dartmouth College Case.* St. Louis, 1879.

Sidney, Algernon. *Discourses concerning Government.* London, 1648; London, 1763. (Jefferson's copy of latter edition is in LC.)

Smith, Joseph H. *Appeals to the Privy Council from the American Plantations.* New York, 1950.

Smith, Samuel Harrison. *Memoir of the Life, Character, and Writings of Thomas Jefferson.* Washington, 1827.

———, and Thomas Lloyd. *Trial of Samuel Chase.* 2 vols. Washington, 1805.

The Speeches at Full Length of Mr. Van Ness, Mr. Caines, the Attorney-General, Mr. Harrison and General Hamilton in the Great Cause of the People against

Harry Croswell on an Indictment for a Libel on Thomas Jefferson, President of the United States. New York, 1804.

Story, William W. *Life and Letters of Joseph Story.* 2 vols. Boston, 1851.

———. *The Miscellaneous Writings of Joseph Story.* Boston, 1852.

Stubbs, William. *Seventeen Lectures on the Study of Medieval and Modern History.* 3d ed. Oxford, 1900.

Sutherland, Arthur E. *Constitutionalism in America.* New York, 1965.

———. *The Law at Harvard.* Cambridge, Mass., 1967.

Tanner, Joseph R. *English Constitutional Conflicts of the Seventeenth Century, 1603–1689.* Cambridge, Eng., 1928.

[Thierry, Jean Baptiste Simon]. *Examen des Droits des Etats-Unis et des Prétentions de Mr. Edouard Livingston sur la Batture en face du Faubourg Ste. Marie.* New Orleans, 1808. (Dated October 15, 1808, not October 22, 1808, as stated in Sowerby #3477.)

———. *Examination of the Claim of the United States, and of the Pretentions of Edward Livingston, Esq. to the Batture in Front of the Suburb St. Mary.* New Orleans, 1808.

———. *Reply to Mr. Duponceau.* (New Orleans, 1809 [?]. Dated New-Orleans, 16th May 1809. No place or date of publication shown.)

Thomas, Charles M. *American Neutrality in 1793.* New York, 1931.

Thomas, Roland. *Richard Price Philosopher and Apostle of Liberty.* London, 1924.

Thompson, Faith. *The First Century of Magna Carta.* Minneapolis, 1925.

———. *Magna Carta: Its Role in the Making of the English Constitution 1300–1629.* Minneapolis, 1948.

Thorne, Samuel E. *Sir Edward Coke 1552–1952.* London, 1957.

Thurlow, Constance E., and Francis L. Berkeley, Jr. *The Jefferson Papers of the University of Virginia.* Charlottesville, Va., 1950.

Tucker, St. George. *Blackstone's Commentaries: with Notes of Reference to the Constitution and Laws, of the Federal Government of the United States; and of the Commonwealth of Virginia.* 5 vols. Philadelphia, 1803. [Tucker's Blackstone]

Wallaston, G. Woods. *Coronation Claims.* 2d ed. London, 1910.

Wambaugh, Eugene. *The Study of Cases.* 2d ed. Boston, 1894.

Warden, Lewis C. *The Life of Blackstone.* Charlottesville, Va., 1938.

Warfield, Ethelbert D. *The Kentucky Resolutions of 1798.* New York, 1887.

Warren, Charles. *History of the Harvard Law School and of Early Legal Conditions in America.* 3 vols. New York, 1908.

———. *A History of the American Bar.* Boston, 1911.

———. *Jacobin and Junto.* Cambridge, Mass., 1931.

———. *Memorandum on the History and Scope of the Laws Prohibiting Correspondence with a Foreign Government, and Acceptance of a Commission to Serve a Foreign State in War.* Washington, 1915.

———. *The Supreme Court and Sovereign States.* Princeton, 1924.

———. *The Supreme Court in United States History.* 3 vols. Boston, 1922.

Washburne, George A. *Imperial Control of the Administration of Justice in the Thirteen American Colonies, 1684–1776.* New York, 1923.

Webb, George. *The Office and Authority of a Justice of Peace.* Williamsburg, 1736.

Wentworth, Thomas. *The Office and Duty of Executors.* London, 1728. (First published in 1641.)

Wertenbaker, Thomas J. *Virginia under the Stuarts.* Princeton, 1914.

Wharton, Francis. *The Revolutionary Diplomatic Correspondence of the United States.* 6 vols. Washington, 1889.

————. *State Trials of the United States during the Administrations of Washington and Adams.* Philadelphia, 1849.

Wilson, James. *The Works of James Wilson.* Edited by Robert G. McCloskey. 2 vols. Cambridge, Mass., 1967.

Wilson, Woodrow. *A History of the American People.* 5 vols. New York, 1902; 2d ed., 1918.

Wirt, William. *Sketches of the Life and Character of Patrick Henry.* Philadelphia, 1817.

Wolfe, Don M. (ed.). *Leveller Manifestoes of the Puritan Revolution.* New York, 1944.

Woodbury, Margaret. *Public Opinion in Philadelphia 1789–1801.* Durham, N.C., 1919.

Woodhouse, A. S. P. *Puritanism and Liberty.* London, 1938.

Woodhouselee, Alexander Fraser Tytler of. *Memoirs of the Life and Writings of the Honourable Henry Home of Kames.* 2d ed. 3 vols. Edinburgh, 1814.

Woolery, William K. *The Relation of Thomas Jefferson to American Foreign Policy 1783–1793.* Baltimore, 1927.

Wroth, Lawrence C. *The Colonial Printer.* 2d ed. Charlottesville, Va., 1938.

————. *William Parks Printer and Journalist of England and Colonial America.* Richmond, 1926.

Index

Accession: 110, 114, 225n.
Adams, Henry: 237n.
Adams, John: 27, 40, 163n., 210n., 243n.
Adams, John Quincy: 79, 167n.
Adams, Samuel: 27
Advowson: 78–79, 80, 83
Akenside, Mark: 16
Albemarle County: xii, 242n.
Alien and Sedition Acts: 202n.
Allodial tenure: 19–20, 62, 237n.
Anglo-Saxon language: 135, 163n., 237n.; *see also* "Norman yoke"
Assault and battery: 93, 217n.
Assize *utrum*: 82
Atkyns, John Tracy: 16, 173n.
Attainder: 185n.

Bacon, Francis: 245n.
Bacon, Matthew: 8, 14, 15, 101, 170n.
Ballow, Henry: 16, 172n.
Barbé-Marbois, François de: 20, 21, 175n., 242n.
Barbour, Philip: 162n.
Barradall, Edward: 75, 209n.
Barrois, Pierre-Théophile: 21, 176n.
Baskett, John: 130; his *Acts of Assembly*, 130, 234n.
Batture: 37, 44, 53, 54, 56, 57, 59, 60, 61, 62, 63, 64, 67, 68, 70, 72, 73, 189n., 196n., 199n., 201n., 202n.
Beccaria, Cesare: xii, 135, 160n., 236n., 237n.
Becket, Thomas à: 81
Bell, Robert: 10
Benefit of clergy: 241n., 247n.

Bentham, Jeremy: 11, 36
Berkeley, Sir William: 127
Beverley, William: 130, 234n.; his *Abridgment*, 130
Bigarre, Peter de la: 56, 57, 58, 195n.
Bill for proportioning crimes and punishments: xii, 135–36, 137–38, 140, 143, 152, 215n., 240n., 243n.; similar Puritan objective, 146, 152
Blackstone, Sir William: xiii, 8, 9, 10, 11, 14, 15, 78, 83, 96, 101, 102, 110, 133, 165n., 166n., 167n., 169n., 170n., 174n., 210n., 211n., 222n., 223n., 226n.
Blair, John: 93, 137, 139, 217n., 219n.
Bland, Richard: 83, 85, 86, 214n.
Bolling, Anne: 95
Bolling, Archibald: 95, 96, 97, 107, 109, 113, 114, 116, 119, 221n., 224n.
Bolling, Edward: 95, 98, 102, 106, 114, 119, 221n.
Bolling, John (of Cobbs): 95, 98, 106, 107, 115, 116, 220n.
Bolling, John (husband of Jefferson's sister Martha): 95
Bolling, Robert (of Chellowe): 95, 96, 97, 102, 104, 107, 108, 109, 110, 114, 115, 116, 118, 119, 221n., 223n., 224., 225n.
Bordeaux case: 200n.
Bracton (Henry of Bratton): 7, 14, 20, 110, 133, 135, 165n., 175n., 247n.
Britton (John le Breton): 135
Brockenbrough, William: 76
Brooke, Sir Robert: 14, 101